THE
PRO WRESTLING
HALL OF FAME

THE HEELS

Also in this series

The Pro Wrestling Hall of Fame: The Canadians
The Pro Wrestling Hall of Fame: The Tag Teams

THE
PRO WRESTLING
HALL OF FAME
THE HEELS

GREG OLIVER & STEVEN JOHNSON

ECW Press

Published by ECW Press
2120 Queen Street East, Suite 200
Toronto, Ontario, Canada M4E 1E2
416.694.3348 / info@ecwpress.com

LIBRARY AND ARCHIVES CANADA CATALOGUING IN PUBLICATION

Oliver, Greg
The Pro Wrestling Hall of Fame : the heels / Greg Oliver and Steven Johnson.

ISBN-13: 978-1-55022-759-8
ISBN-10: 1-55022-759-9

1. Wrestlers — Biography. 2. Wrestlers. 3. Wrestling. I. Johnson, Steven, 1957- II. Title.

GV1196.A1O545 2007   796.812092'2   C2006-906828-3

Editor for the press: Michael Holmes
Cover photo: Bulldog Brower mauls Carlos Belafonte (Brian Bukantis)
Spine Photo: Buddy Rogers (Tony Lanza)
Back Cover: Gorgeous George (The SPORT Collection, www.thesportgallery.com);
Randy Orton and John Cena (Mike Mastrandrea)
Authors Photo: Cindy Johnson
Typesetting: Mary Bowness
Second Printing: Printcrafters

This book is set in Joanna and Officina

PRINTED AND BOUND IN CANADA

ECW PRESS
ecwpress.com

To Cindy Johnson and Meredith Renwick, our wives, who have been constant sources of support and inspiration, as well as message takers, proofreaders, and all-around sounding boards.

Meredith Renwick does her best Missing Link (Dewey Robertson) impression.

The Destroyer gets the better of Cindy Johnson.

The one and only "Nature Boy" Buddy Rogers.

Table of Contents

Acknowledgements_xi

Foreword by Rick Martel_xiv

Introduction_1

The Top Twenty

  1. "Nature Boy" Buddy Rogers_17
  2. Gorgeous George_22
  3. The Sheik_28
  4. Mad Dog Vachon_33
  5. "Wild" Bill Longson_36
  6. Fred Blassie_40
  7. Johnny Valentine_45
  8. The Destroyer (Dick Beyer)_50
  9. Killer Kowalski_53
10. Harley Race_57
11. Danny McShain_61
12. Abdullah the Butcher_65
13. Nick Bockwinkel_68
14. Gene Kiniski_71
15. Boris Malenko_76
16. Hans Schmidt_80
17. Ray Stevens_82
18. "Nature Boy" Ric Flair_86
19. Bull Curry_92
20. "Rowdy" Roddy Piper_96

The Next Five

Terry Funk_103 Killer Karl Kox_107 Ernie Ladd_111
Randy "Macho Man" Savage_114
The Spoiler (Don Jardine)_119

The Pioneers

Chief Chewacki_125 Ted "King Kong" Cox_127
Dick Daviscourt_130 Billy Edwards_132
Abe "King Kong" Kashey_135 K.O. Koverly_137
Heel With a Heart_140 Lord Lansdowne_142
Buddy O'Brien_146 Lou Plummer_149 Dick Raines_151
Ivan Rasputin_154 Frederich Von Schacht_156
George Zaharias_159

The Madmen

"Killer" Tim Brooks_ 163 Bulldog Brower_166
Pampero Firpo_170 "Crazy" Luke Graham_172
King Curtis Iaukea_175 Moondog Mayne_178
George "The Animal" Steele_182
"The Golden Greek" John Tolos_184

The Egotists

Beauregarde_189 Edge_192 "Superstar" Billy Graham_194
Roger Kirby_198 "Nature Boy" Buddy Landel_201
Randy Orton_204 "Ravishing" Rick Rude_206
Bobby Shane_209 "Exotic" Adrian Street_212

The Monsters

Crusher Blackwell_217 "Black Angus" Campbel_219
"Moose" Cholak_222 Eric the Red_224 Kane_227
Jos Leduc_229 "The Mongolian Stomper"_231
Gorilla Monsoon_235 "Apache" Bull Ramos_239
Vader_241 The Zebra Kid_244

The Technicians

Don Fargo_249 **The Legacy of "Iron" Mike**_252
"Mr. Perfect" Curt Hennig_255 The Masked Superstar_258
Big Bill Miller_261
The Rogers-Miller-Gotch Backstage Mystery_264
"Mister Wonderful" Paul Orndorff_267 Bob Orton Sr._270
Pat Patterson_272 Angelo Poffo_275
Professor Roy Shire_278

The Connivers

Tully Blanchard_283 Ripper Collins_286 Chris Colt_290
"Hot Stuff" Eddie Gilbert_294 Dr. Jerry Graham_297
Rip Hawk_301 Triple H_303 Jeff Jarrett_305
Man on the Moon_308 Jake "The Snake" Roberts_311
Larry Zbyszko_315

The Tough Guys

Bad News Allen_319 Mario Galento_321 Stan Hansen_324
JBL_327 The Missouri Mauler_330 Sputnik Monroe_332
Blackjack Mulligan_337 **Death in the Ring**_341
Magnificent Muraco_343 Dick Murdoch_347 Dutch Savage_350
"Dr. D" David Shults_352 Dick Slater_355 Stan Stasiak_357
Ron Wright_360

The Foreigners

The Iron Sheik_363 Ivan Koloff_366 The Great Mephisto_369
Mr. Moto_373 Toru Tanaka_375 Nikolai Volkoff_378
Fritz Von Erich_380 Waldo von Erich_384 Karl Von Hess_386
Kurt Von Poppenheim_389 Baron Von Raschke_391
Tojo Yamamoto_394

Notes on Sources_397

A bloody Mighty Igor tries to escape from The Sheik — and the cage.

Acknowledgements

In the two years since *The Pro Wrestling Hall of Fame: The Tag Teams* came out, it feels like there have been a thousand autobiographies published about pro wrestlers. But we know this book is different. For one, it feels like we *talked* to a thousand wrestlers. The surprising thing? The great insight one gets talking to the "underneath" workers, the carpenters that built stars by making them look good, then laying down and looking at the lights. So a special thank you goes out to them for sharing their memories and thoughts.

Then there are the historians, the folks who really get their hands dirty digging up results from a century ago or finding the clipping of an overzealous athletic commission suspending some bad guy for a perceived infraction. In this wired world, many people can claim to be historians, but a select few really stand out for their long contributions to the realm of professional wrestling research: J Michael Kenyon, Don Luce, Fred Hornby, Lib Ayoub, Steve Yohe, James C. Melby, George Schire, Mike Rodgers, Tom Burke, Dave Meltzer, Tim Dills, Jim Zordani, Michael Norris, Dr. Bob Bryla, George Lentz, Vern May, Tim Hornbaker, Mark Hewitt, Evan Ginzburg, Mike Lano, Brian Bukantis, Mike Mooneyham, Will Morrisey, Crimson Mask, Rich Tate of *Peach State Pandemonium*, and Dick Bourne and David Chappell of the Mid-Atlantic Gateway Web site. Others, like John Pantozzi, Dale Pierce, Greg Price, Greg Mosorjak, and Ken Jugan helped with valuable leads. Then there's Scott Teal, a publishing maven in his own right, whom we are proud to call a friend, especially now that we've both finally met him; his support has been invaluable through the years.

Budding journalist Annie Johnson helped with some story flow and interviews. Staff and friends of SLAM! Wrestling contributed a quote here and there as well, so thank yous go out to Dave Hillhouse, Bob Kapur, Matt Mackinder, Chris Schramm, Jon Waldman, Jason Clevett, Corey David Lacroix, and Colin Hunter.

On the organizational front, Red Bastien, Karl Lauer and Dean Silverstone of the Cauliflower Alley Club have positively jumped at the chance to help us with our projects. Thank you. The physical Professional Wrestling Hall of Fame in Amsterdam, New York, shares more than just a title with our series of books; like us, the staff of volunteers headed by Tony Vellano is striving to keep wrestling history alive. The induction weekends in May are a yearly highlight, from Penny Banner and Ida Mae Martinez singing karaoke to the induction banquet itself. The George Tragos/Lou Thesz Professional Wrestling Hall of Fame, freshly moved to Waterloo, Iowa, aims to do the same with the wrestlers who have a little more serious grappling background. Kudos to Mike and Bev Chapman, and Kyle Klingman, for their hard work. And the Library of Congress staff responded with a smile to endless microfilm runs.

It's been a real pleasure to know that people in the business like Dr. Tom Prichard, Rick Martel, Les Thatcher, Bob Leonard, Bill Anderson, Don Leo Jonathan, and Emile Dupre are there when we need them, with no question too small. Working in public relations at WWE or TNA must be a thankless job, so here's a first — thanks to Dawn Dwyer and Steven Godfrey and their hardworking staffs, interns included, as well as the many who preceded them.

At ECW Press, we have supporters in publisher Jack David and our editor, Michael Holmes, both of whom are fans of wrestling. The support staff there — Kulsum, Crissy, David, Mary, Rachel et al. — has proven to be just as essential to this series. (Though if our names aren't on the cover of this book, you'll be seeing a fork-wielding Abdullah the Butcher in your office soon!)

We've also made many, many friends through the SLAM! Wrestling Web site and the Steel Belt Wrestling Web site, and our connections with both sites have helped tremendously with the books.

The response to The Tag Teams has been quite wonderful, and though we're committed to keeping the secret, thank you to the Hall of Famer who said he keeps his copy in the bathroom — that's the ultimate compliment!

And finally, a thank you to the bad guys who entertained us through the years.

Greg Oliver
Producer, SLAM! Wrestling
slam.canoe.ca/wrestling
goliver@canoemail.com

Steven Johnson
Editor, Steel Belt Wrestling
www.steelbeltwrestling.com
blakeslee_74@yahoo.com

Paul LeDuc holds Killer Kowalski for Jos LeDuc to hit with a chair.

Foreword by Rick Martel

Howard Lapes

Rick Martel, WWWF hero.

When I first walked into a "bad guys" dressing room I was thirteen years old and it was love at first sight. I liked being around those guys right from the start. My brother Michel, who was one of "them," would bring me on some trips with him and I was always amazed to see how — especially in those days — the heels had to fight their way out of the ring because of the heat they had generated. They often found themselves in dangerous situations, and on numerous occasions their actions even caused riots. When they made it back to the dressing room, they would just casually joke about it. Yes, they were a special breed.

At the beginning of my career as a pro wrestler, because of my looks and my young age of seventeen, I had to be a "babyface." Throughout my first fourteen years, I wrestled against the best of the bad guys. I won't mention any names because I don't want to forget anyone. But many of them are in this book, all those characters with different gimmicks. Finally, in the few remaining years of my career, I was able to become a heel. I loved every minute I spent as "The Model" for the World Wrestling Federation — though I quickly realized that being a heel in the '90s was a bit different than being one in the '70s. I was very happy with the response I received from the crowd — the fans hated me — but I didn't have to fight my way out of the ring. Outside the arenas, I didn't have to worry about my car being scratched and in a bar I didn't have to watch my back constantly. That side of pro wrestling has changed — but the fans still get a kick out of "booing" the heels because, let's face it, without the bad guys there wouldn't be any good guys.

When I heard that Greg Oliver and Steven Johnson wanted to write a book about the "bad guys," I thought, *What a great idea, it's about time somebody "puts them over."* Heels are fascinating, each one so unique that they collectively deserve a book written about them. And if you have been around Greg Oliver and Steven Johnson at all, you know that their passion and love for professional wrestling, combined with their dedication and their always extensive research, makes them the best people to write such a book. Not only do I respect and admire Greg and Steven, but I believe we need them to keep all those great memories alive. I am sure that you will enjoy reading this book very much.

I am not in this book because if you look at my career overall, I am considered a babyface. But that's okay, I understand there will be another book coming out by the same team about the "good guys." It may not be as fun as this one but it will definitely be prettier! (Sorry, the babyface in me is coming out again!)

Finally, I want to say *thank you* to all the "bad guys" because they made professional wrestling so much more exciting — in and out of the ring.

Rick Martel
March 2007

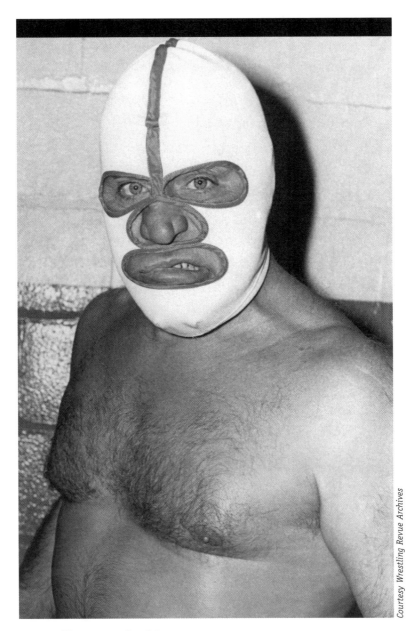

The Intelligent Sensational Destroyer.

Introduction

Back when we were all separated, if you went in the heel dressing room, you would have had a ball. The babyface dressing room — they couldn't walk by the mirror without stopping to look. We used to say, "You're not really that popular. C'mon!" — Davey O'Hannon

This is one heck of a way to make a living.

In 1980, following a match in Albany, New York, long after Larry Zbyszko turned on his mentor Bruno Sammartino, he had trouble getting out of the ring. As Zbyszko worked his way through the crowd, he felt a sharp pain, as though someone had kicked him in the rear end. In the security of the dressing room, he reached back and pulled out a broken metal blade that had lodged in his buttocks.

In May 1976, Ole Anderson was walking from the ring after a heated match in Greenville, South Carolina, when a seventy-nine-year-old man lunged at him and slashed his chest open like a fisherman gutting his catch. Woozy, reeling from the loss of blood, Anderson took more than one hundred stitches. He was back in the ring two days later.

In July 1965, another seventy-nine-year-old man — what is it about that age? — thrust a four-inch pocketknife blade into the stomach of Benji "The Mummy" Ramirez outside a ring in Pasadena, California. The attack sent The Mummy to the hospital in serious condition, but, as befits a mummy, he lived to tell about it.

For the last century, grown men, presumably sane, have been going out in public and doing things that make people yell at them, stone their cars, stab them, shoot at them, threaten their families, and generally make their lives a living hell. They have been called villains, bad guys, roughhousers, meanies, mischief-makers, evil-doers, rule breakers, and, in the most popular vernacular, the heels of pro wrestling. "If you're the hero — the good

The result of "heat" — angry fans (of all ages).

guy — it's a good life," the seemingly ageless Jean Madrid, a.k.a. Gypsy Joe, sighed to the *Charleston Daily Mail* a generation ago. "But, if you're the heel, it's a tough life."

Professional wrestling owes a lot to heels — probably its very existence. Wrestling is based on "heat," a broad and ill-defined term that basically means getting people mad at you, typically by gaining an upper hand on the good guy, or babyface. Without heat, most wrestlers feel there can be little, if any, emotional involvement from fans. Without fan involvement, tickets don't move as quickly — and you wind up with a depressed and sputtering business. As Johnny Powers, a grappling star around the world for two decades, explained: "You cannot have a good match without a good heel. You can have a great match with two heels. But you can only have a so-so match with two babyfaces because life is a morality play, good versus evil. If you don't have that tension created by the heel, you don't have an emotional release. If you don't have a release, what have you got? You've got something that's boring."

No wonder many wrestlers, including Powers, preferred to be heels, despite the accompanying perils. There were financial benefits to being a heel — grappler after grappler interviewed for this book recalled how they didn't really rake in the loot until they switched to the dark side. But being a heel also enabled them to express their creativity in a way that they couldn't do as upstanding, law-abiding citizens. Robert Fuller, part of the legendary Fuller-Welch wrestling dynasty in the South, is one of many who preferred working as a bad guy because it allowed him more freedom in the ring: "As a babyface, you're sort of limited. There's only so much you can do being a nice guy. There's only so much good performance you can do being a good babyface. But a heel, it seems to be unlimited. As much bullshit as you've got in you, you can let every bit go when you're out there trying to get people mad at you." From the managerial perspective, Sir Oliver Humperdink, a heinous sort for most of his career, said the release of pent-up emotions might even have been healthy for mind and soul. "As heels, we were able to be as annoying and politically 'incorrect' as possible. We were able to say and do what everyone probably wanted to say and do, but, for one reason or another, could never, ever get away with. And, by being able to do so, I generally found that my fellow heels were much more 'easygoing' than our babyface counterparts who had to 'toe the line.'"

Not everyone is fit to be a heel, of course, and fewer still are fit to be successful heels. Many in the industry believe in the concept of a "natural heel," a villain who is so convincing because he relies on something within himself to rattle fans, rather than on a wholly conceived, separate wrestling character. In essence, a natural heel's ring identity is an extension of his real-life identity, with the volume cranked up. Stan Lane, who worked as a hero and as a villain during a successful tag team career, believes individual personalities play a key role in determining who will succeed as a bad guy. "I think some people are more predisposed to be nice and humble, and other people, such as myself, are predisposed to be more cocky in nature. It just fits better being a heel; it's a lot easier to make somebody dislike you than it is to make them like you. You can anger somebody a whole lot faster than you can win them over." That's a general rule, not applicable to every wrestler, but Dr. Tom Prichard, a star in various promotions and a top wrestling teacher, believes, based on his own circumstances, that it has merit. He was toiling away at the beginning of his career as a cheery, undersized chap, but after some sour experiences in real life, he found that role didn't fit him. "I was working in Louisiana and I hated being a babyface, and I hated going out there, and I hated working with the guys I had to work with. When I walked out of the dressing room, I didn't feel like a babyface, didn't feel like being a good guy, and having people cheer for me. [Promoter] Bill Watts said, 'Hey, have you ever thought about being a heel?' I said, 'Every day.' I felt more comfortable, it was more natural. I didn't smile — it was just a natural thing to not smile for me. It was easier to be an asshole than to try to be a nice guy." As Watts, famous for his work as head of the Mid-South territory, put it: "You can't be what you're not. In other words, you can't be a great heel if you don't have some heel quality."

A HEEL'S JOB

Larry DeGaris, a sports marketing professor at the University of Indianapolis who moonlights as wrestler Larry Brisco, relates a conversation that he had with a friend who wanted to work as a heel on a local independent show. His pal was anxious to get in the ring so he could kick and stomp the good guy into oblivion. To DeGaris, that fervor represented a fundamental misunderstanding of the heel's true calling — to make his opponent look good. "The number one job is to get the babyface over," he said. "Good heels understand that. Your challenge is to make this other guy look like Bruno Sammartino, not the local ex-gym owner. A lot of heels don't understand that because they want to beat someone up to make themselves look good, as opposed to being a coward. When you're a heel, when you're on top, you're brave. But then the tide turns against you a little bit and you become a chicken."

The line between heels and babyfaces has become blurred during the last twenty years, but DeGaris' insight still rings true — the heel is charged with the responsibility of winning sympathy for his opponent. Tully Blanchard, one of the best workers of his time, said he understood that was the way to make money. "When it's time for the comeback, I am all over the stinking building and they're talking about me. By making him look good, I'm making me look good."

What many fans of pre-1990s wrestling do not realize is that the heel was the one calling for his own blood. Before the introduction of tightly scripted, step-by-step matches, most bouts were laid out in the ring, in progress, with little more than a predetermined finale. The heel led the match like a dog trainer would an excited but unschooled puppy. "The heel is the guy that was truly the ring general, in most all cases. He was the one that ran and set the stage, set the match, and ran the flow of the match," Watts said. "So if I was working in the ring, and the guy was a quality heel, I would let him call my match, even if I owned the territory, as long as he was calling the match in a manner that I thought fit the direction that we were going. You let the heel call the match because he's the one that had to execute it." In fact, in what wrestlers fondly refer to as "the old days," it was common for a wrestler to break into the business as a good guy, then work for several years with more experienced villains who could teach him the subtle ins and outs. "I remember, as a heel, I loved it because you're the guy that controls the way the match is going," good guy-turned-superego Rick Martel once said. "You're calling the match. One of the things that I enjoyed the most about being a heel is that finally I was able to do that."

There's a secondary job for heels, and it's closely related to the first. They have to keep the business in the black by inducing fans to come back week after week to see justice in action — a sort of psychological ploy that for years served as wrestling's underpinning. It's the logical conclusion to what French social critic Roland Barthes explained in a famous 1957 essay "The World of Wrestling": "But what wrestling is above all meant to portray is a purely moral concept: that of justice. The idea of 'paying' is essential to wrestling, and the crowd's 'Give it to him' means above all else 'Make him pay.'" In other words, heels serve an important function as a source of ire, both in their matches and in the grand scheme of wrestling. Frankie Cain, who wrestled both as an Inferno and as The Great Mephisto, took a trip inside the mind of a typical male fan so he could figure out how to get him to keep buying tickets. "The guy's got a job," Cain explained. "He's mad at his wife. His kids are driving him nuts, and you make him madder than when he came into the arena. He's saying, 'There's no justice in the world!'"

HEEL PSYCHOLOGY

Les Thatcher, one of the sport's top trainers, begins seminars by asking would-be wrestlers a question he picked up from Ricky "The Dragon" Steamboat — why is a heel a heel? "One kid will say because he's ugly,"

Thatcher related. "Another kid will say because he's wearing black, or he punches and kicks. None of the above. He's a heel because the other guy out-wrestles him. Out of frustration, out of lack of skill, he has to take shortcuts to stay on top or to get on top. That's why he's a heel."

That's a fundamental point that wrestlers feel has been lost as the sport has changed content and character in recent years. Heels come in all shapes, sizes, and colors. But if there is a single denominator common to all successful heels, it's this: they have to cheat to win because nobody likes a lousy sportsman. "The true heel is not a mean guy. He's a cheater. He's not a very brave individual. He may be tough as nails, but he's not willing to put his body on the line to take the fall from the guy," said veteran Randal Brown, one of the premier builders of wrestling rings in the country. "The true heel is a disgusting person. He's a guy who shakes hands with you and takes your ring and your watch, so you want to see his butt get beat."

Heels have an almost infinite number of ways to draw heat, from their getups, their interviews, and their facial expressions, to their underhanded tricks in the ring. The profiles in this book describe many of these methods in detail. In virtually all cases, though, successful heels draw a careful line between "cheap" heat and "real" heat. Cheap heat is based on actions that elicit a quick, superficial jeer from the crowd. Parading through an arena in Boston wearing a New York Yankees jersey — that's cheap heat. Standing on the second rope and telling a section of the crowd that it sucks — that's cheap heat. Flipping the bird to a fan — that's cheap heat, and veteran wrestlers turn their noses up at it as though a skunk just passed through their midst. "There's nothing cheaper than hollering or yak-yak at the people in the front row," Blanchard said. "That pumping the crowd stuff; that's not going to sell out Madison Square Garden. That's cheap heat. That's because you can't think of anything else."

Real heat — the kind that once had overwrought fans standing on their seats, flipping open their switchblades — is something else entirely. The best real heat, many wrestlers agree, comes during the course of a match, through normal give and take. "They've gone out and wrestled a little bit and every time they do, the good guy comes out on top," Lane said. "So the heel has a decision to make. 'Obviously, this guy is a better wrestler than I am; eventually he's going to pin me. Do I want that to happen or am I willing to cross that line and cheat?' So you start cheating and that's what makes the people mad." Cain, who has studied heel psychology as much as anyone, believes that the best heat can be accomplished by slithering in and out of holds and counterholds, without pandering to the audience. "Once you've got your heat, you don't have to tell them every ten minutes, 'I'm a heel.' You do your wrestling. That's the way that they drew money in the old days without television. Even when I was traveling around the country, heeling was a lost art, and it's a shame."

Sometimes a heel doesn't have to do anything. Just the bare hint that a heel might consider bending the rules is more than enough — a minimalist approach to heat that ensures the audience will react in a major way when the heel finally snaps. "Sometimes, I'd sneak my hand up the guy's back two or three times when he had me in a headlock," said Ken Wayne, a long-time star in Tennessee, now a trainer there. "I wouldn't pull his hair; I'd just wrestle. I'd save myself, so then when I did do something, it meant something." If the heel, after begging for mercy, comes out a victor because of a dirty trick, managerial interference, or some inventive finish, so much the better — as long as fans believe in their hearts that the heel otherwise was headed for ignominious defeat. "You have to show vulnerability," Johnny Valiant said. "You have to show that you can be beat. So when you win by some method of cheating, people get even hotter because they know you're not deserving."

Essential to heel psychology is the role of the referee. In recent years, referees have become almost irrelevant to the mat game, but during the heel heyday they were an important component because they established the rules that were to be broken. "To be a good heel, you've got to use the referee," Jake "The Snake" Roberts stated. "When I say 'use' the referee, respect the referee. It makes no sense if a guy doesn't listen to the referee because then the heat goes on the referee; it doesn't go on the heel . . . Sort of like if you've got a sniper in the bell tower shooting kids in a playground, and you've got a policeman next to him. Who has the heat? The policeman; he's not doing his job. So, to me, honoring the authority in the ring, breaking down and apologizing, begging off to the referee, these things are what makes a heel. You've got to respect the authority."

In this book, we've placed heels in different categories depending on their dominant characteristics. A cautionary note — our categories are not mutually exclusive; heels can belong to two or more. Dick Murdoch is thought of as a big, brawling

Bob Leonard

Referee Jochen Herman administers a count to Jason The Terrible (Karl Moffat) as he destroys Bruce Hart.

Texas cowboy; less remembered is the fact that he was one of the best technical workers in wrestling. But it's easier to compare and contrast different heel styles by trying to categorize them. Our groups include:

• Madmen — Wrestlers who threw the rule book out the window while applying foreign objects to the foreheads and torsos of their opponents.

• Foreigners — Perhaps the most common villain in the postwar world, wrestlers adopted Japanese, Russian, and German guises to disgust and incense patriotic fans, even though most of these wrestlers were true Americans or Canadians.

• Technicians — Wrestlers who employed a variety of holds and technical wrestling skills when they weren't cheating behind the ref's back. Within the profession, these grapplers often referred to as "smooth" wrestlers or "wrestling heels."

• Egotists — The most well recognized category of wrestling villain is probably the bleached blond, narcissistic, pretty boy, who has headlined cards from the time of Gorgeous George to today's Ric Flair.

• Tough Guys — Wrestlers who were best known for hard-hitting, brawling, slugging, realistic-looking action. For tough guys, fisticuffs came as naturally as a Stetson to a cowboy, which is an archetype many tough guys portrayed.

• Monsters — Wrestling can be larger than life, and monster heels often were "larger" than wrestling. Three hundred-pound behemoths have been a draw for years, in part, because of their seeming invincibility.

• Connivers — Some wrestlers have a knack for understanding how and when to manipulate a crowd, even though it might just be through a raised eyebrow or a turn of the head. While every heel is a conniver or a sneak to some degree, some performers stand out for their ability to master audiences.

We've added a category called Pioneer Heels that includes some wrestlers whose careers started in the 1920s and 1930s. That shorthand is our way of singling out wrestlers who charted a course for their rule breaking heirs.

THE HISTORY OF HEELS

Clarence Whistler was the Abdullah The Butcher of the 1880s — he ate glass. Whistler, known as the "Kansas Demon," celebrated his achievements by downing a goodly measure of champagne, then snacking on the flute. He also was among the first wrestlers to be accused of stratagems any budding heel would envy. In a legendary 1881 marathon with William Muldoon, Whistler allegedly wet his hair with ammonia to burn his opponent's eyes and used his long fingernails to scratch Muldoon's body. His deceits remained unproven, and he later wrestled several exhibitions with Muldoon. But the mere possibility that someone bent the rules 125 years ago shows that heel tactics as are old as pro wrestling itself. (Whistler died in 1885, reportedly from ingested jagged crystal, though some writers suggested excess booze was the true culprit.)

In the early years of the twentieth century, what later generations would call villains or heels were identified as roughhousers, or rough-and-tumble wrestlers. One of the first was Leo Pardello, billed as an Italian heavyweight, who earned some infamy for his brawling methods. In 1908, he touched off a minor riot in Chicago after losing a fall to Charles Olsen. Pardello jumped Olsen, and "in an instant the two men were in the center of the ring pummeling each other in approved prize ring style," according to the Fort Wayne Daily News. An assistant police chief and several detectives protected Pardello from enraged fans.

Pardello's was the dominant bad-guy style until the development of slam-bang wrestling — around 1919 — popularized the use of storylines and emphasized wrestling characters. The brainchild, in part, of Joseph "Toots" Mondt, slam-bang wrestling combined boxing, traditional mat wrestling, and lumberjack-style fights into revolutionary, emotion-filled athletic "contests." World champion Ed "Strangler" Lewis, who was to wrestling what Jack Dempsey was to boxing in the 1920s, was the early-day equivalent of a killer heel — his headlock allegedly rendered opponents unconscious and caused lasting neck damage. The new style of wrestling took off like a rocket, so much so that historian J Michael Kenyon observed there was scarcely enough supply to meet the demand. "The mat trust(s) became instant goldmines, with every city, town and country holler eager to stage weekly shows. Nearly three-score, full-fledged wrestling 'circuits' sprang up throughout North America in the early '30s, and, of course, it was an impossibility to provide them all with the legendary, headline wrestlers."

Who then to fill the bill? One of the answers rested with a group of mayhem-loving charlatans who packed audiences from coast to coast with wild antics — the freshman class of character heels. Wrestlers like Chief Chewacki, Ted "King Kong" Cox, and Buddy O'Brien hit the mat scene in the early 1930s, creating a sudden and unprecedented run on goods at the neighborhood illegal foreign object store. In many cases, the character heels were failed prizefighters. O'Brien and George Koverly were two of many who turned to wrestling after exiting boxing. In any event, they were a smash hit with Great Depression audiences starved for diversions. "College men have helped to revive wrestling," William Draucher, sports editor at the Newspaper Enterprise Association, noted in 1931. "The decline of boxing interest also has been a factor. But there is another cause perhaps as great as either of these. It is called showmanship. A great deal of the quality that Barnum worshiped is in the cast of characters of the act itself which provides that one man must be a conniving, unscrupulous villain. . . ."

If fans soaked up the new and outrageous acts, high-minded athletic commissions and lawmakers were less impressed. In 1933, John V. Clinnin, chairman of the Illinois Athletic Commission, said he'd impose fines and suspensions on grapplers who engaged in organized monkey business. "It is no longer a sport. They bite each other, trade blows, and go through other horseplay for no other purpose than to work on the passion of the spectators," he declared. A Michigan legislator introduced a bill to abolish commercial wrestling in 1935, on the grounds that it had become a public nuisance. "When business is slack all a promoter has to do is obtain the services of Gentleman Jack Washburn, either of the better Duseks, Chief Chewacki, or any one of a dozen or more stirrer-uppers," Representative Stanley J. Romanski fumed. "They will fill his hall — with police, if no one else. They come — first-class riot guaranteed, or no pay."

It's unclear when the term "heel" started to become commonplace. Wrestling historian Don Luce said old-timer Lou Newman recognized it when he asked him about it. In 2001 on WrestlingClassics.com the great Lou Thesz wrote that the press might have invented the term. "When I came into the world of Ray [Steele] and George Tragos, the terms were 'clean' and 'rough.' I don't know when the 'heel' term began because I never really thought about it." Regardless, suspensions and fines aside, heels thrived in the 1930s and 1940s, passing themselves off in just about every guise imaginable. "The villains are invariable hairy specimens who might pass as walking testimony to the Darwinian theory except that they must be able to register the whole gamut of emotion on their not-classic countenances and to put more soul into their grunts than the brutish anthropoid," Maine sportswriter Richard G. Kendall wrote in 1937. "Added to these accomplishments the villain matman preferably comes from some outlandish spot on the globe. It is alright, however, if he lives in New York City as long as he looks like he might have originated in, say, Ukrania, or almost any portion of Poland or Russia."

The biggest change facing heels during the first half-century of pro wrestling though came with the invention of the television. "TV in its infancy and professional wrestling kind of grew up together. TV found the perfect vehicle in this constant, flying-around action. It was perfect for the small screen and wrestling changed to accommodate it," said wrestler-author Ted Lewin. "People no longer laid in holds for twenty minutes. There had to be a lot of moving around and a lot of flying and aerobatics to keep people's interests. I think they kind of grew up together." By bringing the action from arenas into living rooms, TV placed a premium on showmanship and visual attractions, and launched the career of Gorgeous George. The gorgeous one was a star of the early television days, and, while historians still debate his impact on box offices around the country, there's no question about the impression he left on millions of viewers. *Entertainment Weekly* put his November 11, 1947, television appearance as the forty-fifth greatest moment in the history of the boob tube. "Who knew a bottle of peroxide and a trunk full of attitude would change pro wrestling — and TV — history?" the magazine mused. "By the late '40s, wrestling (one of the few spectator sports unsophisticated cameras could successfully capture) was often a nightly TV event, and flamboyant George was like programming manna from heaven." New York promoter Bill Johnston told the Associated Press that television helped wrestling in the East "by at least fifty percent."

Even after national TV abandoned wrestling in the mid-1950s, the basic heel formula remained the same for about thirty years. Russians, Germans, and Japanese had nothing less on their minds than the hostile takeover of America. Bleached blonds preferred that their locks remain undisturbed. Masked men concealed their identities, adding a whiff of mystery to their ways. "Satanic arch-enemies are necessary in our melodramas so that even the dimmest of us can see some clear contrast with the crusading knight. The characters we love to hate — the Professor Moriartys, the Fu Manchus — are played by experts. It is the same in wrestling," Joe Jares wrote in his good-natured 1974 romp, *Whatever Happened to Gorgeous George?*

In 1984, the world of wrestling changed forever when WWF owner Vince McMahon seized the industry, recast it as sports entertainment, and marched it to the forefront of pop culture. McMahon's drive, determination, and marketing genius made a lot of money for many people, most of all himself, but it also had a profound effect on the way fans perceived heels. In a world of B-list, celebrity-stuffed WrestleManias, toy action figures, cable specials, and Saturday morning cartoons — *Hulk Hogan's Rock 'N' Wrestling* ran for two seasons on CBS — there was no room for the killer heel who warded off fans with a malevolent leer or a threatening fist. George "The Animal" Steele, became soft, more or less cuddly. Nikolai Volkoff and the Iron Sheik showed up in a Cyndi Lauper music video. As McMahon bought and consolidated territories, pro wrestling became nationalized, and World Championship Wrestling, the Atlanta-based company that offered a slightly more traditional heel product, was the only competitor until 2001, when it toppled. "When Vince made a cartoon out of it, that changed everything," said WWF veteran

Davey O'Hannon. "Then there wasn't delineation between a heel and a baby-face anymore."

WHITHER HEELS

In 1989, McMahon made one of his periodic forays into the mainstream by tapping Tom "Tiny" Lister, a relatively unknown actor, to portray a monster heel named Zeus as Hulk Hogan's antagonist in the forgettable *No Holds Barred* movie. Their rivalry extended into the ring. Zeus fought Hogan in tag team matches at SummerSlam and Survivor Series that year. In December, Hogan vanquished him once and for all, but the episode probably sounded a death knell for traditional heels. "When Vince took Zeus, an actor who had never been in the ring, and never had a match, and drew money by putting him with Hulk Hogan in a pay-per-view, that told me that you did not have to start out and learn the trade," Hall of Fame manager Bobby Heenan said. "You simply had to have someone give you a push. Just think of that."

Pundits have filled up notebooks and computer screens to explain why heels have fallen by the wayside. The foreign heel, a staple of '60s and '70s wrestling, has dried up in the face of geopolitical developments. Instead of hurling invectives at German and Japanese wrestlers, fans drive German- and Japanese-made cars to the arena. And how much could they hate the Iran-sympathizing Iron Sheik if he was a goofy regular on a Saturday morning cartoon show? Paul A. Cantor, a professor at the University of Virginia, observed that the end of the Cold War put promoters and heels in a pickle. "Suddenly, audiences could not be counted on to treat a given wrestler automatically as a villain simply because he was identified as a Russian," he wrote in a 1999 essay "Wrestling and the End of History."

Changes in the business also have contributed to relegate the red-hot heel to the dustbin. Pro wrestling has become a "might makes right" enterprise, discarding the old moral struggle between good and evil. Huge monster heels that caused fans in a bygone day to cringe in horror now win praise when they demonstrate their power and might. "You take a guy like Abyss or some of these other guys, they just go out there and manhandle people and mutilate them," Brown noted. "And people identify with them and start rooting for them because they see them as big tough guys who are not going to take anything off anybody." DeGaris, writing about wrestling from an insiders' perspective, noted the same phenomenon: "Today's pro wrestling audience, skewing heavily younger and male, cheer the strong and boo the weak. In the absence of a framework of 'sportsmanship' that predominated wrestling for so long, it is no longer moral weakness or moral turpitude that is vilified; it is

Mike Lano

Today's fans go to be a part of the spectacle.

simply physical weakness." Mid-Atlantic wrestler and trainer George South believes disrespect for authority now is a badge of honor. "People have the wrong concept of what a heel is. . . Just because a guy comes out cussing and shooting the middle finger, they think that's being a heel, and they think it's cool. Everyone knew Vince McMahon was 'Stone Cold' Steve Austin's boss, and every time Austin stuck his middle finger in McMahon's face, people cheered that. How can you be a heel if that's being a babyface?"

These factors have contributed to the demise of heels, but it's just as clear that heels don't have a chance to flourish in today's business climate. World Wrestling Entertainment is the Microsoft of elbow drops; it committed the old wrestling territories to the dirt so young wrestlers don't have a chance to learn their trade by working five or six nights a week. "So many of these kids are self-trained," Thatcher said. "Some are remarkably easy to educate. Others just look at you with this blank stare like, 'What's he talking about?' because they've never seen it, and they don't have anywhere to go to get the experience they need. There are some things you can only learn by being in the ring night after night."

Even if Thatcher, Wayne, Prichard, or other trainers cranked out great heel after great heel, it might not be enough. Greg Gagne, son of former world champion Verne Gagne, worked for a while as a trainer with the WWE in 2006. Stephanie McMahon, Vince's daughter, released him, explaining that he wasn't working out, though the Ohio Valley Wrestling territory he was assigned to was doing well, and several wrestlers credited him with helping them improve their skills. Regardless, Gagne got a peek at the WWE mentality, and his findings are worth quoting at length because they explain how the heel he knew during his career has fallen out of favor: "The kids watching today don't have a feel for what it really was. When I was up with McMahon, I told him, 'That's what you're missing. The kids aren't learning to be themselves.' Stephanie McMahon said, 'Now, when you go and train the kids, I want you to develop some characters.' I said, 'Stephanie, we don't develop the characters. You can't take a kid and do that.' Guys like myself who grew up in the business, maybe after three or four years, we'd start to find the character. Guys that were in the business five years, six years, seven years — heck, some never find it. But until you find that and can project that to the people, you're not going to succeed, and that becomes a character. Take Paul Burchill. They made him a frigging pirate. The writers wanted a pirate, so they made him a pirate. I worked with the kid down in Louisville. That's not his personality. So when it didn't get over, the writers said, 'Oh, this kid's no good. Get rid of him.' It wasn't the kid's fault. It was them trying to make him something that he wasn't. I was going nuts with them."

Manager Sir Oliver Humperdink makes a point.

Can wrestling return to its past? Can the wrestler we loved to hate suddenly reappear from behind the curtains, without pyrotechnics and video boards, and whip crowds into an angry frenzy? Skandor Akbar, one of the most despised managers in history (he wasn't beloved as a wrestler either), has his doubts. These days, Akbar is in Texas, doing a little training and helping local groups run shows. "People will come to me and they'll say, 'We liked it back when you guys were in. It was real. We loved it.' Sometimes I'll book shows around here and the first thing they say is they want a family show, they don't want that stuff we see on TV, naked women and stuff. I'm sure they're good people up in [the WWE] — I've always had a good rapport with them. But that's their house and they do what they want to do. It's hard to say if it will ever go back to being like we were used to."

Perhaps, then, it's worth a final trip into the past to appreciate the raw hatred that a good, old-fashioned heel could engender. Herman Hickman, a College Football Hall of Fame lineman, dabbled in wrestling for a few years, and penned his remembrances for the *Saturday Evening Post* in 1954: "I know that there have been few legitimate professional matches since Milo of Croton was six times champion of Greece, and Theseus laid down the wrestling rules in 900 B.C. I even have my doubts about whether that historic match between Ulysses and Ajax was a shoot. I do know that I met a lot of good guys who were the straightest shooters I've ever known, and that I got to see a lot of 'faraway places.' I still don't think you can get a better night's entertainment than you will by seeing your favorite 'hero' tangle with a 'villain.' This plot has had the longest run in show business, so it must have something."

ABOUT THE WRESTLERS IN THIS BOOK

We know the question is coming: *Why isn't so-and-so in the book?* (How do we know it is coming? Because it happened with both previous books.)

The *Pro Wrestling Hall of Fame: The Heels* is by no means meant to be a comprehensive list of bad guys during the last century. Chances are someone you booed with all your heart in your childhood isn't here. Our aim is to offer a decent representation of wrestlers who had particular importance, a lasting impact on the sport, or interesting stories to tell. By doing this, we hope readers will have a better understanding of why heels are such an important and fascinating part of this business. And maybe some young wrestler will find something in this compendium that he can refine and use to entertain us for years to come.

For ease of reading, we've tried to group heels into certain categories that we think cover some of their defining characteristics — whether they were monsters, foreigners, madmen, and so on. It's an imperfect system, but we hope this makes for interesting comparisons between heels, and helps to explain how different heel styles evolved.

There are very few wrestlers who were either a good guy or a bad guy their whole careers. We've tried to classify them based on their longevity or heel impact, but there are always going to be disagreements; in some territories, a wrestler may be seen as the spawn of Satan, and in another, fighting on the side of angels. Those good guys, or "babyfaces," will be dealt with in the next volume in this series, *The Pro Wrestling Hall of Fame: The Heroes*. Others are a curious shade of grey, particularly a lot of the grapplers during the last fifteen years, or those that we have decided to label anti-heroes, like Bruiser Brody or "Stone Cold" Steve Austin. Some of these wrestlers will make the next book as well.

Finally, listing the top twenty heels of all time is an admittedly subjective endeavor. To come up with our ranking, many different sources — historians, wrestlers, fans, promoters — were consulted, and heels were rated on a set of a dozen standards. Some of these standards are quantifiable, such as longevity as a heel, the size of the box offices they drew, and the number and quality of territories where they worked as a main-event heel. Some of them are more subjective, such as their ability to work different styles of matches, or the reasons for their success. In every case, we've tried to emphasize a couple of factors we think are most important — their responsibility for significant historical innovations, and their influence on later generations of wrestlers. With a few exceptions, we've kept a lot of the early pioneers from our rankings simply because we don't have the luxury of evaluating their work on video.

"Bulldog" Don Kent argues with a fan.

We don't claim this is the final word on heels — in fact, we hope we're just getting the debate started and the memories flowing. So, on to the stories. And remember, you're free to hiss at will.

The Top 20

1. "NATURE BOY" BUDDY ROGERS

Buddy Rogers in all his arrogance.

You still see him everywhere.

You see him every time Vince McMahon swaggers down the runway to the ring on TV. You see him every time someone clamps on a figure-four leglock. You see him every time someone screams out, "NA-ture Boy!" You see him everywhere because wrestlers, promoters, and fans all agree that he was the most imitated, most talented, most . . . everything heel in history.

The ironic thing is that there wasn't much original about Buddy Rogers. His name was lifted from Charles "Buddy" Rogers, an actor and jazz musician who starred in *Wings*, the first winner of an Academy Award for best picture. "Nature Boy" was a number one hit on the Billboard charts in 1948. The sneer, the strut, the pretty boy looks . . . those were parts of wrestling almost from the start. It's just that all-time greats like Don Leo Jonathan agree Rogers packaged them like no wrestler before. "He really wasn't that good of a hand, but he was a hell of a showman. He could draw houses where other guys couldn't. He just had that thing. He had a way of making those people want to kill him, and he could do it just with a look, a posture," Jonathan said.

Billy Darnell, Rogers' friend and greatest rival, tells of an incident in the early 1950s that puts it all in perspective. "In those days, in Hollywood, you could go in small clubs and see the best entertainment in the world, and never spend a dime for a cover charge or anything. At the Brown Derby, Nat King Cole was there and he had his trio. So I walk in, and I'm sitting down, and there's Nat up there playing something. And Buddy Rogers walked in the door. It was an amazing thing. The spotlight went over to Buddy Rogers, and Nat looked over and saw him and nodded, and he transposed the song he was playing right into 'Nature Boy.'"

Rogers was the sport's top gate attraction for the better part of two decades, until he lost the World Wide Wrestling Federation world title to Bruno Sammartino in May 1963, and essentially ended his active career. In his most famous match, he drew a record 38,600 to Chicago's Comiskey Park in June 1961, when he beat Pat O'Connor for the National Wrestling Alliance championship. While he served some duty as a fan favorite, especially early in his career under his real name of Herman "Dutch" Rohde, he was meant to be a heel. "Buddy Rogers loves being hated. He loves being hated almost as much as he loves being Buddy Rogers," observed famed Chicago sportswriter Dave Condon. As Rogers himself once explained, "It's bread and butter, and cake, too, for me. The more the fans hate me, the more money they pay in hopes of seeing me whipped. This I enjoy."

To say the least, Rogers was not everybody's cup of tea. Many of his contemporaries, while acknowledging his skills, viewed him as a schemer and conniver who knew his position in wrestling, and went to great lengths to protect it. "He was strictly a con man from A to Z. Everything he did was bullshit to keep you down and keep himself up, but he was always laughing and joking along like he was normal," said Bob Orton Sr., Rogers' tag team partner in the early 1960s in the Northeast. "What he was doing was thinking, 'How can I screw this guy?' I could read him like a book and remember every word." Opponent Jackie Fargo called him "Bud-ro," and felt the same as Orton, based on encounters and matches with Rogers. "He was the most no-good son of a bitch that ever put on a pair of wrestling boots. He was a fabulous, fabulous, fabulous worker. He was a natural, and you can't take that away from him. But as far as a person — listen, he would try to hurt you or cripple you any way he could." Before one bout in New Jersey, Fargo recalled saying to Rogers, "Let me tell you something, pally — if you screw with me any way, shape, or form, don't try to leave the ring, 'cause you've got a fight on your hands." Lou Thesz carried a long grudge against Rogers for belittling Ed "Strangler" Lewis, Thesz's mentor, during a ride to Louisville, Kentucky. "The knowledge of his contempt for Ed and true wrestlers was more than I could tolerate," Thesz wrote in his autobiography *Hooker*. Despite years and years of main event matches, Thesz "never let him win, just on principle."

Regardless of what people felt, Rogers was guaranteed money in the bank, with a perfect sense of what to do and not do in the ring. When in 1960 and 1961 a newspaper exposed Tito Carreon, one of Rogers' opponents in the Northeast, as Mexican and not Puerto Rican, Carreon found himself being booed one night in New Jersey. Rogers pounded Carreon into oblivion, and then whispered, "Flag me," a tip-off for his opponent to seize the offensive. Carreon reported his comeback was so intense that excited Puerto Rican fans started throwing chairs in the ring. "We had good matches all the time because [Rogers] knew how to get the crowd going. He had something special about him. There are a lot of jealousies in the business. Everywhere he wrestled he was drawing people. Everywhere. Babyfaces, they loved working with him," Carreon said. Don Arnold battled Rogers for a version of the world title in Ohio in 1952 and 1953, and thought he had a terrific head for business. "He made money for you," Arnold said. "The place was sold out weeks ahead. He was a big attraction and big name. He was the first to do what he did."

The son of German immigrants, Rogers was born in Camden, New Jersey, in 1921, worked the carnival circuit for a couple of years as a teenager, and turned pro thereafter. He said in interviews that he officially turned to the mat to support himself after the death of his father, who was nearly fifty when Buddy was born. For years, he maintained a loose affiliation with the Camden police department. After a brief stint in the Navy in 1939 and 1940, he started to attract attention on the East Coast for his good looks, Adonis-like physique, and cocksure ways. By 1944, *The Washington Post* labeled him "the District's most popular mat star." The following spring, Rohde headed to Texas under the guise of Buddy Rogers, a name older stepbrother John used during a brief wrestling career. In May 1946, Rogers won the Texas heavyweight title, including an apparent swap with Thesz, though Thesz claimed the title change took place in an office, not the ring. In September 1946, Rogers hooked up with Jack Pfefer, a promoter who was alternately brilliant and reviled, but who helped push Rogers to the hilt for about five years.

Adding "Nature Boy" to his persona, Rogers made a splash in California in 1948, when Pfefer arranged a grand coming-out party designed to make the public forget about Gorgeous George. In a letter to promoter Hugh Nichols, who ran the Hollywood venue, Pfefer sought an accordion player and a couple of Amazonian models to accompany Rogers to the ring and tend to his splendid capes. "After the big circus which the gorgeous guy put on in your clubs, we will have to beat this silly stuff with something more unusual, but at the same time something serious and beautiful," Pfefer wrote. Rogers won that night, and didn't lose a match until he fought Darnell that October. It worked out for Rogers — he wrote Pfefer that he

Howard Lapes

Rogers hosts his short-lived WWWF segment, here with Pat Patterson.

raked in $26,349 in 1948: "So Jack we had a great year together again and I'm sure glad to hear we have a good new year coming up." Pfefer's cut was $7,118.

Rogers, a natural for the early days of TV wrestling, officially changed his name from Rohde around 1950. His appeal only increased as he toured the country and won a variety of regional championships with a cold, calculated hostility toward audiences. As a youngster, former Chicago columnist Bob Greene was taken with Rogers and eventually got to know his anti-hero. "Well, the blond hair, the sneer, the gaze of absolute confidence — Nature Boy Rogers was to wrestling what Elvis Presley was to music: electric, jolting, incandescent," Greene wrote. "He was a unique personality," added Darnell, who wore a collar for a year after Rogers accidentally crushed discs in his neck with a botched piledriver. "He was one of those guys who wanted to appear like a hardball, but if you needed something he was there for you. He was like Sinatra. He wanted to rule the roost, but if you needed something, he was there for you." And Rogers was oddly honest with interviewers about his portrayal of a wrestling villain. "Out of character, Buddy Rogers is a pleasant, soft-spoken, handsome gentleman who readily admits the long blond hair, the exaggerated strut, and the scornful stare are all part of an act," Art Abrams admiringly informed readers in the Pittsburgh Post-Gazette in 1962.

Rogers held the NWA title until January 1963, but his reign was marked by controversy about his unwillingness to wrestle outside a handful of major cities. To be sure, his draws were as big as ever. In 1961, he helped to pull $151,000 in four shows in Pittsburgh against Johnny Valentine and "Crusher" Lisowski; Steel City wrestling had been dead for years. He was closely aligned with promoter Vincent J. McMahon in New York, and McMahon made Rogers his first WWWF champion in 1963 after Rogers lost the NWA belt to Thesz in Toronto. "In my opinion, Buddy Rogers was one of the best ever," said Pete Sanchez, a frequent opponent from 1960 to 1963. "He was a very intelligent worker. He could go in the ring with a broomstick and make the broomstick look good, because if the broomstick looked good, and Buddy beat it, he would look that much better himself."

Rogers was WWWF kingpin until May 1963, when Bruno Sammartino dispatched him in forty-eight seconds. The circumstances of Rogers' title loss have been examined almost as carefully as the Zapruder film. For years, backstage whispers, spread in part by a New York sportswriter, held that Rogers suffered a heart attack, and was dragged out of a hospital to wrestle Sammartino. That wasn't the case, according to several people familiar with the event. Rogers backed out of three matches in a row in mid-April 1963, and a physician checked him out after at least one of them. To some colleagues, he explained that a long-standing heart murmur troubled him, though many of his contemporaries remain convinced that he was fashioning an alibi for his defeat. Terry Milam, a friend in later life, quoted Rogers as reporting shortness of breath and palpitations leading up to the bout with Sammartino, who was on track to become champion. "Later on, he went to another physician in New York and the guy says, 'Well, this is not a big deal. We can fix this.' Buddy said he went and had surgery, and when he came out, he was fine," Milam recounted.

After Rogers dropped the title to Sammartino, he quickly became a secondary figure in the business. In late 1963, he hurt his back in a broken-chair accident, forcing him to forfeit a lucrative tour of Europe. He won $15,000 in a lawsuit against the Florida resort that owned the chair, and wrestled only a few matches, mostly in Montreal and Ohio, during the next few years. He made a comeback in 1979 in Florida and the Carolinas, handling some booking for Sunshine State promoter Eddie Graham, and briefly feuding with "Nature Boy" Ric Flair. Otherwise, Rogers' biggest post-retirement headlines came in July 1989, when he lived with wife Debbie in south Florida and was recovering from surgery. Rogers stepped to the plate at a Fort Lauderdale restaurant to stop a disgruntled twenty-four-year-old man from screaming abuses at female employees, and at him. The Nature Boy cuffed him around, earning plaudits from workers and the local police force. "Here he is, sixty-eight years old and he just had a bypass operation and a hip operation, and he stands up to this guy," Police Chief Joe Fitzgerald said.

"He was very outgoing, very confident, no question about that, just the way he walked and carried himself. He looked great until the day he died.

He was in perfect shape," said brother-in-law David Ludwigsen. "The ring didn't come out in him. He was a perfect gentleman, always, a great conversationalist. You wouldn't think he did what he did unless you actually knew it." True to form, Rogers' demise came in June 1992, when he was happily chatting with a woman in a grocery store. He slipped on some cream cheese and landed in the hospital, and then suffered a series of strokes that claimed his life on June 26, 1992.

Rogers in his Florida garden.

Through all the glitz and glamour, all the controversy and championships, Darnell still remembers his old friend as more of a soft touch, particularly in retirement, than anyone would ever imagine. "I found out what a softie he was when an old black Labrador dog was sick, laying down on his doorstep," Darnell said. "And he took the dog to a veterinarian, and got him well, and they were inseparable for a long time. And then, when Buddy died, that old dog lay down and wouldn't get up anymore. Debbie had to take the dog and have him put away."

"It was a lot of fun," Rogers told writer Ray Tennenbaum in 1985. "I wouldn't trade my life for any other athlete, for a lot of people I knew from day one. And I knew that I'd be the best at what I did, and even till this day I know that I was the best at what I did. I feel that, and no one can ever erase that thought."

2. GORGEOUS GEORGE

Enrique Torres remembers wrestling a chap by the name of George Wagner in Texas during the 1940s, and thinking he was a pretty tough customer. Not long after, he squared off with Wagner in California. Only this time, Wagner had curled his hair, donned an effeminate getup, and pranced to the ring as Gorgeous George. "I didn't know what to think," Torres recalled with a hearty laugh. "I knew he had done something. He was acting kind of fruity and it worked for him."

Jeeves tends to Gorgeous George's hair in a photo shoot for *SPORT* magazine.

It worked so well that Gorgeous George became a household name, lathering wrestling with show-business glitz that's still part of the sport today. Lost in the valets, orchids, and gold-plated bobby pins, though, was a simple fact — Wagner knew his way around the mat. "I'll tell you, Gorgeous George was a good wrestler," Torres said. Phil Melby, who battled him in Arizona, concurred. "He'd make a lot of these big guys squeal. They thought he was just for show. But you didn't want to go to the gym and get on the mat with him."

George was one of the biggest stars of the early days of television, and his act regaled fans from coast to coast on televised shows from California. During his peak, from 1947 until the mid-1950s, this Liberace in tights sent newspapers into full pop-celebrity alert whenever he ducked into town for a well-publicized hair appointment. "Each year, they pick a coiffure queen out there," Sam Menacher, one of George's handlers, said, waving a Hollywood flyer at sportswriter Red Smith during one hair-care interlude. "This year, for the first time, they picked a coiffure king. See? George. 'Our King,' it says here. The hairdo he's got, that's the Gorgeous George swirl."

Ardath Michael, the companion of wrestler Don Arnold, has pleasant memories of George — and the way he smelled — from the time she tended to George's locks in Memphis, Tennessee. "He had a certain style that was his trademark. He didn't want to deviate from that. He was an extremely nice person. . . He smelled better than anybody I ever smelled in my life. I don't know what he wore. I asked him one time, and he told me, I'm sure, but I was just a young thing." Certainly, George's hair sometimes deviated from Lana Turner platinum blond — he dyed it brunette, red, and indigo blue for some matches in 1947 and 1948, according to various accounts.

George Raymond Wagner's story was a true American rags-to-riches-to-rags tale. Born in 1915 in Seward, Nebraska, he was raised in Houston, never finished high school, worked at carnivals and small shows as a teenager, and peddled milk door-to-door to eke out a living. Wagner started his pro career when he was about seventeen, and made a mark for himself as a local favorite in Texas in the mid-1930s. "George Wagner, 185-pound native of Houston, is a clean, clever wrestler, who likes the flying tackle and the Irish whip made famous by ex-champion Danno O'Mahoney," the *Galveston Daily News* observed. As Wagner, he enjoyed moderate success for several years, winning the Pacific Coast Light Heavyweight title in 1938, taking his real-life marriage to Betty Hanson in a Eugene, Oregon ring in 1939 from venue to venue, and copping a regional junior heavyweight crown in 1941.

His transformation into Gorgeous George was gradual, and represented a compilation of ploys from wrestling's early showmen. His dazzling capes brought to mind the garb flashed by Danny McShain. Sterling "Dizzy" Davis, a childhood pal of Wagner's in Houston, developed a prissy character and tossed gardenias to fans; George chose orchids. Another influence was his friend Lord Lansdowne, who refused to enter a ring until his valets sprayed it, and took his sweet time folding his precious ring garments. Even in George's prime, Newspaper Enterprise Association sports editor Harry Grayson tipped a cap to Lansdowne as the man from whom George "got the resplendency idea." But, if those wrestlers were first in flight, George was the booster rocket — soaring to new heights, majestic, magnificent, radiating heat and light for all to see. He claimed close to one hundred robes in all the colors of the rainbow, full of ruffles and flourishes, with touches of mink and ermine thrown in. The late Portland, Oregon, promoter Don Owen said the robes helped pull up the curtain on George's performance around 1944, when he made a huge production number of disrobing. "You can imagine how this went over with an audience full of loggers and lumberjacks," laughed Owen. "Here was this guy taking his time and they grew impatient and wanted the action to start. So he would use that and take even longer until the point where it became a part of his whole act. It really drove fans crazy. They were incensed."

Wagner refined the character through the mid-1940s. By July 1945, he was advertised as "Gorgeous" George Wagner, though he was still a favorite in places like Missouri, and he was touted as "the California city slicker with an English valet" when he fought old buddy Davis in Oklahoma in early 1946. By spring 1947, the old Wagner disappeared and he was billed as "The Toast of the Coast." Late that year, he hit Los Angeles for good, and that's when his career took off, thanks in large part to the small screen. Dave Lewis of *The Independent* in Long Beach, California, noted George would more than double his annual income to about $100,000 after becoming Hollywood's latest poster boy. "The magic of television has done more for G.G. than anything else. In fact, the combination of Gorgeous George and television is credited with giving wrestling in southern California a much-needed shot in the arm."

Dick Brown, son of legendary champion Orville Brown, wrestled George several times in the 1950s, and remembered some of his early publicity stunts. Once, George rented a convertible limousine, drove to the corner of Hollywood and Vine, and started throwing money to the masses. "Most of it was change, but there were probably a few dollar bills and stuff. He's driving down there. 'Here, peasants, here, peasants!' Half the people out there were probably making more money than George was making and they're diving and scrambling for the money. He gets the story in the paper, the gag writers get on it, and he's getting national publicity out of it." As Brown concluded, "Nobody got over the way George did."

George's gimmick was big on the West Coast, but it fell flat in his bally-hooed debut in the East. In March 1949, he headlined a card in New York that brought wrestling back to Madison Square Garden for the first time in a dozen years. That drew just 4,197 fans, a weak $14,000 house, and a dismissive review from the NEA: "All Wagner — now Gorgeous George — succeeded in doing was setting rassling back another twelve years, or longer." While he drew big box-office numbers the late 1940s and early 1950s, the consensus is that he was better as an occasional novelty act. "[Primo] Carnera, Gorgeous George, and the rest give the game a great boost for six or seven weeks when they appear in a new city. But after they leave the place is 'dead' for wrestling," long-time grappler Karl Davis said. After George's death, "Nature Boy" Buddy Rogers told writer Ray Tennenbaum that the gimmick was not built for the long haul. "George had a big fantasy world around him for around three years. Every promoter wanted him, because he could pack the house. But, see, when you put bullshit into the house, remember what's comin' out — it ain't gonna be wine and roses. After three years, the bullshit waned away, and there wasn't anything left — and guess what? They had to resort to that good old word called — 'wrestling.'"

But it was darned entertaining while it lasted, and the ring entrance alone was worth the price of admission. A valet named Jeffries — sometimes his friend Jack Hunter — came to the ring, stiffly, with a bath mat, a rug, and a silver tray with George's toiletries. Only after the ring was disinfected, the mats put in place, and "Pomp and Circumstance" cued on the sound system would George deign to enter, tossing gold-plated bobby pins to delirious women as he marched up the aisle. "I like the finer things in life. It isn't an affectation. It is natural and normal. Dirt, sweat — ugh! Jeffries, the smelling salts. I feel faint," George snootily told Alan Ward of the *Oakland Tribune*. Dave

Brady of *The Washington Post* recognized George actually was a true bottom-line artist. "George isn't content with a mere act, he has a Wagnerian production, complete with a small cast and props. The idea is an offshoot of The Gorgeous One's love for attention, color, cleanliness, and the dollar bill, though not necessarily in that order." Others tried to mimic George's success; one Gorgeous George Arena was enjoined by a Chicago court in 1949 from referring to himself as "Gorgeous George."

Courtesy Wrestling Revue Archives

He was a bump-man ahead of his time.

During a typical bout, George forgot about his appearance and became the typical bad guy — punching, kicking, biting, and begging for mercy, tresses be damned. "They were mad at him because he was a show-off, with the curly hair, and the capes, and all that stuff. That's what ticked them off. He was a dirty wrestler too," said occasional rival Bill Melby. "I thought the guy produced real well. The people just didn't like him." Brown also recalled him as "a good, solid worker. He danced around a little bit here and there, but the match generally was pretty solid." But his renown came from his standing in the mainstream. George starred in a 1949 flick called *Alias the Champ*, about mobsters trying to grab a share of the California wrestling market. He hung out with Bob Hope and Eddie Cantor, appeared on *Queen for a Day*, and inspired pop songs. And he became the world's best-known turkey farmer, plowing part of his earnings into a ranch east of Los Angeles. At the 1951 National Turkey Show in California, he exhibited two turkeys, whose feathers were dyed orchid and sprayed with George's famous Chanel No. 10 "atomizer" every two minutes. Shopping for a holiday meal? Gorgeous George "orchid brand" turkeys were forty-nine cents a pound at the market during Thanksgiving 1956.

George had money, fame, acclaim, and even one version of the world title after beating Don Eagle in Boston in 1950. But the orchids in the ring did not smell as sweet outside of it. Betty divorced him in 1952, and he hooked up with a Las Vegas showgirl named Cherie Dupre, who took on the role of valet. John Hall, the celebrated *Los Angeles Times* sports columnist, lived in an apartment adjacent to George at the La Brea Towers in the 1950s. "Heavy drinking had begun to catch up with him. His liver and kidneys were in trouble. Sometimes you could hear him a block away, coughing all night," Hall wrote. "Still, he had the magic. When money ran short, he'd go barnstorming in the tank towns. His name sold right to the end." One night in Buffalo, George showed up loaded before a match with Ilio DiPaolo. Promoter Pedro Martinez sent two seconds out with George to toss him in the ring so DiPaolo could quickly put him in an airplane spin. "Now he gets up from the airplane spin and he staggers all over the place. The people don't know that he's drunk as hell," said Dick Beyer, one of the area's favorites at the time.

In April 1962, Cherie filed for a divorce, charging George threatened to kill her and became belligerent during his frequent binges; the two divorces drained a lot of his holdings. George turned his attention to his bar off Sepulveda Boulevard that featured life-sized mannequins of himself and his robe collection, and wall after wall of pictures with Hollywood stars. When Beyer, by then "The Destroyer," dropped in one day in 1962, he found the place deserted, and George desperate for money. Beyer talked promoter Jules Strongbow into booking a hair-versus-mask match in Los Angeles, with a follow-up a few weeks later. "He said he'd bring his valet, and I said, 'Well George, you're not going to get the mask.' He said, 'I don't care about the mask, I need a payday. I'll shave my head if I don't beat you and I'll have my barbers at ringside.' And that's exactly what happened." George was in and out of the hospital with liver problems. On Christmas Day 1963, he suffered a reported heart attack and died two days later, penniless. His funeral was, appropriately, a shindig. More than five hundred mourners showed up to send off George in his "George Washington" orchid robe, and fresh orchids covered his casket. He was buried in North Hollywood.

It didn't end there, of course. Gorgeous George Jr., Gorgeous George III, Adrian Street . . . every manner of pretty boy that henceforth donned a pair of boots represented a paean to "The Sensation of the Nation." In 1961, George transfixed a brash boxer named Cassius Clay with a stream of trash talk about an upcoming bout in Las Vegas. "And all the time, I was saying to myself, 'Man, I want to see this fight. It don't matter if he wins or loses; I want to be there to see what happens,'" Muhammad Ali recounted to author Thomas Hauser. "And that's when I decided I'd never been shy about talking, but if I talked even more, there was no telling how much money people would pay to see me."

A book on George's life is in the works. "With his bobby pins and his bleached hair, Gorgeous George became the progenitor of most of the performing we see in sports today," writer Bert Randolph Sugar opined. "I can't see a dance in an end zone without thinking, 'That was Gorgeous George.' He changed wrestling into the spectacle that it is."

3. THE SHEIK

Courtesy Wrestling Revue Archives

You didn't have to see The Sheik in person to be scared to death of him. Just stroll to the magazine rack at local newsstand in the 1960s and 1970s, and chances are you'd find his piercing eyes locked in a satanic trance, the embodiment of pure evil. Next to his face, headline writers added terror to his countenance: "Wrestler With a Flame Thrower in His Fingertips!" "The Sheik: Mysterious as the Night." The Sheik was to the wrestling press what Michael Jordan was to *Sports Illustrated* — the perfect cover image to capture a sport.

"I loved the guy. He gave you a lot of great shots, with the facial

The Sheik and The Princess (his wife Joyce) in an early photo.

expressions," said long-time *Wrestling World* editor Lou Sahadi, who shared a Lebanese heritage with The Sheik. "He was a 'good' bad guy, if there is such a thing. The fans loved to boo him. He really drew the emotions out of the fans. He was a great performer."

During a career that lasted almost fifty years, it's safe to say Edward Farhat, The Sheik, drew as much heat from fans around the world as any wrestler who's lived, whether it came from jabbing opponents with a broken pencil, hurling fire at them, or violently rolling his eyes and tongue as he tortured some poor soul. "The Sheik had a magnificent heel face, his eyes, he was terrifying to look at. I remember he saw me at the airport and he put his face right against mine and it scared me to death. I had about two hours of sleep," veteran star Lanny Poffo recalled. Legendary manager Bobby Heenan said The Sheik was his favorite villain. "This guy started hardcore wrestling. He would stick you with a screwdriver. He threw fire," Heenan said. "Plus, he never spoke. He never did an interview. He never spoke a word of English. He terrified people. He didn't take bumps. He didn't have to take bumps. If he had taken bumps, he would have been just another guy. Every time he came to the ring, you didn't know what he was going to do. He was the best heel this business ever had."

Even into the 1990s, when he was in his sixties, The Sheik could still lunge at a crowd and cause fans to scatter like cockroaches, according to Dave Burzynski, a.k.a. Supermouth Dave Drason, who managed him after starting as a writer and photographer for the Detroit promotion. "To go out with him for a couple years, it was just the thrill of a lifetime. I was always scared to death because the heat that guy could generate — I never knew what the heck was going to happen to me. Going to the ring was fine, but the walk back to the dressing room was the scariest moment I've ever had in the business. . . It was justified because of the times we got attacked."

Farhat's parents emigrated from Syria to Michigan, where he was born in 1926. (The family was Lebanese, but Lebanon did not become a separate country until 1943.) He joined the U.S. Army in 1944, and started training after the war with promoter Bert Ruby's Detroit office, while working as a day laborer. With Farhat's vaguely foreign looks, Ruby started him out as The Sheik of Araby, a well-to-do Middle Easterner who incorporated sheik and sultan gimmicks that had bounced around wrestling for years. He wasn't then the bloodlust scoundrel that he would become, and even worked on the Christiani Brothers Circus in 1950 and 1951. But televised wrestling from Chicago popularized his act, which consisted of attendant Princess Salima — his wife Joyce adopting Farhat's mother's name — snakes, incense, and an endless delay in folding his turban. Chicago also appears to have been the breeding ground for his crazed look. Years later, Jim Lancaster, who got his start in The Sheik's Detroit territory, listened to him describe his descent into madness during a talk in a Cleveland locker room. "He said that a cameraman in Chicago said, 'You know what you ought to do. You ought to look at the camera, and act like you're crazy, and act like you're out of your mind, and roll your eyes — that kind of stuff.' And they got to talking and he made a deal with the cameraman — 'I'll be in this corner and I'll do this expression.' That's really where it kind of started, as I overheard it," Lancaster said.

Through the 1950s and early 1960s, The Sheik was a top draw just about everywhere he went. At no point was he considered a superior worker; his matches emphasized violence and wild-eyed antics. Just one example: he started a near-riot in Rochester, New York, in 1961 by knocking out local favorite Ilio DiPaolo with a piece of steel after DiPaolo won by countout.

Even so, former world champion Lou Thesz, who had little time for gimmicks, said The Sheik had remarkable drawing power. Thesz came to admire his foe during their handful of matches. "He was a terrific salesman," Thesz said on WrestlingClassics.com before his death. "Once in Chicago when I didn't buckle to his antics and wanted him to wrestle, he just walked out of the ring and didn't come back. He was a great guy, but not a wrestler." In fact, Eddie Farhat Jr. said The Sheik took refuge from Thesz under a bus, prompting headlines that only accentuated his madman image.

In 1964, The Sheik acquired the Detroit promotion from Jim Barnett and Johnny Doyle, put himself on top, and started a reign of fear along the Great Lakes that's never been equaled. He took the U.S. title in Detroit and held it most of the time until his promotion shut its doors in 1980. Working with Toronto promoter Frank Tunney, The Sheik ran off a 127-match unbeaten string in Maple Leaf Gardens from 1964 to 1974, drawing biweekly crowds of 10,000-plus for matches that seldom ran more than five minutes. He guarded against fan attacks as he walked to the ring by keeping a razor blade in his fingers. "He just had that ability to work everybody into a frenzy. He might cut you. He was known to do it," said Bruce Swayze, whom The Sheik helped get working papers so he could wrestle in Detroit. "The guy was on fire for years in Toronto."

The Sheik probably was at his most infamous when he plucked Ernie Roth, the pint-sized voice of *Big Time Wrestling* in Calgary and elsewhere, stuck a fez on him, and named him Abdullah Farouk. Dressed in brightly colored, mod clothes that made audiences wince for the days of black and white, Farouk became the noble one's mouthpiece, an obnoxious, nattering talker who threatened opponents that The Sheik might, just might, break out the fire in his next match. "Ernie Roth was a trip, wasn't he? He was such a little shit and he was just arrogant, so arrogant," said Irish Mickey Doyle, who broke into wrestling in Detroit. "The first time I worked with The Sheik, we used to do TV in Dayton [Ohio] way back when. I think he bodyslammed me eight times in a row and then put the camel clutch on me, then Ernie Roth comes in and puts the boots to me, this little 130-pound guy. He was a great manager, just that arrogance."

Lancaster noticed a distinct difference between the way The Sheik wrestled on TV, crushing no-names in seconds, and the way he wrestled in arenas, holding out fans' hopes that he could be vanquished. "It was TV where he really convinced you that he was mean. It was never at the house show. At the house shows, they always gave the impression that the babyface could beat him. You went to the arena knowing that Bobo Brazil, Mark Lewin, all those guys were going to beat The Sheik and take the title. It was

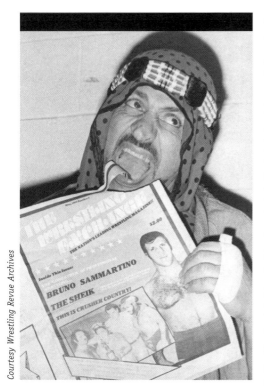

Courtesy Wrestling Revue Archives

Snacking on a magazine.

on TV that he shined. He always worked with the job guys; he always went two minutes. He would bite them and speak that Arabic language." In fact, The Sheik's famous babble, loudly blurted as he manhandled an opponent, was a play on his home area of Michigan. "He was actually saying the name of the city Kalamazoo," Lancaster laughed. "He would say it with that Arabic dialect, but he was saying Kalamazoo. Nobody knew what that language was. We bought everything." His most legendary feud was against Brazil; they fought hundreds of times during a thirty-year period, and Sahadi witnessed firsthand how hot the rivalry was during his trips to Detroit's Cobo Hall. "I was there maybe five or six times. They packed the joint; they absolutely packed it. There wasn't a single empty seat. It was really great wrestling, great theater. The place went nuts. The fans were on their feet for ten minutes."

Fans despised The Sheik, and some opponents felt the same way, saying he tried to hog the spotlight, turning heels into heroes so he could monopolize the bad guy side of the ledger. For instance, when Matt Gilmour got hot as Duncan McTavish in the early 1970s, The Sheik tried to squash him in one match, instead of letting a feud slowly brew. "He wouldn't let anyone else get the heat. That to me isn't what the business is about, to entertain the people, not to block the other guy," Gilmour said. "He wasn't a big man, but he did have the presence, and by doing that he went over, and I hope he made a lot of money because that's what it's about in the long run."

In other territories, Farhat's style was strictly non grata. Larry Matysik of the St. Louis office said there was some pressure to bring The Sheik into the city for promoter Sam Muchnick, after a Detroit promotional war with Dick the Bruiser died down in the early 1970s. The Sheik was a member of the National Wrestling Alliance, which Muchnick ran from St. Louis. "So Sam brought him in. He jumped Pat O'Connor before the match had even begun — we nearly had a riot. Sam said, 'That's it. He's done,'" Matysik said. "The madman thing, The Sheik stuff, that was never going to go here. Never. We had him in twice and that was it, never again."

Stories about The Sheik shortchanging wrestlers on paydays are legendary. Detroit-area fixtures such as "Killer" Tim Brooks, George Cannon, and Tony Marino ran an opposition office to him in the mid-1970s after finding cuts in their paychecks. Jack Reynolds, the voice of TV wrestling in Cleveland, and later an announcer for the WWWF, said The Sheik tried to push him out of the scene in favor of his own ring announcer for one introduction against Johnny Powers. "He and I did not get along, especially in the beginning. He could be a miserable SOB," said Reynolds, who did help The Sheik secure tickets to WrestleMania I a decade later. "He didn't trust anybody."

At the same time though, many of The Sheik's friends and regulars saw a kinder and funnier side. In 1962, Heenan washed The Sheik's car when he was in town for the Indianapolis office. "He was my first friend in the business," he said. "He befriended me, he talked to me, he gave me his car keys to wash and everything. He would give me a ride to the bus stop and give me five dollars. That was a lot of money for a kid." Mickey Doyle, new to the business, got a glimpse of The Sheik's mystical powers one night during a driving snowstorm, when The Sheik commandeered the wheel of an old Ford from crony Mike "Porky Pig" Loren for a ride from Kitchener, Ontario, to Detroit. "It was like a blinding snowstorm going back to Windsor, and then over to Detroit, and Porky's driving about twenty miles an hour, and by this time, Tex McKenzie is with us. He needed a ride back. Sheik goes, 'Lemme drive, pull this damn car over, Porky!' And he pulls over, Sheik gets behind the wheel, and he's going like sixty-five. You could not see a thing, it was a whiteout; Porky was crying, Tex is taking pictures out of his wife, 'Sheik, this happened to me before.' The Sheik says, 'Don't worry.' I'm sitting there; I've been in the business six months, and I'm thinking, 'I've got nothing to worry about. The Sheik's driving.' He got us back home in about two hours. It was unbelievable, right through the snow like Santa Claus and the reindeer."

By the mid-1970s, the Detroit office was going downhill fast, a combination of hard economic times and bad booking that kept the aging star headlining long past his prime. The Sheik continued wrestling through the 1980s — he was always a massive draw in Japan — and worked his final match in the U.S. in 1994. His health was shot as he climbed into the ring for a ceremony in Japan one last time in 1998. He died in January 2003, and his funeral was a perfect testament to the way he carefully guarded his character — the officiating priest called him by his given name just once and by "Sheik" throughout the rest of the service. You'll still associate his name with wrestling, as sons Tom and Eddie Jr. are working to revive his Big Time Wrestling promotion, and Sheik-trained stars like Rob Van Dam and Sabu, his nephew, continue to headline cards. "This guy was the most hated villain in wrestling," Supermouth Burzynski said. "He was a legend and you're not going to find another one like him."

4. MAD DOG VACHON

Mad Dog Vachon leaves bootprints on Jesse Ventura.

Courtesy Wrestling Revue Archives

The saying "It's not the size of the dog in the fight, but the size of the fight in the dog" was not coined for Maurice "Mad Dog" Vachon, but it might as well have been.

Though he towered over no one at five-foot-seven, Vachon, to butcher another cliché, never found a fight that he didn't want to be in — in or out of the ring. In fact, he may have created more bar fights than any wrestler in history. His contemporaries are quick with the stories, often involving alcohol and broken glass.

Outside the ring, explained Dutch Savage, "you'd have to hit him with a hammer or shoot him or he'd kill you." Killer Kowalski chuckled while telling his Mad Dog story. "One time we went to a bar outside Minneapolis. Someone gave him a little flak and he beat the shit out of the guy. Took a jar, or something like that, and hit the guy over the head with it." Mad Dog's brother Paul "The Butcher" summed it up nicely: "The guy would rather fight than eat."

In the ring, it was a similar story. "His kick was when he got ahold of a young wrestler that didn't have much experience, he would beat the shit of him just for fun," said Hans Schmidt. "I never liked that, but that's the way he was. He didn't like to give nobody a chance." Rick Martel had only been wrestling a short while when, in Texas in the fall of 1975, he found himself in the ring facing his hero — whom he had seen beat up fans in Quebec ("It was like a wolf was sent into the crowd, with everybody scattering"). Martel admitted, "I had mixed emotions. I had heard some stories about him, that he was hard on kids, and young guys, just beat them up. For me, it was the ultimate thing; finally I was going to wrestle this guy I idolized. I wrestled him, and wow, what a night it was for me. . . . He gave me a chance to make a match out of it. I had a lot of respect for him after that."

Vachon offers no excuses. Though he was a successful amateur wrestler, who competed for Canada in the 1948 Olympic Games and the 1950 Empire Games, he loved to fight. He learned to be tough in a family of thirteen kids in Ville-Émard, a working-class section of Montreal. Anybody with the temerity to tease a Vachon with the rhyme *Vachon cochon* (Vachon the pig) would suffer the consequences. Quitting school at thirteen, and dabbling in boxing, it was wrestling that kept his interest. Maurice and his brothers would walk three miles just to see the posters in the windows at the Montreal Forum. When they could afford it, they'd pay seventy-five cents to get in to the matches, then sneak down to ringside. "I was one of the biggest wrestling fans in the world then," said Mad Dog. "I knew every one of them, 'Jumping' Joe Savoldi, The French Angel, Henri Deglane."

Finding that medals earned as an amateur didn't put food on his table, Vachon broke into professional wrestling in the early 1950s in northern Ontario under Larry Kasaboski's Northland Wrestling promotion during the summer, and in Texas during the winter. "When I started wrestling professional, I have to admit I was a good-looking young man, had a lot of hair and beautiful teeth. But it didn't take me long to realize that good guys finish last," he once said. Dubbed "Mad Dog" in Portland, Oregon, by promoter Don Owen in 1962, Vachon became box-office gold with his total disregard for the rules, penchant for mayhem, and unpredictability. And though he claims to never have made the big, big money, he found his reward in the riots; to a superstar heel, that was applause.

"After a while, it's an art. You just do it by instinct," said Mad Dog, who, at seventy-eight, is generally a whole lot less ornery now, and lives with his third wife, Kathie, in Nebraska. "One time I was in Texas. They sent out the first match, no response, hardly anybody there. Second match, no response. Finally, when I got in the ring, I got a riot! People started hollering at me. I picked one guy at ringside, right next to the ring. I said, 'Come on, you son of a bitch! Get in the ring!' Then everybody got mad at me because I picked on one guy, and got heat with that. One way or another, I got them going."

But Mad Dog Vachon's success came from much more than the violence, or his bald-headed, bearded look. There was, perhaps most of all, the wide-eyed, spit-flying intensity, and the gravelly, guttural voice. Rene Goulet said Vachon was the best interview in the business: "You had to believe when he was saying something . . . his expression was fabulous."

Greg Oliver

Mad Dog hamming it up for the cameras with Edouard Carpentier in 2006.

"Here was a guy who was a horrible worker, and no matter who you were, you had to adapt to his style, and you never knew what the hell he was going to do," added promoter Bill Watts. "But did Mad Dog draw money? You're damn right he drew money. Why'd he draw money if he was such a bad worker? He drew money because of the intensity of who he was. His interviews were so dominant because he believed that he was the toughest son of a bitch that walked. And he may have been!"

Was Mad Dog ever scared? "I loved it. I loved it. Very seldom did I get scared, very seldom. I knew what to do," he said. "I got hit with bottles thrown from the top bleachers. Remember years ago, they used to sell beer bottles at the wrestling. I got hit right in the face with bottles. One time, when I was wrestling in Bermuda, somebody threw a full Coke can at the back of my head. But beer bottles, twice I got hit in the face. They hit you with chairs."

His greatest days came in the Midwest, where he was American Wrestling Association world champion five times, including the Omaha version of the belt. It was also where he matched up with the yin to his yang. In clean-cut, hometown hero Verne Gagne (who also went to London for the 1948 Olympics, though didn't compete), Vachon had someone to lock up in epic good versus evil battles all around the circuit. He also had somebody to help turn him babyface.

The unlikely switch to fan favorite came in 1979, when Gagne decided he needed real help in battling Ray Stevens, Pat Patterson, and Nick Bockwinkel, all managed by Bobby Heenan. "I'm going to need somebody who's going to surprise everybody. I'm going to get my biggest enemy," Gagne recalled. "The Dog and I tagged up together, and I'll never forget his words. We were doing a television interview, and they were interviewing both he and I at the same time. He said [imitating Mad Dog's voice] 'Verne Gagne, remember this. When the match is over, and we get our hands raised, you go your way, and I'll go my way.' And that's what happened." Actually, Vachon would later coax Gagne out of retirement to battle Sheik Adnan El Kaissy and Jerry Blackwell.

But the roll toward immortality had begun. By the time Maurice decided to retire from pro wrestling for good, he was a folk hero in his native province; and like other celebrated Quebecers such as Jean Beliveau and Guy Lafleur, he had a farewell tour. In his final match, Mad Dog teamed with Jos Leduc to beat Sheik Ali (Stephen Pettipas) and Man Mountain Moore at Le Colisée in Quebec City on October 8, 1986. He was given a Quebec Nordiques jersey with the number fifty-seven on the back, representing his age. Vachon also became a spokesman for various products, including beer and chocolate bars, and reviewed restaurants. Then there was the rap record, with the unmistakable crushed-rock voice of the Mad Dog rhyming off in French to a funky beat. Collectors beware.

In 1987, his fame grew even more through a terrible hit-and-run accident. Mad Dog was walking along the road in Des Moines, Iowa, when he was clipped by a driver. As a result of the incident, he lost his right leg below the knee, but gained a true sense of his impact on society. The cards and letters poured in from young and old, and the Canadian Prime Minister called in his best wishes. Soon, a private corporate jet was dispatched to bring Mad Dog home for treatment. The transformation to Canadian icon was complete.

"I was in wrestling forty-four years, I had about 13,000 matches, and I did everything I could so the people would hate me. I failed miserably!" Mad Dog has said often. Today, he keeps in touch with his six children, seven grandchildren and eight great-grandchildren. He has been honored by his peers with the highest tribute given by the Cauliflower Alley Club, the Iron Mike Mazurki Award; he is a member of the Professional Wrestling Hall of Fame in the Tag Team Division with his brother Paul; and he was inducted into the George Tragos/Lou Thesz Professional Wrestling Hall of Fame in 2003. Up next, perhaps the Poker Hall of Fame. "That's all I do now, watch poker on TV," he said. "I used to tell people Mad Dog is the name, wrestling is the game; if you don't like my face, come and tell me to my face. Don't talk behind my back. I'm Mad Dog Vachon and I approve of this message. Now I say, Mad Dog is the name, poker is the game; if you don't like my hand, maybe you'd prefer my fist!"

5. "WILD" BILL LONGSON

On January 5, 1937, in San Francisco a promising boxer-turned-wrestler named Bill Longson took a bad bump in a match against Man Mountain

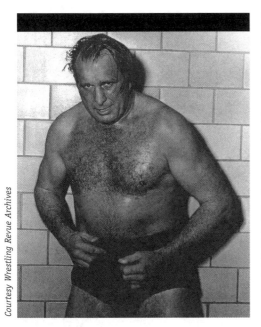

Bill Longson looking wild.

Dean. While performing his famous running broad jump, the 315-pound Dean landed awkwardly and shattered Longson's back. Longson tried to wrestle a couple of more matches, but the pain was so intense that even the tough young man, who busted wild mustangs as a Utah teenager, knew something was seriously wrong. Doctors put him in traction and a body cast, propped his feet higher than his head, and hinted at invalid status. By his physicians' reckoning, his career — started as a way of bringing some money to his family — was surely over.

In fact, it was just beginning.

From that untimely accident, which sidelined him for nine months, "Wild" Bill Longson recovered to become a three-time world champion, the first long-term heel champion in wrestling history, and the biggest money draw of his time.

"He was a wild son of a gun," said an admiring Sonny Myers, himself a former world title claimant. "Bill Longson was a hell of a wrestler, and he didn't give what he didn't take. Boy, he was in there and he gave the people their money's worth. He was a great champion. He was a hell of a guy."

Born in Salt Lake City in 1906, Willard Longson was the second oldest in a vigorous family of five boys. He played football and wrestled in high school, but his education was cut short when his father, a prison guard, lost his job because he couldn't bring himself to fire on an escapee. Longson and a brother went to work to support the family, breaking in wild mustang horses and toiling on road crews that pounded highways into the rocks and dirt of the Salt Lake valley. "I guess I was a wild one even when I was a kid," Longson said after he retired.

But he never was far from athletic endeavors. He continued to practice on the mats and in the ring, and captured the Amateur Athletic Union Boxing and Wrestling Intermountain titles three times from 1927 to 1931. Local promoter Verne McCullough took notice of him and directed Longson into professional wrestling. "At that particular time, it was the Depression. Conventional jobs were few and far between, so the opportunity to make money wrestling really came along at the right time," reflected his son, Dick Longson. Wild Bill still kept up his boxing too, and wasn't afraid to shoot for the top there, though a one-round knockout loss to Jack Dempsey in September 1931 helped him define his ultimate line of work. "Jack hit me with a short punch to the heart and I thought I was going to die," Longson laughed years later.

In wrestling, Longson fared much better, starting in Utah and Nevada before moving to California in 1934. Considered an up-and-coming star, the match with Dean halted his progress dead in its tracks. Immobilized at first, with no medical insurance, he forsook a graft that would support his weak-ened spinal column with shin bone for fear it would cripple him. He moved back to Salt Lake City with his family and worked doggedly at rehabilitation. "The breaks of the game, and sometimes the breaks are a broken back," he explained to one interviewer. In a move seen too infrequently in wrestling and other businesses, California promoter Joe Malcewicz stepped in to help cover medical bills and living expenses.

Canada's Sports Hall of Fame / Turofsky Collection

The ultimate villain, trashing a photo of hero Whipper Watson.

Upon his return to the ring, Longson was hailed as "a miracle man," and moved quickly to make up for lost time. In 1938, he mystified Bay Area audi-ences as the "Purple Shadow," a hooded creature with an inexhaustible supply of dirty tricks. During a July 1938 bout against Terry McGinnis, Oakland fans pelted his lavender hood with a sackful of tomatoes, but Longson was undeterred. Four years later, he donned a mask in Louisville, Kentucky, as "Superman II," pulled off his disguise in mid-match, and choked Orville Brown into submission with it.

Longson held the heavyweight title of the National Wrestling Association, a forerunner of the National Wrestling Alliance, three times in the 1940s. He first beat Sandor Szabo in February 1942, and held the belt for several months. His second reign stretched for four years, from 1943 to 1947, and he held the crown again for eight months before dropping a title bout to Lou Thesz in July 1948. "He was a great wrestler and a great champion. He knew about every trick in the business," said Angelo Savoldi, a frequent opponent.

The reason for Longson's extended reigns was simple — he packed in the crowds. He is the most dominant wrestler in the fabled history of St. Louis, his adopted hometown, where he was at the top of 133 cards from 1942 to 1955, averaging more than 9,000 fans per outing. Loathed by fans — he took a three-inch knife cut on his leg from a spectator in Evansville, Indiana, in June 1943 — promoters everywhere demanded his service. A typical spurt in 1948 found him in Cleveland, Montreal, Toronto, and St. Louis on consecutive nights, pre-interstate highway and pre-discount airfare. "'Wild Bill' was the villain and a more convincing blackguard never pulled on the wrestling trunks," said John Mooney, long-time sports editor of the *Salt Lake City Tribune*.

In the ring, Longson was a true innovator. With a wild shock of black hair dangling over his eyes, he typically mauled opponents at the opening bell with a flurry of punches and kicks. Just as his foe mounted a comeback, Longson unfurled his signature escape, a running vault over the top rope during which he was nearly parallel to the floor, a high-flying move for the times. Back in the ring, he wrestled marathons. In Houston alone, he battled to a two-hour draw against Bobby Managoff in 1942, and a pair of two-hour draws against Thesz in 1942 and 1943. After watching Longson tear apart Ali Baba in a 1942 bout, George A. Barton of the *Minneapolis Tribune* concluded: "He did everything to the squat Turk except rip out a ring post and wrap it around Ali's well-shaved noggin. . . . Judging from his actions, Longson must have taken a vow to make the public despise him."

After Longson softened up his opponent, he invariably broke out the piledriver, a move he popularized, folding his opponents on their necks like collapsed accordions. The Missouri state athletic commission "barred" the deadly hold because of its danger to the welfare of his victims, which only added to its dangerous allure.

Rip Hawk, who worked with him in St. Louis, recalled that Longson was so incredibly active in the ring that he actually gave himself a shiner one night. "We were tag team partners. I'll never forget that match because it was so funny that he gave himself a black eye. He was the type of wrestler who was always moving. I tagged him to go into the ring and he started to move his arms up and down, and he hit himself in the eye. I ribbed him about that for a long time. He was a great guy, a top wrestler and a top gentleman too."

Dick Longson, who traveled the circuits with his dad as a teenager, said his heel style was a natural extension of his rough-and-tumble youth. "He learned the techniques of wrestling as an amateur, but he liked the tough stuff, and I think right away he probably recognized that it had an effect on the crowds that watched the matches."

Longson held his share of other titles too. He was a three-time Pacific Coast champion, Central States champion, and Texas Brass Knuckles champion, among other honors. Even when he cut back on his schedule, he was capable of inciting riots. In Kansas City, Missouri, he fought to a no contest outside the ring with Antonino Rocca in November 1959 in a melee that required police intervention. A year later, he got into a scrap with future legend Gene Kiniski on the *Wrestling at the Chase* TV show. "He came in to break up a fight," said long-time St. Louis wrestling executive Larry Matysik. "It ended up with him and Kiniski, slap, slap, bang, bang. He grabs Kiniski and gives him a piledriver. This is 1960, I can still remember the reaction of the crowd in there, watching it on TV, watching how that audience reacted. It was like, when he delivered that piledriver, 'He just killed Gene Kiniski.' Everybody bought it."

In his private life, Longson could not have been more different. He was married to Althea for fifty-five years, and his two children became successful professionals as a schoolteacher and manufacturing executive. He became a local icon in St. Louis, where he owned a portion of the lucrative promotion — everybody knew Wild Bill. He fulfilled the bright pride of his father, George, who, when he died, had in his wallet no money and no debts, but a sole clipping of his son winning the world championship. It was a long and remarkable career, and it grew from a quiet resolve to overcome a devastating injury suffered in San Francisco on a January day long ago.

"He didn't talk much, he didn't whine. But he must have done a lot of thinking," wrote Alan Ward of the *Oakland Tribune*. "Maybe it's possible the nature of his thoughts pulled him through a pretty tough situation. Thoughts have the power to heal, if they're backed with courage and determination."

6. FRED BLASSIE

In his heyday, no one disdained, detested, and abhorred his audience more than Freddie Blassie. He spat venom in his wrestling interviews, dismissing fans as "pencil-neck geeks." And he wasn't any different in the many stories written by newspaper reporters. "Sure, people are dumb," Blassie told columnist Joe Hendrikson of the *Pasadena Star-News* in 1962. "If people weren't dumb they wouldn't hate me so. They'd pull for me to win because they'd have something to cheer about every time." That same year, he told the *Long Beach Independent Press-Telegram*, "You might say that wrestling is the oldest profession. People have always watched it. They come out to cheer the hero and boo the villain. As far as I'm concerned, they're all a bunch of

Freddie Blassie tries to remove Mil Mascaras's mask.

idiots." When the *Wall Street Journal* caught up with Blassie a decade later, he was working as a babyface, but things hadn't changed much. "Those people will believe anything," declared the "Hollywood Fashion Plate."

The ink-stained wretches did their best to fire back — *Los Angeles Times* sportswriter Jim Murray once called Blassie "the worst villain since Hitler," asserting that he "wrought something of a revolution in the unmanly art of exhibition wrestling" — but Blassie had the bigger audience.

Consider this TV tirade from Los Angeles: "Well, you know, the women may swoon over me, but like I say, it doesn't do them any good. Because the people that I've seen so far, the women around here, the way they dress, I mean, it looks like they're all dressed in potato sacks! The women where I come from, they dress like women. And they want the fellas to appreciate them. And they know how to dress. But the women that I've seen out here, believe me, they're nothing but pigs."

Though his hatred of the fans was a front — he would sign autographs if asked politely — his unwavering arrogance and confidence as a performer stayed with him throughout his career, to the point that some wondered where "Classy" Freddie ended and Fred Blassie, the nice kid from St. Louis, began.

"There was a lot of Blassie that was consistent with his character on TV. I think that it's inevitable if you play a role well that some of that becomes part of your personality," said his biographer, Keith Elliot Greenberg. "What came first, the talent of the Freddie Blassie character with Freddie Blassie the human being, and how much of Freddie Blassie the human being that I got to know in later life was inspired by Freddie Blassie, the character? Certainly his very gruff ways, the way that his voice would suddenly raise very quickly. He was an old man when I worked with him, so sometimes he would get confused and cranky, like somebody's grandfather, but it seemed very similar to the Freddie Blassie that I saw on TV, his impatience."

In his autobiography, *Listen, You Pencil Neck Geeks*, Blassie admits as much:

"Freddie Blassie the man had turned into Freddie Blassie the wrestler. And even with my wife and kids, I'd become — as the boys like to say — a mark for my own gimmick."

"He was never out of character," explained "The Destroyer" (Dick Beyer). He was Freddie Blassie "all the time, even when we played cards." Butcher Vachon agreed. "He believed he was a dirty guy, and he acted like one, calling everyone pencil-neck geek, insulting everyone. He lived his life like a villain."

And oh what a life it was. At his peak, "The King of Men" was a celebrity in Hollywood, with movie and TV stars seeking him out after

James C. Melby Collection

The pose.

his matches at the Olympic Auditorium, and admirer Andy Kaufman casting him in his indie flick *My Breakfast With Blassie*. He recorded two albums, and his song, "Pencil-Neck Geek" is still requested on Dr. Demento's novelty radio show. But even that paled in comparison to his stardom in Japan, where Blassie was caught filing his teeth while coming off the plane before battling Rikidozan for the World Wrestling Association world title. The simple gimmick got Blassie labeled as "The Vampire," and he would bite at opponents' heads until blood streamed. The shock of his viciousness is "credited" for the deaths of dozens of people in Japan. Still, that wasn't enough for Blassie, who once boasted, "In my whole career, ninety-two people dropped dead of heart attacks. My ambition was to kill one hundred, and I failed."

Born in St. Louis in 1918, Blassie was a boxer early in his career, working the carnival circuit. "But nobody wanted to box. They all wanted to wrestle. And I wasn't making a penny. So I decided to become a wrestler. I was wrestling in carnivals," he told the *WrestleTalk* radio show months before his death on June 3, 2003. His first match, he said, was in 1935, in East St. Louis, Illinois. "I didn't know anything about wrestling. All I knew was a headlock, body scissors. The guy beat the daylights out of me, and I made a dollar. My wrestling license cost five dollars. I was getting the daylights beat out of me, and I lost money on the deal." St. Louis got to be a hot wrestling town, and Blassie was able to learn from the likes of "Crusher" Casey, Lou Thesz, and Everett Marshall.

The six-foot, 220-pound Blassie had his career interrupted by a stint in the navy from 1942 to 1946. While in the service, he participated in a few exhibitions to raise money for war bonds. Upon his return to active wrestling, he was known as "Fred The Sailor," and by 1950, was a main event babyface.

Teaming with Billy McDaniels as his "brother" Fred McDaniels got Blassie to Los Angeles for the first time. Back on the other coast, he got hot — real hot — in Atlanta and held the Southern heavyweight title fourteen times. He considered capturing the Southern belt a real turning point in his career. "From then on, there was no stopping me. I became the talk of the South, I just became the talk of the wrestling profession," Blassie told *WrestleTalk*. It was also in Atlanta that he bleached his hair and first became a major heel. "I always figured if I was going to be rough, I'd be the roughest one in the profession," he told *The LAW* radio show. "I went out of my way to be obnoxious and ugly. I could care less, spit in their face and everything."

Greenberg, a lifelong New Yorker, was surprised to learn just how big Blassie was in the South as he wrote his book. "Before he was the Hollywood Fashion Plate, he was a fairly notorious heel in the South. Had he retired at that point, there'd be a fair segment of Southerners that would remember him as this very rambunctious heel that held titles down there," he said.

But as great as Blassie was while based out of Atlanta — he owned a part of the Paul Jones-run promotion for a time, and kept an apartment there for years — Hollywood and Blassie was a marriage made in heaven.

It was all a matter of timing, said Art Williams, who was a fan when Blassie arrived on the West Coast, and later refereed and promoted. "He was just so immaculate, his hair, his ring attire — he would never wear the same ring attire in the same town two weeks in a row — powder blue, matching trunks and boots one week, the next week would be another color, and the next week another color. He just had the fire, that's the word to use, the fire," Williams said. "Once he got through the ropes, just the look in his eyes, the fans, they hated his guts before he was even introduced! They wanted to kill him before the match even started. With his finger off the forehead, throwing sweat at the fans. Pacing like a caged lion before the match started. Just his persona. He hit the right territory at the right time, like the Beatles did."

The disputed National Wrestling Alliance world title match between champion Lou Thesz and Edouard Carpentier in Chicago on June 14, 1957, led to a series of changes. Some promoters recognized Carpentier as the champion, including the Los Angeles office. The World Wrestling Association world title came out of the chaos, and Blassie would beat Carpentier for the belt on June 12, 1961. A short while later, Blassie beat Thesz (who had lost the NWA belt) as well to solidify his claim to supremacy. The WWA belt became an even bigger deal when Blassie switched the championship with Rikidozan.

For the next decade, Blassie ruled Los Angeles, spouting off on whatever he liked, making appearances on talk shows and doing walk-on roles on *The Dick Van Dyke Show*. But that is not to disparage his in-ring skills. "The thing he did that no one is doing today is sell," said Los Angeles publicist Jeff Walton. "Blassie sold the hell out of everything. The bell would ring and the other guy would beat the hell out of him for most of the match, then he'd come back with a low blow or something, and barely roll over and pin the guy. That's how he got his heat."

In 1965, a series of ailments led to a kidney being removed, forcing the forty-seven-year-old Blassie to the sidelines. Until he was able to wrestle again, he sold cars in Atlanta, and his business card read, "Mr. Wrestling, 4 Time World Champion."

Wrestling was in his blood though, and after a cautious return in Atlanta, he ventured West again. By the end of 1969, the promotion realized it was time for a change. "It all started when I jumped in and helped out a couple of Latin wrestlers who were getting beat pretty bad in a tag team match," Blassie said of his babyface turn to the *Wall Street Journal* in 1971. More important, as he wrote in his book, the switch to good guy allowed him to slow down the pace of his matches, but his style never changed. Storied feuds with The Sheik, John Tolos and Kinji Shibuya followed.

Blassie's body was starting to wear out, however. He made a trek to the WWWF, challenged for the world title, then eased into managing as a full-time gig. During his first WWWF run in 1978, Blassie managed "Bad News" Allen Coage, who recalled, "Blassie was my manager, but he was my favorite hero as a talker. He wasn't a great worker — and he'd tell you that to your face — but as a talker, he was just unbelievable. He could just use his mouth and people wanted to kill him." Two of Blassie's charges reached iconic status. Hulk Hogan was one. Blassie was at Hogan's side when he first came in to battle Andre the Giant in the WWWF. Blassie was also the colorful frontman for Muhammad Ali for the boxing champ's 1976 mixed bout with Antonio Inoki. In 1986, Blassie left the scene, content to do public relations appearances for the WWF. He was inducted into the WWE Hall of Fame in 1994, and the Professional Wrestling Hall of Fame in 2004.

During his last years, confined to a wheelchair, Blassie was still an unabashed fan of the WWF. "I hear this all the time, 'In your day, in your day.' In my day, we couldn't keep up with these kids today," he told *WrestleTalk.* "They do things that we hadn't even thought of." He did numerous voice-overs and promos for the WWF, including the great "showcase of the immortals" clips for WrestleMania. "Whenever they need me, they give me a call, send a limo out for me," he said. He was also used in a Knute Rockne type role for the WWF troops as the Invasion angle started in 2001. Blassie issued a challenge to the WWF roster: "Gentleman, there comes a time when every man must fight for that he believes in. Now is the time, get up, stand up, and fight." He didn't share his oft-quoted mantra though: "Win when you can. Lose when you must. But at all times, cheat."

7. JOHNNY VALENTINE

Bill Janosik

Johnny Valentine wraps a strap around a bloody Wahoo McDaniel in Hampton, Virginia.

Johnny Valentine took his time, meeting everything on his own measured terms, whether it was wrestling, finding the love of his life, or staving off death. He took his time against a young Johnny Powers at Toronto's Maple Leaf Gardens, when, for several minutes, Powers couldn't get his opponent to touch him. "The Toronto fans, who were quite sophisticated, at first yelled out, 'Bullshit! Fake! Fake! These guys don't want to fight!'" Powers said. Five minutes went by, then ten, then twelve, as Powers muttered, "Valentine — lock up." "Not yet," was Valentine's reply. Slowly, the crowd turned from skeptical to convinced. After seventeen minutes, it was time. "All of a sudden, boom! He locks up. I'm telling you, a simple collar-elbow lock-up, the damn crowd went crazy, and I knew then I was in the ring with an absolute pure artist. That's how great Valentine was. I think there was no greater artist in that form of wrestling that I've ever seen."

Wrestlers don't agree on much — who was the toughest, which promoter was the biggest cheapskate, who drew the biggest gates. But they do agree that Johnny Valentine was at the top of his profession. "I rate him probably as the best this business has ever seen," said former NWA world champion Jack Brisco. "He was 100 percent professional; he never hogged a match — that was never his intention. He just had that style that made him look so tough that everybody believed he was for real. He just had a charisma about him that was second to none."

Valentine was one of the sport's biggest attractions, and its most authentic performer, ice-blue eyes fixed straight ahead in a singleness of purpose, until a 1975 airplane crash left him disabled. "What was so great was that he didn't believe in high spots, because in a high spot, it's not realistic. If I were to get you into a fight, I wouldn't be throwing you into the ropes, would I?" asked Lanny Poffo. "And his face, he looked like a handsome, cruel man, like a sniper, with no expression, and kind of a deadpan look. His hair would bounce every time."

Valentine was born John Wisniski in 1928 and raised in the mountains near Hobart, Washington, outside of Seattle. His childhood was difficult; friends and relatives describe his parents as dysfunctional. An older sister married, and she and her husband watched the teenager, who ratted around at his brother-in-law's race-car business, and passed hours at a gym. There, the famous Stanislaus Zbyszko saw him and took him under his wing, moving him to a farm in Missouri so Wisniski could train and provide cheap labor for the Zbyszko manor. "Zbyszko sold me on wrestling," Valentine explained in a 1985 interview. "By the time I looked in all his old scrap-books, I was very interested."

Valentine turned pro in 1947 — in Buenos Aires, of all places — and soon determined that the unpronounceable name of Wisniski wouldn't do. So he picked up on the name of a radio show that he loved to listen to at his grandmother's house. "He'd go there and get to listen to the radio some, and there was an 'Inspector Valentine' on the radio. And that's where he decided he'd like the name Valentine," his wife Sharon recounted.

Valentine was a hit early on. As a snotty "Atomic Blond" with Chet Wallick, he was booed in the Midwest, but after a split with Buddy Rogers, he was cheered in the Northeast. "You get the 'bad guy' image because you are successful," he admitted to Shirley Garden of the *Galveston Daily News* in 1970. "People always go for the underdog and because I am not the underdog, they dislike me." Regardless, once he refined his character, time and tempo moved according to his dictates. "Heel or babyface, Johnny was the type of guy who never changed his style. It looked like he was going to knock your head off," said Nick Kozak. "One time, he hit me so hard in the chest — because he liked to bend you backward on the ropes — I know I passed gas."

Valentine pounded, and pounded, and pounded, and the harder you hit him — egad! — the more he liked it. "He'd whack you, I mean, he did, and you'd whack him back. That son of a bitch used to get goosebumps," said Ronnie Garvin. "You'd whack him as hard as you've got and he'd go, 'Heh, heh . . . is that all you've got?'" Bill Dromo fought Valentine for the Southern title in Tampa, Florida, one night and both men entered the ring sunburned. "We pounded the hell out of each other and we were welted. I mean, we were absolutely welted. Even the people, when we walked by, they said, 'My God!' All I said was, 'Uhhh.' I was hurting, and I know damn well he was hurting too."

Valentine even took his sweet time coming to the ring. Bob Roop remembered one approach to the ring apron in Tampa, where Valentine walked in like he was alone in the building. "All of a sudden, it was like he'd been day-dreaming or something. He came out of it. He just very slowly turned and looked at one side of the audience. Just about every person jumped up, and was shaking their fists at him, and screaming at him because he'd been ignoring them," Roop said.

"You could feel Johnny Valentine all the way up to the bleachers," added Dr. Tom Prichard, who admired him while growing up as a fan in Houston. "He just had this aura about him, and you wouldn't dare approach him for an autograph or anything because he'd just scare the hell out of you."

Valentine was an inveterate prankster, and the story of how he allegedly filled Jay "The Alaskan" York's asthma inhaler with lighter fluid is part of wrestling lore. Pepper Martin can set the record straight since he saw it play out in a St. Louis dressing room. "Nobody saw Valentine put lighter fluid in his inhaler," Martin cautioned. "But what did happen was when Jay came out of the ring, he went to his bag, and he's huffing and puffing. He started choking and coughing, and Valentine tried not to laugh." Later that night, York pulled a sawed-off shotgun and blew a hole through Lou Thesz's metal suitcase, thinking it was Valentine's. "Well," Valentine deadpanned when York brandished the gun, "I can't top that." A few days later, Martin and Valentine were stuck in traffic near York's vehicle. York got out of his car, walked back to his colleagues, and tossed a hand grenade through the window. Martin and Valentine scurried for cover; the grenade was a dummy. "Valentine thought that was a great joke," Martin said.

Other wrestlers said York and Valentine combined forces to pull inhaler-and-gun pranks. One night, York "assassinated" Valentine in front of Powers in the Minneapolis territory. "All of a sudden, bam! The gun goes off," Powers vividly recalled. "I went, 'Ah fuck, Jay. You stupid son of a bitch.' I can still feel the tension in my body." Then, from the floor, Valentine sprung to life, chuckling even as York laughed uproariously. Powers explained, "That's kind of what Valentine could do in the ring. Take his time and set things up. He was an artist in a physical form." For the record, Sharon said her husband confided that he never actually put goo in any of York's inhalers, though he said someone else possibly could have.

Sharon experienced Valentine's legendary deliberation in 1971 when she worked as a hair-dresser at a Dallas department store. Valentine asked for her opinion about perfume he planned to buy for his daughter, then methodically reappeared every day during her lunch break. "Finally, I asked him, 'Johnny, how do you know where I'm always going to eat?' His response — he lived in a penthouse apartment across the

Valentine battles The Sheik.

street, and, come lunchtime, he broke out his binoculars and started looking for her. As she chuckled thirty-five years later, "It took me some time to really come around, but when I did, it was like, 'Boom! I'm hooked.'"

Valentine only held one singles world championship — the National Wrestling Federation in 1972. But his talent was so legendary that he was in demand everywhere despite occasional rifts with promoters and competitors. In 1974, he shook up the Mid-Atlantic territory with a smack-your-chest feud against Wahoo McDaniel, who assured booker George Scott that Valentine spelled box-office success. "I told [Scott] to take my word for it, that he works a style, but when he gets over, nobody else will ever be able to get over," McDaniel told journalist Mike Mooneyham in 2001. "It was that slow, rugged, brutal style. He was a brilliant man with the best timing in the world."

On October 4, 1975, Valentine was in the front seat of a twin-engine Cessna that ran out of fuel and crashed near Wilmington, North Carolina. The pilot later died, but two of the six passengers, Ric Flair and Tim Woods, were able to return to the sport. Valentine broke his back and was paralyzed for life. He was in and out of hospitals for a year. When girlfriend Sharon visited him in Florida, he brushed her off. Eight years passed and late in 1983, after Sharon had battled her own health problems, her daughter announced that a man on crutches was working his way toward her Texas house. "Momma, you're not going to believe this, but Johnny Valentine is walking up the driveway."

"Oh my God, please tell him I'm dead," Sharon recounted. "So I locked myself in the bathroom." Valentine would have none of that. "I finally got my head on straight," he told her. He'd been driving aimlessly around the area since dawn, looking for the house and looking for her. He had some questions.

Was she dating anyone? Did she still have feelings for him? Would she marry him?

"I said, 'Oh, I guess so.'"

They were married in a small church in Bowie, Texas, on Valentine's Day, 1984.

Their seventeen years together were not easy. His hospital bills totaled more than $1 million; the couple relied on a Social Security income to make ends meet. For weeks, the dinner staple was beans and rice, beans and rice. "Mostly, we had a very lean existence, but during the seventeen years, I never went one place without him, never even to get gas for the car, never even to get the cleaning picked up from the cleaners. . . We literally ran and played for seventeen years. And every minute of it was great," Sharon said.

In August 2000, Valentine slipped on the front porch of his house, fracturing his back, and landing in the hospital for eight months. Even in critical condition, he paced himself. While doctors and nurses told Sharon "three or four times a week" that he was in the throes of death, he perked up out of unconsciousness one day when his wife started singing, "Seems Like Old Times." "I held his hand and started singing our song to him, and his eyes opened up real big, and he started singing, he finished the whole song. The nurses nearly died — they couldn't believe it — and then he closed his eyes and he was gone again."

Valentine died in April 2001. In interviews, he expressed disappointment that wrestling promoters never tapped his mind after the accident; he thought he had more to offer the business. He's not forgotten though. At training sessions, Prichard, afraid to ask him for an autograph as a child, invokes his name. "There were other things to his persona besides what he just did the ring. That's what I try to tell the guys in the seminars — it's those little nuances and little quirks that are so important." Valentine's son, Greg, still works slowly, like his old man. In 2006, Johny Valentine was inducted into the Professional Wrestling Hall of Fame. "The reason I loved to work with him was, most of the time, he ended up with his face all beat up and mine too," said Jose Lothario. "I loved to wrestle with the man because he was one of the best, and I don't think there will ever, ever be another Johnny Valentine."

And he's still at Sharon's side. "He always asked me, long before he got sick, to have him cremated. 'Momma, keep me as close to you as you can, always.' And he's as close to me as he can be. I have him sitting right here beside my bed."

8. THE DESTROYER (DICK BEYER)

Not since Hugh Hefner built his fortune with *Playboy* have women's undergarments done so much for one man. The mask that Dick Beyer, "The Intelligent, Sensational Destroyer," wore to become an international celebrity was fashioned from a girdle. Beyer went into California in 1962, expecting to be a fan favorite, when Jules Strongbow told him he was going to wear a mask and wrestle as The Destroyer. A clean-cut, all-American type for most of his career, Beyer didn't have a mask, so Vic Christy lent him a miserable woolen contrivance that stretched around his head and body, and buttoned in the crotch. "I got

The Destroyer as U.S. champ.

claustrophobia, I couldn't breathe, I couldn't do anything in the ring," Beyer said. "I tore the mask off and I threw it at Hardy Kruskamp, who was the promoter in San Diego, and I said, 'Hardy, tell Jules Strongbow up in L.A. that he's seen the first and last of The Destroyer.'" Fortunately, Ox Anderson tossed him a more comfortable mask made from a woman's girdle. "Gee, this is great, I can see, I can breathe, I can probably eat with it," Beyer remembered thinking. The next day, he went shopping for girdles at Woolworth's in San Bernadino, California, and the rest is history.

"The Destroyer?" Fred Blassie asked during a 2003 radio interview with

Jeff Walton of the Los Angeles territorial office. "Greatest masked man there ever was. He was very scientific, knew all the ins and outs. He had an answer for everything. The Destroyer would have to go down as one of the top ten wrestlers of all-time." Oddly, it was Blassie who got Beyer to Los Angeles in 1962. The two squared off in Hawaii, and Blassie excitedly returned to the Los Angeles office, proclaiming Beyer the best babyface in the country. In the meantime, Beyer planted the seeds of his bad guy image by shaving his head and adopting the sarcastic personality of the Intelligent, Sensational Dick Beyer. Hawaii is also where he learned the figure-four leglock, his long-standing finisher. "I was trying to get the heat by telling the Hawaiian people how intelligent I was," Beyer claimed. "That I was a Syracuse University graduate, and I wasn't a graduate from one of these Hawaiian schools, I wasn't a graduate from one of these West Coast schools. I was from the East Coast where the intelligent people are."

Intelligence aside, Beyer was closely identified with the East Coast before he gained worldwide fame. A native of Buffalo, New York, Beyer wrestled Don Beitelman, later Don Curtis, in the Niagara District Amateur Athletic Union finals in 1951, and lost 5–3, but local promoter Ed Don George took notice and told him to keep his options open. At Syracuse, Beyer won three letters each in wrestling and in football, and played in the 1953 Orange Bowl (an — ouch! — 61–6 loss to Bart Starr and Alabama). In 1954, George sent him to Columbus, Ohio, for seasoning, then Beyer came back to Buffalo, and kept a spot on the Syracuse football coaching staff. "I was in the right place at the right time when I got a chance to go to Syracuse. I was in the right place at the right time when I got a chance to meet Ed Don George."

Beyer was a talent, no doubt, as *Wrestling Life* picked him as its 1955 Rookie of the Year. "This is an unbelievably fast rise for one so recently out of the ranks of the amateurs," Syracuse sportswriter Jack Slattery informed readers. "He doesn't have blond hair. He doesn't go into the ring barefooted. He doesn't have a valet. Perhaps his singularity, in that he simply wrestles, has made him stand out." But as Beyer recounted years later, there was a glass ceiling on a hero of his size. At five-foot-ten and 210 pounds, Buffalo promoter Pedro Martinez considered him too small to be a main-eventer, and Beyer mortgaged his house to guarantee one night's gate in Cleveland, Ohio, for a shot at reigning bad guy Fritz Von Erich. So when the chance came to switch his colors, Beyer jumped. "I wrestled as Dick Beyer for eight years. And wrestling as Dick Beyer for eight years, when I'd lose, people would say, 'Ah, that Dick Beyer, he can't win.' It's kind of like baseball teams that lose or football teams — the people don't want anything to do with them. When you're a good guy, you have to win. But when you're a villain . . . I changed to being a villain as The Destroyer and I had people come to watch me just to see me get the hell get kicked out of me."

The wrestling brass said the mask was great because it hid Beyer's looks while letting him turn up the volume on his personality and showcasing skills unusual for a villain. Now, he was a great, athletic wrestler with a growling voice that everyone loved to hate. "He was one of the best real wrestlers who ever lived," said Los Angeles promoter Mike LeBell. "We had a thing that he never had his mask taken off. The only trouble he had was whenever he went places, he went without his mask and some of the fans are too smart — they can recognize you. So he wore his mask eating and the whole thing." Art Williams, who refereed and helped to promote Bakersfield, California, said Beyer was "in a class all by himself . . . probably the best I've ever seen." On a scale of one to ten, Williams asserted, "I'd give him a twelve."

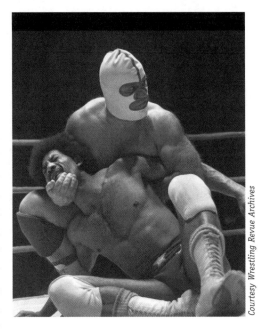

Courtesy Wrestling Revue Archives

Tying up the Dark Angel in Detroit.

Strongbow wanted a masked champion for the World Wrestling Association, and Beyer had three turns with the belt from 1962 to 1965. In 1963, he made his first tour of Japan, where he was a smash against Rikidozan, the Japanese wrestling legend. Their televised match attracted nearly seventy million viewers and was the second-highest rated TV program in Japanese history. Beyer also was in the AWA regularly from 1967 to 1972 as "Dr. X," a nod toward not wanting to rip the mask off The Destroyer. Beyer briefly held the AWA crown, but considered the piece of synthetic fabric to be his real title. "If you beat me two pinfalls out of three, I'll take the mask off, and it went over big," he said.

"The mask was the reason for his success," said Harley Race, a star in the AWA at the time. "He had a unique thing about him also — Dick could out-wrestle most of the guys that were wrestling, and if he had a babyface down, it got heat. If the roles were reversed, and he outwrestled somebody, and they got up and started stomping the shit out of him because he had, then he was a babyface." Beyer said he did most of his heel work coming off the ropes, using, for example, a clenched fist to slug his foe. Quietly, he then whispered to a ref, "'Put that fist up and ask me if I hit him with the fist.' Then I turned to the people and said, 'No, I never hit him with the fist. Open hand.' So with that little exchange you establish heat between yourself and the people. It wasn't on the referee."

Tag team partner Don Manoukian liked the way Beyer treated both his profession and the mask with respect, instead of as some kind of gimmick. "You'll see a lot of bad guys, they'll have some humor to them. They'll throw in some comic relief to get themselves over. Dick was a good amateur wrestler, and he was a serious professional. He was very convincing. He was very believable as a bad guy. He was a very convincing guy. Of course, with the accessory of the mask, it fit. He respected the business, and he'd wear that mask until he was in his bathroom at home. He was serious about keeping his identity."

In 1973, Beyer inked a pact with Shohei Baba and NTV in Tokyo to wrestle in Japan for six years. He helped Baba establish All Japan Pro-Wrestling as one of the major forces in the business, and starred on a top-rated musical-comedy series called *Uwasa No Channel* that included skits, singing, and a bit of nonsense. "I'm as popular in Japan as any star in the United States," Beyer legitimately claimed to his hometown Buffalo paper in 1975. Fellow wrestler Angelo Mosca put it succinctly, "It was like walking with God in Japan."

Beyer returned to North America in the late '70s, and wrestled for several more years before becoming a football, wrestling and swimming coach at Akron Central School in Akron, New York. He's a member of the George Tragos/Lou Thesz Professional Wrestling Hall of Fame, the Professional Wresting Hall of Fame, and the Buffalo Sports Hall of Fame, among others. The English version of his autobiography is expected in bookstores in 2007. He still makes regular trips to East Asia; every summer, he takes a group of youngsters to Japan to compete in a national wrestling tournament. And the mask stays put. "When I go to Japan now, I'm somebody. I go through customs, and immigration, and so forth with the mask on. I lived the part, and I still wear it."

9. KILLER KOWALSKI

Meet the woman who did what nobody could in a thirty-year wrestling career — tame "The Killer." Theresa Dodd, twice widowed, met Walter Kowalski almost a decade ago. But in the spring of 2006, Killer Kowalski (that old softie) proposed while they were driving. "A lot of women who used to like him are going to get mad to hear that," laughed Dodd. The wedding was a quiet affair at the chapel at St. Theresa's in North Reading, Massachusetts on June 19, 2006. With a twinkle in his eye, Kowalski explained the decision to get married for the first time. "Well, she told me, she's seventy-six years old, and she says, 'I'm pregnant.' I said, 'Wow.' She said, 'You'd better marry me.' I said, 'I will, I will, I will.' That's why I got married."

Yes, there was indeed a time when Killer Kowalski was a matinee idol. "He was such a good-looking guy. six-foot-eight, he weighed over 300 pounds, and had long hair and looked like Tarzan. He looked real good, whatever he did," said Paul "Butcher" Vachon. "The women just loved him and the men hated him. I heard about women fainting when

Killer Kowalski shares an evil smile with The Sheik.

Killer Kowalski came into the ring. So it's hard to picture him now, almost eighty, and sort of bent over a little bit. But in those days he learned his business."

And what a business it was. Kowalski, who started in 1947, would be on anyone's list of the greatest wrestlers of all-time, and he faced the greatest names, all of whom had enormous respect for him. "Kowalski's strength is utterly fantastic. Unless you have faced him in the ring, no amount of words can make you realize the fantastic power that man holds in his body," said Lou Thesz in *Wrestling Revue*. "I would say that Kowalski has everything a great wrestler must have: speed, a perfect sense of timing, courage, and balance. And he can think."

"I had tremendous imagination," Kowalski explained with a shrug. "I was like a magician when I walked to that ring. I performed things that people had never seen before."

Born in 1926 in Windsor, Ontario, the son of Polish immigrants, Walter Kowalski (not his birth name, though, as of 1963, his legal name) followed in his father's footsteps, and was training to be an electrical engineer at an automotive plant when he started wrestling. Having worked out a little with local promoter Bert Ruby (who reputedly told him he had two left feet and should go home), Kowalski hit the road in late 1947, and competed mostly in Ohio as "Tarzan" Kowalski. In other places, to play up his Polish roots, he was Wladek Kowalski. His first break came in St. Louis, where he found a teacher. "My mentor was Lou Thesz," said Kowalski. "He tested you to see how tough you really were." By July 1949, Kowalski had his first NWA world title shot, losing to Orville Brown.

Promoters sat up and took notice. Kowalski was a box-office draw with a rare physique for the day. "When I first saw him I thought he was the most magnificent specimen of a human being I'd ever seen in my life," Jody Hamilton told the Georgia Wrestling History Web site. "He was working out at the gym and was six-foot-six and about 280 pounds, and he was ripped, and just looked phenomenal."

What made him a hit? It was more than his claw hold and relentless style. Jacques Rougeau Sr. has a theory: "His vicious way of wrestling. People thought the guy was a maniac, but really he was one of the nicest guys in the world. But he was a hard worker, always worked hard in the ring. Always in good shape. You were always sure to get a lot of action with this guy. Never had a bad match," Rougeau emphasized. "People really believed in him. That's why he went over so big. He looked mean. He was the nicest guy in the world, but in the ring, he looked like a real killer."

Kowalski's career will be forever intertwined with another incredible physical specimen — Yukon Eric. In January 1953, they were paired for the first TV broadcast of wrestling in Canada. Then, a year later in the Montreal Forum, came wrestling's most famous kneedrop. Kowalski leaped from the top turnbuckle onto Yukon Eric, whose leg was tied in the ropes. Eric tried to turn his head, but Kowalski's shin bone grazed his cheek and ripped off his foe's cauliflowered ear. Referee Sammy Mack picked up the ear, but since Yukon Eric couldn't continue, Kowalski was the victor. Two days later, Kowalski visited his victim in the hospital, and, seeing him bandaged up like Humpty Dumpty, started laughing. The press caught the act, and dubbed him "Killer," and opportunistic promoters across the continent did the rest. "They used that to the maximum, which was great, because people really believed he did it on purpose," said Rougeau.

While his fame was in ascension, Kowalski found himself out of wrestling, following a car accident near Ottawa, Ontario. He reassessed much of his life, and had to rebuild his physique. Doctors were astounded at his recovery, especially given his strict vegetarian diet. Soon he was back, but it was a different Kowalski.

"Kowalski was one of the greatest I ever saw," recalled Bob Orton Sr., "back before he got on the religion and the vegetarian kick, and he had that car wreck and hurt his arm. He started wrestling different after that. But before that, he was always good." Following their many matches in New York, Bill Watts credits Kowalski with really

Killer Kowalski twists an arm.

making him a success in the WWWF. "The original Killer was a specimen with just an awesome physique. But at the time I'd met him, he'd become a vegetarian, where he didn't have that great physique. He was tall and thin. But he had a relentless style, he stayed on you. He had unbelievable aerobic cardiovascular conditioning. He would never stop," said Watts. "For me, I'm the kind of babyface that liked the heel to stay on me. It was so simple with Kowalski. He was going to attack me viciously. Whatever he decided to attack, he was kind of like a pit bulldog in that he was going to stay after that point on your body no matter what you did — over, and over, and over, and over, and over. So it was real simple."

Many titles found their way to the waist of Kowalski — he held the Quebec International/World title eleven times between 1952–1962 — but he considers the International Wrestling Alliance world title in Australia among his greatest accomplishments. Though he was awarded the belt upon arrival Down Under in 1964, he would capture it for real five more times. Until 1971, he'd stay for in Australia for six months, and then head to North America for the remainder of the year. "Kowalski was the first big star, he came down there with [Jim] Barnett in '64," said Aussie star Ron Miller. "He was a good interview, very impressive individual. The way he wrestled was just non-stop action."

Though Dominic DeNucci knew Kowalski from Montreal, they'd never had a real program against each other until they clashed in Australia. "Walter looked like an animal. He was good, he had good timing and everything else," said DeNucci. "One time, I remember in Melbourne, the people wanted to kill him. In the ring, he said to me, 'Goddamn, get up and start to beat the shit out of me or these people are going to kill me!' Kowalski always wore purple shoes, purple trunks. His suitcase was one of those aluminum suitcases. On the bottom, he'd put a towel, and he'd put everything straight. He never put the shoes back in the suitcase before he cleaned them."

Kowalski was equally fastidious about what went into his body. A lifetime vegetarian, he never smoked (or allowed smokers in his car) and forsook alcohol beverages. It kept him in decent enough shape to make a comeback in 1992 for a single match against John Tolos in the Frontier Martial Arts promotion in Japan. (They went to a double countout.) Kowalski was a deep thinker, silent for long stretches of road trips and reading heavy subjects in hotel rooms. "I watched him go through his diets and that kind of stuff, talked to him a lot about it. He was into that metaphysics," said Don Leo Jonathan. "He was interested in religions for a time. He was looking for many things, but he was a student of theology." Kowalski's biggest vice was a love of photography, and he had a book of his work published in 2001.

By the 1970s, Kowalski had settled outside Boston, Massachusetts, and become an American citizen. John Minton, who would later become "Big" John Studd, was his first wrestling student. They would team up under masks as "The Executioners" in the WWWF, and even claim tag team gold. However, the hood on Kowalski's uniquely chiseled frame didn't fool anyone.

The experience as a trainer prompted Kowalski to open a wrestling school. The media loved the idea of a public training school for wrestling, and Kowalski was in demand again, appearing on *Late Night with David Letterman*, and in the pages of *People* and *Maclean's*. He also wrote a wrestling column for the *Boston Herald*. Today, he no longer runs a school, but has lent his name to one close to his home. A number of his charges went on to notable careers: Triple H, Chyna, Mike Shaw ("Norman the Lunatic"), Perry Saturn, John Kronus, Matt Bloom ("A-Train"), Kenny Doane of the Spirit Squad, John Walters, and April Hunter. "I can spot these guys by the way they perform in the ring," Kowalski reported. "And Hunter had so much athletic ability that I said, 'This guy's going to make it.' And he sure did. And Chyna, I talked to WWF and said, 'Look, you guys need a girl like this,'" Kowalski explained. "The whole thing is, live the dream and you'll make it."

10. HARLEY RACE

On eight different occasions, Harley Race was National Wrestling Alliance world champion. That meant that on eight different occasions, he had wrestling's greatest heat-getter in his possession. "Ninety percent of the places that you went, you went in there, anyone who booked you always wanted their fans to cheer their local guy. Whether you're a heel or a babyface fan, you want to see that title change hands in front of you," said Race. "I just let the title be the biggest part of the heel."

Harley Race drops a knee on Mark Lewin.

That's not to say that Race couldn't be a heel in his own right, with dastardly tricks and mean stomps to his opponents — he most certainly could. The self-professed "greatest wrestler on God's green Earth," Race was as tough as they came, and fans recognized that. Their hero would have to go through hell to take that gold from his waist.

Race doesn't believe that he ever really studied the art of being a heel. "With me, it just came kind of natural. In the making of a good heel, you've got to be where you respond to the people, you acknowledge the people; you treat your opponent and referee in the same fashion, and then have the moves and the technique to pull it off."

Of course, few others can say that they worked on the farm of former world champion Stanislaus Zbyszko, and his brother Wladek, as a teen, then that they helped bathe the 700-pound Happy Humphrey. But those are only part of Harley Leland Race's credentials. Born April, 11, 1943, in Maryville, Missouri, he was kicked out of high school at age fifteen. He stayed on the family farm until he got up the moxie to approach Gust Karras for a spot on his wrestling show in a traveling carnival. Old pros like Buddy Austin, Ray Gordon, and Bobby Graham got Race ready for pro wrestling. He debuted at age sixteen, and began driving Humphrey around before landing a role as John Long's tag team partner (Harley going by "Jack Long"). He also survived a car crash that killed his new bride Christmas night in 1961, and kept him on the shelf for twenty-one months.

The first major spot for the six-foot, 238-pound Race came in the AWA, where he was "Handsome" alongside "Pretty Boy" Larry Hennig, whom he had met in Texas. "Harley came in here as just a young kid to Minnesota. Harley's about seven or eight years younger than I am," said Hennig. "Harley came to Minnesota and wrestled on TV. They just threw us in one day together, and all of a sudden, it was unbelievable. We were a good team because we didn't do the same things. I was more surface transportation and he was more air express. It worked out real good for us." The pairing ran from 1964 to 1969.

It was in the AWA that Race's star began to rise, and he became respected as one of the best bump-takers in the business — his diving head-butt can still be pictured in the mind's eye. His reputation as a tough guy lives on as well, and not just because of the homemade tattoos on his arms. "Harley could whip just about anybody. Boy, we had some pretty good fights out on the street there and never lost," said Eddie Sharkey, who went on to explain promoter Verne Gagne's position on these unofficial matches. "Verne never really cared if you got in a fight. If you lost, you were out. As long as you won, it was fine."

When "Mad Dog" Race bought into the Kansas City promotion in 1970, in part to start a family, it didn't stop his combative ways. "For years, we challenged everybody," recalled Roger Kirby, who was the Central States and Florida tag champ with Harley. "We never backed down from anybody, truck drivers . . . weightlifters. Anybody who wanted to challenge us in the ring, if you could beat us in ten minutes, we'd give you $1,000. Neither one was ever beaten, and this went on for ten or fifteen years. But Harley was tough. Marks are unbelievably stupid."

Race also has the respect of his peers for his booker work, which included stints in Amarillo, Florida, Atlanta, and in Kansas City and St. Louis, where he was hands-on, and still involved when on the road. He still has all his old booking records. "I've got them here in my desk. They go back to the late '70s through the '80s when I hooked up with Vince [McMahon]," said Race.

Race welcomed the added responsibility behind the scenes and enjoyed the challenge of making new stars. "I always kept myself in a position of power that if something happened, or somebody left, I could step back in and take over," he explained. "It's always easier, and you can keep your heat a lot longer, if occasionally you go out there and work with a young talent that you're trying to get over anyhow. You can make that talent and keep your heat at the time, and then you're just putting somebody else in line that can draw money for you."

Attention to detail is what Rick Martel remembers about Race. "Everything's paced with Harley, it was always about the technicality of the moves, how he was doing those moves. That was important to him. Everything had to be precise, how he landed — when he landed the bump, everything would hit at the same time. The coordination this guy had was unreal."

Some memories stick around. "Harley was such a great heel," recalled Dr. Tom Prichard. "On TV in El Paso, Texas, he took a brick. He kept hitting himself in the head with a brick and he got a hard way [blood] with it. That was real. He was busting himself open, live on camera. He was crazy. He's a beer-drinking, whisky-drinking, smoking, filthy, dirty rotten son of a gun. In real life. He's really not, but in a way he is."

His first NWA world title reign is still his sweetest memory from the business, though he held other prestigious belts, including the PWF world title in Japan, and the Missouri state and Central States belts on many occasions. Working earlier with the Funks in Amarillo meant that he had their trust, so when the NWA decided to take the title from Dory Funk Jr. to get it to Jack Brisco, the Funk family balked, and Race was the interim champion. What few counted on was that he would be back again and again as titleholder.

His partner in the Heart of America promotion, Bob Geigel, credits Race's longevity to good health and the ability to fit where he was needed. "He talked like wrestling fans understood him," said Geigel. "He could change his style with the different wrestlers in the ring. You knew that if he went someplace to work as a heel, he could work as a heel, he could work as a babyface, it didn't make any difference."

In late 1985, having turned over the NWA world title for the final time to Ric Flair, Race told his partners in the Kansas City promotion that he was done, and was jumping to the WWF. It was a shocking move to many traditionalists, who saw the growing WWF as a cartoonish fad that insulted the history of wrestling.

Soon after his arrival, the company decided to make Race its "King" in the second King of the Ring tournament. Race saw the title as his transformation from hated heel to beloved elder statesman. "I hated it. I was always my own man, and I didn't care for the glitz, I was just Harley Race," he said. Given Bobby Heenan as a manager meant automatic heat anyway, though Race admitted that the WWF style of fan hatred was different than what he was used to. "Well, it was a cheaper-type heat," he said. "I didn't change my style, I was just a little more cockier at doing it." After runs against "Hacksaw" Duggan, Hulk Hogan, and Junkyard Dog, Race left in 1988, competing even after hospitalization for peritonitis.

He resurfaced in 1991 as a manager in World Championship Wrestling, and took two more men — Lex Luger and Vader — to the world championship. An auto accident in 1995 derailed his career. It took a few years to recover and decide what he wanted to do with his life. Race let his body heal, then tried bounty hunting.

With his third wife, B.J., whom he met in 1990, Race opened up the Harley Race Wrestling Academy and World League Wrestling, based out of Eldon, Missouri. He's been sharing his knowledge there since 1999. Of course, "Handsome" Harley teaches the art of being a good and bad guy. "There's an art to being either one of them, and if you learn them both, that's the best of both worlds," he explained. "It's much easier if you start right at the beginning when you've got them. Then you bring them up and you start testing them. I've got a couple of kids now where I'm in the process of one night or one weekend, they're going to be a heel. The following weekend, I'm going to put them with somebody and they're going to be the babyface. I want them to learn both ways."

Kansas City announcer Bill Kersten knew Race before he ever became a wrestler. "He was successful because he was a great worker, and a business person," Kersten said. "Harley was always looking on the positive side of his profession and he was always looking for something better. He has found that now, with the WLW and getting young folks, men and women, interested in the profession. I have never known him happier than he is now."

Over the last few years, few have had more honors bestowed upon them than Race has. He has been inducted to the Professional Wrestling Hall of Fame (Class of 2004), the George Tragos/Lou Thesz Professional Wrestling Hall of Fame (2005), the WWE Hall of Fame (2004), and, topping it all off, the Cauliflower Alley Club's Iron Mike Mazurki Award in June 2006. "Like I said with every award that I've gotten, it's always fabulous when a group of your peers honor you for anything. The Iron Mike Award, I guess as far as awards are concerned, would be the highest in wrestling. Of course it makes you feel good."

11. DANNY MCSHAIN

More than fifty-five years later, there is a touch of wonderment in Ted Lewin's voice as he recalls the first time he laid eyes on the charmer who would become his brother-in-law and wrestling model. Danny McShain, the former light heavyweight wrestling champion of the world, pulled up to the Lewin house in Buffalo, New York — he was dating Lewin's sister Sallee — and exited his stylish Chrysler convertible with faux-wood paneling.

"He got out of that and he strutted across the street. I thought, 'Wow, what a character!' He didn't walk across the street. It was what he did in the ring, the same strut. The way he dressed, everything about him was very California, very showbiz. It suited him, even to the little pencil mustache. The way he carried himself — it wasn't a character he invented. It was him. That was always Danny."

From 1933 to 1967, McShain turned heads, broke bones, incited riots, bled rivers of blood, and popularized the wild, fight-to-the-finish wrestling style associated with Texas. His bright eyes took such a beating from boxing and wrestling that he had virtually no peripheral vision. So he turned his head to engage people, fixing his eyes straight ahead, glaring at friends, fans, and opponents, like an owl.

"He had style, class, and charm, all of the above. He was one of my idols," said Red Bastien. "He was a class act, in my book. He was the heel, but there was a charm in the way he did it. You couldn't have a bad match with him. I don't know what it was he had, but he had it."

Danny McShain at his best . . .

Department of Special Collections, University Libraries of Notre Dame

Born in Arkansas on October 30, 1912, McShain's family moved to California when he was young — his father had asthma and the then-clean air helped him breathe better. Before he got into wrestling, McShain was a boxer — starting as a teenager, he had about sixty bouts. As Sallee recalled, his switch to wrestling was rooted in self-preservation. "He didn't want his brains scrambled." In any event, McShain took to the West Coast lifestyle like a duck to water. After a stint in the Coast Guard, he spent his formative years in the sun of show people — he was briefly managed by Dick Lane, a theatrical performer later to gain fame as the "Whoa, Nellie!" voice of televised wrestling in Los Angeles. "The flickers are calling him. Dangerous Danny has the requisites because he is handsome and alert," writer Dean Snyder reported of McShain in 1940.

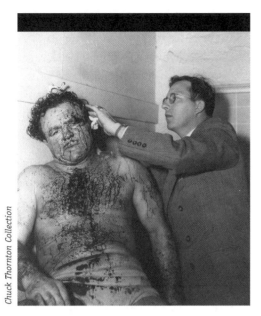

Chuck Thornton Collection

. . . and his worst.

In the early 1930s, McShain made his mark on the light heavyweight scene with his strut, dazzling satin robes, and fast-paced and bloody action. He was Pacific Coast middleweight champion in 1935, and won the first of his world light heavyweight titles two years later, beating "Wild" Red Berry, whom he fought off and on for more than twenty years. During the course of his career, McShain was the most prominent champion in the lighter weight classes, and one of the biggest drawing cards in the business in every territory. More than a dozen times he held various light heavyweight crowns, defending the NWA belt for almost two years in the early 1950s. During other tours, he was Gulf Coast heavyweight champion, Texas junior heavyweight champion, North American champion, and Louisiana champion. "Every time he walked or strutted, I wanted to hit him," joked Danny Hodge, the Hall of Fame light heavyweight. "But the people, the fans, they loved it. I guess if I could have strutted, I would have done it too."

Most of all, McShain was a rule breaker of the first order. In January 1936, a grand jury in Amarillo, Texas, hauled him in for questioning after he sparked a near-riot of 1,500 fans for squirting tobacco juice in Bob Castle's face to gain an easy pinfall. But his contemporaries had the utmost respect for him. "He was a real cocky guy. I'll tell you what, for the weight that he had, and for the people that he wrestled, he should have got beat a thousand times, but he didn't. . . . Danny McShain was a fantastic wrestler," said Sonny Myers, a favorite opponent.

"I wrestled him so many times it was unbelievable — Texas, Oklahoma, California," added Angelo Savoldi. "Danny was a good wrestler. I have to admit that. He was very active and very, very good. He was a helluva showman. He was a great showman, a great entertainer, and a good wrestler. He knew his wrestling."

And his blood. While McShain did not invent the practice of nicking his forehead to add color to a match, he became one of its foremost practitioners. In February 1940, he retained his light heavyweight title when a referee stopped a match with Bob Gregory after McShain was blinded by his own blood. Pictures of McShain before and after were a promoter's dream: first, smooth and debonair, looking for all the world like a local bank president; and then ravaged, hair tussled, blood flowing, his forehead a graphic relief map from cuts and scar tissue. "Blood is absolutely nothing — just an occupational hazard of the game — the same as broken noses are to fighters," he explained to one Australian journalist.

Lewin squared off with his brother-in-law on the East Coast in the 1950s and was amazed at his ability to suspend disbelief. "He was as light as a feather to work with. I worked a few matches with him. He could grab you by the hair, draw back to throw a punch, and punch you square in the nose. It looked like your nose should be spread out against your face, and, of course, you went down like you were pole-axed. People would go, 'Oh my God!' and you never felt anything. It was really remarkable."

In the mid-1950s, McShain became a fixture in Texas wrestling. He fought Bull Curry in the inaugural Texas brass knuckles championship match in 1953; though he lost that one, he held the title three times in the decade. McShain moved on to barbed-wire matches more than a generation before they became popular in Japan, tar-and-feather matches, and once fought Curry in a match in which the loser — Curry — was painted green for St. Patrick's Day. Not that McShain would have minded; he was a regular in the Irish day parade in Houston. Still, whether he won or lost was irrelevant, said Nick Kozak, who remembered that friends called McShain "Twinkle Toes" because of the way he strutted.

"Danny's philosophy was, he used to tell me, whether he was on the opening match or the main event, he wanted to tear the house down. He was the kind of guy who could be beat in the middle, and when the thing was through, they're still hooting and jeering at him. He's got that cocky walk, that twinkle-toes walk. They said, 'You cocky son of a bitch. You just got whipped and you still piss me off anyway,'" Kozak recalled with a chuckle.

In Houston, McShain took heart on a teenaged dishwasher at the D'George Hotel, where wrestlers stayed before their Friday night bouts. He befriended the young man, poor and black, furnishing him with tickets to shows, and dispensing fatherly advice. "Being black, Danny didn't care," said the young man, Plasee Conway, who became "Tiger" Conway Sr. "He was a super guy. He had his own style, it was a beautiful style. He'd take that cape in the middle of the ring and swirl around. Man, I thought that was the greatest thing. He was a super guy, not just because he took me under his arm. He had a beautiful attitude."

In private, McShain couldn't have been more different than his wrestling character. "Danny was never ever a wise guy or a smartass. He was very respectful of women. Even the grannies who used to holler and raise hell with him, they got so tittery they were almost silly," Sallee said. "Basically, Danny was a good person. He'd help anybody out of anything. I'm sure people don't think of him that way, but that's he way he was." He wrestled through 1967, and worked as a referee and promoter in Texas for many years. His last years were rough. Pneumonia, arthritis, and the aches and pains he accumulated in his lifetime robbed his body of its usefulness. He was confined to a wheelchair and died in July 1992 at seventy-nine. But, before he died, he let friends and family know one last time that wrestling was bred in his bones.

Years before, McShain helped Conway break into the business, and Conway appeared at one barbecue in Texas in honor of his friend's birthday. As Conway and Lewin remembered, family members brought McShain from a nursing home for the celebration — he was in and out of lucidity at that point, only occasionally aware of what was going on around him. He slept much of the day. Suddenly, he roused himself one last time. He looked up, saw Conway, and asked, "Where we working tonight, Tiger?" Conway replied, "We're off tonight, Danny." And McShain replied, "That's good, because I'm tired."

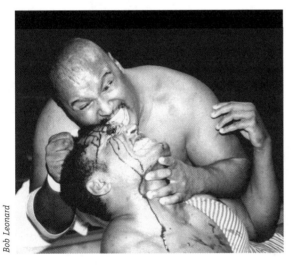

Bob Leonard

An early battle between Abdullah and Carlos Colon.

12. ABDULLAH THE BUTCHER

One of the few things that ever stopped Abdullah the Butcher was a skyjacker. In February 1969, Abdullah and Matt Gilmour (Duncan McTavish) were headed from San Juan, Puerto Rico, to Miami on an Eastern Airlines jet when a gunman ordered the plane to touch down in Havana, Cuba. Gilmour headed down the aisle to take matters into his own hands, only to be stopped by a steward who told him the hijacker was holding a pistol to a stewardess' head. "And I've got to tell you, as soon as Abdullah found out we couldn't go down there, he went into his little act.

'I'll get 'em!' Meantime, he made sure we couldn't go down there first. He suddenly got really brave!" Gilmour said.

The incident caused The Butcher to miss an appearance in Montreal, where his demented ways had set the city on its ear. But it was just one missed match, and that was almost forty years ago. The Butcher is still wrestling. "Oh, heavens, he's got to be two days older than water," Gilmour said. "But that was his life. I think he spent hours looking in the mirror calling himself Abdullah the Butcher."

Is there anything Abdullah wouldn't put in his mouth? Probably not. Referee Bobby Simmons can't forget the time in 1975 the Butcher showed up in Georgia, a state accustomed to straightforward wrestling. "First week here, he ate raw fish on TV and then he ate a light bulb. He reached up, unscrewed a light bulb out of a socket, and ate it. I mean, I couldn't believe this. The people were afraid of him. Heck, I was afraid of him," Simmons said. "They went nuts when he got here. There had never been anybody in Georgia doing the things he did, and acting like he did, so the people went bananas."

Stuffed into a pair of judo pants, with a forehead like a botched excavation project, the enormous Butcher has frightened and fascinated fans around the world since he became "The Madman from the Sudan" in Calgary in 1967. Veteran announcer Jack Reynolds was on a tour of India with Abdullah for a month in 1996; by then, the Butcher was pushing fifty-five. "We were checking into our hotel in Amritsar. There must been well over 200, 300 people in the lobby waiting to see the professional wrestlers who were scheduled to come and check in. I had to baby sit Abdullah. When we walked in the lobby, I'm not exaggerating, the whole lobby, they cleared out when they saw Abdullah. One of the funniest things I've ever seen in my life."

The Butcher was born Larry Shreve in Windsor, Ontario, apparently, in 1941, and his childhood was filled with martial arts work. At one point, a much slimmer Shreve taught judo and karate to the Windsor police officers in his backyard. He was tending several gyms when he met the likes of Gino Brito and George Cannon, and started wrestling in the Detroit area. That's where Gary Hart first encountered him, long before the raw fish and the light bulbs. "When I knew him in Detroit, he didn't have the Abdullah the Butcher persona. He was a karate guy; a lot of people don't know that. But Larry was a very good martial arts guy."

With Dr. Jerry Graham, Abdullah won a version of the Canadian tag team title in Vancouver, and worked mostly north of the border in the late 1960s. In the process, he built a mansion of mayhem on the foundation laid down by the original Sheik — biting, gouging, bleeding, and using anything he could tuck into his tights. With Eddie Creatchman as manager, the whole routine had fans screaming for revenge during Abdullah's run in Montreal. There was nothing scientific about it. "The guy liked to have blood in every match," said Jacques Rougeau Sr., who figured he must have fought Abdullah fifty times. "You'd just touch him, and he'd cut open right away. He'd ask you to do it. 'Gimme a good punch' and cut himself open. He'd start bleeding and go like a wildman. It was something new, an attraction." Throw in the martial arts background and you had a jaw-dropping spectacle, friend and rival Johnny Powers said. "The Butcher looked like a weird man, a great, big, huge black man. But all of a sudden, he'd throw a damn side karate kick to your throat and it'd hit you right smack in the throat and it was a perfect shot. People would say, 'Oh, did you see that?'"

Why, Abdullah was even mean to little kids. Wayne Coleman, later "Superstar" Billy Graham, started out in Calgary in 1970 when Abdullah was hot there, and learned what it meant to be a first-class villain. "One of the things that stands out in my mind was watching the matches in Calgary with Abdullah. We're standing in the back, and fans could actually come around and ask you for an autograph. So Abdullah, a little kid asked him for an autograph, and he took his piece of paper, ripped it up and broke his pencil," he said, laughing at the memory. "But this was Abdullah at his best, this old-school heel at his purest, his purest form, Abdullah the Butcher — can't speak English, hates everybody, vicious." No wonder the *Winnipeg Free Press* issued a public Merry Christmas to him in 1969 — "because we're afraid of him."

Not everybody enjoyed working with Shreve. When Tommy Young was first starting out as a wrestler in Detroit, Abdullah gently slit him in the ring to draw blood. But after he became a ref, Young thought an Abdullah match was a nightmare. "He was miserable because he'd come into the ring with a gimmick the size of a yardstick, and you couldn't miss it if you tried, and he'd just do stuff right in front of me, and make me look like an idiot. He didn't work with me." Gilmour recalled a hysterical trip across the U.S.–Canada border that brought Abdullah out of character for one of the few times. "The customs guy looked at him and said, 'Where are you from?' He says, 'Sudan.' Customs guy says, 'What?' Abdullah said, 'Sudan.' He said, 'What?' Abdullah goes, 'Windsor.'"

Abdullah was a little bit unique because, although he was black in a time of racial unrest, according to Gary Hart, he seemed above color, both in his appeal within the sport and in the way he carried himself. "Abdullah grew up in Canada, where the prejudice, if it's there, is under the surface; it wasn't as overt as it was in this country. You've got to remember that we're talking '60s and '70s when these guys were really making their mark in wrestling. Abdullah never had that 'You're doing this to me because I'm black.' That may seem like a small thing, but it isn't," Hart explained.

It's hard to single out one particular spectacular event or program with Abdullah, but a one-month stint in summer 1972, when he won the National Wrestling Federation world title from Ernie Ladd, then set a Montreal attendance record with 26,000 fans against Johnny Rougeau, isn't bad for starters. In Japan, he aligned himself with Shohei Baba's All Japan Pro-Wrestling, and toured the country two to three times a year for most of the 1970s. At more than 300 pounds he won the promotion's big Grand Carnival in 1976 and 1979. His matches there with The Sheik against Dory Funk Jr. and Terry Funk remain gory classics, as does his feud with Carlos Colon in Canada and Puerto Rico. The Butcher's last run with a major North American federation was with World Campionship Wrestling in 1991 and 1992, where he teamed with Cactus Jack (Mick Foley).

"Abdullah is amazing. We all know how old Abdullah is, the gargoyles on the Notre Dame church were carved from his visage, and that was 612 years ago. I don't really know how old he is but he keeps going. He has always looked like a chocolate sundae melting," Kevin Sullivan cracked to journalist Alan Wojcik.

Abdullah — Terry Funk calls him "Spanky" — still works the independent circuit for a buck here and there, though now he tends more to his business interests. Who would have ever envisioned Abdullah the Butcher Management Co., Inc. overseeing restaurants that serve ribs and Chinese food in Atlanta and Korea? "When you've got a few dollars, you have the opportunity here if you know how to make it work for you," Abdullah said. As Powers summed it up: "I really believe the character of Larry Shreve that came out of Windsor actually created the best heel for his time. In my opinion, he took The Sheik's gimmick and took it to the next stage. If you are asking about villains, I think the Butcher is number one."

13. NICK BOCKWINKEL

As one of the most articulate heels of all time, Nick Bockwinkel had a secret weapon during his heyday, and for those familiar with his eloquent discourses on the state of the world during interviews, it shouldn't surprise: it was a dictionary. Well, actually it wasn't one dictionary, but many. He had a little notebook in which he jotted interesting words, and began to learn them and their meanings.

"I used to use the four-, five- or six-syllable words as best I could," expounded Bockwinkel. "If I ran across one I didn't know, I had a little dictionary. I would have this little dictionary, with seventy or eighty words, that

AWA World champion Nick Bockwinkel and NWA World champion Harley Race.

I would always be perusing. I had it with me all the time. Automatically, some of these words just starting coming to me in my interviews because I was familiar with them."

Memphis announcer Lance Russell praised the arrogance and condescension of "Tricky Nick": "He made it a point to let that come across, and he played that so beautifully . . . n o s e - i n - t h e - a i r, smelling something bad, you lowly peons. Nick had that down to a T. The guy could really wrestle." Larry Hennig described both sides of Bockwinkel: "articulate and meticulous."

The son of pro wrestler Warren Bockwinkel, Nick was born December 6, 1934 in St. Louis, and switched high schools six times. Though he grew up around wrestlers, Nick said his father encouraged him to play football. He got a wrestling and football scholarship to Oklahoma, where he studied physical education, but two knee injuries derailed his gridiron dreams. "At a college like that, number one in the nation, they don't keep you if you're a freshman and have two knee operations," said Nick. "My dad said, 'Well, come on home. We'll start you wrestling.'" (Perhaps his dad always knew wrestling was in his son's future; he used to send out a photo of a sixteen-year-old Nick, at a well-built 185 pounds, with his publicity, saying that he'd be available in four years.)

His father was his main trainer. "I had been raised by him showing me moves and holds from the time I was six, seven, eight, nine, ten years old. So there was a whole lot that I knew," Bockwinkel said. "So my dad taught me an awful lot and I always had good people around me. If there was somebody I liked, I'd see them and say, 'Show me how you make that move.' And the guy would show me and I would try to duplicate it, see if I could get it down."

The early days of his career, which began in 1955, were spent around Los Angeles as a babyface, where he also finished a degree in marketing at UCLA.

Wrestling was a way to pay for school. "As a babyface? I was okay. I was all right. I was good if I had a hot enough issue, and depending on where it was, that sort of thing," said Bockwinkel, who admitted he patterned a lot of his style after Wilbur Snyder, later a tag team partner. Around L.A., the father-son Bockwinkel team got a good push. Nick later teamed with Joe Blanchard around Indianapolis, and bounced from L.A. to Houston, to Buffalo, to Calgary, to Hawaii. He was known as "Dick Warren" while in the Army, stationed in Monterey, California, as "Roy Diamond" briefly in Texas, and as "The Phantom" in Nebraska.

In Atlanta, he really hit his stride, and found his calling as a heel. Bockwinkel had a series of matches with Dory Funk Jr., and his frustration at being unable to upend the fellow second-generation wrestler for the NWA world title marked his subtle transition. Bockwinkel recalled his interview that anounced the turn: "I said, '*Webster's Unabridged Dictionary*, page 1,348, the far right column, the thirty-sixth word down. It is "Funk." F-U-N-K. Definition: to retreat in terror, to be afraid, to be not confident.' I slammed the other half of the book closed. I said, 'Thank you' and I walked off. The TV station said that they got more response, the office got more response, just out of that little tidbit. For all intents and purposes, God love it, all the other guys who just wanted to growl, and bitch, and moan, and groan, they actually gave me a category to be in all alone, all by myself."

Though Funk Jr. has heard the definition of his last name a few times from opponents, he considers Bockwinkel in a rare class. "Back when I was champion, he was one of the best wrestling challengers for the belt that I had. I've got to put him right in there with Jack Brisco and Harley Race, Johnny Valentine and Wahoo McDaniel . . . they're all great. The matches in Georgia were the most memorable," Funk Jr. recounted. "He was very technical, and put a lot of thought into his interviews, his talk, his work in the ring, his persona."

From there, Bockwinkel was off and running, and by the time he arrived in the American Wrestling Association at the end of 1970, his skills could not be denied. He held the AWA world title four different times from 1975 to 1987, and the AWA tag belts with Ray Stevens three times. Bockwinkel honed his character, and played perfectly off "Sir Robert of Heenan," his manager in the AWA.

As world champ, Bockwinkel's arrogance shone. "They had a lot of respect for the champion, even if they disliked him," said challenger Manny Fernandez. "They grudgingly respected him." As a tough guy, Harley Race wouldn't think of bailing out of the ring when things got rough, but Bockwinkel would. "Nick would slide out of there, then he'd kind of point toward his head, saying, 'I'm a lot smarter than that. I ain't going to take a beating.' Nick was excellent at doing that," Race said. But Bockwinkel could also take bumps with the best of them.

Brockwinkel acknowledges that it was about more than the wrestling. "I knew how to wrestle a little bit, but I was not a Danny Hodge in any capacity. I worked hard, I worked enthusiastically. I didn't want anybody to see any holes in my work," he said. "By that, I meant the guy at ringside, the tenth row of ringside, the fifteenth row of ringside. So I laid them in. Now I didn't lay them in with the knuckles as much as the whole forearm. Well, if you can't take the pounding . . . then God almighty, it's not a sewing circle!"

In 1987, Bockwinkel could see that the AWA was in its dying days and that Vince McMahon had won the wrestling war. He gave McMahon a call, and was hired as a backstage road agent, a position he held for almost two years. Lanny Poffo is one of those WWF grapplers who benefited from Bockwinkel's wisdom. "I felt Nick Bockwinkel was the epitome of being a champion because of the way he carried himself in and out of the ring, on the plane, at all times," Poffo said. "I was on tour with Nick Bockwinkel in France and Italy. At the end of the tour, I was wearing my laundry, and he still had pressed pants and shirt, not a tie but an open collar and a sport jacket. I looked at him and said, 'He's a champion, not me.'"

After being downsized from the WWF, Bockwinkel worked in financial services until his retirement. These days, he spends a lot of time on the golf course, visits his two daughters and his grandkids with his second wife, Darlene, and is the president of the Cauliflower Alley Club (he jokes that he is "the curator of vintage material," meaning that he hauls and stores the club's memorabilia; the irony is that photography was a hobby while on the road). He was inducted into the Professional Wrestling Hall of Fame in 2003. Bockwinkel has been mulling writing his life story. He already has the title picked out: *You're Right Dad, They Suffer From Cranial Anal Imperfection*.

14. GENE KINISKI

"Big Thunder" Gene Kiniski still keeps up his daily training regimen, which includes swimming and walking around his 4,000-square-foot property in Washington, near the Canadian border. He also continues a habit he developed and used while wrestling, which he credits for a lot of his success: reading two newspapers a day.

Being topical was a big part of the success for Kiniski, who would easily rank on anyone's list as one of the best interviews of all time. Who else could go on the Canadian Broadcasting Corporation in 1957 and call out Prime Minister Louis St. Laurent, wondering why the country was still under

British rule, flying the Union Jack and singing "God Save The Queen"? Or call the head of the CBC's foreign-language broadcasts "a complete idiot" and an "imbecile" — while on the CBC?

"I was so fortunate because they always wrote articles on me," said Kiniski, admitting that he loved the controversy. "They wanted me to do that shit, they'd feed me that stuff." That is not to say his interviews were ever scripted. "I used to leave hours ahead, or even the day before, if I could just get on a radio program," he said. "I'm at my best when the pressure is on, and it's just impromptu." (Like the time in 1978 that he derailed a Peter Gzowski TV interview by asking the host, "Has anyone ever told you that have beautiful blue eyes?")

Canadian sports writing royalty like Jim Coleman and Trent Frayne loved to write about him. "When a columnist runs into a dull, uninspiring day, the gloom can be dispelled quickly by placing a long-distance telephone call to Gene Kiniski, the sweetest Canadian this side of Guy Lombardo's musicians," Coleman wrote in 1968. Frayne described wrestling in its purest form, good versus evil: "Kiniski is always in the black corner, a really rotten man with a repertoire of eye gouging, throat stomping, crotch kicking and assorted other illegalities that drive the customers to paroxysms."

Perhaps Kiniski's greatest chronicler was Dick Beddoes, whom Kiniski first met when he was just fifteen years old, in a gym in Edmonton, Alberta. Later, when Beddoes rose to prominence as a writer and a TV host, he'd regularly use his old friend. "Your correspondent had a reunion the other night with a delightful ogre named Eugene Kiniski, who is a big twig on the rassling branch of the human tree," Beddoes once wrote. It was on Beddoes' show in Hamilton where Kiniski was dubbed "Canada's Greatest Athlete."

A young Gene Kiniski.

Chuck Thornton Collection

The phone lines lit up, but Beddoes defended his assertion — Kiniski could wrestle, play football and hockey, and was an all-around athlete.

Often Kiniski is described as a football-player-turned-wrestler, but really, wrestling was his first love. He rolled around on the mats at Edmonton's YMCA as a teen, and got addicted to grappling. A champion amateur in Alberta (even tangling with Maurice Vachon at the 1947 Canadian championships) and, later, at the University of Arizona, football was a seasonal distraction for Kiniski. He elected to play pro ball in Edmonton rather than for the Los Angeles Rams because there was more money at home. His parents, Nick and Julia Kiniski, were well-known in the community, and Julia was a politician. Gene lasted just four years in football when a knee injury toppled him.

In 1953, back in Tuscon, Arizona, Kiniski started wrestling professionally for Rod Fenton. He knew many pros from his days at the university. His first big break came in 1955 in San Francisco, where the rugged Kiniski was paired with the noble "Lord" James Blears. The Lord had seen Kiniski in Los Angeles. "He was great, knocking people down, knocking the posts down, the big giant. So I said, 'That's the man for me,' and we teamed up. We were tag team champions for three years," recalled Blears, who said it was a rough go. "We were attacked every night. In California, Gene and I, I'm not kidding you, had to fight our way out of the ring. We couldn't get out of the ring. The fans wanted to kill us. In those days, you could go out swinging. Now, you hit one guy, you'll get sued. Back then, you just battled your way out of the ring. Gene, he'd say, 'Let's go! Okay Lordski, let's go!' He always called me Lordski. . . . Boy, he'd go swinging those arms, and I'd be behind him, protecting his back."

Kiniski's wrestling technique never really changed much beyond Blears' description. He only knew how to go forward, liked to shoot a bit in the ring with others who had amateur backgrounds, and had a stamina that was unparalleled. "I had a lousy physique but I was always in such superb shape. My stamina was so great that I was exceptionally strong. If you look at me, I'm just big — my bone structure, my hands, my size fourteen shoes, six-foot-five, 275 pounds. You had a lot to reckon with when you went up against a guy like me," Kiniski explained. "If you take a defensive posture in the ring, people can go to sleep on you. You want to give them goddamn action. And that's what I did."

Others reckon the same. "He had a goofy-looking body, but he was the best conditioned athlete I'd ever run into," said Hurricane Smith (Bob Grimbly). "He had me blown up in about ten minutes."

"Just a great psychologist," praised John Quinn. "He wasn't a powerhouse, he didn't come across as a big, strong man — but he was. And he never developed into what looked like a fit man — but he was. He had a mouth on him that wouldn't quit."

"I hated working with him. He was stiff. It was a hard night out when I worked with him," said "Cowboy" Dan Kroffat. "If I had to go thirty minutes with him, God, it took three days to recuperate. He just chopped the shit out of you."

Of course, talking about Gene Kiniski without talking about "Whipper" Billy Watson is like trying to build a house without nails; they were an essential part of each other's careers. They wrestled across Canada and into the U.S. from 1956 to 1967. Kiniski

Kiniski, NWA world champion.

knew his role. "When I wrestled him, people went in there to see me beat," Kiniski said. "And I'd just go out — I had a flamboyant style. I'd just give them action, action, action because I'm a rough, tough son of a gun. And as a result, we just drew so much money." Throughout the matches, it was Watson in control. "He was coaching, and I was doing all the offensive work."

All the notoriety paid off for Kiniski — at more than just the bank. He was American Wrestling Association world champ in 1961, and World Wrestling Association world champ in 1965. Promoters in the National Wrestling Alliance saw something in him, and he was chosen as the heir to Lou Thesz, whom he toppled for the world title on January 7, 1966. Kiniski held the prestigious title until February 11, 1969, dropping it to Dory Funk Jr. "Gene Kiniski was like a second father to me. He helped me through many situations, especially a very serious knee injury in Vancouver," said Funk Jr., explaining that he'd wrap his knees and go work. "Kiniski had probably the toughest attitude I've ever known. He really was Canada's greatest athlete."

While he was world champ, Kiniski lived outside St. Louis with his wife, Marion, and their two sons, Kelly and Nick. Given his dad's notorious attitude, Nick said that he was trained not to say who his father was. "They say,

'What's it like to have a famous father?' I don't know — I've never had any other father," said Nick Kiniski. "I just knew that my dad was a tough son of a bitch. I'd go watch him wrestle, sit in the stands, and not say who I was for sure."

While still world champ, Gene bought into the Vancouver promotion with Sandor Kovacs and Don Owen. The family moved to the Pacific Northwest. In 1973, the Kiniskis divorced, and Gene became the home-maker. "He was wild and crazy, but every morning, he'd get up, make sure I had breakfast, drive me to school," said Nick. "After school, I always ate good meals — vegetables and salads, there were no TV dinners; it was always a full-course meal. The house was always spotless. He did my laundry, he did my bed." Not long after the divorce, Marion committed suicide. Gene Kiniski becomes uncharacteristically tongue-tied when talking about the incident. "My wife was a very, very attractive girl, exceptionally attractive. She just couldn't handle aging. The boys were growing up and she was so depressed. She said, 'I'd just give anything if I could buy the boys some toys and stuff like that.' It was just one of those things that I didn't realize was happening. We got divorced. Of course, she started drinking and I never real-ized she had a drinking problem. It was a very, very sad thing."

Kiniski's in-ring career would run until 1992. He got to see both of his sons become good amateur wrestlers before they became pros. In retire-ment, Kiniski took a few acting roles and worked out with the Simon Fraser University wrestling team in Vancouver. He also was a bartender at his son Nick's bar, where today he just goes to hang out and play poker. Nick can rattle off story after story about his dad. "These guys are thrown out of the bar. The one guy tells my dad to fuck off, so my dad goes down and slaps him. Another guy says, 'You can't do that.' So he's chasing these three young kids in the parking lot, and he can't catch them. I said, 'Fuck, Dad, you can't be doing that, because I'm going to get sued. It's not like it used to be.' So he's back there bartending, like a bull in a china shop. It's about a half hour later. He says, 'Fuck, I don't know what's better, fucking or fighting.' I look at him, and I say, 'Either I don't know how to fight, or you don't know how to fuck. They're not the same.' He's seventy-six years old and he's saying that."

On his All-Star Wrestling broadcasts in Vancouver, Gene Kiniski insisted on the last word over host Ron Morrier: "I'd like to take this opportunity to thank my fellow Canadians and American viewing audience for allowing me into their TV, and as usual Ron, you did a superb job." He can claim that when people paid their dollar for a ticket, they got a ten-dollar value when they saw Kiniski.

He'd do it all over again if he could: "Thank Christ I knew how to wrestle. Thank God there was the wrestling business. Could you imagine working for a living?"

15. BORIS MALENKO

You can still hear the fondness in Ricky Hunter's voice, even though Boris Malenko smashed his gift wristwatch to smithereens. On Flordia television in late 1968, in one of Malenko's classic subterfuges, he raced from backstage to destroy a fifty-dollar watch that a fan gave to The Gladiator — Hunter under a mask. "People, they saw tears coming out of my eyes and it continued the situation for several more weeks. We'd go to the Bahamas and people would say, 'Can we buy you a watch because we feel so bad?'" Hunter recalled.

Boris Malenko.

The Gladiator got his revenge — he destroyed a small statue of a knight that Malenko commissioned in honor of himself, extending a feud that packed arenas in the Sunshine State. "He was a heel, but people responded to him and appreciated him," Hunter said. "He was just, for the lack of a better word, the glue that held everything together in a good match. I don't know five other heels that were as good as he was."

Boris Malenko — The Great Malenko, or, more formally, Professor Boris Maximilianovich Malenko of the School of Hard Knocks — was a character cut from a heel fabric long since out of production, a master strategist who was worlds ahead of his contemporaries in manipulating fans' emotions.

"In my book, he was one of the best. I would put him in the top five in my lifetime," said former NWA world champion Ronnie Garvin, who had a hot run with Malenko in the Knoxville, Tennessee promotion in 1978–79. "You could have a riot with him just doing nothing. Other guys could go out there with baseball bats and axes, you name it, and not get half the heat."

Born in 1933 in Newark, New Jersey, to a Polish immigrant father and

American mother, Larry Simon was raised in nearby Irvington, and did some amateur wrestling at different YMCAs as a teenager. He drove a truck in the New York Garment District, and got into wrestling full-time in the mid-1950s. For several years, he worked under his real name in the East. He went to Texas as "Crusher Duggan" in 1957, where he was the state heavyweight champ. In 1961, he teamed with Bob Geigel to win the AWA tag team championship as Otto Von Krupp, a German bruiser who sported a front tuft of hair, like The Mongols or The Missing Link years later.

In 1962, Simon officially became Boris "The Great" Malenko in Florida. He was not the first Malenko — Frank Fozo and John Kearney worked as Malenkos in the 1950s. New York promoter Vincent J. McMahon has been wrongly credited with inventing the character; Malenko's son Jody and several wrestlers said Karl Gotch gave Simon his new persona. Simon took it and ran with it, portraying a mad indignant Russian who would have been a perfect fit in a Stanley Kubrick film. "He was just a convincing character," said Jerry Prater, the long-time Florida wrestling publicist. "He played the Russian villain magnificently. When he was really into it, he was one of the best heels I've ever seen." Malenko's promos were mini-masterpieces, his voice rising and falling in a Russian accent as he twirled his mustache, one eyelid drooping, then falling shut. "I called him 'Cyclops,'" Angelo Mosca chuckled. "His facial expressions were great. A lot of the older guys always told me, 'Your face is your money.' That's what I learned from Malenko."

Malenko's feuds with Florida promoter Eddie Graham, who billed himself as the top babyface in the state, are the stuff of legend. Malenko advertised himself as king of the Russian chain match — "the way my ancestors fought" — and their bloodbaths touched off a boom period for Florida wrestling. "I loved watching and working with him," said Ricky Steamboat. "The way that guy could sell, bleeding all over the mat — I was in high school when I was watching some of that — and at the same time, he'd entertain you. He had that one eye open and the other one closed, selling his ass off as he and Eddie literally beat the living hell out of each other."

Malenko's bag of tricks also included the famous broken denture angle, first perfected in 1966 against Sam Steamboat, who ran into the ring to halt a Malenko beatdown. When Steamboat popped Malenko in the mouth, he spit out his false teeth, and Steamboat stomped them into the canvas. For years, Malenko lost his teeth from coast to coast, always ranting about the expensive bridgework that his opponent now owed him. "Larry Simon for my money was a great heel," wrestler and announcer Les Thatcher said. "As much showmanship as one saw on the surface, there was a ton of good solid ring psychology behind everything he did. Laugh at him during his promos, you had to take him seriously once the bell rang."

Malenko played audiences like a conductor, his movements changing moment by moment to evoke the desired reaction. Jody Simon, who later wrestled as Joe Malenko, recalled a match in Tampa, Florida, where Billy Robinson and Tony Charles put on a clinic, using every move in their English-style repertoire. "If they had left the ring and gone back to the dressing room and remembered something, they would have gone back out to the ring," he said. A few matches later, Malenko pulled out a simple Three Stooges trick — the old two-finger poke to the eyes. "The place exploded," Jody said. "You could not hear yourself think. People were flying out of their seats." Charles quizzically asked how a borrowed bit from Moe Howard could top his own best efforts. The answer — Malenko had demonstrated more than a hold.

"My dad had impeccable timing," Jody said. "He wasn't a guy who had a great cadre of holds. He had a few things that he could do, but he did them at the exact right minute. He would literally let a crowd boil, and then, not a second before, not a second afterward, he did the right thing, and people would just go nuts."

Even then, he'd cross up the audience, just to keep fans on their feet. Hunter, who worked as a subtle heel as The Gladiator, said Malenko liked to go behind an opponent, take him down, and cross him into the ropes. But, instead of going for a quick fist or elbow, he backed off and curtsied to his foe. "It would completely blow the logic of wrestling. People loved him and hated him at the same time, but by golly, they were back in line next week to see him again. When you had Malenko in there, if you had a bad match, it was your fault."

Throughout the 1960s, and 1970s, Malenko starred in Florida and the Carolinas, with runs in places like Texas and California thrown in. He was Florida brass knuckles champion whenever Graham wanted to hype rougher action. In Florida in 1971, he turned into a fan favorite during an angle with Rene Goulet and Dick Murdoch, but went back to his nefarious ways soon enough. A few years later, he formally split with Graham — the two never got along, and most insiders blamed the headstrong Graham. Malenko took his business elsewhere. In Tennessee, he disappeared from televised interviews for weeks, saying he was tired of Ronnie Garvin's taunts. Instead, he sent a servant Russian woman to explain his absence to TV announcer Thatcher. A couple of weeks later, Garvin further humiliated his rival by kissing the woman — and she responded as though she got into the smooch.

The next week, she presented Thatcher with a Malenko-scripted note that disclosed she was wearing a veil because of a "mark of shame." Actually, the veil was designed to cover the effects of major surgery on her jaw. "I reached over and lifted her veil and I almost fainted," said Garvin, still aghast more than twenty-five years later. "Her face, it looked like she got hit with a base-ball bat." The unspoken implication was clear — Malenko roughed her up for her kiss. That night, Garvin fought Malenko in the tough-and-tumble town of Harlan, Kentucky: "I swear to God, I thought somebody was going to kill him. For a month, he had so much heat, it was unbelievable." For years, Garvin honored Malenko with the "Garvin stomp," a series of boots around the body of a prone foe. "Nobody has realized that I copied Malenko. That was his gimmick in Florida . . . I copied it ten or fifteen years later and I even used it on him."

Malenko was involved in independent promotions for years, and his sons wrestled in the United States and Japan. Dean works with the WWE as a road agent, while Jody is a Tampa businessman. Malenko became known for his wrestling "school" in Tampa — a rundown, rat-inhabited room in the back of an old mattress factory.

According to trainee Bob Cook, Malenko was brilliant at conveying ring psychology. "He always used to say, 'You exaggerate everything, whether you're punching, throwing a forearm, facial expressions. You're not sup-posed to be a normal person walking around the face of the earth, so when you're walking around or doing an interview, don't act like one.'"

In 1994, Malenko was stricken with leukemia, a terrible disease for a health-conscious man who didn't drink, didn't smoke, and carefully placed a towel over his head after matches to avoid catching a cold. "Everybody constantly laughed because the hospital floor was like his indoor track," Jody Simon said. "He wouldn't run, but he'd take his pole with the chemo hanging off and he'd walk around the floor, and he'd walk, and he'd walk a million and one times." Malenko developed a severe infection before a second round of chemotherapy, and died of complications September 1, 1994 at sixty-one. An era in off-the-charts villainy and good humor passed with him.

"He had a way of taking a day you were having a miserable time and turning it into a positive," Cook said. "Even the last time I talked to him, a couple days before he died, I called him to see how he was doing. He said, 'I'm not doing too good, kid, but the hell with that. How are you doing? How's WCW treating you?' And he's cussing them — 'Ah, they wouldn't know talent it if they saw it.' He never did anything but positive things in my life and I'll never forget him."

16. HANS SCHMIDT

In a public world where he was the target of fan ire on a nightly basis, the big-booted, despicable German heel Hans Schmidt needed to find a quiet place where he could get away from it all. He found that peaceful haven in the deeps.

Ever since being introduced to the sport of skin diving by a neighbor in Newport Beach, California, Schmidt was hooked. "It was very interesting. I liked to go deep. It was a good, exciting sport," said Schmidt. "It was quiet there for a change. Nobody was yelling at you when you were underwater."

In the ring, the former Guy Larose was portrayed as a loner, a "Teuton Terror" who lived only to mete out punishment. But the reality is that he was well-liked by his peers — despite the many boot marks he left on their bodies. From his home north of Montreal, Schmidt's battered vocal cords come to life while telling stories of old chums he took into the water.

Hans Schmidt shows off a title in his heyday.

Chris Swisher Collection

Bill Melby was schooled in diving by Schmidt near Chicago. "My first dive, he says, 'Here's what you breathe through, do this, do that.' He showed me the stuff. We dove, and we dove down fifty feet on the first dive. I thought, 'What in the hell am I doing down fifty feet? I don't even know what I'm doing down here!'" laughed Melby. Diving didn't work out for Bobby Managoff — he couldn't see underwater without his glasses. Sky Hi Lee? He got lost. "We were in Hawaii . . . he took off on his own and didn't have any experience," Schmidt remembered. "That day, the boat we were with, there was no anchor. I had told him to stay with the anchor! He was looking for the anchor and we lost him. I found him, but it scared the hell out of me. I said, 'No more.'" The six-foot-four, 250-pound Schmidt fired a salvo against the tough reputation of Don Leo Jonathan — a noted underwater adventurer — as well. "I went diving with him one time in Toledo in a quarry. He was scared shitless. He didn't want to go down. The quarry, it's very clear when the sun is shining, but it's a funny place to go, with a lot of small tunnels. If you have a rope, you can go in those tunnels, but without a rope, you'd better not go, to find your way back. Don Leo didn't want to go there at all."

In 1949, the twenty-four-year-old native of Joliet, Quebec, found himself working as a pro wrestler, sometimes as "Guy Rose" or "Guy Ross," sometimes under his real name. In 1951, his life changed for good. "It was hard with a French name like that," he said. "When you got to the States, people were making jokes, funny names and stuff like that. I met a promoter in Boston, Paul Bowser. He was German and he told me I looked like a German. That's when he gave me that name, Hans Schmidt."

During the early years of televsion Schmidt became a huge star out of Chicago on the DuMont network. Babyfaces like Verne Gagne, Ronnie Etchison, and Yukon Eric would face Schmidt hundreds of times during their careers. DuMont announcer Jack Brickhouse once called Schmidt "the roughest wrestler I have ever run across."

"You have to remember the era. He was Johnny-on-the-spot shortly after the Second World War when the television era really started in the U.S.," said Paul "Butcher" Vachon. "At an early age, he had become bald. He didn't have to shave his head or anything. He was tall, he had a stern look on his face that was not put-on — it was just a natural scowl that he had. And they made a German out of him. It took a lot of guts."

However, unlike contemporary German villains Karl Von Hess and Fritz Von Erich, Schmidt never played up the Nazi side of things; instead, Schmidt preached against sportsmanship in his interviews, vowing that he would do anything to win. "He kept himself in great, great shape. He was a big, rugged, lean-boned guy," said Gene Kiniski. "He had the persona of being a storm trooper."

Schmidt had his act down, perfecting the backbreaker as a finisher. "It's the way you move, it's the way you talk — it's a different way of doing everything. But I was not that bad. I was a nice guy!" Billy "Red" Lyons agreed, on the nice guy part at least. "I enjoyed working with Hans, we had a lot of laughs. We'd laugh about the match afterwards. We would potato each other, maybe he got me tonight, and tomorrow night when he wasn't expecting it, I'd get him."

There were few corners of the North America where Schmidt didn't terrify fans. In his heyday he'd typically head out from Chicago to Florida, and then hit both Denver and New York, all during the same month. He made five trips to Japan. He was never much of a titleholder since he rarely stuck around long enough to make it worthwhile for a promoter to crown him.

By the 1970s, Schmidt had settled into a quieter life in the mountains north of Montreal. Yet he couldn't get away. "I was on my way out. I didn't want to wrestle anymore, but they were bothering me. They were calling me everyday. I wanted to quit earlier, but they didn't want to let me go. They said, 'You're still good, we need you.' The territory was down, so they said, 'Could you help us?' So I did for a while." His last run in Quebec for the Rougeaus, and the Buffalo, New York-centered National Wrestling Federation, exposed Schmidt to a whole new generation of fans; he even found himself in the odd position of being the babyface in a feud with Waldo Von Erich.

Today, Schmidt lives a quiet life, though the lake he and his wife live on has become a playground of the rich during the thirty years they've been there. He's dismissive of today's wrestling, and quick to deflect conversations away from his own glory days. Yet he can't get away from his past. A couple of years ago, two Japanese reporters showed up unannounced at his doorstep. "They came into my place by cab, a taxi from Montreal. You know how they found me? They called the taxi company, and they asked if the driver knew who I was and where I lived. By chance they found one guy who knew where I lived. They hired him and he took them to my place, where I saw them. I couldn't believe it," Schmidt chuckled, imagining the hour-and-a-half cab ride from Montreal. "They stayed about half an hour then they took off."

17. RAY STEVENS

It's the funeral that sticks out in Don Manoukian's mind about his friend Ray "The Crippler" Stevens. "It was full of cowboys, bankers, doctors, merchants, chiefs. He had a cross-section of friends. It was remarkable, and he was a remarkable guy." But, in true Ray Stevens fashion, Manoukian and his wife were out until the wee hours at a wedding the night before the funeral. Manoukian awoke to the alarming fact that he had to get from Reno, Nevada, to Fremont, California — a four-hour drive — in three hours. "Somehow we did it. Ah, Jesus Christ, I put my clean clothes and shoes on in the mortuary side of the banquet room, the reception room. What a day. I remember thinking, 'Boy is this appropriate. This is exactly something that goddamn Ray would do.'"

The life story of Carl Raymond Stevens — born September 5, 1935, in Point Pleasant, West Virginia, and raised by an aunt in Columbus, Ohio — is full of rich tales that couldn't be scripted by the best booker in the world.

First, the cowboy. Besides teaching Stevens how to wrestle steers, and rustle cattle on the ranch, world champion cowboy and Rodeo Hall-of-Famer Jack Roddy also ran with Ray. Roddy's brother owned a bar, and Jack recounted one Stevens incident taking place there. "There were two big

Ray Stevens prepares for the Bombs Away against Jose Lothario.

Hispanics in there. They were all drinking," Roddy began. "They said, 'Ray, for a hundred dollars, we'll whip your ass.' Ray said, 'Nah, a friend of mine owns this place.' So they really looked for it. As they kept drinking, they finally got down to a dollar. When they got down to a dollar, Ray jumped off the stool. He went, 'You know I can afford that.' And he whacked one, and he flattened him, and he grabbed the other, and he rolled him on his back. He grabbed his hand, and he broke five fingers, and left. These guys pushed and pushed, but they pushed with the wrong guy."

Now, the racer. "Ray was such a versatile guy. The guy could do almost anything he made his mind up to," explained Joe Leonard, champion motorcycle and stock car racer. He and Stevens became good buddies, and soon Ray wanted to race too. "He was big, but he had a great, big motorcycle. These little ones get around the corner better," Leornard recalled. "I said, 'Ray, all you've got to do is get off the line, and you just use up all the track.' He said, 'What do you mean?' I said, 'Just go as fast as you can go. Use all the track. Don't worry about staying in one little line.' Sure enough he won." Leonard then tried his best Ray Stevens impression, dropping into a big, gruff, joyous voice, "'Well, I guess there's a new champ around here!'"

Then there's the second wife, who can attest to the many, many tales of Stevens going out for a loaf of bread and not coming back for days. Carol Blanc and Stevens married in 1972, having met in California, and moved to Minneapolis together when Ray went to the American Wrestling Association. "He had the greatest laugh, he had the greatest personality. He was just great," she said. "He was real whimsical. If he wanted to do this, we'd do that." Stevens loved to race snowmobiles in Minnesota, and had four so that friends could compete; the machines complemented the boat and a hydroplane.

The couple moved to Montana, and then Stevens just disappeared. "I couldn't find him for over a year. He didn't contact me or anything. After a year and a half, I thought, 'Well, okay Ray. This is it.' So I filed divorce papers here in Montana. We got a divorce. The odd thing was, the day our divorce was final, he called me. He said, 'Why did you divorce me?' I said, 'Ray, I haven't heard from you for a year and a half. I think that's a pretty good reason.'"

Though Stevens' first wife, wrestler Therese Theis, with whom he had four children, isn't around to tell her stories, one yarn has grown through the years. It's even true. Stevens and Theis had a big fight, and she left in their station wagon. He chased her down on his motorcycle, jumped through the window and took the wheel.

Back to Manoukian. "First time I met Ray, we're traveling constantly between L.A. and the San Francisco territory. I was a bachelor. I thought he was a bachelor. We were having a great life. About two months into the relationship, he hits himself in the head one time, and said, 'Jesus Christ, I forgot to call my wife.' I said, 'Holy Christ, are you married?' He said, 'Yeah.' I said, 'How long have you been married?' He said, 'All my life.'"

Time to tag in the tag team partner. "Ray, no matter if he was sixty years old, when you were around him, you could say he was eighteen," recalled wrestler Pat Patterson. "Always fun, always happy, nothing bothered him. He was a fun guy to be with, really a fun guy. And in the ring, he was a master, no question about it. I learned a lot from him. I learned a lot from Roy Shire. I learned my psychology from Roy Shire."

Thanks to Patterson for bringing it home. Without Roy Shire, there is no Ray Stevens. Ray was just a teenager in Columbus when he started hanging around the Toe Hold Club. "He used to ride his bicycle down there and would hang around the wrestling office. Everybody loved him. Carl [Ray] was big for a young kid. Big and chunky," Frankie Cain told *Whatever Happened To...?* That 160-pounder wouldn't give up on his dream to be a wrestler. "He used to bug me constantly. He'd be up in the office all the time," said Donn Lewin, who was also in Columbus. "Finally I said okay. So I got Jim Henry, the guy who started me, and started working with him and teaching him a few things."

Debuting at the age of fifteen, by 1952, Stevens was working a program with Gorgeous George in Columbus. Soon after, Roy Shire took the youngster under his wing as his tag partner, Ray Shire. The schooling of a master had begun and Shire shared his heelish shortcuts as well as bump-taking lessons. Stevens would grow into a five-foot-seven, 237-pound man, with bleached blond hair, a tribute to his hero "Nature Boy" Buddy Rogers.

Another early influence was Don Fargo, who worked with Ray as brother Don Stevens.

Stevens with manager Freddie Blassie in the WWWF.

Stevens developed into the best bump-taker in wrestling history. "Stevens, I think, going through the twentieth century, was the all-around best worker of any of them in the profession," said Nick Bockwinkel. "When I ask my cohorts about that, when I say, 'Who was the best?' — time and time again, it's Stevens."

"Stevens was so fluid, his timing was unassailable," wrote "Superstar" Billy Graham in his autobiography. "Nothing was ever rushed or delayed. He took big bumps on a hard ring, and watching him sell made a believer out of me. In my opinion, there wasn't anything that 'The Blond Bomber' couldn't do. There'll never be another one like him."

Stevens was an "old-school, hard-nosed, hardcore" heel, Graham added. "Ray Stevens, he was my wrestling hero. Like I called him in my book, he was the neighborhood bully. He was the tough guy on the block. If I was going to be a heel, I wanted to be like Ray Stevens, who was just too hard, too tough, too unique."

Paul Diamond compared it to working with God. "I remember working Channel 2 in 1963. 'Bombs Away off the top rope is the finish, Paul.' 'Don't hit my teeth, Ray.' He flew through the air. His knee breezed by my neck. I sold it like a million bucks. I lay there twitching. Ray pinned me 1-2-3," said Diamond, launching into another memory. "He said, 'Throw me into the turnbuckle. Just throw me into the turnbuckle.' He goes flying into the ropes — he was the guy who did this first, and Flair does it now. Ray Stevens would only take that bump in a main event. He went boom! He did it ten times better than Flair, Flair goes over like a big piece of turd. Stevens would go over like a ballet dancer, fly over that top rope and land on the cement outside. People thought I killed him. So when he beat me, he beat somebody who threw Ray Stevens flying through the air."

Confident in his abilities, Stevens wasn't afraid to share his knowledge either. "I was so fortunate that I was around Ray when he was at the zenith of his career," said Bill Watts. "It was phenomenal to get to work with him. I learned so much — he took time to teach me. That's the way it used to be done." Roger Kirby said Patterson, who learned a lot from Ray, would help as well. "Pat and Ray would sit down and explain stuff, and this was back when I thought I was a pretty good worker. But they still helped and explained. They taught me so much psychology, which was so important."

For all his skills, championships, and headlining bouts in wrestling, however, Stevens had great difficulty reining himself in. On more than one occasion, an extracurricular activity like go-karting or motorcycling resulted in an injury that would derail an angle. He smoked and drank (Crown Royal was a favorite choice), and lived every day like it was his last. "He was exuberant. He didn't care about anything," said frequent opponent Red Bastien. "He just went through life and lived the life. *Vive la vie*, he picked up that expression, *vive la vie*. He did, to the fullest."

As he aged, Stevens gained weight and relied more on his mind in his feuds and his interviews, where he uttered his threats from the side of his mouth. Yet he was still believable, whether working with rising stars like Flair or Ricky Steamboat in the Mid-Atlantic territory in the late 1970s, or Superfly Snuka in the WWWF. In the AWA, he got a chance to co-host *The Superstars of the AWA* with Larry Nelson, allowing his wit to shine. Stevens would end his forty-one-year career in 1991.

In 1995, the mayors of San Francisco and Oakland jointly proclaimed April 5 "Ray Stevens Day," and he was honored as a true local legend. He suffered a heart attack in late 1994 in Minnesota, and, on May 3, 1996 in Fremont, California died in his sleep from heart illness at age sixty.

"Ray was probably the most gifted athlete — hand-eye coordination, nimbleness; there was not anybody in the business that had his innate ability to pick up things," said Manoukian. "Ray probably reached seventy-five percent, eighty percent of his potential, and he was great. He had the real great, laid-back attitude. He'd give what he thought was 100 percent, but he had so much more."

18. "NATURE BOY" RIC FLAIR

Q: Nature Boy, is the art of being a heel gone from today's wrestling? A: "No, but they won't let me do it," Ric Flair jokes, chuckling with his familiar slightly off-center smirk. It's pretty obvious that he misses the days gone by. "The powers that be have different opinions on that, and I have a different opinion on it too. It's just a business change. They just don't have that killer heat guy that walks around where they want to kill you."

Sharing his insights into the life of a bad guy in Toronto, Flair told a tale about the storied Maple Leaf Gardens, where the wrestlers would stay in a hotel a couple of blocks up the street. "We always had to fight our way there, and fight our way up the steps of the door. It was brutal. That was heat. But it was good though. The fans wanted to kill us, that's what wrestling was. It's better now and more lucrative now, but it was really fun back then to have that kind of heat."

Fans today are better educated and think differently, seeing wrestling as entertainment, and only getting mad in certain places. But Flair also credits improved security at venues for the change in the dynamic as well. He

Pete Lederberg

Ric Flair perfected the figure four leg lock — here on Sting.

doesn't miss Hatpin Mary! "It was a fun time in my life to make people that crazy, but it was dangerous. Things have changed all the way around."

While Flair still works a full-time schedule in the WWE at the age of fifty-seven, most fans don't want to remember him that way, losing to members of the Spirit Squad with alarming regularity, albeit with an evident joie de vivre. Instead, it's the vintage Flair — circa 1974–1984 — that brings goose-bumps and smiles.

Born February 25, 1949, in Memphis, Tennessee, he was adopted as a baby and grew up in Edina, Minnesota, as Richard Morgan Fliehr. A decent athlete, he wasn't a great student at Wayland Academy in Beaver Dam, Wisconsin, or the University of Minnesota, where he spent a year and a semester, and played freshman football. "I went there to play football, but I didn't project to the NCAA scholastic part of it, and when I found out I

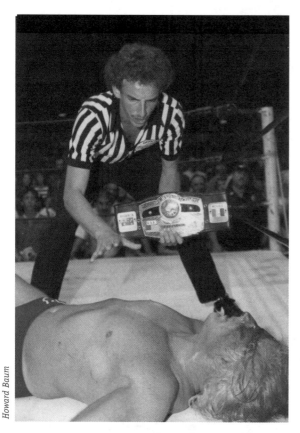

Howard Baum

Flair was also the master of escaping with his title — here, the NWA belt is returned by Bill Alfonso.

couldn't play football, I lost interest," Flair said in 1986. He knew Greg Gagne from school, and Gagne suggested giving wrestling a try. Fliehr dropped out of Verne Gagne's training camp twice, selling life insurance to make ends meet, before sticking for good in 1972. From this point, it's easy to let others take over.

TINKER TODD: *When Johnny Heideman and I went up to Minneapolis — we had just come back from Japan, just before I retired, so it would be '72, they asked us to train three guys, and Ric Flair was one of them. Well, I'm at the end of it now, I want to get out of it, I'm building this house, I bought this property. I didn't have any enthusiasm. The snow cancelled out St. Paul or somewhere, or Denver or somewhere, so they asked me to train these guys. But he don't turn up in the morning. The other guys do and Johnny takes them down to the armory. Well, all of a sudden, about thirty minutes later, I'm enjoying the program, and in walks Ric Flair. He was genuine. His car, his battery had gone bad — he drove a green Cadillac. So I took him on down, I worked him out hard and my famous words are: "This kid will never make it in the business." I come back and Rip Hawk was looking for a guy because at that time Swede Hanson had a heart attack or something. He asked me if I'd work with him, and Bronko Lubich wanted me to work with him as his partner. I didn't want to; I was building a house and getting ready to get out of the business. So I told Rip, "I've just the guy for you, up in Minneapolis by the name of Ric Flair. He looks like you, in my opinion, and I think you could shape him up good." And Rip Hawk got in touch with Ric Flair and brought him in as a nephew or something.*

It's 1974, and Flair is in Charlotte, North Carolina, preparing to work for Jim Crockett Sr., and George Scott was the booker.

GEORGE SCOTT: *I'm the one that gave him the name Flair. He came in to wrestle. His parents, he was adopted. His father was a doctor. . . . I said, "Go with Ric Flair." Then I got Buddy Rogers to give him the name Nature Boy. . . . Buddy had retired and quit, and Buddy was one of my best friends. I brought him up to the Carolinas, and he wrestled a couple of matches, he did a bunch of refereeing, and stuff like that. . . . Flair wanted to be a cowboy. I said, "You ain't going to be a cowboy!"*

RIP HAWK: *He was greener than grass. He was a pretty good guy. He picked up pretty fast. We were together for about a year. He embarrassed me a lot, the way he acted, not in the ring, but out of the ring. He used to do stupid things. He did one when he got in with this Mafia guy's girlfriend. They were going to bump him off, in Norfolk. They were friends of Swede [Hanson] and I, and they were heavy Mafia out in New Jersey, but they owned a couple clubs in Norfolk. They were kind of cooling-off spots for me. And I had Flair with me one night, at one guy's club, and I told Flair, "Leave that broad alone." He said, "Yeah, yeah, I won't bother her." Then, all of a sudden, he was in big trouble. Swede called me and Swede said, "We've got to get him out of there — they're going to kill him." It took a lot of talking. Those guys liked us, they loved us.*

BOB CAUDLE, MID-ATLANTIC WRESTLING ANNOUNCER: *He came into the Mid-Atlantic area really young. He had a good physique on him, he had that long hair, and of course he had that mouth on him. Flair was always able to talk. Right away, he was a hit and a success.*

The promotion saw something in Flair, and began grooming him for a main-event run. But on October 4, 1975, a Cessna twin-engine 310 plane with Flair, Tim Woods, Johnny Valentine, Bob Bruggers, and David Crockett on board, crashed near Wilmington, North Carolina. The pilot was killed, Valentine paralyzed, and Bruggers never wrestled again. Flair broke his back in three places, and was out until February 1976.

After a heated feud with Wahoo McDaniel, Flair was paired with Johnny Valentine's son.

GREG "THE HAMMER" VALENTINE: *I was my father's son so I naturally wrestled like him. I got that talent from my dad so that's why I think Flair and I are compared so much. Beyond that, Ric Flair and myself — after my father's accident — were put together by the promoters. Then, we became the World tag team champions in 1978. We had those belts a long, long time too. I picked up things from Ric, and he picked up things from me. That's where we got our similar styles. I have a lot of respect for Ric.*

Then came singles battles with Ricky Steamboat over the U.S. title. Flair and Steamboat were both still young and hungry. Neither knew they'd still be working against each other for the National Wrestling Alliance world title fifteen years later. Flair brought out the best in Steamboat, and it worked the other way as well. In fact, Flair once called Steamboat "the greatest good guy of all time."

REFEREE TOMMY YOUNG: *Him and Steamboat were the greatest matches I ever did. It was just like bread and butter, they just went together those two, and every match was a classic.*

RICKY STEAMBOAT TO RADIO HOST JIMMY VAN: *He was snug. His punches, and kicks, and chops, and stuff like that. He was living up to the image, obviously you have to realize what era of wrestling that was. That was an era in our business in which kayfabe was dominant. You know, make your punches look good, or stick 'em in, work tight, work snug.*

MIKE MOONEYHAM, CHARLESTON POST & COURIER: *I met Ric in the mid-'70s when he had only a few years under his belt. He already was an established main-eventer and working a U.S. heavyweight title program with the late Bobo Brazil. He was talented beyond his years, and had an undeniable presence. I remember talking to Sandy Scott, who worked in the office at the time, and discussing how he was a can't-miss prospect who had world title written all over him.*

Flair was subtly changing the way fans thought about bad guys. He could threaten their heroes and carry out on his threats, but after the matches, he was a live wire, and did become the kiss-stealin', wheelin'-dealin', jet plane-flyin', limousine-ridin', son of a gun, in interviews that he always bragged he was.

NEWT TATTRIE TO GEORGIAWRESTLINGHISTORY.COM: *Ric Flair is the same all the time. He's only interested in one thing, making money and looking good. He's an amazing guy. One day he was working in Puerto Rico in a sixty-minute match, the next week a ninety-minute match, and then he had to get on a plane to fly to Minneapolis to wrestle the next day. And he still hasn't let up since. Ric Flair is the most amazing wrestler I ever knew in my life. Nobody could even compare with him.*

STAN LANE: *I kind of liked wrestling, but it wasn't till I saw Ric Flair that it became cool. His heat wasn't from saying, "I'm a badass, I'm going to beat somebody up." He was out there talking about partying, and his women, and his girlfriends, and how he would walk in bars and women would pass out. That was cool stuff and that's what really attracted me to it. I'm saying, "This guy is cool as hell. He's built, and he looks good,* he's got these women and these big cars, and he's bragging about it. He's made the common folk hate him." He made it cool to be a heel.

As wrestling transitioned into a national business, Flair changed the traditional sense of heel–babyface. As NWA world champion, he traveled territory to territory, and played whatever role was needed, something his predecessor, Harley Race, had perfected as top dog.

HARLEY RACE: It even kind of got so that when I was going into the Carolinas, Ric was a heel everywhere he went, except when he worked with me. The reason for that is that he had been there, he had taken it, and they wanted to see that guy as champion... If you're smart, which Flair is, you don't change your style. Let the people decide. You put the people in a position where they've got to go against what they would really go, really like to do. But that's when you become a great worker, when you can dominate how people are going to react.

BOB CAUDLE: He's one of those guys — and there's not many of them — that were successful being a heel, then a babyface, then back a heel, then back a babyface. He turned a number of times that way. Even as a heel, the crowd always loved him because he put on a good show, and he was flamboyant with the long hair and the fancy robes. He could talk it up either way.

"NATURE BOY" BUDDY LANDEL: I don't think he can have a bad match. I think, in my opinion, he's the best that's ever been, probably the best there will ever be. When you saw him walk into a restaurant, you knew he was the world champ. You saw him get into the ring, you knew he was the world champ. Anywhere he went, he just represented. He was dressed to the nines. I've just got the utmost respect for the man.

Still going strong after more than thirty years, Flair has had to change his way of wrestling to match the different wrestlers, the heightened requirements, and, the expectations. In 1974, it's doubtful anyone thought he'd be working ladder or thumbtack matches in 2006.

RIC FLAIR: I don't know if I've had to change my style, but I've had to make adjustments. The biggest thing for me is the fact that I just had to adjust to the differences in the style of wrestling. The fact is that most of the guys when I started had ten, fifteen years of experience . . . now we've got kids that are coming in the business that are wrestling three, four months, wrestling a year, year and a half. It's hard. But they're making it, and it's something they should be very proud of. It's hard right now to develop that kind of talent real fast.

In fact, Flair is over today as much as he has ever been. He may not be on top, but he's a legend. The fans react to him with reverence now, instead of hatred.

ERIC BISCHOFF: *You can't be Ric Flair and be in the business as long as Ric Flair's been in the business without becoming a kind of a Babe Ruth icon. Ric was always the guy who wanted to be a heel. But there's a certain point in your career where you've got to recognize that no matter what you do, the fans are not going to hate you, therefore you're not going to be an effective heel no matter how much you want to be.*

KEITH ELLIOT GREENBERG, FLAIR'S BIOGRAPHER: *Flair has become a babyface because of his contributions to the wrestling industry. How can you not love Ric Flair and admire him? Regardless of what your opinion of certain segments of his life might be, you have to respect what he's sacrificed for the business, and still does after all these years — how could you not cheer the guy?*

TOMMY YOUNG: *Out of all the guys I'd refereed down through the years, I would have to say he's the greatest of them all. He is to wrestling what Arnold Palmer was to golf. Not Jack Nicklaus — Hulk Hogan is Jack Nicklaus. He's got most of the records, and he got bigger, just like Jack Nicklaus got bigger than Palmer. But Palmer is the king of golf; he's the one who made it popular, who brought the people out. When it comes to who's the man, it ain't Hulk Hogan. It's Ric Flair. He's the king.*

19. BULL CURRY

According to legend, Bull Curry got his nickname from taming a wild steer that escaped into the streets of Hartford, Connecticut, back in the 1930s. It's just as likely that the steer took one look at him and decided life was better back in the pen. "What he had going for him was his million-dollar face — he looked like the devil himself," said Emile Dupre, who fought Curry in the Canadian Maritimes. "He had eyebrows right across that were almost two inches thick. He had that tough-looking body."

Apocryphal stories aside, Fred Koury Sr. looked like something from a genetic experiment gone horribly awry, and wrestled exactly as you would expect. "He was the first guy who scared me," said Detroit-area veteran Jim Lancaster. "The way he came to the ring — he would just hit guys in the

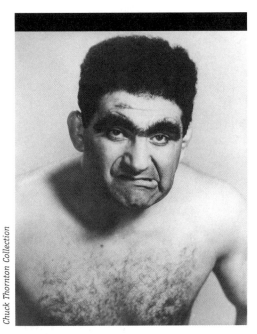

Chuck Thornton Collection

"Wild" Bull Curry.

head and make them bleed. That's all he did. He never had a finish. He'd just pull out some brass knuckles, knock them out, and cover them."

Think Ric Flair has been in the business for a long time? Consider this: as of 2007, Flair would have to wrestle for another fifteen years and box Jack Dempsey to boot to rival Curry's longevity. In 1953 promoter Norman Clark of Galveston, Texas called Curry "the most consistent drawing card I've ever had." Twenty-six years later, Curry, sixty-five, was still main eventing in Galveston against Eddie Sullivan.

Born May 2, 1913, in Hartford, Curry was one of five children and learned early on how to handle himself in a heavily ethnic neighborhood. As a teenager, he was working on the circus circuit, taking on all comers before Detroit promoter Adam Weismuller broke him into the pro game. "He could work it or shoot it — that's what you had to do in those days to survive," said Curry's son, Fred. Curry was a pro by the age of nineteen, wrestling in the Northeast and Michigan. *Ring* magazine ranked him among the world's top light heavyweights in 1936. His bust-'em-up ways drew national attention in July 1940, when he lost a two-round boxing bout to Jack Dempsey in Detroit. Blake Henkel of United Press International said the event set "a new high for ring comedy" with in- and out-of-ring escapades, especially when Curry fell into the lap of a Michigan athletic commissioner who promptly swatted him in the face.

Curry's big move came when he shifted from New England to Texas in 1953, and took his wildman gimmick with him. But, in his debut there, long-time referee Tommy Fooshee recalled, Curry fell flat. "When he first came to Texas, the first two weeks there, he didn't do anything, they were ready to fire him, send him home. But in Galveston, they had five or six balconies in that old auditorium there, and he was running through the balconies. The people bought it." Curry became a sensation in Texas with wild and bloody brass knucks brawls against Danny McShain, Duke Keomuka, and Pepper Gomez. He made little pretense of wrestling; his actions more resembled those of an out-of-control gremlin. "He'd find a mark in the audience, take their shoe off, bring it into the ring and hit the other wrestler with it," Fooshee said. Son Fred added, "He was the original hard-core man. They made the brass knuckles title for him in Texas, and no one could beat him. His punch looked like it was taking your head off."

Courtesy Wrestling Revue Archives

Bull Curry ignores the crowd's taunts.

Generations of wrestlers watched with wonder at one of Curry's signature moves — clutching his sensitive right ear when he was hurt. "No matter where you hit him, he'd grab his right ear. It was amazing," said Nick Kozak, who fought him in Texas. "Stomp his foot, he'd grab his ear. Hit him in the gut, he'd grab his ear." But Curry also could slug it out, and that's when he got the crowd going. "Bull had that deal where he'd make a side-step, then come with that left hook into the gut, that wide sweeping left hook, and you knew it was coming. He kind of opened his hand and it popped. If you stayed open for him, it went 'whop,' and the people, they almost had orgasms, for heaven's sakes," Kozak said.

Louie Tillet said some wrestlers disliked working with Curry because they felt he seldom showed the effects of their offense. But Tillet didn't balk when Houston promoter Morris Sigel and associate Frank Burke lined him up for a series of matches. Tillet called on Curry in a hotel room, and laid out a scenario for making a few bucks. "I said, 'I'll give you one match, and I'll give you all the opportunity that you need. I know that you can draw the money. Let's see what we can do.' We went to Fort Worth, Texas, and had a hell of a match. He sold the shit out of me. He just knew upfront that I was not going to put up with the bullshit. That's it. After that, we worked all through Texas — Dallas, Fort Worth, Houston, San Antonio, Austin when Leo Garibaldi was booking out there. We had a great time."

Dallas TV announcer Bill Mercer felt Curry's trademark unpredictability first-hand one night when he got popped in the chops. "I'm sitting right at the edge of the ring, right below the apron. He's running up and down, slamming against the ropes. He's running around and people are screaming. All of sudden, he looks down and I'm looking up, and he kicks me in the face. My first thought was, 'Oh, I hope I didn't say some bad word.' But I was just stunned . . . You didn't know what in the world that guy might do."

Well, he might request his opponent to toss him headfirst into a beer salesman. Dick Brown worked with Curry in Texas when Bull noticed a vendor peddling beer to front-row patrons was paying no attention to the match. "Bull said, 'Throw me out onto that son of a bitch.' I threw Bull out of the ring and he plowed into the guy's back, with bottles of beer flying all over the place. Bull climbed back into the ring and I guarantee you the beer salesman watched what was going on in the ring after that," Brown said. "He was the character of characters."

The "human cactus," as newspapers labeled him, was so big in Texas that he eventually got cheered, even though his tactics didn't change a lick. "He was around here so long before I was that when I wrestled him he was automatically a babyface," said "Killer" Karl Kox. And, in an account by Christie Mitchell of *Galveston Dailly News*, his cover is definitely blown: "Rumors that wild man Bull Curry pushes ducks into water and robs grandmothers of their inheritance are totally false," Mitchell wrote. "He is a kind, gentle bull who likes flowers and reads poetry."

After 1968, Curry pretty much stuck to the Midwest, where his son was becoming a breakout star. Curry's shtick became so popular there that he again heard his share of cheers, according to manager Percival A. Friend, who refereed some of Curry's bouts. "Foreign objects were Bull's mistress," Friend said. "He often used a huge drapery ring that was either gold or silver in color and would conceal it very well from referees. He was a great draw where ever he went and could be accepted as either good guy or bad guy depending on the issue at hand."

By the '70s, Curry was eligible for a senior-citizen discount, and moving tentatively. "Bull was not really an aggressive guy; he was more of a defensive guy. You'd have to bring the play to him; he wouldn't bring it to you," said Dan Miller, who laughingly recalled one incident with him in Marion, Ohio. "I went to take him over, just from a side headlock. When I got back to the dressing room, The Sheik told me, 'I never saw a guy's neck get so long in my life. The head went, but the body stayed where it was.'"

In later years, Curry told Lancaster he was disappointed he never got a run with The Sheik's coveted U.S. belt. "He said he was a hotter heel than The Sheik was, and at that point, when he came in Detroit for that first time, I would buy into that," Lancaster said. When the Detroit promotion started to slide downhill in the late 1970s and early 1980s, the Currys ran spot shows in Ohio and Michigan, and Bull was a fixture on them, even though he was approaching seventy. Bobby Fulton of the Fantastics said Curry was still magic as the grandfather of hardcore. "He gave me my first chair shot," Fulton recounted whimsically. "I remember one time in Portsmouth, Ohio, on Thanksgiving night, he picked up a chair and started hitting me, and all of a sudden the people started picking up their chairs and throwing them. There was a magnetism about him."

Curry died in March 1985, ending one of the longest and wildest careers in wrestling history. "He'd have them standing when they entered, and they'd be standing when he left," said his son Fred, a Connecticut businessman whose own son, "Rocket," is a third-generation wrestler. "He always stole the show."

20. "ROWDY" RODDY PIPER

Leo Garibaldi was the man who set Roddy Piper loose upon the world. Up until Garibaldi decided to allow Piper free reign, he was essentially a lower-card wrestler. But the down-in-the-dumps Los Angeles territory was starved for new talent in the mid-'70s — particularly heels — so a drastic measure was taken. "I booked him in a match, and I just gave him to somebody to eat him up. But the guy would not be eaten up," Garibaldi said. "He was playing the bagpipes, he was jumping around, and flashing his skirt. The people went crazy. They didn't know to hate him or to love him."

That really is the essence of "Rowdy" Roddy Piper. He was a heel that fans loved to be entertained by, and he was a babyface that could fire back with the best of the motormouth bad guys.

"Piper is always a lively, funny type of character. That's his nature. He could either make you laugh, or make you angry, or whatever. Either way, he will catch your attention," said Johnny Rodz, who, as Java Ruuk in L.A., was the first grappler Piper ever managed.

"Playboy" Buddy Rose made the babyface Piper a star in Portland in the late 1970s, and when Piper came back shortly after his headlining match at WrestleMania, they had a friendly bet about who would be booed by the crowd. Rose had the advantage of the local TV, but Piper was the hated national star. "I went out to the ring first, and got booed. I didn't have to do anything to get booed. I was just the heel," said Rose. "He came out, and

Mike Lano

Referee Lou Anthony raises Roddy Piper's arm after Hot Rod's first victory as heel in Los Angeles.

they gave him a standing ovation. He came out with that heel-Roddy walk, and everything going. He stopped and looked at the people, shook his head, and did the jumping up and down on one leg like he did as a babyface when he was in Portland. . . . He learned something that night, and so did I — it didn't matter what you did anywhere else in the country, if your home was Portland, Oregon, and people knew you lived in Portland, you were their babyface."

To Piper, it all came down to self-respect, and if he took whatever he was doing seriously enough, then the fans would too, no matter what his role was, or what the people wanted him to be. "Every time I went out there I tried as hard as I could because we used to have a rule — you never knew who was there," said Piper, a 2007 inductee into the Professional Wrestling Hall of Fame. "Plus, you had pride, you had a pride in what you were doing. And if somebody called me a phony wrestler in a bar, pfffft! Yep, you got my attention right away."

There's that word "attention" again. Piper had the ability to fire an audience's imagination like few others. And he knew it; his on-air smugness was really a type of confidence. At the height of his run as a national figure, he was given the microphone for Piper's Pit segments on WWF syndicated television, at his request, he says, as he couldn't wrestle due to his ear, which was still healing after the Dog Collar Match with Greg Valentine at Starrcade '83. It proved to be the star-making move of his career. "The reason I started Piper's Pit was if you can watch me wrestle on TV, why pay to see me?"

Piper was a scrapper, who fought for every tidbit that he got along the way. Born Roderick Toombs in Saskatoon, Saskatchewan, in November 1956, Roddy's father worked as a police officer for the Canadian National Railway, and the family moved to many different outposts over the years: The Pas for Roddy's first year of school, Dofin; Port Arthur; Dawson Creek; Winnipeg;

Montreal; Toronto; plus Glasgow, Scotland; and Melbourne, Australia. As a teen, he was a child of the streets. He needed structure, and found it in a Winnipeg gym. Wrestler Al Tomko was the local promoter, and Piper slept in his gym. "I had a television production company at the time. He was sort of a local wrestler, he was into boxing before he was into wrestling," Tomko said. "A neighborhood kid. We took him and trained him. Then I'd let him use the television so he'd learn to talk. We had a circuit around Manitoba to train these guys, we'd do the small towns so they would learn how to wrestle before they hit the big time."

Following the lead of his primary trainer, the equally diminutive Tony Condello, Piper was brought into the AWA in mid-1973 to make others look good. How many people remember his October third loss to a rookie Ric Flair in Minneapolis? Piper had the kilt and the bagpipes almost from the start. Piper's first territory was Central States. "Bob Brown came down one day and said, 'There's a kid up in Winnipeg who is going to be a hell of a performer. I think you can use him and make some money with him.' It was Roddy Piper," recalled promoter Bob Geigel. "He made up for his size with his brain."

An almost forgotten tour of Texas in early 1975 resulted in an awkward spot for Piper, but illustrates how he could make the best out of any situation. Promoter Paul Boesch was a very patriotic man, and played the national anthem before his shows. The record began to skip, and Boesch apologized, and introduced Piper to play an impromptu version on his bagpipes. "There's only eight notes on these things! So I went out and screeched out a version of the American national anthem. And those people erupted. It was so bad it was good," said Piper. "That's what got me my first interview. And if he hadn't have done that, I might never have gone nowhere. . . . There's little bits all the way through my career of those kind of things. Nothing premeditated, and that's the best thing."

In summer 1975, just before he cracked the public consciousness in Los Angeles, Piper worked out in the Maritimes, where tough old-timers like "Mad Dog" Vachon and "The Beast" (Yvon Cormier) took him in. "I don't think that I called him a geek, but he was a little small," said The Beast. "But after I got done with him, trained him, and he gained weight, I knew he had the heart and desire to be good."

To this day, Piper gives credit to those who helped him. "I owe my whole career to everybody but myself," he said. "The structure by which I was taught. You need to keep your mouth shut at all times, write nothing down, keep everything in your head, shut your mouth, and give it your all at all times." Piper is pretty matter-of-fact about the way his life was going on the streets. "I think I probably would have died if I didn't have the discipline that they instilled in me."

When Garibaldi gave Piper his shot as a heel, he was careful not to put the six-foot, 230-pound Piper in against a giant. To capitalize on the heavily Latino audience, Piper got to work with Chavo Guerrero Sr., who was seven years older, and a second-generation veteran. "Brother, he was just box-office all the way," said Guerrero Sr., still in awe of Piper on the microphone. "He would come up with the weirdest things, man — not weird, but something to draw the people. One time he came out with a donkey, and called it my mom. It meant something to me, so naturally he got heat. Every time we got in the ring — we used to do a lot of cage matches, chain matches, and all kinds of matches. We actually had to beat the hell out of each other. The people, they'd see us so much . . . We liked it. Piper and I had that rough style. We respected each other, but we used to lay them in, man."

Piper worked so much with the Guerreros that his style had changed, and it took the advice of another old-timer to bring him back. "Johnny Valentine gave me that little piece of philosophy and, at that time, I learned instead of working with Chavo Guerrero and the lucha libre, he told me, 'Get your feet on the ground and start acting like a fighter.' That became 'Rowdy' Roddy Piper."

This new "Rowdy" Roddy Piper could be a heel or a face with ease. He loved the business he was in, and proved it by being a joy to be around, and sharing his knowledge. "Hustler" Rip Rogers was one who benefited from Piper's advice in Portland. "He was always very nice to me, tremendous talent in the ring. Never took liberties with me. Let me call matches I did not deserve to call, because he knew that I needed to learn," said Rogers. "He was passing it down to me, and here he was about the same age as me, but he was just so good to me."

George Scott was booking the Mid-Atlantic territory. "I saw him in Oregon and he was playing the pipes," said Scott. "I brought him in and I said, 'When you walk out before your match, I want you to play the pipes and walk around the ring.' It was ungodly real. Our ratings went up in three months something like thirty percent, and it was from him playing the pipes, and stuff like that. He got over like that." Piper's legend grew, as he worked as a color commentator in Georgia Championship Wrestling alongside Gordon Solie, and did compelling interview after interview.

As 1984 began, he was in the WWF, initially as a manager, but later as the wrestler who really kick-started the rock'n'wrestling connection; all it took was a well-placed boot. At *The War to Settle the Score*, broadcast on MTV from Madison Square Garden, Piper beat Hulk Hogan by disqualification when singer Cyndi Lauper and actor Mr. T jumped into the ring, setting off chaos.

"A lot of stuff happened that wasn't going to happen, like the New York City police jumping into the ring, and also I got to tussle with them," Piper said of that night. "Next thing I know, I see something blond coming out, and I turned and kicked. You can see it, I tried to pull the kick. Field goal! Cyndi Lauper! Oh, and it exploded. All of a sudden, McMahon went, 'Whoa.' Now promoters got into it." Piper almost considers the first WrestleMania an afterthought, even though it was his feud with Hogan, Lauper, and Mr. T that drew the audiences live and on closed-circuit TV.

The rest almost writes itself. Piper became such a superstar, that it was inevitable he would turn babyface again. He did, and was equally effective in that role. Later, he would reprise his

Declaring his supremacy as U.S. champion.

feud with Hollywood Hogan in World Championship Wrestling, with their roles reversed. Other roles followed too, on TV, and on the big screen. Dirk Benedict (*Battlestar Galactica*, *The A-Team*) worked with Piper on one of those early flicks, *Body Slam*, and could see he had it. "I realized immediately that he understood the trick of performing in film. You will notice how real and simple he is playing his 'character,'" Benedict said. "Acting in film is very different from stage, and very, very different from the performance required in a wrestling arena, which has to be big, and a bit over the top, to register for those fans in the cheap seats. He had a natural instinct for being real, and honest, and got continually better as the filming went."

Recently, Piper has found an outlet for his creativity through a stand-up comedy act. Though still involved with wrestling on occasion, whether it has been pushing his autobiography (which he wanted to call *If You're Gonna Die, Die in the Ring; It's Good for Business*, in an unsubtle jibe at unscrupulous promoters), or a DVD, or a new film, Piper has remained grounded by his wife, Kitty. She and their six kids live in Oregon, and have stuck by him through the highs — both in the ring and chemically-induced — and the lows, including his radiation treatment for lymphoma in 2006 and 2007. He has paid the price to reach the status of icon.

Lanny Poffo first met Piper in 1978 in Portland. "He had the best personality in the dressing room I've ever seen. He was the best interview I'd ever seen, and his work was more bang for your buck than I'd ever seen. He was totally unique, and he was a very happy guy, fun to be with. Then I saw him in 1985, and he was a physical wreck. What he did, he gave too much to the business," said Poffo. "He kept taking bumps, hurting himself, and taking more bumps. . . . When he'd talk about the business with you, he came from left field. He was an interesting person, he was interested in the business, he loved the business. He had so many ideas. He had a great career."

Mike Mastrandrea

Piper still has the gift of gab, seen here addressing the crowd at a 2005 Toronto Blue Jays game.

Courtesy Wrestling Revue Archives

Before he was "Macho," Randy Savage was an average grappler, taking on Chief Jay Strongbow.

The Next 5

Howard Baum

Terry Funk battles Dusty Rhodes.

TERRY FUNK

Few things in life gave Terry Funk more pleasure than riling up a crowd. At his induction into the Professional Wrestling Hall of Fame in May 2004, he bragged about one near-riot on August 30, 1971. Funk was wrestling at New York City's famed Madison Square Garden, alongside his father, Dory Funk Sr. The two Texans were battling the Kangaroos, Al Costello and Don Kent, in a bout that went forty-five minutes to a curfew draw without any falls. The crowd was really tense, about to snap as the show was coming to a heated conclusion. The younger Funk explained: "Who actually came down, I don't know if you remember this at all or not, Vince [McMahon] Jr. came down there, and he said, 'Daddy said to get out of the ring!' And he was pretty young at the time, and I said, 'Get your ass out of here!' I certainly wouldn't say that to him today! I'd do anything but go ahead and argue with him or anything else if he gave me some of that money."

Such is the complex nature of Terry Funk. At one moment, he can be serious, telling tales from the arena or road, of accidents, lost friends, or mentors; the next, he can be sharing a joke in his unmistakable gnarled, squeaky

Ernie Ladd, left, relaxes backstage with Terry Funk.

voice. It's the former world champion who dedicated his autobiography to all the enhancement talent. It's that contradiction of the polite, soft-spoken man who apologizes for his need to spit out his chewing tobacco with the madman of the ring, who would stop at nothing to incite a crowd. Add it all up, and that is what makes Funk still such a fascinating character.

It also marks one of the real debates of his legacy. What was Terry Funk? Where does he rank all-time? He was a hero at home in Amarillo, Texas, where he was the son of the promoter, who was also heavily involved in charity in the community. But in Memphis, say, he was public enemy number one for a while for his attempts to eradicate any connection between Jerry Lawler's head and his torso. Funk was NWA world champion from December 1975 to February 1977, but his older brother, Dory Jr., beat him to the pinnacle, holding the same title from 1969 to 1973.

The comparisons between the brothers come from their peers. "What a character he is. I worked with him sometimes, and I just used to shake my head," said "Cowboy" Dan Kroffat of Terry. "This guy was somewhere between a space cadet and a nutcase. He was wild. His brother was nothing like him. When I worked with Dory Funk, those were two different matches completely, night and day."

Bill Watts agreed. "Dory Funk Jr. was, I think, one of the greatest champions that we ever had, whereas I think Terry Funk turned the championship into kind of a cartoon." A close friend of the Funk patriarch, Les Thornton, was even more direct about Terry's reign. "That was the start of the goofy champions."

Terry does have his defenders though, with his brother and frequent tag team partner first in line. "I think that's an exaggeration. Terry is far out. He does crazy things. He also learned from the same teacher that I did, that's his father, Dory Funk Sr.," said Dory Jr. "We both had to learn wrestling from the basics, starting with amateur wrestling, competitive amateur wrestling, and on into the pros. Few people know how really good a wrestler Terry is, because they like to talk about the wild and crazy things that he does. But he does have a solid wrestling background along with that."

"Terry's a little strange, and the quirky bit came right from Dad," said former AWA world champion Nick Bockwinkel. "He was a solid worker. He was every bit as good as Dory was. Dory was totally serious. Terry's work was so good that it allowed him to be just a little bit whimsical. In other words, if he got nailed real good, he might stagger back like a drunk versus an athlete getting knocked down."

Manny Fernandez, a protegé of Terry Funk, dismisses the goofy talk. "When Terry was world champion, there was no such thing as a goofy champion. Terry was very serious as the world champion, very, very serious. There was no goofing around. His style, everybody thinks is goofy. That's fine, I don't think it is. Terry's style is what Terry makes it for the situation, like a chameleon. Whatever was required of him to get that thing over and done, that's what Terry did," Fernandez said. "With Funk, it was crazy, up and down, goofy things outside the ring, around the ring, to entertain the people."

Born June 30, 1944, while his father was away in the U.S. Navy, Terry Funk grew up around wrestling. His father's garage in Amarillo was a sparring ground, where contemporaries like Bob Geigel and Verne Gagne would mess around with Dory Sr. Cal Farley's Boys Ranch, which his father helped to run, had Terry on the mat by the age of four. "All those other kids, they went ahead and thought about being cowboys, being Indians, and playing with their cap guns. Not me. I thought about a lot of other things," Funk said. "I thought about wrestling, back drops, and all that kind of stuff, one tackle and get it again and that kind of crap."

During summers, the family traveled with Dory Sr. on his circuit — northern Ontario. "It was a great place to go. They popped it, he and the Vachons. Gosh, it was just a little territory, but they were drawing, selling out

North Bay every week. It was unbelievable," said Terry. "They'd have him against the Mad Dog. They'd had a riot every week and have to fight their way out of the arena. They'd play 'God Save the Queen'. . . It stopped them for a couple of weeks, then it didn't work."

Terry would attend West Texas State, where he was a tight end on the football team, but it wasn't a surprise when the six-foot-one, 235-pound Terry followed his father and older brother into wrestling. From his debut in 1965, until present day, when he still puts on the tights, Funk has entertained and enraged audiences.

"The riots were a form of flattery. The greatest thing (for a heel wrestler) is to do your job so well that someone wants to kill you. What could be more wonderful?" Funk mused. "People who have done terrible things to me, and wanted me to charge them, well I wouldn't. I mean, do I want to put someone in jail because I convinced him or her that I needed to die? I did it to them. That's how I look at it, and that may be sick, but it's also beautiful."

Strange as it may seem, he is nostalgic for the days when his life was in danger from the crowd, as opposed to the last decade, where he transformed into a hardcore wrestler that seemed intent on one more table spot or one more barbed-wire match.

"I loved the era of the riots. In Puerto Rico there'd be riots where I'd have to fight my way to the back, San Antonio, the Dallas/south Houston area. It was absurd. They would have to stop the matches because too many people would be hitting the ring. In Kentucky, I can remember when they took forty guns off of people coming to the show. I've had guns pulled on me and knives too," said "Terrible" Terry. "Corpus Christi is where I got stuck with a knife in the neck. Fortunately, it wasn't that big a blade. It went all the way into the hilt, and I thought it was a dart or something, so I left it in. When I got to the back and saw it was a knife, my eyes got as big as saucers when I realized what it was, and that someone had tried to kill me."

As great — or crazy — as Terry was in the ring, he was equally memorable on the microphone. "Terry is one of the great storytellers," said Jimmy Hart, dropping into a Funk impression, and telling the story about having an old dog that they had to take out behind the barn. "'That old dog didn't bite anybody anymore.' That left your imagination, 'Oh my God, did he shoot the dog or what?' 'That's what I'm going to do to you, Jerry Lawler. I'm going to take you out behind the barn and you're not going to be the King.'" Or, as Memphis announcer Lance Russell said, "Terry Funk understood *exactly* the character that he was."

In Miami in 1989, Bob Cook got a lesson on how far Funk would go to keep up his character. "He was sitting there on this forklift, telling me a story and laughing. Some security guard came over and said something to him about getting off the forklift. Terry just gave him a dirty look, and cussed at him, and didn't get off," said Cook. "Later, he's out watching the matches by the curtain, and a kid came over and asked for his autograph. And Terry cussed at him, and told him to get away, and I asked, 'Terry, why were you mean to a little kid?' He said, 'Bob, if these people out here see me being nice to a little kid now, they're not going to believe I'm a bad guy when I get in the ring.'"

Away from the ring, Terry used his interview style to land one of the lead roles in *Paradise Alley*. The press release for Funk's character said that Terry "answered that [casting] call by sending a two-and-a-half-minute videotape to writer-director-star Sylvester Stallone which was so brutal, so threatening and so utterly ridiculous that the part of Frankie the Thumper was his, hands down." Other film roles and stunt work followed, but wrestling always called back when the casting agents didn't.

Having walked out of the WWF during its 1980s heyday, Funk reinvented himself as a hardcore icon, who was "middle-aged and crazy" and enjoyed stretcher matches and at least one no-rope, explosive barbed wire, time-bomb, landmine, double hell death match.

In 2005, he was honored by his colleagues for his contributions to the business with the Iron Mike Mazurki Award at the Cauliflower Alley Club reunion. Like Funk's wrestling style, his speech had a little of everything: emotion, humor, self-reflection, and insight. "This is a wonderful, wonderful gathering. It's more than just a gathering, it's a blood gathering. We all have the same blood, it's for a crazy, excuse me, but, goddamn insane business," he said to laughter and applause. "I love everybody, and I love everybody in this room. I truthfully love this business with all my heart. It's just the greatest thing. It's a trip I'll never forget, and never want to end."

KILLER KARL KOX

Well, here's a candidate for *America's Dumbest Criminals*. In October 2006, an intruder tried to break into the shop behind the Dallas residence of one Herb Gerwig, better known as "Killer" Karl Kox. "I snatched the son of a bitch and took him down. I took him down in a front facelock and held him down. My wife called 911 and said, 'My husband's got this guy who was trying to break into his shop. He's seventy-five years old and you'd better send some help.' The cop that came and investigated recognized me. And he said, 'God, you didn't need any damn help,'" Kox said with a laugh. "I'm still a good heel."

The guy was just lucky Kox didn't put his brainbuster on him. When he was at his peak in the 1960s and '70s, nobody, but nobody, messed around with Karl Kox. A lot of villains would try to get a rise of out a crowd, then tone down things just a tad to keep fans from rioting. Not Kox. "Nah, I toned it up. It's just the way I was," he said. "There was nobody tougher than Killer Karl Kox," marveled Don "Lawman" Slatton, who promoted Abilene, Texas, and wrestled him regularly. "The son of a gun could go. To get a crowd roused up, there was nobody in his class. He just looked like he didn't like you. He was something else."

Killer Karl Kox.

Chuck Thornton Collection

Kox came into being after the wrestler known as Herb Gerwig passed into the night. Born in 1931 in Baltimore, Gerwig got into his first big scuffle at the city's Forest Park High School when he was booted from a softball game and suspended from school for whacking a teacher-umpire who slapped him in the head. From there, it was on to the Marine Corps during the Korean War, then to Cleveland and a construction job, where he moonlighted as a high-level softball player. An old wrestler named "Gentleman" Fred Bozak found him and tossed him into the ring at age twenty-three. "They threw me in with some old guy I didn't know. He bent me like a pretzel." Gerwig said. As turned out, he had just met Ruffy Silverstein, a Hall of Fame amateur and one of the greats of his day. But during Gerwig's apprenticeship, he also watched and learned from wrestlers like the Gallagher Brothers, who mixed violence and comedy in their matches, a formula he'd use wisely.

Gerwig wrestled for six years in places like Buffalo, Pittsburgh, and Cleveland, before The Sheik hooked him up with Joe Dusek, the promoter in Omaha, Nebraska, in 1961. There, Dusek switched Gerwig's name to "Killer

Carl Cox." "I didn't have the background and the knowledge to be a baby-face," Gerwig claimed. "I played semi-pro football and ice hockey as a heel. It was easy for me. It just came natural." When he headed to the Amarillo territory, he switched to "Killer Karl Kox" — KKK — and the racial overtone was none too subtle. "He had the greatest gimmick ever. KKK — he didn't have to say a word," Ernie Ladd recounted. But the threatening initials were just a little something to madden the fans. "We didn't look back at all that stuff," explained Tiger Conway Sr. "We went out to do our business, and we did our business. He was so fantastic. Him and I were so close, like we were brothers." The friendship even survived an application of the brainbuster, a headfirst inverted suplex that was allegedly "barred" around the world, Conway said. "He dropped me on my head years ago, and I almost lost my whole head and neck. They had to get the 911 to get me. And I still love him."

Dallas wrestling announcer Bill Mercer thought Kox also had the ideal look for a heel, one straight out of Hollywood: "He had a style of just walking into the arena, and looking. His face was sort of De Niro, the glare that he had, or guys like Duvall, that glare. He'd glare at people, and the place would just go nuts. Then he'd stand around and look at them." Kox was, well, different. Slatton is laughing even as he tells the story: "He would come in the ring with one boot on, and where the other boot was supposed to be, he'd just have a sock. On one foot, he had a wrestling boot and a sock, and on the other, he just had a sock. Everybody would say, 'What's the matter with this crazy guy?' He could think of so much crazy stuff to do."

Kox earned a lot of his infamy overseas, with nine trips to Japan and five to Australia. In Perth, because of death threats, police formed a cordon around him as he walked through a soccer stadium to wrestle Billy Robinson. "The police had to escort me maybe 100 yards to the ring. And the cop said to me, 'I hope the bastard that shoots you is a good shot, hits you and don't hit me.'" In Hong Kong, authorities threatened to stop matches because of fears of rioting. Promoter Jim Barnett once suggested Kox cancel a planned trip Down Under. "I was living in Amarillo, Texas at the time," said Kox, breaking into a perfect mimicry of Barnett's high, droll voice. "'Karl, my boy, I think you'd better cancel out because you have so many threats on your life that I think it wouldn't be worth your while.' I said, 'Hell, no. I'm coming anyhow.' We drew a helluva lot of money." And all those threats and curses rolled off Kox like water off a duck's back. "I loved it. I wouldn't have it any other way."

"Karl gave 100 percent. He actually never really changed his style. He was like Johnny Valentine," said Nick Kozak. "He never changed his style. People liked him or hated him. He was always thinking of something." Jimmy

Garvin, who worked with and against him in Florida, can testify how Kox tipped an audience with idiosyncrasies, such as listening to an imaginary friend named Alex who hovered near his shoulder. "He'd do something and for a second, you'd go, 'Ooooh, that guy's kind of weird.'" But that masked some serious work, Garvin said. "Karl was a great operator in the ring as far as psychology and his work ethic. He was a hard worker, he didn't pull punches when he came to work. He thought about what he did, he drew the mental picture in his mind, and he went out and did it."

The late Cal Pullins learned that when Kox clocked him in the throat with a pipe the timekeeper used to ring the bell. Then, Kox stuck the weapon in his tights, out of the referee's line of sight. "When the time was right," Kox began, "I had him scoop slam me, and slam that damn thing on my back. And the people went crazy. I pulled that pipe out of the back of my tights, and threw it out there where the referee could see it, and had him disqualify me. It got over so great, Pullins told me, 'My God, I never looked so good in my life.'"

Kox had a pretty fair sense of humor outside of the ring, too. Dick "The Destroyer" Beyer traveled with him in Japan and remembered how Kox played games in lounges with a glass marble that looked like an eye. "All of a sudden, he'd take this marble and he'd drop it into his beer. Then he'd close his eye up tight and he'd call the waitress over. He says, 'My eye!' He looked up, and she looked down at the beer, and they'd pick up the beer, pour it out, and give him the glass eye back, and then he'd make believe he was putting the eye back by covering it up. We did this every night, in every bar we went into."

Kox trimmed down from about 230 to 215 pounds as he wound down his wrestling in the early 1980s, and even though he was a thinner, balding, older man, he still packed a wallop. One night in Weslaco, Texas, in 1983, Dusty Wolfe was standing next to him when the Sheepherders started a riot at a gym. Authorities were trying to control the crowd, when one rowdy they slung toward Kox mouthed off to him, "Fuck you, too!" Wolfe picks it up from there: "The punch didn't travel six inches, and it sounded like a baseball bat hitting a side of beef. He hit the guy so hard you could smell that he had just shit on himself, as he passes out from a punch that did not travel six inches. He said, 'Well, I don't think he'll talk to me like that again,' turned around, and went back to the dressing room. That was when I realized that I will never mess with him."

After he quit the ring, Kox put his talents to use keeping an eye on jail prisoners for the sheriff's department in Dallas. "I used to tell them, 'You know why I'm wearing white and you're wearing blue? Because they haven't caught me yet.' Oh, they liked that." He still has some ties to wrestling through his son Cody, a ring announcer for the Arlington, Texas promotion, and his wife, who helps him sell memorabilia online. "I miss it," Kox said. "Believe me, I miss it."

ERNIE LADD

Chris Swisher Collection

The giant Ernie Ladd.

Now, this sounds like Ernie Ladd — whacking an opponent with a foreign object, earning a fine, being threatened with a suspension, then cooing about his accomplishment. And that was in football, not wrestling. "I'm not going to lighten up on anybody," Ladd bragged after he was caught swinging his helmet at an opponent on the old Houston Texans. "I don't care if they ever like me. I play to get paid." That militant attitude, and his massive frame, made Ladd one of the most feared defensive tackles of his day, and, later, one of the biggest draws in wrestling. "He was a great promo guy. He just had that ability to get the fans excited," said friend Bruce Swayze. "He just had that great look — being six-ten with a crown on his head certainly didn't hurt matters either."

With hands the size of baseball gloves and size-eighteen boots, yet able to run a 4.9 in the 40-yard dash, Ladd was an athletic freak and a shrewd businessman who left the gridiron primarily because he could make a bigger buck on the canvas. "He gave me a lot of advice," said Chavo Guerrero Sr. "He told me, 'Guerrero, the color of this business is not black, yellow, whatever. It's green. It's called money.' I learned a lot from that man, a lot." By the time Ladd hung up his boots in the mid-1980s, he had taken care of his family, but also left a lasting impression on the business.

Tony Atlas recalled the esteem others held for Ladd: "I went into Georgia to wrestle with Ernie, and I saw Ernie sit down at the table with Jim Barnett, Ted Turner, and Ole Anderson, three of the most powerful men in wrestling. And what came out of Ernie's mouth was just as important as what came out of Ted Turner's mouth. He had that sort of respect. He crossed boundaries."

Ron Martinez, son of Buffalo promoter Pedro Martinez, and a part of the National Wrestling Federation front office, called Ladd "one of the true gentlemen of the business, even though he and Dad argued over payoffs. I remember that one day Ernie had had enough; he hadn't seen his wife and kids for something like three months, and was dying to get home to see them. Dad, who was great at seeing other peoples' needs and satisfying them, sent four first-class plane tickets to Mrs. Ladd and the kids and flew them to Buffalo. Ernie never forgot that and always mentions it when we talk."

The hard-nosed ways of the "Big Cat" started long before he entered wrestling. Ladd grew up in the segregated South, and starred at Grambling College for Hall-of-Fame coach Eddie Robinson before entering pro ball. For five years, he and Earl Faison formed a fearsome tandem for the San Diego Chargers, frightening quarterbacks, and batting down passes. But Ladd's tenure in San Diego was tumultuous. He claimed the team kidnapped him to prevent him from dealing with the NFL Chicago Bears, and contended Charger honcho Sid Gillman benched him in 1964 to prevent him from collecting a $16,000 bonus. A four-time American Football League All-Star, Ladd played out his option to sign with the Houston Oilers before heading to Kansas City in 1967.

In the meantime, he was giving wrestling a whirl, and moonlighted during the off-season throughout the 1960s. Tiger Conway Sr., who knew racial discrimination all too well, took him under his wing in Houston when some other black wrestlers wouldn't: "I taught him how to get in the gate, and taught him everything that I knew about wrestling. He went on and had championship matches with the top people. He was a great, true athlete. He is a real pioneer."

In 1969, when Ladd's knees started to give out, he hit the wrestling circuit full-time. He grossed about $100,000 in his first year, but also missed being a part of the Chiefs Super Bowl IV championship. "It looked like a foolish decision at first," he said. "Right there, I was out $25,000, a lot of friends reminded me. I wasn't in that kind of a money class in wrestling, yet." For Ladd, the key came in 1970 when he landed with Pedro Martinez, whom he credited with allowing him to be a full-fledged heel, even against blacks like Bobo Brazil, derided by Ladd as "Coconut Head." Ladd asked, "How could a guy this big be a babyface? It meant more to me at the box office to be the first black heel." To further darken his image, he laid out in the sun to tan his light skin. To round out his act, Ladd freely stole from other performers — he swiped Terry Funk's "egg-suckin' dog" line, picked up a crown like Bobby Shane and Jerry Lawler would wear, and emblazoned his ring jacket with "Promises, Promises," after seeing football star Joe Namath with similar apparel. "I was a great thief," he said with a chuckle. "Plus I had the gift of gab."

He was so imposing, so commanding, that his character transcended his skin color. Dominic DeNucci, one of his favorite opponents, recalled three black women getting worked up at Ladd one night in Akron, Ohio: "He beat the shit out of me, and the lady got up and yelled, 'Come on, Dominic, kill that nigger!' The woman was black!" Atlas, who commends Ladd for helping to bring him into the WWWF, agreed fans focused on the wrestler, even though the heel vowed in public "to beat the black off" him. "That's the thing the fans looked at — that loud mouth, that bully, that cheatin', dirty, rotten Ernie Ladd," Atlas said. "He was not seen as black. He was seen as Ernie Ladd."

He held more than the twenty-odd belts during his career; colleagues were impressed by the way Ladd was a student of the business, analyzing wrestling like he did football. "Ernie learned more really watching each and every bout. That's where he got his learning from." Conway said. "All I had to do was take him with me, explain to him what I knew, and he would watch every night, like these football coaches watch these videos of the mistakes you're making." Bill Watts, who later made The Big Cat his booker in the Mid-South, said Ladd "opened my eyes in a way that nobody had, in that he made me understand first of all, the depth of his intelligence, in that how he actually studied the industry and the business he was in. He did the same in pro football."

If Ladd wasn't busy thinking, then he sure must have been eating. As a rookie in 1961, Ladd put on an exhibition for a New York sportswriter. Here's the take: two shrimp cocktails; three dishes of coleslaw; three servings of spinach; three baked potatoes; eight rolls with butter; a half-gallon of milk; three desserts; and four 16-ounce steaks. "He's lost his appetite," joked Irv Roberson, an alarmed teammate. After wrestling one night, Ladd took DeNucci for some grub at a restaurant in north Cleveland favored by blacks. As DeNucci said: "We got a small room in the back, with just me and him. And I mean the guys and girls that were working there, they brought fried chicken, barbecued spare ribs, and we drank three or four beers. We were supposed to go to Detroit or something, but ten miles up the road, we went to sleep!"

Ladd didn't carry his battles with the front office into the ring, where he did everything he could to make a giant of his size appear vulnerable. The undersized Guerrero was standing to the side during TV interviews in California when he heard Ladd speak. According to Guerrero, "All of a sudden, he goes, 'I want to wrestle' — and he looks — 'that guy.' I turn around and there's nobody there, man. I said, 'Aw, man, here they go making fun of me again. This is a joke.'" But Ladd convinced the office to book Guerrero as his opponent, showed up typically late, and laced his boots at a deliberate pace before stealing the show. "The next week, we sold the damn place out and from then on, we just went around," Guerrero said. Johnny Powers had his doubts about Ladd when The Big Cat entered the Buffalo territory, but became a fervent admirer of the one-time NWF world champ. "I ended up totally respecting him because he was very unique, very creative, would give to the business and would put people over," Powers said. "All those knee operations, and his flying splash off the top rope was equal, not as pretty, but equal to Jimmy Snuka's, and Snuka is iconic for that."

In the final years of his career, Ladd stayed closer to home, starring and booking for Watts; to this day, he is one of the most prominent African-Americans ever to hold authority in a wrestling office. He was North American champion in the Louisiana–Texas territory five times from 1978 to 1984, when he started to wrap up his ring career; he also served as a manager from time to time. A devout Christian, he was involved in a variety of civic projects and ministries, and was an active supporter of the George Bush family in presidential politics. Back in the 1960s, the elder Bush wanted to meet black leaders while he ramped up a Senate campaign. "I wasn't going to no hotel to see no Republican," Ladd said. Bush agreed to meet Ladd and allies on The Cat's terms. "He came to my house. My brothers all got after him politically. He weathered the storm, shot us down, and that's how I became a Republican." Ladd accompanied Bush in 2005 on a visit to Hurricane Katrina evacuees in Houston, another facet of a complicated man who was more than just a good hand in the ring. He fought a nearly four-year struggle with cancer before succumbing in March 2007 at 68. Just before his death, he had one last conversation with his dear friend Watts, who told him: "Ernie, I am afraid the Lord will call you home before he does me. And I'm concerned, because the way you eat, there may not be enough food left in Heaven for a banquet when I get there!"

RANDY "MACHO MAN" SAVAGE

A little known fact about "Macho Man" Randy Savage, who has been one of the most famous professional wrestlers of the past two decades: he was selling Herbalife part-time when he got the call on June 17, 1985 to leave Memphis and come to the bright lights, big city of the WWF.

It's not the kind of tidbit that Savage gives up. A guarded man with a touch of paranoia about anybody and everything, Savage doesn't give many interviews.

The Spider man later morphed . . .

And when he does, it is often in character, or with a specific product to plug, like his recent CD, *Be A Man*, with the title track calling out Hulk Hogan.

But there are people who know Savage well, perhaps none better than his brother Lanny Poffo, who explains what it's like to be on the other side of the wired Savage's unrelenting attacks. "I wrestled him many, many times before we got to the big time. In our own promotion, I was the main babyface and he was the main heel. Also in the Maritime provinces, when we had bought in to the territory with Emile Dupre. We did very good business. He was the heel, I was the babyface," said Poffo. "What I loved about working with Randy is he knew everything that I could do well, then he called the match. He's very creative and very artistic, and he's got a passion for detail. He made sure that I looked so good in that match, no matter what the finish was. He was totally unselfish, and then he would do something terrible to me, then, boom, I'd be down. He was all business at all times. He had his gimmick down. He's was the most imitated man in show business at the time — 'Oh, yeaahhh' everybody does him. He made himself unique."

Oh, yeaahhh, there's that voice. "When I first heard him, I thought, 'That'll never work.' That was that voice, that growl, and almost totally stupid," said Memphis announcer Lance Russell. "But it did work, and still to this day, for whatever he's doing." Savage has always been a master of making the unexpected work, his brother agreed: "Even his hair, which was a negative, he turned it into a positive. That was just part of the thing, the wild hair and then later on, the balding hair. It fit him."

The son of wrestler Angelo Poffo, Randall Mario Poffo — born November 15, 1952 in Columbus, Ohio — wanted to be a baseball player. Randy was an all-state catcher at Downers Grove North High School in Illinois, and signed with the St. Louis Cardinals in 1971. He made it as far as Class A ball, playing with four teams in three different organizations: the Cards, Reds, and White Sox. Injuries contributed to his failure to rise higher. Disappointed and angry, Savage turned his rage into a positive thing, reshaping his six-foot-one, 190-pound baseball player body into a muscled 230-pounder, suitable for the abuses of a wrestling career.

Given his genes, he was a quick study. Angelo Poffo decided to start his own outlaw promotion to properly showcase his sons. "It was good for them, but they earned it the hard way," said Angelo. "Lanny was a good acrobat, and Randy was a real good, hard worker." Bob Roop was one of the original partners in International Championship Wrestling, and saw Savage's commitment to getting better. "He was talented. I didn't think about it really, because he was with his dad, and we were running this little opposition," said Roop. "He was developing the act, using the voice, the gravel-in-the-throat voice, the body language, and all that. He was kind of just starting out on it. It was interesting enough, and his work in the ring was decent. He got bigger by the time he went with Vince. He had weights in the living room of his house."

Rip Rogers learned a lot from Savage. He dismisses any talk of favoritism about Angelo pushing his children; they had talent. "Randy Savage was so far ahead of everybody, so far ahead of everybody. He used to carry me in the Maritimes for full thirty-minute matches, and I didn't know how to tie my boots," said Rogers. "He'd been around the business. At the time, I was twenty-three, and he was twenty-four. Then a couple of years later, at one time we had fifteen television markets. So he's running the TVs, he's writing the TVs, he's a performer, he's a champion, he's telling us every finish and what to do."

The inter-promotional war between the Poffos, based out of Lexington, Kentucky, and the Jerry Jarrett and Jerry Lawler company in Memphis is still a source of intrigue. Wrestlers on both sides admit to carrying guns in case of trouble. In 1985, Jimmy Hart would be the conduit by which Savage made his way to the WWF, but when he first met Randy, he was coming at his car in Lexington with a baseball bat. "He had some other wrestlers with him, because at that particular time, they were running opposition to us on Channel 24 in Memphis. Every week, they would challenge everybody," Hart

Howard Lapes

. . . into The Macho Man, at his peak.

said. "I was getting out of the car, and I had Killer Karl Krupp with me and Dream Machine. We got out of the car, and Krupp said, 'Oh my God, there's Randy Savage! My God!' We got out, and he says, 'Jimmy Hart, let me tell you, tell Jerry Lawler that I want him with the utmost intensity.'"

Though Lawler was out of action at the time with a broken leg, the eventual closing of the Poffo promotion meant that a Lawler-Savage match was a big money maker. Piledriving Ricky Morton through the timekeeper's table cemented Savage's wild reputation as a risk-taker willing to do anything to win. His flying axe handle off the top turnbuckle to the floor became a trademark, as did his flying elbow.

Intensity is actually the key to believability, Savage said. "Getting into the angle a million percent and having that translate in the ring is probably the secret. It's not really a secret, you have to build up to something, and the longer you build it up, as long as it is interesting, the bigger the explosion will be when the match actually happens," he told journalist Jason Clevett. "Wrestling is emotional, you have to be into it in order to translate that to the wrestling fans, and that is what they deserve."

In the WWF, Savage proposed to booker George Scott that they utilize his wife, Elizabeth Hulette, as his manager (Savage had married the Frankfort, Kentucky belle on December 30, 1984). Borrowing heavily from "Exotic" Adrian Street, with whom he'd feuded, Savage began wearing ultra-fancy robes, and treated Miss Elizabeth like a second-class citizen. The evolution of their relationship through the years was soap opera at its best, culminating in an in-ring marriage. In reality, Savage's ultra-possessiveness rubbed many the wrong way, and he'd often lock his wife in a room to prevent others from talking with her. The couple divorced in 1992, though even that was used in a storyline in World Championship Wrestling, with Ric Flair bragging about Elizabeth sharing Savage's money with him.

Savage was given the responsibility of being WWF world champion at a key time in the promotion's history — with Hogan away pursuing other interests. Savage rose in respect with the fans and backstage, and was a true team player through the years, whether he was comical as the "Macho King" or insightful as an announcer. "I liked Macho Man just 'cause he was flashy and in your face, and always jumping off the top rope," current WWE star Johnny Nitro told a Canton, Ohio newspaper. "He was athletic, and he wasn't afraid to tell everybody how great he was."

Kevin Nash told the *Pro Wrestling Torch* that Savage was the "captain" of the team. "He was the guy who kind of held the ship together. When he left, losing him was a bigger loss morale-wise than losing Hogan. When he left and went to WCW, that really was a ball-shock because he did *Raw* in Bushkill, and then he was gone."

In WCW from 1994 to 1999, Savage had four world title runs. "Savage is one of those guys who doesn't get the credit he deserves in regards to WCW's rise," said Bryan Alvarez, co-author of *The Death of WCW*. "Everyone points to the nWo as this major turning point, but in reality Savage's house show matches with Ric Flair really started to boost business prior to Scott Hall ever appearing on Nitro." But he wasn't an easy guy to work with, said frequent opponent Sting. "Randy was high maintenance, just put it that way," he said. Trying to recreate the dynamic he had with Elizabeth, Savage brought in his twenty-two-year-old then-girlfriend, Stephanie Bellars, as Gorgeous George. In the end, Savage's WCW contract just expired, and he departed the scene.

For the last few years, Savage has tried to branch out. He did a rap album, and has tried his hand at acting, with his biggest role coming as Bone Saw McGraw in *Spider-Man* (the irony being that Savage once wrestled as "The Spider" to protect his baseball career). He will also be on the eighth season of *The Surreal Life*. TNA brought him in for a few appearances, but learned that his unstable nature was more trouble than it was worth. "I am done with my wrestling career unless Hulk Hogan accepts my challenge, then I will be right there, and we will have the first 'real' fight in professional wrestling history," Savage said in 2003.

His legacy? "Colorful, could talk, and I'm telling you, no matter what anybody says, that's still what this business is all about — it's being visual and being able to talk," said Jimmy Hart. Though he never had the success of his older brother, Lanny Poffo is proud of him. "I'm happy for Randy. He deserves it. I was sad the day in 1975 when he got let go from his third major league team . . . You know what? Ten years later, he's in Madison Square Garden jumping off the top rope onto the floor, landing on 'Quick Draw' McGraw. The fans had never seen anything like that."

THE SPOILER
(DON JARDINE)

It's a backward compliment that could only work in the twisted world of professional wrestling: "Donald was made to wear the mask." Gary Hart certainly doesn't mean anything, well, mean about it; he simply feels that when Don Jardine put on a mask in 1967 and became "The Spoiler" under his stewardship, he changed who he was — and became a major superstar. "He was one of those guys that didn't have a whole lot of personality in his face, but was an extremely good worker," continued Hart. "Once he put on the mask, he was off and running. . . . All Don really needed was some packaging and some direction."

Jardine concurred, and explained how he changed with his face hidden. "I think your body takes over then, the movements from your arms and legs, and everything else. Your face doesn't necessarily do everything," he said. "If the people are 300, 400 feet up, they certainly can't see the emotion on your face, but they can certainly see the motion from your arms, or your legs, or whatever you're doing with them, a lot better than a facial expression, unless you're at ringside."

It was a twelve-year struggle for Jardine to climb that hill to full-time main-event status as The Spoiler, and later as "The Super Destroyer." Born in rural New Brunswick in 1940, and raised in Moncton, Don and his brother Herb were big wrestling fans. "Many, many times, Don and I would walk down to the Stadium. To get in, we'd try to carry the wrestlers' bags," said Herb Jardine. "We'd always find a way to get in." What Herb didn't know was that his brother would grow into an impressive physical specimen himself.

Courtesy Herb Jardine

Don Jardine at the start of his career.

The Spoiler at the height of his dastardly deeds.

Emile Dupre, who later trained Jardine at the local YMCA, recalled seeing the youngster around town. "He was a kid, about fifteen, sixteen years old. He used to hang around Main Street. In fact, I used to see him at the Capital Theatre. He knew that I was wrestling and he approached me. I was looking at his height — he was six-four, six-five. He was a big, tall kid, big, natural big legs, muscular legs. I told him he should work out with the weights to get a bigger upper body, which he did in no time at all. He blew up — I saw him the year after that."

During a charity appearance at the Moncton Eaton's department store, "Whipper" Billy Watson met Jardine and came away impressed. In 1959, Jardine got a telegram from the Toronto office, and figured they just wanted to give him tickets. Dupre had to explain that they wanted him to wrestle in Maple Leaf Gardens. Babyface Jardine was born. A star, however, was not.

"I knew that I was good," said Jardine. "They had all those old-timers there that didn't want young kids in the business. They resented anybody coming in at that time, especially young guys that had talent. I wasn't the only one. There were a lot of other guys that were in the same shoes as me." He toiled away on shows in Calgary, North Bay, the Maritimes, Indianapolis, Amarillo, the American Midwest, Oregon, and down to California (where he was "The Butcher" during one stay, without a mask, but wearing a glove; during another tour, he was in the Masked Enforcers team with fellow Maritimer Clyde Steeves). In 1963, Jardine made the first of nine trips to Japan.

But all that was a warm-up for The Spoiler. Fritz Von Erich had met Jardine on the road, and assured him that one day he'd own a territory and bring him in. True to his word, Von Erich hired Jardine, gave him The Spoiler name, and Gary Hart as his manager. "I was the one who created that persona that he had because when he put on that outfit, to me, he looked like the Phantom," said Hart. "That's how I envisioned him. If you remember, I said he was from Singapore." To combat perennial babyface Von Erich in Dallas, it was decided to allow The Spoiler to use a variation of the Iron Claw hold — The Hart Krusher, which was delivered with a black glove with the fingers cut out.

"Donald wasn't your typical bad guy. What made Donald a bad guy was me being with him," said Hart. "The fans always liked him. Once he put the mask on, the fans loved him. What made them dislike him was me being his manager." Jardine recognized that as well, and changed his wardrobe accordingly. "If you were new to a territory, if you had a reputation of drawing money, then you had to know what to say on TV, how to get yourself over in the different outfits and everything. When I started, I always wore black, because black is more of a heel thing. Then later on as I stayed in a territory, my outfits got lighter and lighter, because I knew eventually the people would end up liking me."

Fans and his peers are still in awe of abilities in the ring that were a good twenty years ahead of the time for a man his size — walking the ropes, moves off the top rope. "If you look at The Undertaker today, you see a glimpse of what The Spoiler was. He was magnificent," said Hart. Former world champ Jack Brisco was also impressed. "I was amazed that a guy his size could move the way he could move."

But as much as Jardine was respected for his in-ring talents, he was criticized for his difficulties with promoters and bookers. All those years of being misused had left him wary. "Don wasn't a butt kisser. And if you wanted to take Don on, Don would beat the living crap out of you," said his former tag partner Dutch Savage, launching into an account of confrontation between Jardine and Amarillo promoter Dory Funk Sr. "Funk made the mistake of slapping him one night. We had to leave the territory. Jardine just cold-cocked him, down he went. We had to pull him off of him. We knew that Funk was going to get the sheriff after us, so we had to head for the New Mexico border as fast as we could."

The Spoiler in 2005 with his wife.

Another popular tale told by numerous people is of AWA promoter Verne Gagne telling Jardine that he was going to lose his mask. An argument went back and forth, and Jardine said, "Verne, you might as well try to take it off in the dressing room because you're not taking it off there!"

In reality, Jardine *did* lose his mask on a couple of occasions — he was unmasked in Texas by Billy "Red" Lyons and Red Bastien, on another occasion by Fritz Von Erich, and in Australia by Mario Milano. But Jardine also did it by choice in July 1972, to be able to work in Madison Square Garden against Pedro Morales (whom he had already had a heated feud with in California). MSG had an arcane rule prohibiting masked workers. "I didn't want to use The Spoiler because I was still down South, and in several other territories with the mask on," said Jardine. "It was a big decision, what am I going to do when I put the mask back on? They had so much coverage and everything. I said okay, and gave it a try. It went okay. I don't think they associated with the two — a true wrestling fan probably did." (Yet in December 1972, Mil Mascaras was allowed to wear a mask in MSG, ironically against an unmasked Don Jardine.)

In the fall of 1973, Jardine began menacing the Mid-Atlantic region as The Super Destroyer. "I have the highest respect as a wrestler for Don

Jardine," said veteran Bill White. "He was a very formidable foe in the ring when he wanted to be. You looked at him and he showed you, with that mask he was a heel, no matter what he did. Whether he threw a punch or pulled hair, you knew it was deliberate." After a two-year run, battling names like Swede Hanson, Sonny King, and Wahoo McDaniel, he left abruptly, and the promotion had Rufus R. Jones announce that he had unmasked The Spoiler — and even showed a photo of Jardine unmasked. "I would never let a talent like Rufus Jones remove my mask. He didn't have the notoriety to remove it. I liked him as a person," Jardine told the Mid-Atlantic Gateway Web site. "The unmasking did not happen. I wanted to leave because I wasn't making the money that I had worked so hard to create for the promotion."

By the mid-'80s, Jardine was done, his body beaten up. (Completionists would want to make note that he was hired, briefly, by the expanding WWF of the time.) He tried promoting around Tampa, Florida, a little. "That was okay, but I was dealing with guys that were difficult, trying to get people to show up . . . There was some good talent there, a lot of talent."

Post-wrestling, he lost some money in the Texas oil crunch, and headed back to the Maritimes to help with his ailing parents. In the mid-'90s, he met his third wife, Becky, who was a Royal Canadian Mounted Police officer. They moved to Alberta, with their young son. Jardine found creative outlets in poetry and writing, sculpting in clay, and carving in wood.

His declining health was the major factor in his life, however. He battled leukemia for a few years, along with the regular aches and pains associated with a violent business like wrestling. "It takes a toll after you take thousands of bumps. I figure I probably took a quarter of a million bumps on my back, because I had over 10,000 matches." In December 2007, after fighting leukemia and pneumonia, Jardine suffered a heart attack and died at sixty-seven.

Like the villain he portrayed, Jardine made no apologies. "It was a tough business, very tough, now that I look back at it. At the time, I probably didn't think that. But now, jeez, how the hell did I do all that?" he said. "I don't regret it, but there are a few things that I could have done differently. After a while, you just get tired, you get worn out."

"Dirty" Dick Raines gives an outdoor exhibition of his skills.

The Pioneers

CHIEF CHEWACKI

Chief Chewacki.

His name sounded like it had a touch of craziness to it, and that's exactly the way Chief Chewacki wrestled. Carpet tacks, steel wool, coat hangers, stove lids, Mercurochrome, pepper, ether-soaked cloths, horse prods . . . you name it and chances are Chewacki tried to smote his opponents with it in the 1930s and 1940s. Variously billed as an Indian chief and eastern European gypsy, and spelled Chewacki, Chewchki, and Schewke, one thing is for certain — Chewacki is the father of illegal foreign objects.

"It seems that he has a knack of suddenly becoming the possessor of added equipment at certain stages of his matches," wrote Walter Haight, a sportswriter for The Washington Post. So outlandish was his reputation Haight joked that Chewacki once pulled a bomber from under his arm "and the plane circled over his rival's head and made five direct hits."

Relatively little is known about Chewacki's personal life. His real name was George Mitchell, and he was from Oklahoma. For many years, promoters, sportswriters, and Chewacki himself peddled the notion that he was an ex-boxer named Billy Daniels, who once knocked out former heavyweight champion Max Schmeling. However, historians have determined that was merely a publicity ploy. While his battle-scarred face and flattened nose attested to some sort of pugilistic background, Chewacki was primarily a Depression-era wrestler who would do anything for a buck.

In 1931, Texas promoter Morris Sigel spotted Chewacki, at the time a fan who had worked in a cheese factory in Denison, Texas, and introduced him to wrestling as Chief Georgie Shewchka. "The redskin didn't know how to wrestle but he did know how to swing his fists and make faces," said sportswriter Albert Reese of the *Galveston Daily News*. Chewacki explained his antics by claiming that an unusual ancestry of gypsy and Indian blood caused him to detest all white people. "My father was Waso Danelo, a Yugoslavian gypsy, and he taught me to hate white people. My mother was a Cherokee Indian named Sebanca Chewaki, and she taught me the same thing," he told the United Press in 1936. "After I saw a wrestling match, I quit prizefighting and turned to wrestling because I could hurt 'em more that way."

Chewacki made a splash upon his California debut in 1933 — he lost his first match there despite trying to clobber his opponent with the top of a writing board desk — and was a huge box-office attraction for a decade. Perhaps his most notable feud was with 317-pound Man Mountain Dean, whom he laid out with chloroform in New Orleans in 1933. Outweighed by ninety pounds, Chewacki claimed he hated bearded white men even more than the unbearded kind, and vowed to pluck Dean's whiskers one by one. Rematches in Los Angeles packed the Olympic Auditorium; Chewacki allegedly "broke" Dean's jaw with a series of punches during one free-for-all.

Chewacki's typical match involved several minutes of rough-and-tumble action, including well-placed bites to his opponent's face and body. Then he would get tossed from the ring, and the fun really kicked into gear, as Bill Henry recounted for the *Los Angeles Times*: "He gets in a frenzy, grabs anything handy, such as somebody's straw hat or cane and tears same into bits. With variations. He occasionally grabs the timekeeper's hammer, and climbs back into the ring, and assaults his opponent."

Chewacki was suspended by just about every athletic authority that ever sanctioned a match. The mayor of Cleveland barred him indefinitely in December 1933 after he roughed up Hans Kampfer, leading to a riot in which two persons were injured. The Alabama athletic commission shelved him in March 1934 for whacking George Zaharias with a blackjack; the commission also fined him $100. He earned a suspension from the Indiana athletic commissioner in 1934 for unusual tactics in a bout with "Irish" Pat O'Shocker. Chewacki clamped a leg scissors on O'Shocker, who yelped in pain and pointed to Chewacki's tights. An in-ring strip search by referee Heze

Clark revealed Chewacki had planted tacks and sandpaper under his ring apparel. "A fellow is too restricted nowadays," Chewacki moaned to George Considine of The Washington Post. "When you want to give the public the best you've got, somebody always comes along and says, 'Don't do that!'"

Yet Chewacki was quite even-tempered and even whimsical outside the ring. In 1936, he employed a bit of levity before a San Diego prosecutor in answering a charge of assault with a deadly weapon — in this case, a bent clothes hanger he wrapped around the neck of Gino Garibaldi had prompted a riot. "I had a hard time thinking up that joke," he said. "You need to think up these jokes to please the crowds. I was having a hard time thinking up something to do last night." With Garibaldi's assistance, Chewacki avoided prosecution — though he earned another suspension from the state athletic commission.

Even when he was innocent, Chewacki had an uncanny knack of landing in hot water. In 1938, he was sailing through Maryland at eighty-five miles per hour with his wife and wrestler Bronko Valdez, when he was halted at gunpoint on suspicion of robbery. Officers were on the lookout for two men and women in a high-powered car that, like Chewacki's, bore Oregon tags. After two hours, Chewacki was released when the service station owner who was robbed told police officers they snared the wrong man. "They oughta be catching speeders on that road — not looking for burglars," Chewacki muttered.

Chewacki turned from creating riots to serving his country in the navy during World War II. He was stationed at bases in Oklahoma and Illinois, and reportedly was hit by shrapnel twice during a tour of the South Pacific. He made a return appearance in Oakland in 1945, and wrestled occasionally through the end of the decade before fading from the scene. So successful was his gimmick that another wrestler, Lenny Montana, eventually passed himself off as Chewacki. In later years, every time The Sheik or Abdullah the Butcher reached for a pencil or fork, they were giving a nod to the self-styled king of the Romany gypsies. Wrote Considine: "He was seen as the person-ification of all that is wrong, all that is to be despised. That was the Chief's intention and he was profoundly successful."

TED "KING KONG" COX

Ted "King Kong" Cox was born near Crazy Woman Creek outside of Buffalo, Wyoming, May 8, 1902, and seldom has a place of birth been more appro-priate. Cox was one of wrestling's pre-eminent bad guys in the days before television and pay-per-views. A tough, rowdy, unabashed showboater, Cox might have caused more trouble in more places than any wrestler in history

— all while the turnstiles clicked to the sound of paying customers. "Cox played the bad-guy role to the hilt," recalled retired *Fresno Bee* sportswriter Bruce Farris, who watched Cox tear up Ryan's Auditorium in Fresno nearly sixty years ago.

Cox, five-foot-eleven and about 220 pounds, grew up in Colorado and was a potato farmer when he began wrestling as a circus strongman as part of the carnival circuit in the early 1920s as a way of earning extra cash. Wrestling was more lucrative and he moved into it full-time in 1931. Even before he was dubbed "King Kong," he was busy wrecking things. In November 1931, he was disqualified against Dr. Pete Visser for, among other things, gnawing on his adversary's ears. Following the loss, Cox

Ted Cox.

charged around the ring like a bull and took a few extra pokes at referee Louie Miller. Naturally, he required police protection. The next month, "Bulldog" Cox merited a suspension from the California athletic commission for rough tactics. "Referees, spectators and policemen: protect yourself at all times," warned Alan Ward of the *Oakland Tribune*, who called Cox "wild as a March hare on the mat." In July 1933, he got another ninety-day suspension in California for chomping on Abie Kaplan. Sonny Myers, who faced Cox, recalled he was a pounder, not a wrestler. "You had to keep your eyes open all the time or he'd knock your head off. He was just an ornery devil."

In the early 1930s, Cox moved his family to Lodi, California, and earned the sobriquet of the "Lodi Wildman" or "Lodi Lunatic." On July 19, 1934, he sparked what wrestling authorities in Vancouver, B.C., called the wildest riot in the city's annals. After being disqualified against Jack Forsgren, Cox punched referee Bill Draper and hopped out of the ring. He was quickly hemmed in by a mob. "A little, slugging hombre in a faded blue shirt with a homemade cigarette drooping from the corner of his mouth went to work on Cox's head with rights and lefts," the *Vancouver Province* reported. Forsgren and his second broke character, came to Cox's rescue, and yanked him by his legs through a trap door under the stage even as fans were pulling his torso like cheap taffy in the opposite direction. It took twenty minutes to disperse the mob. "I didn't mean to hit Draper," Cox moaned. "He just got in the way."

A month later in the same venue, with an extra retinue of policemen and wrestling authorities at ringside, Cox repeatedly spit at fans, then tore apart Dick Daviscourt, wrenching his left ankle until an anguished Daviscourt gave up. With Daviscourt limp on the floor, Cox suddenly became concerned about his stricken foe's plight and carefully picked him up to carry him backstage to a nice round of applause. The dark side got the better of him quickly — he dropped Daviscourt, who plopped to the floor six feet below. He pulled the same stunt in Spokane, Washington, where angry fans chased his car across railroad tracks; he admonished Fred Palmtag, a relative who worked as his second, to beat a train across the tracks to safety.

One of Cox's favorite tactics was a true stroke of genius — and financial loss. "He always made sure he was the first one to enter the ring," said Chris Palmtag, Cox's great-nephew, who regarded him as a second grandfather. "Back in the old days, they had the microphone in the center of the ring — they'd drop it down. When they'd go to introduce the other guy, he'd grab it and say, 'You don't have to introduce him because he won't last long enough for anyone to remember anyway.' And he'd rip the thing out of the ceiling. A lot of times he had to pay more money than he'd win to replace that thing."

On and on the mayhem went. In February 1934, the Portland, Oregon boxing commission docked him $100 for taping sheet lead to his fists and smacking a referee. Eighteen months later, Reno police arrested him for disturbing the peace after he got into an argument with a referee and tumbled with him into the aisle. In April 1936, Nebraska authorities followed suit after Cox failed to appear for a hearing on his "ungentlemanly conduct." No problem — he headed back to California where he took a swig out of his ammonia and water bottle before the bell rang for the third fall, spitting it into the eyes of Jake Patterson. When the Texas state championship trophy was awarded to a rival in 1941, Cox smashed it to bits, then sold the scrap metal for $1.27, Chicago columnist Arch Ward duly reported.

As the "Masked Marvel," Cox held the Toronto promotion's version of a world title in 1938; the chairman of the Ontario Athletic Commission halted one title bout in the middle of the match because he feared the Marvel was inciting a riot. Cox headlined everywhere in North America, Australia, and New Zealand with his diamondhead twist, a form of a neckbreaker, and a cobra clutch. He beat past and future world champions Dave Levin and Buddy Rogers to win the Texas heavyweight title in 1945 and 1946. He wrestled until about 1955, did a little promoting, and settled into a comfortable role as a Lodi dairy rancher with his wife and two children. He was a familiar face in town until his death in 1976.

For years, he worked as a masseuse at the YMCA in Stockton, California, soothing sore muscles next to a poster in which he mimicked a King Kong pose. Even then, Chris Palmtag said he was a larger-than-life character. "Uncle Ted used to drive an old convertible Jeep, a red one. One time we were coming around the corner from the Y and there's this big, 300-pound guy that was beating on a Chihuahua with a flyswatter. Uncle Ted drove that thing right into the guy's yard and said, 'My name is Ted Cox, and I wrestled so many matches and I won so many of them, and I'll be damned if I'm going to let you beat up on a Chihuahua.' He picked up the dog and took it home. The guy didn't say anything to my uncle. He was something else."

DICK DAVISCOURT

Dr. Benjamin F. Roller was one of the most important figures in the early days of professional wrestling. A medical school graduate, professor, athlete, and lecturer, Roller maintained that wrestling built character in young men, and sent many of his charges into the pro ranks. And few of his recruits became as successful as a powerfully built native of Washington state named Nicholas Dewiscourt.

One of the earliest and best ring ruffians in a long career that spanned from the 1910s to the 1930s, Dewiscourt, known as Dick Daviscourt, was a key figure in the transition between the tough but antiseptic wrestling of the turn of the twentieth century and the later

Department of Special Collections, University Libraries of Notre Dame

Dick Daviscourt.

out-and-out mayhem that attracted fans begging for retribution.

"They want action. They cry for gore," he once explained to *The Ring* magazine. "Toss a man out of the ring; stand on his chest. Boot him as he is about to rise to his feet, stick your finger in his eye or clout him on the chin and you'll see how the customers will flock to see you the next time out."

Born June 11, 1888, in Washington state, the youngest son of an immi-grant brewer, the adventurous Daviscourt — a brother anglicized the surname — played football and baseball, wrestled at a YMCA, worked on an Alaskan steamship, and toiled with a surveying crew for the Copper River railroad, his son, Richard, recalled.

In the early 1900s, Roller, then a professor of physical culture at the University of Washington, took notice of the budding athlete. "He wrestled my father — I think he was about eighteen years old — and he got an offer to go back east," Richard said. Yellowed clippings in fact reveal Roller to be the victor in one bout between the two in Ellensburg, Washington.

It was clear that Daviscourt had found a career path, and soon he was head-lining in every corner of North America. By the early 1920s, he emerged as one of the top challengers to world champion Ed "Strangler" Lewis. In 1921, Lewis touched off a feud when he "dislocated" Daviscourt's neck vertebrae with his famous headlock. A couple of years later, in Wichita, Kansas, a bout between the two ended in a free-for-all punchfest that required police inter-vention. Lewis and Daviscourt squared off dozens of times, and Daviscourt was one of the few wrestlers to hold a pinfall over the kingpin of the 1920s. Daviscourt's list of conquests reads like a wrestling hall of fame: Jim Londos, Toots Mondt, Wladek Zbyszko, Milo Steinborn, and Jim Browning.

Big for the era at 230 pounds, Daviscourt got meaner in the ring as the Roaring Twenties progressed, earning derision as "Rough House Richard." Like many of the day, he relied heavily on front and reverse headlocks, but also invented his own brand of a finishing maneuver he called the Chaw-hammer, a right forearm to the chin. That, he noted one time, was his response to a prohibition against closed fists and elbow smashes. In St. Louis in 1925, he reportedly earned a thirty-day suspension for punching Londos in the jaw and head; the St. Louis Post-Dispatch said a sergeant and several policemen escorted Daviscourt to safety, and authorities stationed guards in the dressing room to prevent a melee. Two months later, Daviscourt and Browning promoted a hot angle with fisticuffs at a Wichita gym. Some of that was undoubtedly promotional hype — but it added a gloss to Daviscourt's reputation as a wrestling meanie. The Frederick [Maryland] Post tabbed him "the mat game's most savage and ferocious warrior."

During the middle of warfare between Daviscourt and Browning in 1926 and 1927, Dick Hawkins, a columnist for the Atlanta Constitution, summed it up: "Dick Daviscourt is the champion villain of the wrestling profession. He talks back at the audience, refuses to shake hands with opponents, argues with the referee, and climbs through the ropes — all with the purpose of making the crowd hate him so sincerely that they will pay money to see him beaten or even hurt. And yet they call this a civilized world." Apparently, the tactics did wonders at the turnstiles — Atlanta newspapers noted with amazement that Daviscourt drew a much larger house than Lewis.

From there, Daviscourt stepped up the pace of his rule-breaking. He lost by knockout in a May 1931 bout in Baltimore, but not to scheduled opponent Gino Garibaldi, whom he had encased in a stranglehold. A local grocer, Thomas Lusso, infuriated at Daviscourt's disregard for the rules, rushed the ring and waylaid him. Daviscourt suffered a pigeon-egg sized lump and cut under his ear; the bout was a no contest. The Nevada athletic commission pulled back Daviscourt's purse after a 1932 match because he illegally used his fists. The same year, in Syracuse, New York, before a bout with Londos he coated his body with oil to become slippery as an eel. The referee naturally ordered Daviscourt to clean up his act, though not before the villain "called Londos all sorts of a piker and took a swing at the champion within the first three minutes of action," the *Syracuse Herald* reported.

What fans didn't see was how hard Daviscourt worked to earn their wrath. He was among several grapplers who contacted trachoma, allegedly from a wrestler from India — the bacterial infection that then, as now, is the world's leading cause of blindness. Living in San Francisco, Daviscourt had to take a year off. "They wore black eye patches during the day. He'd run on the beach and my mom would run with him to guide him. He still kept his eye patches on and he saved his eyesight," his son said.

Quiet and soft-spoken in person, Daviscourt wrestled until he was about fifty, and operated an orange, lemon, lime, and avocado farm in California from the late 1920s until about 1940, when he and his family returned to Washington. He later worked for his brother's bakery and owned a tavern before the toll of all those headlocks and Chaw-hammers caught up with him in January 1960.

BILLY EDWARDS

It was the grandest show (or scam) on earth — educated horses that amused children and adults, fortune tellers trained in the occult, midgets who puffed cigars the size of their arms, and, of course, wrestlers. When professional wrestling was cutting its teeth as part of the carnival circuit in the United States, Billy Edwards was already figuring out how to incite crowds for profit on the way to earning recognition as the sport's first, great colorful heel.

Born in 1889 in Nebraska, but living much of his life in Kansas City, Missouri, Edwards started wrestling as a teenager, and one summer in the 1900s, hooked up with the Al G. Barnes Traveling Carnival Show. His task was

A rare Billy Edwards card from a set released in Australia in the 1920s.

simple: egg on all comers with a lure of $100 if someone could whip him. All Edwards had to do was ensure the carnival bets were covered, make his opponent look good enough that excited fans upped their wagers, and win.

"Of course, we were reasonably safe," he remembered in a 1929 interview. "We toured the small towns, and while I met a lot of town champions, none knew the rudiments of wrestling. They were strong, but strength alone is not enough." The crafty Edwards estimated that he worked the carny circuit regularly for about five years, and even turned up on a Snapp Brothers tour in Reno, Nevada, in 1924. The "Kansas City Butcher Boy" took the sneaky tricks he learned on resin and sawdust mats, and applied them in gymnasiums and arenas around the world.

While he was known for stomping and slugging referees as often as opponents, Edwards' calling card was one of the first of the well-publicized submission moves. He called his trademark hold the chiropractic headlock, developed with the assistance of Kansas City chiropractor Paul Jameson. Edwards purported to deaden muscles supporting the spinal column with pressure near the eyes and ears, then render his foe unconscious with a whiplike motion that snapped neck vertebrae out of place.

So renowned was his headlock that opponents routinely greased their scalps so they could escape the hold, like a dog slipping its leash. When challenged in Galveston, Texas, by a chiropractor, who suggested that chiropractors did not embrace brutality, Edwards angrily fired off a letter to the editor, describing the hold's basis in science. "Dr. Jameson and I spent many weeks before I could get satisfactory results," he said. The hold helped him claim a version of the world light heavyweight championship in 1931.

Joyce Critchfield, Edwards' niece, remembered him well for his flashy attire — he wore diamond rings and always sported a big elk's tooth on a chain around his neck — and the trauma he caused her mother. "My mother and dad were married quite young, and my dad took her to a wrestling match. Evidently, Uncle Billy twisted the rope around this other's fellow neck, and my mother fainted. And she refused to ever go to another match, and dad was not to mention him again," Critchfield laughed. "But he was a big, jovial guy. He was a very kind, nice man, but he played the villain in the ring."

Edwards' innovations extended beyond grinding the skulls of fan favorites. His melees with Ira Dern in 1924 and 1925 are considered to be forerunners of the Texas Death Match. "As Billy hammered Ira to all corners of the ring, the crowd went wild. Edwards was finally disqualified, but Texas-rules wrestling had been born. The promoter reasoned that if the crowd liked it that much, the faithful would continue to pay to see it," Missouri sportswriter Gene Sullivan reported. "This box-office genius kept the rules simple. Only the stranglehold was barred."

In 1931, Edwards made national headlines when he brawled with Jack Dempsey, imported as a special referee to keep the hooligan in line. Edwards shredded Dempsey's shirt during a match with Jim O'Dowd in Dallas, then refused to release the chiropractic headlock after using it to conquer O'Dowd. When Dempsey tried to break the hold, Edwards took a swing at him. The ex-champ responded with a left and a short right that lifted the villain off the mat — just as Edwards wanted. "Had to eat soup for three days," Edwards said years later. "Just couldn't chew. But what a gag!"

Bill Hensel, a retired petroleum technologist in Texas, recalled that Edwards regularly bought limburger cheese at the Hensels' small grocery in Dallas. On one occasion, Edwards tucked away some limburger for a long drive to Houston. Hensel's father protested that the cheese would go bad during the long, hot drive, but Edwards had other ideas. "As he left to enter the ring, he placed a large handful of it in his left armpit. He entered the ring and met his adversary in the center for the usual pre-match instructions," Hensel said. "Catching the wrestler off-guard, Billy grabbed him and crammed his face, nose and all, under the armpit filled with the limburger. As the story goes, the opponent fainted and had to be carried from the ring."

All those days of carnival travels and in-ring mischief paid off handsomely. In 1927, Edwards bought a seventeen-acre farm near Dallas, where he raised chickens and thoroughbred hogs, and built his own gym. His thirty-two-year career ended January 22, 1941, when he died following a car crash on a back road near Hillsboro, Texas. His death inspired a huge outpouring from mat fans and a spate of stories that fondly reflected on his showmanship and his amiable nature. Wrote Felix McKnight for the

Associated Press: "Old Billy, a glowering, conniving figure in the ring who was the greatest wrestling attraction the Southwest ever knew, was really a gentle guy."

Department of Special Collections, University Libraries of Notre Dame

ABE "KING KONG" KASHEY

If you can't beat the other guy, you might as well beat the ref. That was the thought in Abe Kashey's mind during a March 1938 bout in Winnipeg, Manitoba, against an up-and-comer named Lou Thesz. Four times, Thesz tossed Kashey into the crowd, but Kashey responded by chucking referee Alex Stewart into press row, and choking the arbiter with a leglock around the throat. A disqualification was in order, as it often was for Kashey, and he was pelted with foodstuff during a hasty retreat.

Just another day at the office for Abe "King Kong" Kashey. From the 1930s to the 1950s, the Syrian assassin was one of wrestling's bad boys, with a thick, sinister accent; a hairy, menacing look; and a flair for treachery that entertained and enraged fans. Born November 28, 1903, in Syria, Kashey was a former steelworker and amateur weightlifter who turned pro around 1930. He was a top amateur in the metropolitan New York area, and first wrestled as "Turk Abad Kasah" in Washington, D.C.

Kashey made his biggest mark for promoter Tony Stecher in the Minneapolis territory, where he was "the first really big star of the promotion," according to wrestling historian James C. Melby, author of *Gopherland Grappling: The Early Years*. In describing Kashey's ring style, the *Brainerd Daily Dispatch* concluded: "He merely puts into practice what his perusal of the wrestling rule book tells him is not popular and definitely against regulations of ring warfare." Still, Kashey, who popularized the atomic drop as a finisher, denied he was the instigator. "I've never broken a wrestling rule in my life without just provocation," he said in a newspaper interview. "After all, it's not against the law to protect yourself."

He did a pretty good job of protecting himself in one of the first, big boxer-wrestler bouts. In October 1934, a screaming throng of 8,000 in Minneapolis saw him escape a third-round knockdown, then score a fourth-round pinfall against Minnesota heavyweight Charley Retzlaff, with Jack Dempsey as special referee. Two nights later, Dempsey and Kashey traded blows in La Crosse, Wisconsin, after Kashey whipped another wrestler, and then turned his wrath on the former world champ-turned-ref. (Retzlaff exacted a measure of revenge by kayoing Kashey in a 1940 bout in Fargo, North Dakota.) Kashey even got a few movie roles in the 1940s — what could be more fitting than his part of Tongolo the Terrible in one Tarzan flick?

Kashey's issues with referees extended to a prank set up by fan-favorite Sandor Szabo, who egged "King Kong" and referee Al Stecher by telling them separately they were saying nasty things about each other. One night in Sacramento, California, Szabo disclosed to Stecher that Kashey was looking to flatten him, and the ref had better get his shots in first. Kashey retaliated and alarmed promoter Joe Malcewicz found his featured attraction standing over a prone Stecher. "I am a gentleman and will not hit you while you are down," Kashey announced in his halting manner. "Sandor," Malcewicz told United Press International, "has never stopped laughing."

Billy Wicks recalled one night in the early 1950s, when Kashey taught him a lesson. Wicks was just starting his career, in Brandon, Manitoba. "Al Mills was kidding me. He said, 'Hey, Wicks, you got the ol' man out there tonight. You got ol' King Kong. He's gonna cover you like a blanket.'" A talented amateur, Wicks twice tried some basic moves on Kashey that led to a break on the ropes. "Referee comes to break it up, just before he does — I'm down on my hands and knees — Abe turns around and smacks me right in the nose with his elbow. Bang! I mean, he smacked me. He said, 'Hey, sonny, this is professional wrestling. This is not amateur.' I got the message right away. This ol' man is going to whip me if I'm not careful."

Kashey had a legendary series of brawls with Dick Raines across North America, and was a California state tag team champion with Mr. Moto in 1950. He also was the first opponent for future champion Verne Gagne in 1949. They met again in St. Paul on January 2, 1953, with wrestler Vic Holbrook as special referee. Gagne came out on top, and in a post-match scuffle, Kashey cut Holbrook above the eye, prompting the crowd to attack the ring.

The meanie turned into a bit of a softie late in his career, when son Al started wrestling. The two first partnered in 1952, and later wrestled a lot in the upper Midwest, where Al came out of the audience to rescue his dad, who, ironically, was serving as a referee when Al Mills and Tiny Mills roughed him up. Father and son teamed regularly in the mid-1950s, before Abe called it quits around 1958. They also had a health studio together in California. Even in retirement, "King Kong" was a fearsome visage. "My grandfather was a terrifying guy from the viewpoint of a child," said grandson Valente Jacobia, who recalled that his grandfather and grandmother Marge went through their share of loud, animated vocals: "My mother would send me to the back room to wait. But do you know what he'd do? He come back and find me. 'Where's Valente?' And he'd always give me a silver dollar. He gave me I don't know how many silver dollars. When I was sixteen years old, I bought my first vehicle in part from all the silver dollars he would give."

Kashey died of heart failure September 24, 1965, in Los Angeles. His son continued to wrestle for several years, homesteading in Arizona, where he built a thriving real-estate practice. During the summer, he'd load up the family to spend time with relatives in Wisconsin while he worked in the Midwest-based American Wrestling Association. Al died in 2005.

K. O. KOVERLY

A right uppercut, a left hook, and boom! George Koverly was nicknamed "K.O.," and every prominent wrestler from the early 1930s to the late 1950s knew why. None of that pantywaist forearm smash business for the 230-pounder from St. Louis — his talent rested with his fists, and they kept him in main events in every corner of North America for most of his twenty-five-year career.

Godjo Kovacevich was born in Yugoslavia on November 3, 1902, and emigrated to Canada and then the United States with his parents at a young age. The family settled in St. Louis, which had a sizable eastern European population. Koverly became a two-sport athlete of the hard-hitting kind, pursuing boxing and wrestling simultaneously. In June 1932, he dropped Joe Salvo in a two-round preliminary bout in Sacramento, and then lost a four-round decision to Jack Casper two weeks later. At the same time, he was wrestling as "Handsome" George Koverly before switching to the more apt "K.O." nickname. "Wrestling is much tougher than prizefighting," Koverly, who spoke with a distinctive eastern European accent, told Alan Ward of the *Oakland Tribune*, though some of his contemporaries thought he lacked a top-notch fighter's ability to withstand a punch.

His fists always were heavily taped — doctor's orders, he explained, saying he had suffered so many broken knuckles that he needed the tape to get a grip. Of course, he used the tape to rake his opponents' eyes and dipped it in water for a final, hard-as-a-rock, knockout blow. In California, he held the San Francisco-based Pacific Coast heavyweight title three times in the mid-1940s, feuding primarily with Dean Detton. When he wasn't winning, Koverly was busy getting disqualified, as he did in February 1937 in New York City, where he punched out Steve "Crusher" Casey, referee George Bothner, and required a police escort. Even in defeat, he frequently refused to leave the ring, ambling about to a

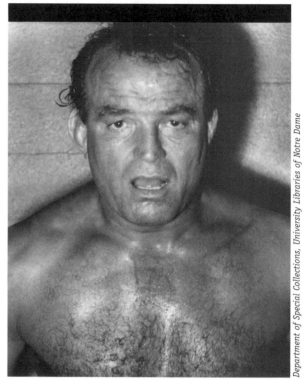

K.O. Koverly.

hailstorm of paper cups, drinks and coins, taunting the audience and protesting to anyone who might listen. It earned him reputation as a "one man gang," according to Louis Effrat of *The New York Times*.

Fan insurrections followed him everywhere — Koverly suffered a cigarette burn at the hands of an audience member in Toronto, following a five-minute riot after a tussle with "Dirty" Don Evans. In Washington, D.C., Koverly turned mat meanie LaVerne Baxter into a hero by simply reaching over the referee's shoulder during opening instructions and cold-cocking Baxter with a left. Promoter Joe Turner barked at him in public, saying, "If Koverly again attempts to pick an argument with a ringsider, his purse would not only be held up but he would be set down for life as far as local matches are concerned."

The slugger's most memorable performance occurred in August 1938, when he squared off with Dr. Patrick O'Callaghan, the Irish Olympian, in Los Angeles. The ruddy-cheeked O'Callaghan won the gold medal in the hammer throw in the 1928 and 1932 Summer Olympics, and, with his athletic credentials and ethnic appeal, saw himself as a world title claimant. He tamed foe after foe during a tour of the United States before encountering Koverly.

Braven Dyer, long-time sports columnist for the *Los Angeles Times*, recalled taking "society" folks to witness O'Callaghan, in the grand manner of a theater opening, and assured them what they were about to see was staged.

Somehow, the message didn't get through to Koverly. Whether at his instigation or a promoter's prodding, Koverly beat the living daylights out of "The Wild Irish Rose." Dyer's horrified friends could barely stand to peek at the mauling from behind their programs. "First, he smashed poor Pat across the nose. Blood flowed like a claret. Then he went to work on Pat's ears. With three or four slashing swipes, he sliced the doc's auditory appendage to ribbons. . . The referee finally stopped it. To the best of my memory, Pat was never off his feet. Neither was K. O. Koverly," Dyer wrote. The incident ended O'Callaghan's flirtation with wrestling, but only added to Koverly's image, as Eddie Briatz of the Associated Press dubbed him "the new big, bad wolf of the wrestling combine." He accidentally broke Ted Cox's jaw with an errant punch, and former world champions Lou Thesz and Bill Longson recalled him as one of the most rugged characters that they encountered.

For many years, Koverly ran a popular St. Louis restaurant called The Mural Room, which out-of-town sports teams frequently habited. Even there, he could pack a punch. On one occasion, a man entered The Mural Room, brandished a gun in front of alarmed patrons, Longson, and his wife, and threatened to shoot Koverly for an alleged dalliance with a woman. "George, in his calm way, said, 'Let's not create a disturbance here. Let's step outside,'" Longson's son, Dick, recalled. "So they stepped outside the door and George knocked him cold with one punch, and told him to be on his way. . . . He was a legitimate tough guy."

Thesz liked Koverly after he got to know him, and called him a colorful guy who used fisticuffs liberally. "I saw him once in Boston where he came out of the ring when the crowd was after his ass, and he punched his way through it, dropping citizens left and right, all the way to the dressing room," Thesz told Kit Bauman, his collaborator on *Hooker*. Another time, a man Koverly kicked out of his restaurant returned to stick a gun in K.O.'s back. "The guy said, 'Outside, you son of a bitch!'" Thesz recounted to Bauman. "As they're going through the door, George somehow mousetrapped the guy, took away the gun, and then beat the dog crap out of the guy before calling the cops. George was not someone that you wanted to back into a corner and make angry."

Nick Bockwinkel recalled seeing his dad, Warren, fight Koverly, just as Nick was starting his career in California. "He was a little bit quirky, a little bit of an enigma, though not in a destructive way. But you know when you went in there with him that you'd better stand your ground," Bockwinkel said.

Koverly continued to wrestle through the mid-1950s, was associated with security at a Las Vegas hotel for years, and retired to Santa Monica, California, where you could find him playing checkers in a local park. He died in 1989.

Heel With a Heart – The Original Dutch Mantell

Today's wrestling fans know the name of Dutch Mantel – he was a top star in Tennessee for years, and has been an important figure in the creative end of several promotions, most recently at Total Nonstop Action Wrestling.

But fifty years before the current "Dirty Dutch" (Wayne Cowan) made a name for himself, the original Dutch Mantell, this one spelled with double "l's," was leading one of the most fascinating and productive lives of any heel in history.

Born in 1881 in Luxembourg, Alfred de re la Gardieur listened intently to tales of his father's travels to the United States, and developed wanderlust at a young age, according to H. Allen Anderson, Mantell's biographer. After his father died in 1891, he lived

Courtesy Cal Farley's Boys Ranch

Dutch Mantell shows off his finest.

briefly with an uncle in Germany, then, at fourteen, stowed away on an English merchant ship to the West. He ended up in Australia, where he took up boxing and wrestling, and found a friend and mentor in actor Robert B. Mantell, the source of his name.

Mantell finally got to the U.S. in 1900, where he wrestled on the East Coast before joining the navy and becoming an American citizen. He was a lightweight, seldom tipping the scales at more than 150 pounds, but he separated himself from the pack with tactics considered rowdy for the times – punching, kicking, gouging, and generally acting as an irritant to spectators. "The Lon Chaney of the mat," the *Charleston Gazette* once called him. From 1913 to 1915, he became one of the first wrestlers on the silver screen, as a member of Mack Sennett's silent "Keystone Kops" film comedies, but he

Dutch Mantell goes for a run with Cal Farley.

was soon back on the wrestling circuit. At one time, "Rough House" Mantell, as he was known, stoked crowds by putting up $1,000 to anyone who dared meet him in the 145-pound class. "Mantell bested such big-name welterweights as Mattie Matsuda and Jack Reynolds, but never was able to gain official championship status because of his uncouth, crowd-inciting techniques," Anderson explained in *The Handbook of Texas*. In 1972, Dory Funk Sr. would recall him to writer Jimmy Dodson as "the type of wrestler to storm into the ring smoking a cigar and as soon as the bell would ring he would shove the cigar into the eye of his opponent."

In the early 1920s, Mantell barnstormed through Texas, where he came upon a baseball player and wrestler named Cal Farley. The two hit it off, even though they were ring foes, and Mantell became a fixture in Amarillo. Wide-eyed kids followed him like a Pied Piper as he strolled around town with high-heeled boots, a sombrero, and a huge police dog. One of the youngsters, sportswriter-to-be John Bloomer, wrote years later that "a menacing mien" only added to Mantell's appeal – Bloomer acknowledged he usually stayed a careful eight paces behind the dog. Mantell helped Farley's tire business, appeared regularly on Farley's popular radio show, and promoted wrestling in Amarillo with him. But most of all, he and Farley shared a passion – helping kids in need. With assistance from Mantell and community leaders, Farley established the Maverick Boys & Girls Club and Kids Inc., to provide productive activities for children in the community. Eventually, Farley's vision would lead to the creation in 1939 of the famous Cal Farley's Boys Ranch, where troubled youths could escape dangerous streets and impoverished conditions. To this day, the ranch is an international leader in residential and community-based programs for children.

For his part, Mantell always extended a helping hand to people, at least outside the ring. He once estimated that he earned half a million dollars in his lifetime, but, according to the Newspaper Enterprise Association, he was so generous with loans that friends eventually took over his finances because he gave away his fortune. In 1940, a year after Farley's ranch was chartered, Mantell was beset by cancer. He died January 31, 1941. His worldly possessions consisted of a small apartment house and a car. Everything else went, under the terms of his will, to the Maverick Club and Cal Farley's Boys Ranch. The Associated Press observed his death by memorializing both his profession and the cause that was dear to his heart. "He was a pal of underprivileged kids everywhere and a favorite of fans who watched him maul opponents."

LORD LANSDOWNE

Before "Nature Boy" Ric Flair, there was "Nature Boy" Buddy Rogers. Before Buddy Rogers, there was Gorgeous George. And before Gorgeous George, there was a creative lad from Ohio who would become a British "lord," hobnob with the Hollywood elite, land on the periphery of two murder cases, and revolutionize professional wrestling. Wilbur Finran became Lord Patrick Lansdowne Finnegan, the first of the colorful pretty-boy wrestlers, and the genius behind innovations such as entrance music, in-ring spray guns, and tea breaks between falls. So entertaining was

Lord Lansdowne is dressed by his valets.

Lansdowne in his prime that Ohio sportswriter Bill Snypp preferred him to the great matinee idol of the 1930s: "We have seen Jim Londos at his best . . . Londos was quite a showman then, as he is now. But we will take five minutes of Finnegan's antics and give Londos away for a full evening."

Born in Springfield, Ohio, in 1905, the young Finran displayed none of the characteristics that would bring him later fame as an effete, haughty Cockney. He attended parochial school in Springfield, and got involved in gymnastics, swimming, and wrestling at a local YMCA. As a teenager, he peddled newspapers to make ends meet — his father split for California when Finran was young, according to his daughter, Rita Helsel.

In the late 1920s while working as a pressman, Finran debuted in preliminary matches in his hometown and quickly fell in league with Jack Reynolds, a top welterweight of the era. Within a few years, a combination of wrestling connections and a fertile imagination catapulted him to stardom. By 1932, he assumed the role of an ethnic Irish hero for Columbus, Ohio promoter Al Haft as Pat "Duke" Finnegan. As his persona evolved, he revised his peerage from "Duke" to "Lord" Finnegan in Detroit, where he ended a drought of 184 consecutive non-sellouts for promoter Adam Weismuller's dormant area in a title match against champion Reynolds. Reports of the day claimed Finnegan brought in gates of $4,500 in the city, a sensational sum for the times.

Further south, Finnegan converted to a full-fledged Brit in late summer 1933, when he toured Oklahoma with Reynolds as the long-cloaked, monocled Lord Patrick Lansdowne Finnegan. The following spring, the Reynolds-Finnegan alliance ran into a legal snag. The National Wrestling Association barred Reynolds from wrestling Finnegan in Cincinnati in April 1934, after Reynolds' wife and another man were implicated in two fatal shootings. Reynolds was cleared, but, within a few months, he and Finnegan headed west.

The trip was a fruitful one. In his new guise as Lord Lansdowne of England, Finran hopped out of the audience during an October 1934 tour in Hawaii to challenge Rubberman Higami. With his curly hair coiffed, and a monocle fixed in his eye socket, Finran advertised himself as a representative of the tony, if non-existent, House of Barrington. The self-proclaimed royalist became the first consequential grappler to be accompanied regularly by music, as he instructed bands at wrestling shows to strike up "God Save the King" as he entered the ring, according to a variety of news accounts.

With his pioneering flair and cat-quick ring work, Lansdowne, 175 pounds dripping wet, became the rage among smaller performers. He scored the biggest win of his career in January 1935, when he beat Reynolds for the welterweight title in San Francisco — it reportedly was Reynolds' first loss in fourteen years. Known for his leverage work, his armbar, and a finisher called the Lansdowne special — a series of flying mares followed by a swinging neckbreaker — he "threatens to become as popular among the small wrestlers as Jim Londos has in the heavyweight division," the Los Angeles Times opined. "After a match, it takes him half-an-hour to get back to his dressing room as he is mobbed by feminine autograph seekers."

Lansdowne played his role to the hilt. As to his confusing aliases, he explained to Braven Dyer of the *Los Angeles Times* that his real identity of P. Lansdowne Finnington from Somerset, England, was too weighty for simple Midwestern scribes. "This arose because of my last name, which caused some of the writers a great deal of trouble. I never bothered about correcting them when they billed me as Lord Finnegan."

By then, though, Lansdowne was becoming known for more than just rasslin'. In December 1935, he and a friend, actor Charles York, were set to escort Hollywood starlet Thelma Todd to a cocktail party, where they planned to pose as English noblemen. In one of Tinseltown's great "Whodunit" mysteries, Todd was found dead of carbon monoxide poisoning the night before the party. Lansdowne was directed to testify before a grand jury investigating the fatality because he might have been one of the last people to talk to "Hot Toddy." The grand jury foreman waved off his claims, calling them "a publicity band wagon," and her death was ruled an accident. But in O. J. Simpson–like fashion, the unresolved case remains a source of fascination.

As he refined his gimmick and worked more as a heel, Lansdowne introduced apparel and antics that wrestlers copy to this day. His ring wear consisted of a flowing, purple velvet robe, under which he sported a black tunic — the costume allegedly cost $2,000. He was accompanied by one or two valets, variously known as Tweedles, Twittles, and Jeeves. If his valets carelessly tossed his garments under the ring, an aggravated Lansdowne called an immediate halt to the proceedings, and showed them how to fold the robe properly — an early version of the stall. Once inside the squared circle, Lansdowne inspected the condition of the mat, invariably found it filthy and disgusting, and directed his valets to remedy that condition with an atomizer, which they regularly turned on referees and opponents.

So captivating was his gimmick that it merited attention from *Variety*, the Hollywood trade newspaper, which suggested Lansdowne might be responsible for the rebirth of vaudeville in Columbus. Even the *American Institute of Banking Bulletin* sat up and took notice of a 1938 match in Louisville, Kentucky. "The bell rang for the start of the bout. The lord stepped forth, raised his right hand, announced he was not quite ready. Then he went into a queer routine of exercising, which he termed the Kozak warm-up exercises. By this time the crowd was mad and let it be known . . . The house was sold out, and sold out for the next eight weeks." But make no mistake — Lansdowne was more than just a tea-sipping, 1930s-era sports entertainer. His skills on the mat drew rave reviews from coast to coast. "Lord Lansdowne is undoubtedly the smoothest, most agile wrestler ever seen here," concluded Howard Pearson in the *Deseret News*, the Salt Lake City, Utah newspaper.

His greatest influence on wrestling started in late 1937, when George Raymond Wagner passed through Ohio, working on some cards with Lansdowne, and taking note of the prissy scoundrel. Years later, world champion Lou Thesz said Wagner told him that he borrowed in part from Lansdowne to transform into Gorgeous George, whose valets, atomizer and irritating fastidiousness became a national rage. In fact, Lansdowne and Wagner were friends — the Lord used "Pomp and Circumstance" as entrance music late in his career, as did George. The Gorgeous One visited Lansdowne in Columbus, as well. "He came over and saw my dad a few times," Helsel said. "I was always fascinated with those bobby pins of his. I was just a kid and didn't really understand it, but I was awed."

Frankie Cain, later to gain fame as The Great Mephisto, was just a youngster selling programs at matches in Columbus when he first saw Lansdowne. So awed was Cain that he would remember Lansdowne more than sixty years later as the precursor of a new wave of wrestling characters. "I watched him and I admired him when I was a kid," Cain said. "When I'd seen him come to the ring, I couldn't believe it. I couldn't believe that entrance. He was the first gimmick guy that I'd ever seen."

Lansdowne curtailed his active touring around 1941 and started concentrating on his extensive business interests. He owned attractive lounges and supper clubs in Springfield; Dayton, Ohio; and Sarasota, Florida — well-mannered butler Jeeves actually was Jack Rogers, one of his bartenders. At one point, Lansdowne was worth an estimated half-a-million dollars, his daughter said. In Florida, when the wrestling bug bit, he recreated himself as the White Rajah of Shalomar, in a maharajah getup that looked like Johnny Carson's campy Carnac the Magnificent.

On the trail of success and acclaim though, would come extreme sorrow and pain. His young wife, Jean, died in July 1943 at twenty-four of tuberculosis. Lansdowne appeared in Columbus in July 1950, when he was disqualified for repeatedly roughhousing Angelo Poffo. But he soon encountered difficulty keeping up his vigorous physical routine — and even walking. He went to the Mayo Clinic and was diagnosed with amyotrophic lateral sclerosis, known as Lou Gehrig's disease, around 1951. "I think it was really hard for him. I was a kid, and I didn't understand what it would be like to be so active and all of a sudden, you're not able to perform anything like you did," his daughter said. Lansdowne suffered with the disease for years, losing his ability to move and speak before succumbing in November 1959 at fifty-four in an apartment in Columbus. He is little remembered today, a bit of a surprise considering how brightly his star once shone. After all, as the *Columbus Evening Dispatch* recalled upon his death, Finran's inventive personage "presaged the current type of 'glamour wrestler.'"

BUDDY O'BRIEN

Pound for pound, it would be harder to find anyone in the annals of wrestling who created more mayhem in a shorter period of time than Buddy O'Brien. Though some circumstances of his brief life and times remain a mystery — even to his relatives — more than sixty-five years later, it's clear that O'Brien was a founding father of the anything-goes school of wrestling. Consider these news accounts.

> PHOENIX, ARIZONA, NOVEMBER 1936: Buddy O'Brien spent a night in jail after he pulled a handful of paper from his trunks, set it ablaze, and rubbed the flaming soot in opponent Al Haffert's eyes. Then he knocked out the referee. He was arrested for starting a fire in a public building.

> SANTA MONICA, CALIFORNIA, SEPTEMBER 1937: Police kept guard as more than 2,600 restless fans milled around an arena for more than an hour after Buddy O'Brien handcuffed LaVerne Baxter to the ropes and beat him senseless with broken pieces of a ringside bench.

> EL RIO, CALIFORNIA, JANUARY 1938: Buddy O'Brien was entombed in 4,800 pounds of ice in an alleged attempt to break the world's freezing record of 26 minutes, 40 seconds, but lasted only slightly more than a minute. When he came out, the gag nearly turned into calamity, when a 300-pound cake of ice skidded across the mat and almost crushed a female spectator.

To O'Brien, born Arland C. Miller in upstate New York in 1909, that sort of mayhem came naturally — in fact, it was an extension of his personality out of the ring. "He was a showman. He started a lot of that, the way they do wrestling nowadays. In fact, he was worse than they were nowadays," his younger brother, Stuart Miller, said, laughing. "He would do anything. He was always ready for trouble. But he had a big heart."

O'Brien came from a huge family — he had thirteen brothers and sisters. Early in his life, he threw himself into exercise, running up and down railroad tracks near the family's home outside of Wellsburg in New York's Southern Tier. "He must have been sixteen or seventeen then, but I can remember him training, running up and down the railroad tracks in the wintertime, shorts on, a pair of gloves. That's what he did," Miller said of his

Buddy O'Brian
Foto By Casasola

older brother.

Short and stocky as a fireplug, O'Brien started out as a boxer in the nearby Elmira area, with little success, and headed to California as a wrestler during the Great Depression. He picked up the surname because he looked Irish, and, important to a villainous wrestler, bled easily from his nose — hence the nickname "Bloody" Buddy O'Brien.

By 1936, the charming rogue was considered among the country's elite welterweights in *Ring* magazine's annual rankings, in a small group trailing only champions Jack Reynolds, Johnny Stote, and "Wild" Red Berry. As he moved to main-event status, his presposterous actions grew into the stuff of legend. In a match against popular Nick Lutze, O'Brien employed several choke holds, ground powder from a tobacco sack into Lutze's eyes, threw a stool at his foe, and then choked him with a towel after the match was over. That display brought "six or eight" fans into the ring to try to tear into O'Brien, according to one news report. His ashes-in-the-eyes gambit in Phoenix, which earned him a spot in the "Ripley's Believe It or Not" strip, came the same month as a Ventura, California judge fined him $100 for inciting a riot — he had tossed a sack of flour in Kaimon Kudo's eyes after police demanded O'Brien vacate the premises. In Seattle, he snuck a cake of soap in the ring to rub into Stan Mayslack's eyes behind the ref's back; O'Brien popped the soap in his mouth when the referee turned away. "He may not be the best 'rassler' in the business, but he is the most hated," concluded Larry Mulvaney of the *Ventura County Star*.

In a September 1936 bout, O'Brien, acting as a second, slipped Brother Jonathan, father of the legendary Don Leo Jonathan, some sandpaper with which to blind Sandor Szabo. The local police force employed tear gas to gain control of the ensuing melee. Law enforcement officers regularly restrained O'Brien from continuing his mischief after matches were over. He also caught the overseeing eye of the California Athletic Commission, which suspended him at least four times from 1937 to 1940. Further north, in Washington and Oregon, he wrestled as General Harold O'Brien. In a single night in Seattle in October 1937, he married Dorothy King of Hollywood in the ring, then went haywire during the night's main event, smearing powder in Pat Fraley's eyes, and battering the referee. "I cannot recall reading an account of any of his matches in the pre–World War II days, up and down the Pacific Coast, in which he did not do his level best to inspire a full-scale riot," concluded wrestling historian J Michael Kenyon, a long-time Seattle area sportswriter and radio host.

With the exception of his father, the rascally O'Brien was close to members of his family and brought them gifts when he returned on trips home, Miller said. But even there, O'Brien was no stranger to misadventure. During a return visit to Chemung County, New York, he learned that cockfights were conducted near his family's property. "The roosters were very valuable," his brother said. "So he stole the roosters. The owners, they put an ad in the paper, a big ad for a reward, so he went back, and gave them a song-and-dance that he got the roosters from some place."

The neighbors didn't buy the ploy, and called the police to follow up. But when officers visited the Millers' house, O'Brien was nowhere to be seen. "We had a big sofa — they were leather in those days — and you opened them up, sofa-bed like," Miller said. "They took the mattress out of there and Arland got inside of it. The State Police came and they sat on that sofa, and he was in there. I'm telling you, he was something."

Back on the West Coast, O'Brien continued to toss the rule book to the wind. Charged with disturbing the peace, he showed up for a court appearance in a bright blue shirt, baggy slacks, snazzy red suspenders and an upturned collegiate hat. In Hollywood, he was involved in an incident with Frank Marlowe — a bit actor who appeared in more than two hundred movies and television shows, and who was sometimes billed as O'Brien's brother, Sonny — involving a woman's stolen coat.

O'Brien's demise came quickly and unexpectedly. In October 1941, a policeman confronted him on an allegation of suspicion of robbery. O'Brien charged the officer "in typical wrestler fashion," the Los Angeles Times reported. Sent to an area hospital, he died a few days later. He was just thirty-two.

After O'Brien's death, his wife told Stuart Miller that her husband's freewheeling, reckless ways had caught up with him. O'Brien apparently tried to impress a female friend by walking in a store and snatching a fur coat to present to her. Police called to the scene allegedly battered him, and he never regained consciousness, Miller said.

"He was always getting in trouble and they were after him anyway, because he was always causing trouble. He probably gave them a hard time all the time," Miller said. "He had no fear of anything. He was just a big showman. He would do anything. I never saw anybody like him."

LOU PLUMMER

Department of Special Collections, University Libraries of Notre Dame

Lou Plummer.

Bob Plummer is obsessed with his grandfather, "Larrupin'" Lou Plummer, a man he never met. "When I was a kid, that's all my dad would talk about," he said. Intrigued as an adult, he started looking around, and discovered that Lou Plummer was in both sets of the Parkhurst wrestling cards, produced in Canada in the mid-'50s. Bob wanted more, but was not pleased with what he found. "I just had this obsession to find out where he was from. The more I found out, the more I got turned off with who he was, and what kind of person he was. He really was a bad guy in real life, no matter what he portrayed."

Larrupin' Lou (or Lew) Plummer definitely portrayed the bad guy. He was a thumper through and through, never mistaken for a mat technician, and never a top, top star. "He was tough, a big old grisly, street kind of brawler, he wasn't a great wrestler, he was a brawler," said Stan "The Big K" Kowalski. Former referee Tommy Fooshee recalled seeing Plummer in action in Texas, and one particular move stood out. "He'd get a hammerlock, and work his way in front of you, and he'd hit you in the nuts. That was a DQ, of course. That was a beautiful move. It would kill the match, and then you'd have to sell, hold your balls, and roll around."

Born in 1907, Plummer was raised in Waukegan, Illinois where his father, having left the navy, was a railroad detective. Lou grew into a six-foot-one, 250-pound piece of prime beef. His brother, Robert James, went to Notre

Dame, but Lou never did go to college despite constant billing as a grad of Notre Dame. Reports persist that he played semi-pro football for the Catonsville Eleven and for the Bethlehem Grays, near Baltimore, and that is where he became acquainted with grappler Jim McMillen, who suggested a career in wrestling.

By the end of 1931, Plummer had a few bouts under his belt, mostly around Maryland, showcasing flying tackles and shoulder blocks. He was soon moving up the card, having left football behind. "[Plummer] in nearly three years has developed into a first-class wrestler. He was green at first, but gradually picked up the showmanship and class so necessary in the grunting racket," explained one newspaper account. "The hotter the action, the better Plummer likes it. He is at his best when the going is rough. He and his opponent usually are in and out of the ring a dozen times during the course of a bout." He took on all the big names, from Bronko Nagurski, to Milo Steinborn, to Lou Thesz.

His grandson's fascination with all things Lou Plummer led to the discovery of a 1932 short film entitled *Pardon My Grip*, which features Plummer against Abe Coleman. "I wrote to every big movie collector in the country and the world," said Bob Plummer. Eventually, he heard from a collector who had the original, which had four different bouts in the film. "The guy says, 'But I've got to get fifteen dollars for it.' I said, 'Sir, the money's in the mail.'"

Less interesting for Lou's grandson has been the uncovering of his grandfather's personal life. He married Lillie Linville, and the birth of their son, Robert Jr. (Buddy), followed shortly. Based out of Maryland, they were together ten years until Lillie presented an ultimatum: wrestling or family. "He said, 'I'll see you later' and he left.' My father didn't see him after that until 1953, the year I was born," said Bob Plummer. A subsequent marriage for Lou lasted just a year.

During World War II, Plummer served in the Coast Guard, wrestling around Baltimore until 1943 when he went overseas. "Lou Plummer, who has wrestled in Chicago and other main spots, hit the Sicily beach with the first amphibious landing craft, and claims to have taken the first Nazi flag there," the *Chicago Tribune*'s Arch Ward reported in April 1944. Plummer was honorably discharged in 1944, having suffered an eye injury. Adapting to regular life proved tough, and Plummer drank heavily. He married a third time, to a woman from Texas, and took to preaching as a southern Baptist minister.

"He's reported to have boomed his sermons to over 200,000 persons since he went into this work, which has changed him, incidentally, from a swashbuckling pro athlete to a devout man who does not even take coffee," reads *Wrestling Fan's Book* by Sid Feder. "As a sailor during the war, dark-haired

Lou was in the Mediterranean, and as a result of a naval action, he and six other men were adrift on a raft for fourteen days. . . . While they were praying for rescue, Lou vowed to preach the gospel if saved."

Plummer wrestled only sporadically in the years after the war, until "Dirty" Dick Raines came by the gas station where Plummer worked in Waverly, Texas, and convinced him that they would make a great tag team. By December 1952, they had dethroned Whipper Billy Watson and Pat Flanagan for the Canadian Open tag team title out of Toronto.

Plummer kept up both the wrestling and the sermonizing. "He was an easy-going guy. He liked to quote the Bible to you," said Sandy Scott, who battled Plummer in Calgary. "There was a story going around where he got stopped down in Toronto by the Ontario Provincial Police. He got out of his car, and walked up to the cruiser with his Bible, and started to quote the Bible. The officer just said, 'Hey, get back in your car, but just keep it down low. Don't speed.'" Scott also recalled a trick that Plummer used in the ring. "At times, he would be having a heart attack in the corner. You'd back off, and look at the referee. He'd grab you then, and start working on you."

By 1959, his wrestling career was over. He became heavily active in the Masons, and took to the golf course frequently. But Lou Plummer never did reconcile with his son, who didn't see him after 1953, though they talked a few times. His grandson is not exactly sure what happened at the conclusion of Lou Plummer's life, which ended September 22, 1985. He had been living in a trailer in Huntsville, Texas, as a virtual recluse. Bob Plummer isn't even sure who found the body or where his grandfather's possessions went. He and his father made one last attempt to see Lou Plummer in 1985. They were told not to come by Lou. "I'm dying. I don't want you to see me like this. I'm ashamed of myself," he apparently said.

DICK RAINES

Officially, there is no master ledger of wrestling disqualifications. But "Dirty" Dick Raines claimed he earned his nickname because of the hundreds of times he got the thumb. Few opponents would doubt him. Raines was a top villain for three decades, a certified brawler whose knowledge of conflict was so exhaustive that even his country would tap into it during World War II. "I must have wrestled him fifty times in the Georgia territory. He was a hell of a card," said southern star Tom Drake. "Just a big ol' Texas cowboy — that's what he represented."

Though closely identified with Texas, Charles Richard Raines was born in Muskogee, Oklahoma, on February 17, 1911. He was one of five children

— four boys and a girl. His brothers spelled their surname "Rains," but Dick decided it looked better with an "e," his daughter Charnelle Vanaman recalled.

At seventeen, he got into the grappling business by taking on all comers at carnivals, and it didn't take him long to establish a reputation for violence. When he was nineteen, he started in Los Angeles for Billy Sandow, and in April 1931, just after Raines' twentieth birthday, he worked a bloody melee with Joe Malcewicz that the *Los Angeles Times* called "one of the roughest bouts put on here in a long time." He quickly hit the top, squaring off in his first few years as a pro against champions such as Jim Londos,

"Dirty" Dick Raines.

Canada's Sports Hall of Fame / Turofsky Collection

Orville Brown, and Ed "Strangler" Lewis, and even taking two straight falls from a young Lou Thesz in Evansville, Indiana, in 1935. Raines also became known for his devastating over-the-knee backbreaker; in ranch-clearing spirit, he claimed the idea came to him when he was breaking branches for a fire. If he did not invent the hold, he was its most famous practitioner, and state athletic commissions regularly "barred" the crippling maneuver. "'Dirty' Dick Raines, he was a rough-and-tumble guy," recalled long-time star Enrique Torres, who squared off with him. "But he was a good wrestler."

Weighing in at 240–250 pounds, with garb that looked like he just dismounted his steed, Raines was the first, great, scufflin' Texas cowboy. He had all the heinous tricks down pat — a standard match involved a liberal dose of elbow smashes, kicks, gouges, and punches — even in Texas, where he was sometimes a local hero. Typical was a 1939 match against popular Don McIntyre, whom Raines dispatched with a backbreaker, while tossing chairs at the referee, and goading spectators in "a histrionic performance worthy of a Barrymore," according to the *Mankato Free Press*.

That year, Raines won his first major title, the Hawaii heavyweight crown, on his way to becoming one of the first major American wrestling exports to Australia and New Zealand. "Dick was the most 'unpopular' wrestler ever to visit New Zealand," said long-time New Zealand wrestling journalist Dave

Cameron. Raines made thirteen trips to Australia, and, during his first tour there in 1939, introduced the backbreaker and bulldozing headlock to New Zealand, Cameron said. "Some of the advance publicity which preceded Dick's visits to Australia and New Zealand announced: 'Mothers! Hide your children! You hombres had better quit town! Real trouble is looming.'"

In fact, Raines was a big, fun-loving fellow, according to his daughter. "He was a character. He loved people. He loved the limelight. He was a ham," Vanaman recalled with a laugh. He was just as big a ham in New Zealand as at home. During his trips to Auckland, he stayed with good friend and frequent rival Ken Kenneth, and accompanied Kenneth and his daughter on morning drives to school. Years later, Cameron interviewed Kenneth's daughter, who remembered that Raines had to lie down in the back seat of the car "so the kids didn't see them together after the previous night's radio broadcast."

In January 1943, Raines left wrestling to enlist in the U.S. Army, where he helped to write a hand-to-hand combat book, and taught judo and karate at stations in Washington, D.C.; Georgia; Washington state; and Texas until March 1946. He faced his biggest challenge later that year. In a September match in San Antonio, Charro Azteca tried to use Raines' trademark back-breaker against him. Raines took a bad bump and fractured his pelvis. "By the time he drove back to Dallas, he was paralyzed," his daughter said. "For the first few weeks, they told my mom that he wasn't going to live. He re-taught himself to walk. He refused to go back into the ring until he could go back into the ring with that guy who had broken his back." Sure enough, after a months-long absence, his first singles match was with Azteca in Houston on February 7.

Raines' top territory was in the upper Great Plains, where he practiced his brand of bedlam on and off virtually his entire career. In April 1952, he was disqualified in Winnipeg, Manitoba, for raking Rebel Russell's forehead across a rope, bloodying him, gouging at the blood, then ripping the shirt off referee Kostas Davelis. "That's what I get for fighting clean," Raines grumbled. "Imagine that, getting disqualified just 'cause Davelis panics when he sees a little blood." In 1954, he earned three disqualifications in Minneapolis, the territorial seat, in little more than two weeks. He was booted for hitting Bronko Nagurski with his lucky horseshoe, which led to a fifty dollar fine, and tossed against Pat O'Connor and Abe "King Kong" Kashey. In St. Paul, an infuriated fan stabbed him in the chest with a penknife. "He was tough as hell. He could handle himself. He didn't worry about anybody getting in the ring and working him over because he could hold his own with anybody," Drake said. "But he was personally a nice fellow. I thought a lot of him."

Kashey was Raines' favorite opponent, and the two ran a heel-versus-heel program as part of wrestling's roughest feud from the 1930s to the 1950s. "The territory only had room for one man to claim being the roughest and toughest, so whenever Raines was booked against Kashey, their ensuing bouts were all-out wars," said historian James C. Melby, who saw the two fight in Minneapolis. In a 1952 match in Winnipeg, Raines and Kashey combined to rip the bottom rope from its moorings and shred referee Wally Karbo's shirt. During the bout, Raines twice snatched a handful of hair from Kashey's chest and threw it to the mat. "It was a Pier-8 brawl of the first order that had the crowd in an uproar from start to finish," wrote Maurice Smith of the *Winnipeg Free Press.* "Eventually, Raines, who had an advantage in both height and weight, proved to be the superior of the two ring ruffians," concluded Melby, author of *Gopherland Grappling.*

With fellow heel Lou Plummer, Raines also captured the Canadian Open tag team title in 1952, and continued to wrestle regularly through 1957, with a few appearances on and off after then. In retirement, he became a referee in Texas and promoted in Waco. Eventually, arthritis and the pains of a lifetime of hard work caught up with him. Raines died at sixty-eight in October 1979. "The last two years, he was just very, very feeble. Every step he took was immense pain," Vanaman said. "But he never regretted anything. I know he really enjoyed his life."

IVAN RASPUTIN

In early twentieth century Russia, Rasputin was a controversial "Mad Monk," known for his rise to power in the Romanov court after he allegedly healed the hemophiliac son of Tsar Nicholas II. In the squared circle, Ivan Rasputin was doing anything but healing opponents.

Ivan Rasputin was Hyman Fishman, one of the first wrestlers to adopt a Cossack or Russian persona in the pre-Cold War days. Until 1955, when his health forced him into retirement, Rasputin filled a top spot in virtually every territory with his rowdy tactics and a physique that took on the attributes of a "human hair brush," in the words of Frank Moran, a sportswriter from Lowell, Massachusetts.

Fishman had legitimate Russian credentials; his parents were Jewish immigrants from the Ukraine who fled to Massachusetts to escape an intense outbreak of anti-Semitic violence. He was born June 3, 1912, in Chelsea, Massachusetts, and grew up there and in nearby Revere Beach. Known for his speed and upper body strength, Fishman wrestled at a local YMCA and

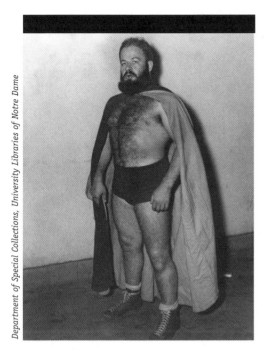

Ivan Rasputin.

gravitated toward football in high school, but also got in his share of non-sanctioned scuffles because of his ethnicity.

"He met someone that promoted wrestling around the area," his daughter Merle Askeland recalled. "He told Dad that if he was going to fight all the time anyway, he might as well get paid for it. So, he took the name of Max Fishman and wrestled in outdoor matches for cash when he was still in high school."

Under his real name, Fishman wrestled in New York City in early 1935, but soon underwent a wrestling makeover during an inspection by noted Columbus, Ohio promoter Al Haft. "He said, 'We need a new image for you, if you want to make money,'" Askeland said. "He questioned my dad about his heritage and looked at him — hairy and barrel-chested — and said, 'I've got it.' Hence, Ivan the Terrible. My mom made him a velvet cape with a bear on the back and that was it."

In his new guise, Rasputin became a holy terror on the mats. Implied in his promotional literature was a thinly veiled allusion to the original Russian Mad Monk. "From this sinister figure does Ivan spring. His appearance doesn't belie the stories either told of him or his depredating ancestor," the *Charleston Daily Mail* observed shortly after his transformation. His appearance only added to the spectacle. Rasputin "is so hairy that someone must have dropped a bottle of hair tonic on him when he was a baby," joked sportswriter Jack Singer of the *Los Angeles Times*.

In the ring, Rasputin was a crouching powerhouse with a low center of gravity and one of the foremost practitioners of the bearhug finishing maneuver. "Ivan was a very good performer," former champion Lou Thesz recalled for WrestlingClassics.com.

In 1938, Rasputin took the Pacific Coast title from Sandor Szabo, whom he later called his "most despised" opponent. The burly bruiser was in demand around in the country, wrestling high-level events in California, the Midwest, Buffalo, Columbus, and elsewhere, using his fists, feet, and, photos reveal, even his teeth as weapons. "The public wants action and blood," he confessed to Ralph Postlewaite, a friend who wrote for the *Mansfield News-Journal* in Ohio. "The boys give it to them."

In 1946, Rasputin broke his back in a match against Leo Numa in Boston. "He left, showered, got in the car to go home and couldn't get out," his daughter said. A Boston physician repaired the injury with a prototype treatment now known as a spinal fusion. "That doctor also delivered me so I know the story well. My dad went to pay him for me and the doctor said, '$100.' My dad gave it to him, and the doctor turned to my mom, and said, 'Here, Sybil, go buy yourself a new dress.'"

Rasputin quit wrestling for a while to launch an antique business in Arcadia, California, but family members knew his heart was not in it when they unexpectedly found a Going Out of Business sale sign on the door one day. He re-entered the ring, centering his work mostly in and around Chicago, where he became nationally known via televised wrestling shows. He also toned down his image a bit in light of harsh anti-Soviet feeling after World War II. The Russian bear robe disappeared from his getup, replaced by a red velvet jacket with his name embroidered in gold. "I used to like to try to rile the crowd into charging the ring to try to take me apart in years gone by. But now I'm satisfied just to bring the people to their feet and let them cool down quickly," he told the *Troy Record* in 1949. He even had cameo roles in two movies: *Mighty Joe Young*, and *Friendly Persuasion*. But an easier-going guise was not enough to prevent fans from screaming for his blood. Rasputin took a monkey wrench to the noggin in March 1950, from an irate fifty-eight-year-old watchman in Joliet, Illinois. He had to be carted out of the ring while an attendant sewed his scalp together.

Rasputin wrestled his last match in 1955, when he lost his license because of high blood pressure that doctors feared could lead to a heart attack. The Rasputin gang moved to California, where he ran a couple of liquor and grocery stores. In retirement, he and his wife bought a travel-trailer and the two roamed the country until Rasputin was diagnosed with deadly skin cancer. He died in 1976. "My father was a very warm, lovable, cuddly man despite his persona," Askeland said fondly. "We used to tell our friends he was really mean and would beat us often, and then giggle."

FREDERICH VON SCHACHT

Sometimes, a wrestler can take his character a little too far. Witness the case of Herr Frederich Otto Von Schacht, a.k.a. Frank Altinger of Milwaukee, Wisconsin, one of the earliest of wrestling's hard-hitting German bootjacks. In spring 1939, more than two years before the United States entered World

War II, Von Schacht transformed his glowering Prussian gimmick into that of an overt Nazi. A year later, as Adolf Hitler's army was overrunning western Europe, Von Schacht entered the ring in Philadelphia, wearing a cape bearing an Iron Cross and delivered a Nazi salute. Police rescued him from a mob attack, and a chair aimed at the German missed him and stunned a judge instead.

A week later, fans in Kansas City mistook Von Schacht's Iron Cross as a swastika and rioted after he was disqualified against Bobby Bruns. Von Schacht retreated to the safety of the dressing room and refused to return for the third fall, while the ring announcer soothed tensions by declaring Von Schacht was Milwaukee-bred, and not Hitler's grappling emissary. So, a few days later, when Gust Karras, the promoter for St. Joseph, Missouri, touted the wrestler as "the Nazi

Frederich Von Schacht.

blitzkrieger," Von Schacht, with fifteen extra policemen stationed at ringside, saw fit to inform the house he was "an American and proud of it."

After that, Von Schacht's allegiance to the Third Reich was more muted, but it certainly didn't detract from a long and remarkably successful career spent maddening fans and causing trouble for wrestling's top heroes. Beverly Altinger, wife of Jack Altinger, Von Schacht's nephew who wrestled as Jackie Allen, recalled that she and her beau had to avoid close association with "Uncle Fred."

"He used to stop and pick us up, and take us to Chicago when he was wrestling. We never went in with him. He always had bodyguards and everything because people hated him so because of that swastika on his cape. So we would go in later like we didn't know him," she said. "With his bald head, and he was just a big man, and, of course, back then during the war in the '40s, they hated him."

Chuck Thornton Collection

Altinger learned how to wrestle at a Milwaukee YMCA and developed his physique hoisting barrels at a local brewery. A powerhouse for his era at about six-foot-four and 240–250 pounds, he first appeared under his own name around 1932. In 1935, he became Hans Schacht for legendary promoter and gimmick-maker Jack Pfefer, and morphed into Frederich or "Fritz" Von Schacht when he changed his base of operations to Chicago in 1938.

Whatever his exact billing, he was a born mauler who developed a reputation for his in-ring abilities and showmanship. "I had a talk with Frederich Von Schacht and have him lined up to come in when you want him," Columbus, Ohio promoter Al Haft wrote Pfefer in 1940. "He is ready money and will help you a lot as he is big and a great worker. Let me know. He works sensational shows with [Orville] Brown and Bruns."

Von Schacht roiled tensions even after he toned down the Hitler salute. Still advertised as a former Bavarian storm trooper, he provoked a riot in Los Angeles in December 1940 for attacking Bobby Managoff during an intermission. "In an instant, the ring was crawling with customers, all of whom were bent on shoving somebody else at the Teuton, and ringside was a sea of enraged humans," said Al Wolf of the *Los Angeles Times*.

Ironically, Von Schacht would figure in the battle between the Allied and Axis powers. In 1942, he enlisted as an assistant in the medical corps in the U.S. Army, serving in England and Michigan until 1945. While in service, he even wrestled a few pro matches as Sergeant Fritz Von Schacht, dutiful American solider. After the war, "The Prussian Crusher" continued as a contender against all the top champions of his day, such as Frank Sexton, Lou Thesz, and Bill Longson. "His own reach appears unlimited — and he owns a perpetual sneer, and looks at his opponents in the ring like he was not only going to take 'em apart, but to also eat them up," *Pittsburgh SportsWeek Magazine* said. In 1947, he even taught a heinous trick or two to a young fan favorite named Fred Blassie. "Fred Von Schacht, towering smooth-dome, beat a hasty retreat to the showers past fist-swinging fans after trashing Fred Blassie something horrible to win with a chinlock and head smash," reported *The Globe and Mail* of Toronto.

In 1950, Von Schacht beat Ronnie Etchison for the Pacific Coast Heavyweight title. That year, he also held the San Francisco version of the world tag team title twice, once each with Ray Eckert and Tom Rice. Even in the twilight of his career, he combined with Verne Gagne in 1952 to set an attendance record in Milwaukee (12,800 fans) that stood for thirty years.

Von Schacht — he legally changed his name from Altinger — moved to Florida in 1951, and wrestled until 1954. For many years, he operated a motel on Treasure Island, and remained in the state until his death in 2001 at age ninety. "He was like a pussycat. He was so different. You'd never know he was the same man that went in the ring like that. He was a sweetheart," Beverly Altinger said.

GEORGE ZAHARIAS

Courtesy Wrestling Revue Archives

George Zaharias.

We probably know more about George Zaharias' love life than any other heel in wrestling history. His wife, Mildred "Babe" Didrikson, who many call the greatest woman athlete in history, once was asked what the most thrilling moment of her life was. Babe didn't mention her Olympic medals or golf trophies, but quipped, "The first night I slept with George."

They met in January 1938, when they were part of a threesome for the Los Angeles Open golf tournament. Photographers crowded around the odd trio — Presbyterian minister C. Pardee Erdman would best them that day — and Zaharias, ever the showman, put a few holds on Didrikson. He didn't let go until her death in September 1956.

"I bought this diamond, you know, a two-carat ring, and I said to her, 'This will make some girl happy.' Babe laughed and said, 'That would make *me* happy," recalled Zaharias in the Didrikson biography *Whatta-Gal!* They lived together in St. Louis, and eventually found enough time together to get married on December 23, 1938 in the home of St. Louis wrestling promoter Tom Packs. George arranged their honeymoon for April; they took a boat to Australia where he had some wrestling matches, and Babe did golfing demonstrations. The new couple turned a profit from their honeymoon.

The practicality of Zaharias' honeymoon was a result of growing up dirt-poor in Pueblo, Colorado, where his Greek parents had settled, and worked for a rancher. George was the oldest child, born Theodore Vetoyanis on February 28, 1908. He helped raise his siblings before working on a farm, and a steel mill near home. In Oklahoma City, he lived with an uncle, and learned hat-cleaning and shoe shining.

Zaharias had an acute case of wanderlust that would stay with him all his life, and ended up in Columbus, Ohio, where he trained for a couple of years under Al Haft, going from a hefty 265 pounds to 235. "After one year, I still knew nothing about wrestling. I hadn't earned a quarter, but I had earned this big cauliflower ear," Zaharias wrote in an article for SPORT magazine in 1949.

After his in-ring debut in South Bend, Indiana in 1928, Zaharias floundered as a babyface until he turned heel in 1930 in Memphis, Tennessee. He proved to be a natural coward, and was soon known as "The Crying Greek from Cripple Creek," a town forty miles from Pueblo.

Zaharias would cheat to his heart's content, but when his foe would rise up and fight back, George would cower in the corner, pleading and trembling, begging for sympathy as tears ran down his cheeks. It was melodrama at its finest. The *Chicago Tribune* called him "the foremost ham of this grappling art" and famed scribe Shirley Povich of *The Washington Post* once wrote: "Zaharias could hire out as a nightmare, himself, if he chooses to put on his best fighting face."

At his peak, Zaharias was one of the top names in the business, perhaps second only to Jim Londos in the 1930s in national name recognition in the grappling world. Two younger brothers, "Onion Head" Chris and Tom, and a nephew, Chris Davelis, helped propagate the Zaharias name (Greek for sugar) as Babe Zaharias. There was a natural rivalry with the Duseks, the other family kings of roughhousing. "George Zaharias once told me he had four lasting injuries sprinkled about his body, each one named after one of the Dusek brothers," wrote Dick Patton.

Besides backing his wife's golfing career — Zaharias supported Didrikson as an amateur golfer, and is credited with being one of the architects of the LPGA golf tour, which she started with Fred Corcoran — he also promoted wrestling in Los Angeles at the Olympic Auditorium. He moved to Denver in 1945 to run the matches there. He participated in many money-making schemes, including a pro football team in San Diego, a Beverly Hills custom clothing store, a Tampa golf course, and a Denver hotel. "[George] was kind of headstrong, and pinched pennies to the point that he would make people unhappy up and down the road," Lou Thesz said in 1999. "He always wanted a little extra something for nothing. And anytime you go to dinner with George, you know who's gonna pick up the tab . . . not George."

Stopping wrestling made his weight balloon — Zaharias eventually had a fifty-two-inch waist — and he developed a diabetic condition in 1954. Babe would joke, "When I married him, he was a Greek god, now he's nothing

George Zaharias chows down at a 1953 golf tournament with his wife, Babe Didrikson.

but a goddamn Greek."

After Didrikson died of cancer in 1956, Zaharias was at loose ends. Though their marriage was tempestuous at times, they stuck together despite the constant demands of travel. Their lifestyle on the road eliminated any possibility of adopting children. The Crying Greek remarried to a nurse in 1960, but it didn't last. In November 1966, he wrote promoter Jack Pfefer that while his health was improving, Babe's loss still weighed heavily on him. "I can't go in the boxes for Babe's pictures now. I mean the Vodka Kid as you named her. I don't want to open up the scrap books now, so let it go." Zaharias suffered a stroke in 1974 and was confined to a wheelchair. He died May 22, 1984 in Tampa.

Andrea Kellaway

In a quiet moment, George "The Animal" Steele shows off his induction ring from the Pro Wrestling Hall of Fame.

The Madmen

"KILLER" TIM BROOKS

Steven Johnson

Killer Tim Brooks chokes Billy Red Lyons.

In Detroit in 1972, the most familiar position for the clean-cut, twenty-five-year-old Timmy Brooks was back to the mat, staring up at the lights. However, having paid his dues over the previous four years, he disappeared for a few weeks, grew out his hair, and came back as "Killer" Tim Brooks. Under the tutelage of The Sheik (Ed Farhat), Brooks developed into one of the toughest SOBs that ever created havoc in the ring.

With long, scraggly hair on a balding head, an unkempt beard, and leather jacket draped over a six-foot-one, 240–260-pound frame, Brooks portrayed someone who could be just as comfortable in a barroom brawl as a wrestling bout. "I think I had a rugged look, with the tattoos, the beard, the long hair. I was a fighter, I was not a technician," Brooks explained. "I was a furniture mover, a fighter. I think what the people liked about me, when they knew I was going to have a match, it was going to be a fight. It was going to be chaos. It was going to be wild. It wasn't going to be your average wrestling match. Also, I think they knew I was going to take it to that babyface's ass."

Unlike his cousin, Dick Murdoch, Tim Brooks took his time getting into pro wrestling. Sure, they were close growing up, often wrestling on a mat with their uncle Farmer Jones in the backyard of his Texas home after the sun went down. But whereas Murdoch started refereeing by age fourteen, and followed in his father Frankie Hill Murdoch's steps as a wrestler shortly thereafter, Brooks didn't get into the mat wars until after a stint in the army from 1963 to 1966. Brooks was a member of the Military Police. "We went into a lot of bars, and whorehouses, and such, and broke fights up. I don't know if it prepared me [for wrestling], but it got me being active in a rough kind of way. The real craziness came in wrestling, not in the army."

Brooks didn't think wrestling was for him. He was in Amarillo, Texas, for his aunt's funeral when Murdoch made an interesting proposal. "When the funeral was over, Dick said, 'Why don't you come and travel with me and go to a few shows? We can drink some beer and have some fun,'" recalled Brooks. Every night, the wrestlers would show him a few skills.

His first match was in Odessa, Texas, in 1969, and he had to be convinced by Murdoch and Terry Funk to replace a no-show. "They said, 'We'll take care of you.' The most famous words in wrestling," laughed Brooks, remembering the fifteen-man battle royal. "They just beat the hell out of me, man, and threw me over the top rope. That was my first match. That was my beginning."

By the early '70s, Brooks had made it to Detroit and settled in. It was a good location to find work in Michigan, Ohio, West Virginia, Ontario, and Quebec, and even WWWF TV in Hamburg and Philadelphia. He may not have been on top, but he was learning.

Farhat is the guy who really schooled Brooks. "He was my father in pro wrestling. He gave me my first break," Brooks said. "He helped because he showed me, he taught me, he made me watch his matches, he talked to me." Later in his stay in Detroit, Brooks became The Sheik's tag team partner, which propelled him up the card to face top names like Bobo Brazil, Tex McKenzie, and Pampero Firpo.

When 1976 came along, Brooks decided to hit the road again. "You can only stay in a territory for so long. When I was The Sheik's partner, I would be the guy to lose and do the jobs. Once you do so many jobs, you need to move on somewhere else because the people know that that's what is going to happen."

Brooks felt he had the skills to be a major figure in any promotion. "My strength was being capable of going out on a card and I could get heat. I don't care who was on the card, or where it was . . . my time being with The Sheik made me capable of going out, and following a lot of matches, and getting heat when there were good people on the card, good heels."

After returning to Amarillo for a stint (returning to Texas would become a regular trend), Brooks went to Calgary for Stampede Wrestling. "I can say nothing but good things about the guy," said "Cowboy" Dan Kroffat, who battled Brooks over the North American title. "Easy to work with. He even had a look about him that was far out there. In some ways, he didn't even look like a wrestler; he looked like a coal miner." Brooks also had great success in Japan — often teaming with Bruiser Brody — and in Georgia, where he famously sold the National title to Larry Zbyszko after beating Paul Orndorff.

In Portland, Oregon, Brooks dominated the territory with Roddy Piper, once memorably bringing out a wheelbarrow full of title belts on TV. It's also the place where the wild life really took over. "Bruiser Brody was probably my biggest friend in wrestling, but Roddy was really a good friend. I enjoyed the time that I spent around Roddy Piper. We had fun in our apartment that we shared. We traveled together and had fun on the road. We had fun in the ring as a tag team. We just enjoyed everything we were doing," Brooks said. "That took plenty of time off my life! If I die tomorrow, I'll blame it on Roddy Piper."

Today, Brooks can recognize the errors of his ways. "There was an outlaw in me, and I didn't always do what everybody wanted me to do. I'll be the first to admit that I don't do drugs anymore, but I had a drug problem. That didn't help me, you know what I mean? Drugs didn't do anything for me. It hurt me. Sometimes people can be their own worst enemy, cut their nose off to spite their face, jump out of the fucking skillet into the fire." His drug of choice? "I didn't have a drug of choice. I did everything, all different kinds of drugs. I never did inject any drugs, but I swallowed, snorted, smoked."

Dutch Savage was one of those promoters who had a rough time with Brooks and Piper. "They did a lot of toot together," Savage said, explaining that their temperament changed when high. "It's like a dynamite keg all the time. You had to walk around them with kid gloves."

As a booker, manager, and friend, Gary Hart saw all the sides of Brooks. "Killer Brooks had a tremendous drug problem. You name it, he took it," Hart said. "He was a complete and total druggie in every way. My rule with Tim was, do not get high before the matches. I don't care what you do after the matches, as long as your name don't get in the newspaper or on the radio, you do what you want. But of that generation, there were quite a few guys that were doing Quaaludes, cocaine, marijuana, acid, like the rest of the world."

A family crisis forced him to clean up after twenty-five years of drug abuse. Both Brooks and his second wife had a drug problem, and squealed to authorities on each other, while filing for divorce. The court ordered them to clean up, or give up their two sons, aged five and six months. Brooks checked into a veteran's hospital and had a sixty-day lock-up that got him dry; then had a six-month stay for "mental hygiene." Both he and his wife cleaned up, and went back to court, where the judge sent them to his chambers with instructions to reconcile if they wanted their sons out of protective services. "I guess we talked about twenty minutes. We came back out, and told the judge that we wanted to make a go of our marriage, we wanted to stay together, and most of all, we wanted our children back," recalled Brooks. "My boys were there within an hour, and the judge released us."

Today, one of those sons is learning the ropes at his father's wrestling school in Waxahachie, Texas. Though Brooks now works a regular job, setting up and taking down displays at trade shows, he says, "There is life after wrestling. It's not the same, but there is life." It seems impossible for him to get completely get away from wrestling. "It's in your blood, brother. You can't get the sickness out. It's in your blood. It's called the wrestling disease."

BULLDOG BROWER

Courtesy Wrestling Revue Archives

As wild as Bulldog Brower might have been — eyes bulging out of his skull as he swung shovels at pregnant women, clobbered opponents with folding chairs, fought off fans, police and security, or pulled out a pistol to protect a colleague — to his son it's the PTA meetings that stand out. "He'd be the complete center of attention when we got to the PTA meetings. He'd get there, and it's 'Whoa, there's Bulldog.' Heads would turn, and there's my dad in a $2,000 suit, when everybody else is dressed in blue jeans and T-shirts," recalled Richie Gland, one of three of

The wild side of Bulldog.

Brower's children. "He liked being a star. My dad really liked being famous," explained one of his daughters, Marcie.

"He was a great father. He actually went to court and won his kids from his wife. That's pretty awesome when you think of the reputation that he had as a tough guy on TV," said Johnny Powers. "I watched him in my territory watch over those kids like a damn protective mama dog for her brood."

After his divorce from their mother, Susan, in 1975, to make the family situation work Brower — born as Richard Gland — settled his three kids in Delaware, where he grew up. That was his third, and last, marriage. His winter schedule would take him away from home for extended stays, but family members (or the occasional girlfriend) filled in the void at home. When daughter Marcie was old enough, she took over the household. Then when school was out, all three pups would travel with Bulldog.

"Every summer, we'd meet different wrestlers. You'd meet so many good friends, then the summer ends, and you're gone, and never see them again," said Marcie Gland, recalling, in particular, friendships with the children of Afa and Sika Anoa'i.

Time on the road allowed them to see a lot of Dad's pranks. "My dad used to get really, really good tans. He really turned black. I remember him telling someone that it was Coca-Cola over his body. I remember all these girls spreading Coca-Cola all over their bodies. They'd be sticky, with bees coming up around them for an hour or so, while he laughed at them," said Marcie. But he did it at home too. "He was pretty laid-back at home. He pulled the odd thing on me," said Richie. "He rearranged the wires in my car, so when I went to start my car, I couldn't figure out what was wrong with it. He'd be in the background, laughing his ass off." Richie launched into another story. "He actually caught me and a girlfriend of mine in her car. I was wondering why the car was going up and down a little bit too fast, and it's him going, 'Come on boy! Go boy!' I'm going, 'Jeez.' My dad had a weird sense of humor." Brower also ran with a couple of Delaware motorcycle gangs, but hated motorcycles; it was more about hanging out with friends and fellow tough guys.

Brower was born in Wilmington, Delaware, in 1933. As a health-conscious young adult who frequented the local YMCA, he joined the Marines. His first marriage didn't outlast his time in the service. His second brought him to Toronto, where the wrestling bug really caught him. Initially working as the "Delaware Destroyer," he was dispatched to Calgary to learn his trade. "I broke him in here. He came out here when he was just a pup," Stampede promoter Stu Hart said in 1997. "Whipper Watson was out here working for me at the time and Whipper says, 'Who's that kid that you just had in the opening match there? Is there any chance of me borrowing him when you're finished with him?' I sent him down to Toronto then, and Bulldog Brower became a superstar. He wrestled Whipper Watson about 500 times. Watson got rich wrestling him."

Hart is not exaggerating. Brower and Watson hooked up dozens of times, and Brower cleared some serious coin very early in his career. "When he first came to Toronto and started making big bucks — $100,000 a year would be like $2 million now — so he was one of the boys that really got good paydays. It went to his head a little bit, but that was kind of normal," Powers said. "He had multiple personalities. He either liked you or he didn't. He harbored grudges," said Bruce Swayze.

Rene Goulet first worked with Brower in the Maritimes. "He was arrogant because at the time he was pretty close to Frank Tunney. He was the top guy at the Garden. He was cocky about that," said Goulet. "We're working and he told me to duck. He had a piece of a two-by-four like Jim Duggan used, and I thought he was going

The mild side of Bulldog.

to hit it like a baseball, sideways. But when I was bent over, he went down on my back. Oh man, he hurt my back, that son of a bitch."

Stints in Australia, the WWWF and the rebel International Wrestling Association promotion proved that Brower had the ability to work with just about anyone, provided they were willing to be hit by things. He was, after all, perhaps one of the best "furniture movers" in wrestling history. "He was actually quite talented. He threw one of the best elbows of all time. He could rare back and throw that right elbow perfectly — in my opinion, the best elbow to the jaw ever," said Powers.

Bulldog Brower was Bulldog Brower all the time. "He liked being a bad guy. He liked his image as a bad guy. He liked being the size, and a rough-house-type person," said Dewey Robertson. There are countless examples of Brower being interviewed on regular news shows, and reacting to a question with a mad rant, designed to protect the business and further terrify viewers. In London, Ontario, in 1961, a cameraman filming in studio for CFPL-TV laughed so hard at Brower's manic behavior that the Bulldog punched him, and tore up the studio. It resulted in the station going off the air for thirty minutes, and stopped the wrestler interview segment altogether.

The most famous Brower incident happened in 1972 in Boston. While working for the WWWF, Brower was the one who came out to save

Blackjack Mulligan who had been stabbed following a bout with Pedro Morales. Brower and Mulligan made it to the hotel adjoining the Boston Garden, and Bulldog flashed his pistol to scare off irate fans climbing the fire escape to get at Mulligan again. Brower then carried Mulligan to his car and drove him to New Jersey, where doctors put him on antibiotics.

Robertson attributed part of Brower's unpredictability to steroid use. "He wasn't a big muscled guy, but he was a big guy," said Robertson. Brower's son, Richie, confirmed that his dad used steroids for a time. "My dad had weak points in his life. At one point, he actually used steroids for a bit. . . . I remember seeing two of the bottles at home, and I remember seeing two of the syringes that he used. These vials were ten years old, and he just stopped using. He just realized it was stupid."

Yet to the average fan, Brower was a larger-than-life character that hooked them right in, and kept them coming back. "Bulldog Brower was one of the great old-time heels that made me want to get into the wrestling business," said TNA manager James Mitchell. He remembered an angle in the IWA in the Carolinas where Brower attacked Mighty Igor on his birthday, smashing Igor into the birthday cake, and strangling the puppy dog he'd received as a present. "The feud went on forever. 'Brower Power' indeed! It's a shame they don't make them like that anymore."

By the early '80s, Brower's career was virtually done, though he'd appear on the occasional show — Paul Heyman even brought him in to be honored on an early ECW event. His father was an ironworker in Local 451, and Brower kept his membership up throughout his wrestling career. He found himself a foreman in Delaware when he stepped on a nail. The doctor didn't realize how serious the wound was, and allowed him to go to Saudi Arabia for a wrestling tour. Brower was diabetic, and the wound never healed correctly. Gangrene set in, and he was flown back to the United States on the Concorde. "I picked him up at the airport, and I could smell it," said Marcie Gland. His foot was amputated. "That totally devastated him," said Marcie, adding that her father still tried to wrestle a few more times afterward.

For such a physical man, the amputation was tough. "He got a little bit depressed," said Richie. "He looked for different routes of outlet. He went to a church for a bit for a religious thing. He just one day said, 'God, they're a bunch of crooks' and just left that." During the last years of his life, Brower was on hemodialysis and that was the main part of his day. Once, while out with Richie, he fell and broke a hip. Doctors opened him up and found a huge infection in his chest. The madman known as Bulldog Brower went into a coma and never came out of it. He died September 15, 1997, at age sixty-four, after the family agreed to pull the plug.

PAMPERO FIRPO

Dory Funk Jr.'s greatest memory of Pampero Firpo is not in the ring, but from the road. "I made the most harrowing trip from the HIC Arena in Hawaii after wrestling there to the airport with Pampero Firpo driving. I feared for my life. He did get me to my flight at the airport on time. Man, the way he drove, I could not believe it!" said Funk Jr. "He was a wildman outside the ring, he was a wildman behind the wheel."

Pampero Firpo heads to the ring.

In the ring, Firpo, or "The Missing Link" as he was known in Hawaii, was equally unpredictable. His style was indeed that of a "Wild Bull of the Pampas," all action and strength, and little science. During his thirty-year career — 6,881 matches, twenty-one foreign countries, by his count — Firpo was a heel until the 1970s, with his frizzy, caveman hair, guttural roars, and smashed-up nose. And don't forget his little shrunken head named Chimu.

"In my situation, I had to be a bad guy," Firpo told *Ring Around the Northwest*. "For my style and my vocabulary, I think as a heel I was to be hated more than anyone else. When I switched to babyface the fans didn't know what to do. That is when you have complete control of two different personalities. Not too many people have that gift. I am not praising myself, just saying things I feel are true."

One of those heels who tried to get heat on the miscast babyface Firpo was "Killer" Tim Brooks, who worked with him in Detroit. Brooks learned to "stay on him hard, because a guy that looked like him, it was not easy to get heat on him because the people weren't going to feel sorry for a rugged guy, a rough-looking guy, they don't feel sorry for that guy easy. So a heel really has to put out to build heat on a guy like that."

Whether as a good or bad guy, Firpo's big move was his claw hold, *el garfio*, which went over an opponent's face. Firpo was ahead of his time with the catchphrases, and no doubt could have made a fortune in merchandising in today's WWE. "I weel take care of beez-nes!" he'd shout, his eyes sparkling with maniacal glee, and then end the interview with "It is I, it is me, Pampero

Rose Diamond

Paul Diamond and Firpo pose in 2001.

Firpo, the Wild Bull of the Pampas . . . OOOOOOOOH YEAH-HHHHHH!!!!"

Born Juan Kachmanian, in 1930 in Argentina, the son of a boxing promoter, he grew up around sports. Kachmanian was into boxing and track and field before being drafted into the army. He learned the basics of wrestling at home, and in August 1957, arrived in Texas, and found work with promoter Morris Sigel as "Ivan the Terrible," a name he'd use until the early '60s. Though his English was non-existent (but he would later speak seven languages), Firpo claimed the Texas title within three weeks. The tours of St. Louis, Chicago, and Nebraska all built him for his runs in the Northeast's Capitol Sports in the late 1950s and early 1960s, often battling his idol Antonino Rocca. He'd return to the New York rings as a formidable challenger during Pedro Morales' WWWF title run.

Firpo "wasn't a good mechanic or a good guy, wrestler-wise, but he was Pampero Firpo. He had a look about him that was believable," said Larry Hennig. Al Tomko said Firpo was stiff to wrestle. "He was a short but stocky guy, a hard guy to move around. He wasn't that easy to work with. He didn't take bumps or anything."

In Hawaii, Firpo became an institution, and his battle cry was imitated by the locals, as well as by "Macho Man" Randy Savage years later. "In Hawaii, after the governor, I was the most popular man," Firpo said. It was also where Firpo underwent life-saving surgery, where a foot-long perforated part of his intestine was removed. But it didn't stop his wrestling career, it just forced him to change his style.

"Firpo always told guys never hit him in the stomach or he'd die," recalled Jim Lancaster, who worked with Firpo in the mid-'70s around Detroit. "You'd get in the dressing room and we'd be talking over the match and he'd say, 'Jeem, you hit me in my stomach, I die. Don't hit me in my stomach; I die.' Then he'd start talking to you about some kind of surgery he had twenty years ago."

With its natural ties to the Pacific Coast territories of Los Angeles, San Francisco, and Oregon, Firpo would work regularly until the late 1970s, and occasionally until his final match in 1986. Mando Guerrero only worked with Firpo at the end of his career. "He had already had a heart operation, so he was using a lot of gimmicks to stay a heel, because he had the voice for it. But his body could not endure punishment anymore. He wouldn't get up for anybody. He wouldn't do no flying, no wrestling. It was just a bunch of fighting and scratching, so you had to use a lot of psychology with him."

Firpo recognizes that he wasn't an ordinary character that had a lot of longevity, even if he did. "I always have that heavy respect for the wrestling fan. Even if I make them upset, even if I make them angry, even if I make them applaud, because psychology is so important," he told *RATNW*. "I can cause a riot and I can cause peace to break out. Make it that way, you become a headliner. Now, in wrestling, you have four positions — preliminary, semi, special attraction, and then the main event. Above that, you have the Box-Office Attraction. I will tell you without hesitation and not any bragging that I believe I was the top one, the Box-Office Attraction. Wherever I went, I always was headlining."

Wrestling enabled Firpo to bring his family to America, which he considers his greatest accomplishment. After wrestling, he worked for the U.S. Post Office near his home in San Jose, California, though he is now retired and his hair is no longer as wild as it once was.

"CRAZY" LUKE GRAHAM

A little piece of tape went a long way for "Crazy" Luke Graham. One of his trademarks was a taped thumb — doctor's orders for an old injury, of course — that he jabbed into the throat of a helpless opponent. Georgia referee Bobby Simmons was a willing culprit during prematch instructions that helped to advertise Graham's gimmick. "When I would touch the thumb, he would flinch, like it was hurt, and I would flinch too, and he would explain it was very sore. Of course, ninety percent of his matches that he won he did by loading up the thumb and throwing a thrust to the throat, so it worked well for him and me too."

Graham was the younger "brother" of the famous pairing of Dr. Jerry and Eddie Graham. But, though he was billed as "Crazy Luke," he was probably the sanest member of the clan. Colleagues describe him as a quiet, soft-spoken Georgian, with a Colonel Sanders-style goatee that gave the impression he mistakenly wandered off the plantation grounds and into an arena. "He was a long way from crazy. Eddie and Jerry were crazy," said Newt Tattrie (Geeto

"Crazy" Luke Graham hears the crowd's taunts.

Mongol), who used Graham a lot when he promoted in Pittsburgh. "Good guy, good worker. You could never say anything wrong about Luke."

Born James Grady Johnson in Georgia, Graham was a big wrestling fan growing up, and fell in love with the brash and bloody Dr. Jerry. He broke in for Tony Santos in Boston in 1961 and was working as Pretty Boy Calhoun when Frankie Cain suggested he hook up with Jerry — then in Canada — because the two looked so much alike. After a good run in western Canada, the reconstituted Grahams entered New York in 1964, with Luke adopting the persona of a slightly touched, manic heel. "What got him over, especially in New York, was the other Graham partners. That's what got him over, and he had the crazy gimmick, shake his head, and things like that. He was a good deal," said veteran Rene Goulet.

The Graham combo won the WWWF U.S. tag titles, but Luke only stayed with Jerry for a couple of years before striking out on his own in 1965 as World Wrestling Association world champion in Los Angeles, where he swapped the belt with Pedro Morales. "It was time for me to be a singles wrestler. I always did a lot of tag team wrestling, but 'Crazy Luke' was probably better for singles wrestling," he said. The "crazy" angle worked like a charm too, as he grasped his ears in mock horror every time fans chanted "Crazy Luke, Crazy Luke."

Actually, Simmons said Graham had a droll, amusing sense of humor even when he was wrestling. In one small south Georgia venue, Graham was working with Ray Candy when he spotted a 400-pound rowdy sitting by himself in a back row of chairs. Graham broke into his madman ritual and started shrieking at him. The spectator yelled back, and, little by little, worked his way to ringside, where Graham, in full crazy mode, sat down on the middle rope and invited the guy into the ring.

"I walked over and said, 'Excuse me, this is really none of my business yet, but it could become my business — would you tell me what we're going to do if this big sucker comes in here?'" Simmons recounted. "And he turned and looked at me, just as serious as he could be. 'If he does, let's make sure you and me don't have a double knockout when we're going out the other side.' That's the kind of guy he was, just fun-loving, easy to work with, and just a pleasure to be around."

Graham wrestled regularly in the WWWF in the 1960s and 1970s, heading off to places like California, Hawaii, and Georgia, before returning for a good run at the top in the Northeast. He had another championship team with Tarzan Tyler — Goulet and Karl Gotch finally ended their reign in 1971 — and later worked with younger "brother," Billy Graham. Crazy Luke Graham Jr. said Graham's wild-eyed antics and facial expressions set a benchmark for later wrestlers like Lonnie Mayne and George Steele. "He was part of a group of guys that don't get all the appreciation they deserve. Even if people didn't remember who Luke Graham was, he was part of the first family of professional wrestling. There was a chemistry there that was mimicked. He could work with just about anybody, and make them look good, and get over himself in many different territories," Graham Jr. said.

Dean Silverstone used Graham as U.S. champion in his Pacific Northwest promotion in 1974 and recalled a rib that Graham good-naturedly accepted. The promotion paid for his plane ticket from Atlanta to Seattle and promised him $1,200 for his work. "He arrived with thirty-three cents in his pocket, so someone told him that this office pays off one week after the event takes place," Silverstone said. Graham panicked and started borrowing spare change from wrestlers and fans. "After his final show, he came into the office and asked if he could get currency for his twenty-plus-something dollars he had begged for in coins. His pockets were pulling his pants down. I remember his face when we paid him off his guarantee, but I made him keep his coins. Luke was a great worker."

Graham retired in the late 1980s, though later he managed and teamed with Luke Jr. In 2001, they attempted to build a national, publicly traded company named Galaxy Championship Wrestling, but that effort wasn't successful. A life of hard living on the road eventually caught up to him. He had a pacemaker installed, but died of congestive heart failure in June 2006 at sixty-six. "He was a man who, if you knew him, you couldn't help but be in awe of him — a real caring, sensitive type of guy that never took himself too seriously in the later years," said Luke Jr.

KING CURTIS IAUKEA

Bob Leonard

King Curtis Iaukea introduces Larry Lane to a table in Stampede Wrestling.

The tales of King Curtis Iaukea are legion, and flow like fine-aged wine from his contemporaries. A notorious bleeder, partier, beach bum, and all-around mad-man with an unparalleled gift for storytelling on the microphone, he is impossible to forget. But today, he's waiting for his pigeons to come home.

"It's a hobby that I used to do as a kid. Now I'm retired and I've just got the beach, then I come back and fly my pigeons. It's our racing season," the seventy-one-year-old Iaukea explained from his home in Honolulu. Retired is a relative term, of course. He and his wife, Jeannette, still operate a beach concession stand on Waikiki beach, a catamaran business, and a carpet-cleaning business. "If you live in Hawaii, you need more than one job," joked Jeannette.

Iaukea still has a wonderful rippling cadence to his speech, rising and falling like the surf stirring over the rocky shoals before hitting the beach with a rush. It's easy to be drawn into his stories, just as it was easy for him to draw blood from both his own and his opponent's foreheads.

"I thought a little red brings in the green," Iaukea explained. But "Da Bull" was never one to do a "little" of anything, said Rick Martel, launching into a story about Curtis' fortieth birthday. They were wrestling in Wellington, and Curtis had brought his father to New Zealand for the matches. Having consumed more than his share of adult beverages, Iaukea stepped into the ring with Martel, and vowed to show the young punks in the dressing room how to properly "get juice" from a forehead. "Here comes the finish, and finally I hit him over the head with something," Martel recounted. "Then he goes [makes sound of cutting] right across. Ugh, man, it poured thick, real thick. Even Mark Lewin was disgusted. He fucking let him have it at the end. 'You son of bitch.' The front row just went 'Ewwwww.'

Here I am, I'm holding him, and it's going down my forearms. He's laughing. . . . That was his birthday that day, and he did it right."

That love of blood, though, led to the end of his active wrestling career and almost cost him his life. Iaukea contracted a nasty bug in Singapore in the late '70s. "I got a virus in through my cuts through the mats. It hit me right at the beginning of '79. I got to Japan, boom. Oh my God, nothing but a clear liquid coming out," he said. After recuperating in Hawaii, he gave it one last try in Florida, where he'd had a great run in 1976 against Dusty Rhodes. His friends couldn't believe the transformation of the six-foot-three, 280-pound madman. "One of the saddest things was after his illness in Florida, he was so weak that I had to help him up a small step at the Sportatorium on a visit to the office one day," said Sir Oliver Humperdink. "Such a huge man with an even bigger persona needing help to maneuver a rather small step."

Growing up in Hawaii, Curtis Iaukea was destined for great things. His grandfather served as a diplomat in the courts of King Kalakaua and Queen Lili'uokalani, and his father retired as a Honolulu police captain. It seemed that Iaukea would be a star on the gridiron. Out of high school, he ended up at the University of California at Berkeley, where he lettered in football in 1956 and 1957 as a 223-pound lineman. When he was a junior, he started wrestling on the side to make a few bucks. He elected to follow a coach to Vancouver to play for the Lions in the Canadian Football League rather than stay in school.

The rebellious life that he picked up at the ultra-liberal Berkeley influenced his decision to quit the CFL after two seasons. "In the meantime, wrestling is going, and I've got a contract with Japan. I got tired of fucking whistles blowing in my ears, brother! That's a hard way to make a buck."

A thirty-year pro wrestling career would follow, all thanks to the Lord — the Hawaiian institution and wrestling legend "Lord" James Blears, that is. "He changed my whole life around. I was a football player," said Iaukea. "The Lord met me when I was surfing, out on the water, when I was a senior in high school." His main trainer was another ex-football player, Joe Blanchard. "He was a good athlete and more. He was a natural. He was excellent and could have been better than he was too," said Blanchard, who would bring Iaukea to Indianapolis when he was booking there. "He got off on the wrong track and let himself get fat, and he got doing drugs and that kind of crap."

Iaukea is not one to shy away from touchy subjects like drugs. "That's just medicine for the mind. I came out of Berkeley, you've got to remember, bro! You've got to remember that I went to Berkeley in '55, when it all started

TOP: Ivan Rasputin works out in his own unique way.
BOTTOM: Lord Lansdowne signs a contract to face Lem Stecklin.

TOP: George Zaharias and his wife Babe Didrikson fulfill their household chores.

LEFT: Buddy Rogers interviews Gorilla Monsoon.

RIGHT: Gorgeous George's valet Jeeves atomizes the dressing room for germs.

RIGHT: Freddie Blassie is interviewed by Vince McMahon Jr.

LEFT: Don Fargo chokes Tex McKenzie.

BOTTOM: AWA tag champions Nick Bockwinkel, Bobby Heenan and Ray Stevens are escorted by Chicago's finest to the ring.

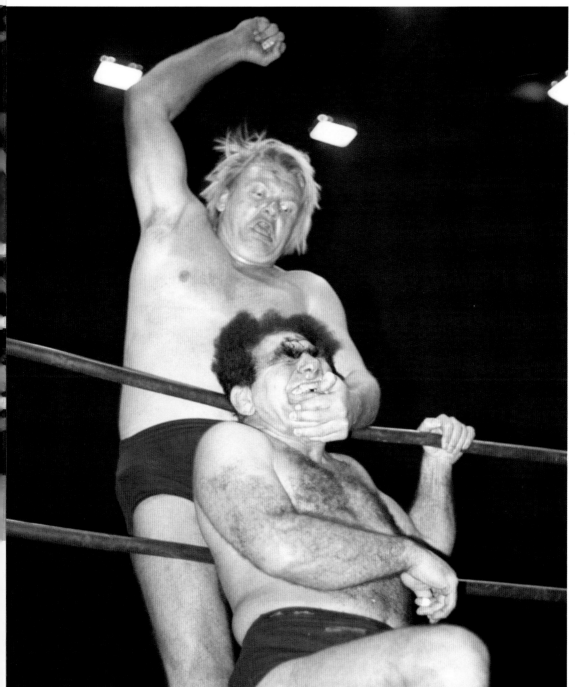

ABOVE: Johnny Valentine drops another hammer on Bull Curry.

RIGHT: "The Mongolian Stomper" Archie Gouldie.

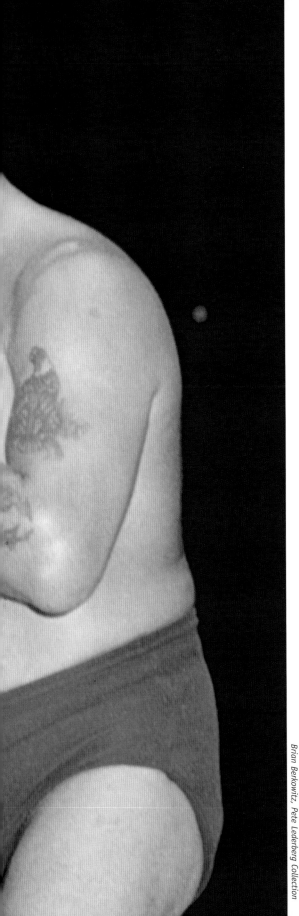

LEFT: Harley Race measures Wahoo McDaniel for another fist.

TOP: WCW World Champion Ric Flair in Japan.

ABOVE: Ernie Ladd makes his claim.

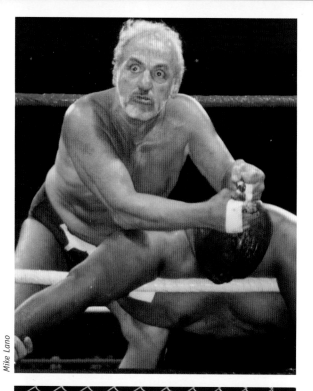

TOP: The Sheik carves into Abdullah the Butcher.

ABOVE: Blackjack Mulligan and The Masked Superstar
(Bill Eadie) wage war in a cage.

RIGHT: Curtis Iaukea crucifies "The American Dream"
Dusty Rhodes.

CLOCKWISE FROM TOP LEFT: Pat Patteron talks with Mark Henry backstage in the WWE; Stan "The Lariat" Hansen makes his noisy (and messy) way to the ring; The Spoiler (Don Jardine) tries out his claw hold on Adrian Street; Gorilla Monsoon interviews "Mr. Perfect" Curt Hennig.

Mike Lano

Mike Lano

OVE: Vince and Linda McMahon, and their daughter Stephanie and her husband Triple H at a screeing of HHH's flick *ide: Trinity*.

ABOVE: Randy Orton.

LEFT: NWA World champion Jeff Jarrett.

Mike Mastrandrea

ABOVE: Edge shows off his WWE championship before the 2006 Unforgiven pay-per-view.

Mike Lano

LEFT: Kane removes his mask.

BELOW: "Crazy" Chris Colt strangles J.L. Sullivan (a.k.a. Johnny Valiant).

Terry Dart

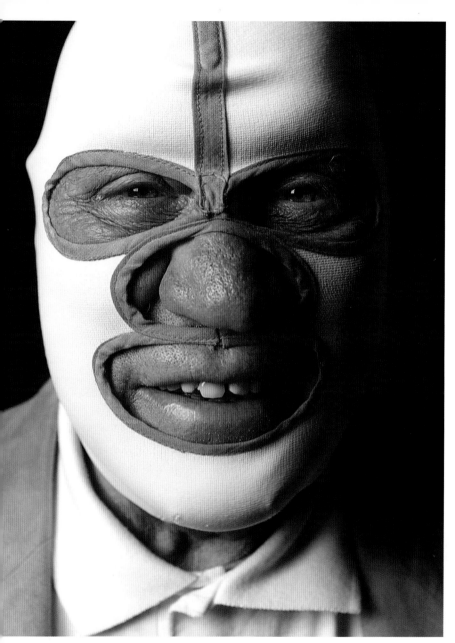

LEFT: The Destroyer (Dick Beyer) still masked in 2006.

BELOW LEFT: Terry Funk and Mil Mascaras at the Cauliflower Alley Club reunion in Las Vegas in April 2005.

BELOW RIGHT: Nikolai Volkoff, right, chats with old foe Bruno Sammartino.

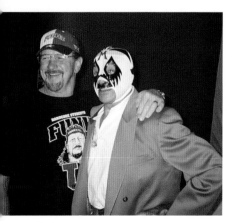

Mike Lano

Shuhei Aoki

LEFT: Newlyweds Killer Kowalski and Theresa Dodd.

BELOW: Bob Orton Sr. chats with Bill Kersten at the Cauliflower Alley Club reunion in Las Vegas in June 2006.

Greg Oliver

BOTTOM: Jake "The Snake" Roberts shows off his dental work in 2006.

Adrea Kellai

before the '60s. That's when Timothy Leary found the cookie, acid, yeah!"

A sixth sense allows Iaukea to anticipate the next question. "Did that help me in my interviews, you want to know?" Well, yes, that is the query. As decent as Iaukea was in the ring, his bulk masking a smooth athlete, and his big splash flattening opponent after opponent, he will be most remembered for his interviews. It's been more than "seven long years" since the world was blessed with his rambling, intense interviews, back to the camera, belt over the shoulder, the words rising like lava from a volcano. His shtick wasn't that different in Hawaii in the 1970s as it was as a manager in the WWF in the late-'80s.

The drugs may have helped, he admitted, but he never took them before a match. "Your timing is off. You're going to hurt the person you're with, and yourself. You really can't take it because of the paranoia, you can't take it before you go to work either, I mean, before you're cutting interviews — that's erroneous."

The booze flowed through his wrestling days too. Ivan Koloff lived in the same apartment complex as Iaukea on Bondi Beach in Australia, and said that Curtis encouraged him to drink wine when he was training, as a part of his diet, to help the flow of blood. "Curtis was turning me on to it because it would give us a buzz, right? He had himself a guy that was a friend of his that would bring a jug of it around every second day — or was it every morning? — and leave it at his door," recalled Koloff. "I remember every time we'd come in, he'd rap on my door. 'Come on, Ivan, time to have a glass of wine.' Of course, one glass of wine would lead into two or three. We'd laugh, and have a great time, and usually have a couple of the other boys over."

Australia was home to Iaukea for a long time. "King Curtis is probably the ultimate personality . . . In Australia, he was one of the great interviews at that time, and he was a talent in the ring as well. So he had it all," said wrestler and promoter Ron Miller. "Australians loaf around the beach anyway, and he's from Hawaii. There was a natural flow." Mark Lewin, Iaukea's best friend and the name with which he is most often implicated, was the booker for much of his time Down Under. "The wild days of Big Bad John and Thunderbolt Patterson. That was a wild bunch down there under Jim Barnett, oh my God. That went on for five, six years or so," said Curtis.

Though he held his share of titles and worked main events, Iaukea recognized that there was a shelf life for his act. "I know about the scorched earth, and all that stuff. I know my reputation and Mark Lewin's, because I read the jabroni sheets, right, every week. I'll tell you, they'd only use Lewin and I when they really needed to."

Gary Hart was one of those bookers who used Iaukea and Lewin, and despite their reputation, said they were a credit to the business. "There was no one like Curtis. Curtis was more than a main-event wrestler. Curtis was an attraction much like Andre the Giant, or Mad Dog Vachon, or George 'The Animal' Steele. I'm not saying that they were the same, but I'm saying that when you saw these guys, you said, 'Whoa, look at this!'"

Today, having battled a few health issues over the last few years, Iaukea is still a vibrant, jovial beach bum, who counts his lucky stars. "I used to pinch myself in the locker room, because when I was growing up, I used to sell papers outside the old Civic Auditorium. Sunday evening was the wrestling at eight o'clock. I can remember when I was eight, nine years old, and Hans Schnabel was the greatest heel here. I just died to see Hans Schnabel. [From him] I got that long, faraway look and the dragging of the leg."

And he owes it all to the Lord. "He changed my life all for the better," said Iaukea. "My first match, he took me in a tag team, and put me right on top with him. Boom! He'll tell you I'm the only one he knows that started in the main event and ended as one, in Dusty's arms in Miami. And I never won a match, bro."

What, are you saying that you are not a legend, Curtis? "Nah, far from it. I was just a good jabroni, brother. I put everybody over."

MOONDOG MAYNE

Chavo Guerrero Sr. gets silent for a moment, collecting his thoughts and reining in his emotions. He takes a deep breath and tells the story about being the last one to see "Moondog" Lonnie Mayne alive. They had just wrestled each other in the main event of a show in San Bernadino, California, on August 13, 1978. After showering, Guerrero headed out to the empty parking lot, and as he was pulling away in his car, he noticed Mayne nearby in his vehicle. "He turned the car and got out. He started puking, man. So I drove back and said, 'Hey, brother, you alright?' He said, 'Yeah, yeah, man, I'm just alright,'" said Guerrero, who waited for Mayne to get on the highway, and then passed him, waving goodbye.

No one knows exactly what happened next, but Mayne jumped the median and slammed into an oncoming car, killing the driver and Mayne. Guerrero and Mayne's family believe that he collapsed while at the wheel. Despite the wild tales of Mayne's lifestyle, they are adamant he was sober. "He wasn't drunk, I'll tell you that, because I saw it," said Guerrero. According to Shawn Mayne, Lonnie's younger brother, the autopsy showed that there had been internal bleeding, and low levels of alcohol, since he'd

Capt. Lou Albano tries to control Moondog Mayne.

had so much in his system from years of partying.

What Moondog Mayne left behind was a cadre of family, friends, and co-workers who light up when telling stories about him, a wife, Diana, and four children — not to mention the Los Angeles version of the U.S. heavyweight title, complete with a great big dent caused by a fan with a .22-calibre pistol only a few days before at the Olympic Auditorium. That belt now hangs in the home of Lonnie Mayne Jr.

The three sons of wrestler-turned-boxing promoter Kenny Mayne of Salt Lake City all wrestled professionally at one point, but it was Ronald Doyle "Lonnie" Mayne — born September 12, 1944, in Fairfax, California, and named after promoter Johnny Doyle — who made it a career. Lonnie was around wrestlers growing up, and despite being a very good football player at the College of Southern Utah, and flirting with the pro game, he began wrestling in California. His father made a call to an old friend from Columbus, Ohio, Tony Borne, in the Portland territory, and said he was sending Lonnie north. Would he look after him as a favor? "Tony Borne was really the strength behind Lonnie's start in his whole career," said Shawn Mayne. "Tony just really brought him along. Lonnie had been around the business all his life, so he had that natural feel for it."

"He came up here, and the guy had more ring color than any wrestler that I've ever met. He just had a way about him, a charisma about him that the people adored," said Borne, who would go on to have ten Pacific Northwest tag title runs with Lonnie, and a feud that lasted years as well. Their first title win came at the expense of Pepper Martin and Shag Thomas. Martin would also be Mayne's first major singles feud. Mayne broke Martin's leg in a match, setting up a heated rematch. "When he came to the Northwest, the wrestling fans in the Northwest had never seen anything like Lonnie Mayne. He would do crazy stuff. And he just got over," said Martin. "But I got a funny feeling that Lonnie was a little odd in the first place; he was a little different. He just got over like a million dollars. I made a lot of money with him in the Northwest."

The blond-haired, bearded, funky-dressing, constantly disheveled Mayne had little fear in the ring. He was as comfortable leaping from the top rope as he was taking a bump from the crow's nest announcing position in Portland. "Lonnie Mayne was doing bumps like Mankind, Mick Foley," recalled Don Muraco, who worked with Mayne in Hawaii. "He'd take bumps from the top turnbuckle to the floor, and stuff like that. I could have seen him taking a bump off a cage, given the opportunity and the venue. He was like that." The Moondog had a very aggressive style, unrelenting and vicious, and a drink or two in his system made him even wilder, said Ron Bass: "He was one of the first one of the high flyers. Period. He'd be soused to the gills, but you'd never know it in the ring. He was a top flyer, man."

In 1973, Mayne upped the nuttiness in New York, where he challenged for Pedro Morales' WWWF world title. The *Wrestling 1974 Annual* described his actions, and called for his banning: "Maybe he will eat a drinking goblet and then scratch himself with the jagged remains. He has swallowed live gold-fish with glee. Mayne's self-inflicted tortures are much milder, however, than those to which he subjects his victims. Mayne tears at his victim's face, his fingers as dangerous as any foreign weapon. He has broken opponents' jaws by reaching in their mouths and yanking down. He is renowned for using anything which might cause profuse bleeding. There are few men in wrestling whose use of the ring post to inflict punishment is as grotesque a work of art. Mayne is the best of them."

Away from the ring, Mayne was equally wild. He gambled and partied, and loved his Southern Comfort, perhaps almost as much as he did motorcycles. The Maynes had an uncle, Pete Cazier, who used to race bikes for the Harley-Davidson factory team. Family lore has Lonnie being about eight years old, waking up grumpy Christmas morning. "They all came in the room, and Lonnie looks around, and didn't see a motorcycle, and he says, 'That dirty old son of a bitch didn't bring me a motorcycle.' Then he went back to his room. He was mad that Santa Claus didn't bring him a motorcycle like our uncle," Shawn Mayne remembered. Tony Borne's son, Matt, used to hang out with Lonnie when he was a pre-teen. "Lonnie used to take me motorcycle riding with him," said Matt. "Actually, I got really good. Me and my dad would go up there with him sometimes. Lonnie just treated me like I was his. Everything Lonnie did, I wanted to do because Lonnie just liked the toys and stuff."

The mention of Jolly Ol' St. Nick is appropriate as well; one of Lonnie's favorite sayings was "Every day is like Christmas to me." Shawn Mayne, eighteen years younger than Lonnie, tried to explain: "Whenever Lonnie was in town, it was like Christmas morning, it really was. It was exciting, it was fun, and when he left, you really felt he was gone. You missed him. I'm saying that as his brother, but you talk to the rest of my family members, people around him, and they felt the same way. He loved to have fun."

Tom Andrews knew the Maynes from Salt Lake City, and he and Lonnie had great times on the road together as wrestlers. One time, they went shopping with their wives in Oregon. "As we walked in, he had a pair of handcuffs. He handcuffed his wife to the front door. We walked off and left her. She was opening and closing the door for people coming in and going out. She was handcuffed to the door handle!" Andrews chuckled.

By 1978, Mayne was apparently ready to stop wrestling. He was working the Los Angeles territory to be closer to his family, and planned to do a final trip before he quit. "He was home a week before he died," said Shawn Mayne. "He told my mom and dad, and I can remember it like it was yesterday, that he was going to do one more tour of Japan, and by Christmastime, he was quitting the business and coming home. But the drinking did catch up to him, it did."

Guerrero recalled a final rib that Mayne played on them after he was gone. "We used to go to Bakersfield. As the announcer gets up and the bell rings to start the first match, Lonnie would turn off the lights, he would turn off the breaker, and turn it right back on. When he passed, Piper did the same thing. At first when he did it, we were like, 'Whoaaa! Wait a minute now!'"

GEORGE "THE ANIMAL" STEELE

With George Steele, one word springs to mind — turnbuckle. "The Animal" had a habit of ripping apart turnbuckle pads with his bare teeth to testify to his madness. And guess what? It wasn't an act. "I said, 'How the hell do you chew through leather turn-buckles like that?'" asked friend and referee Dick Woehrle. "I took my thumb and ran it over his teeth. They were like razor blades! I said, 'My God, aren't you afraid you're going to bite your tongue off?'"

George Steele clamps onto Tony Marino.

Well, if he did, it would have bled green. Steele used green breath mints to tint his tongue in the school color of Michigan State, his alma mater. "He had the green tongue, he was just a good heel," said Frank Durso, a regular in Pittsburgh, where Steele made his first big splash. "His face is what got the people mad at him. He really didn't talk nasty to the fans, but they just disliked him because of the way he looked."

When Steele first entered pro wrestling, no one knew what he looked like. He started as the masked Student in the Detroit area around 1962. The disguise helped him hide his real identity of Jim Myers, local schoolteacher and coach, while he worked out with Gino Brito and other wrestlers. "There was Jim 'The Brute' Bernard, George Steele — Jim Myers then — George Cannon, myself, Tony Parisi, a couple of others," Brito recalled. "It was an old church there, in the basement, we had the whole basement to ourselves. We had weights and everything."

¿Steele's shift to the pro ranks was financially motivated. "I made $4,300 a year teaching when I first started," he recalled in a 2004 interview. "My first summer wrestling, I made $22,000." Bruno Sammartino scouted Myers in Detroit, and brought him to Pittsburgh and the WWWF as Steele in 1967. Named after the Steel City, Steele was a brutal, killer heel at first. A generation of fans who knew him only from his throaty grunts would be surprised to learn he did his own promo work in Pittsburgh. "The way the guy looked, he had a look, much like Brute Bernard, much like Abdullah, in a different way, but had that scary persona about him," said Gary Hart, who managed him as the Student, and thought his teaching job kept his act from wearing thin. "He wasn't on TV every week. You got to see him in the summer time. You got to see him around Christmas, on holidays when he would take off."

The turnbuckle entrée started by accident. In Pittsburgh, someone tossed a small, promotional couch pillow at him in the ring one night. "I took a bite out of it, tore it up, threw it up in the air, and people started going nuts. This was live TV. Eventually, I put the pillow over this fellow's head. The stuff was floating down like snow," Steele said. Someone — he thinks it was Tony Parisi — joked backstage that maybe he could eat a turnbuckle next. When a match with Chief Jay Strongbow was going nowhere, Steele looked at a turnbuckle and said to himself, "I wonder . . ." Bingo! A legend was born. But Steele is absolutely clear about one thing — despite the green tongue and knife-edged chompers, he was not a gimmick wrestler. "There's two people in this body. The persona I use in the ring, I don't practice it. I've never planned it."

Veteran Davey O'Hannon, who has known him for years, agreed that The Animal was no gimmick. "There were heels that the fans would go to and get close to. George, on the other hand, had the fans really wary of him, really afraid of him, because he was that scary a heel," O'Hannon said. "People didn't want to approach him because they didn't know what they were going to get. They weren't positive about this guy. He had a look of that Hannibal Lecter kind of personality."

Known for his flying hammerlock, Steele got regular billing against top WWWF draws like Sammartino, Pedro Morales, and Strongbow. "In the early years I hated working with George 'The Animal' Steele because the guy scared the hell out of me," said former WWF ring announcer Gary Michael Cappetta, "and he can still do a good job of it when he's in character today." Steele wasn't about to take guff from referees, or no stinkin' athletic commissioners either. Woehrle presided at a match one night in Philadelphia where Steele was in full animal attitude. "The head commissioner happened to be sitting there at ringside and he's got his $400 suit on, and George is throwing stuffing all over him," Woehrle said. The commissioner told

Woehrle to stop the match, and the ref consulted with Steele. "I finally said, 'Look, George, the commissioner said don't throw shit on him like that.' 'Screw him!' he said, and he goes over and rips open another turnbuckle with his teeth, grabs a handful of stuffing, and throws it all over the commissioner." Woehrle had no choice but to disqualify Steele, who responded by popping him in full view of the ref's daughter and friends. "Oh, George did not like that," Woehrle said.

When the WWWF went national in the mid-1980s, Steele became a full-time wrestler and a feud with Nikolai Volkoff, the Iron Sheik, and Fred Blassie turned him into a fan favorite. "One of the funniest matches I remember with George is that after he turned, he came into a six-man tag match with Jim Brunzell and myself, and wore the Killer Bee mask," said Brian Blair. "He was a tough guy; he was more of a brawler. But for him to all of a sudden become a good guy — he was better as the bad guy." Steele agrees, and, similar to why he took up wrestling in the first place, points to the bottom line. "I had gone from being one of the wildest heels in the history of wrestling to a cartoon character. I love working heel but the cartoon character helped us improve our lifestyle." He also battled Randy Savage over Miss Elizabeth, and made a brief comeback in 1999 as one of the Oddities. "Once Vince [McMahon] mellowed, softened his image for marketing purposes, the people took to him, they liked George. People like bizarre, they like oddities," Hart said.

Lost in the shuffle is the fact Steele was a good amateur wrestler and a terrific coach. He's a member of the Michigan High School Coaches Hall of Fame and the Michigan High School Football Coaches Hall of Fame. These days, he lives in Florida and spends a lot of time promoting the Professional Wrestling Hall of Fame in Amsterdam, New York, which inducted him in 2005. "In all of wrestling, I may have been the luckiest person. A lot of guys had to go from one territory to the other. I would just teach and, on the weekends, go back in the Northeast, which would have the biggest paychecks. And I wasn't there all the time, so I didn't get stale."

"THE GOLDEN GREEK" JOHN TOLOS

It's been a painful year for someone who made his living with his mouth as much as his muscles. Since the spring of 2006, "The Golden Greek" has been battling back from the effects of a stroke. The words come out much slower now, and the struggle to get them out is evident. "Right now, I'm talking to you, but sometimes I can't even say nothing," Tolos admitted. But in his heyday, few who could talk better than Tolos. It was a gift, and it was spelled T-O-L-O-S.

John Tolos chokes Killer Kowalski.

"Tolos was one hell of a talker. That's what got him over," said Art Williams, who refereed and ran towns for the Los Angeles promotion, where Tolos was Americas champion nine times from 1971–80. "Tolos was a better talker than he was a worker — much to his credit, that's not a knock. That's what got him over."

Los Angeles publicist Jeff Walton agreed, "Tolos without a flaw was one of the best talkers ever."

Frequent opponent Mando Guerrero did his best to put into words what made Tolos the best. "John Tolos was a master at his craft. He actually was from what is now known as the old-school, where he could carry the people to a heated end," Guerrero said. "John had that, he had that character of his, that mouth, the way he talked. One of the first guys that would carry on an interview that would make you sick, making fun of people, to capture what ticked the guy off. He was a master at that. He could do it quick. He had that sense of capturing what was good about the guy, his opponent, and know how to use that against him in an interview."

Tolos had something that could not be taught. "He's got a personality that when you see him looking around at the people, saying something to the people, the people want to kill him. He's just got that arrogance to be a good bad boy," said Jose Lothario. Tolos also had a career that spanned from the advent of television to the international success of the WWF (though his time as a mouthpiece manager in the Universal Wrestling Federation and WWF is properly forgotten by most). In an interview with Ring Around the Northwest, Tolos said he saw the change approaching. "Eventually with all the TVs coming in, everything started to blend together. Every territory started to become the same. Your style got over everywhere. The main thing was your talking. That was the big thing, the interviews, mighty important."

Never known as a truly great worker — his peers gave him the Golden Potato Award at the 2004 Cauliflower Alley Club reunion for hitting too hard — Tolos had an innate ability to do the right thing at the right time. Tolos once asked Rick Martel to come up with just four highspots for their match. Martel told Tolos his choices, who put them in the order he wanted. "When you go in the ring, 'Okay, number one!' He would put it in at the right time," said Martel. "He wouldn't go out there and have 10,000 highspots — we only had four. But they were just at the right time, and man, the reaction you used to get out of them!"

Growing up in Hamilton, Ontario, Tolos occasionally went to the wrestling matches at the Municipal Pool. But his interest was in amateur wrestling, which led him to the YMCA. His older brother, Chris, started learning the pro game from "Wee" Willie Davis, so John did too. As an eighteen-year-old, John toiled at Victoria Cap Co., learning garment manufacturing alongside the boss' son, and future wrestling colleague, Jack Laskin.

Hitting the road in 1951, Tolos went to Amarillo, Texas, to really begin his career. For the two decades, Chris and John Tolos were as formidable a team as there was, with each willing to fight to the death for the other: "Right brother Chris?" Known as the Wrecking Crew, they fought all the great teams of the day. But as with a lot of brother teams, one shone above the rest; John had the personality to be a star. "Actually when Chris Tolos went to Canada, when John started going other places, I think that killed off Chris Tolos' career," said journalist Bill Apter. "Kind of Rick and Scott Steiner in some ways."

In California, Tolos worked on his tan and ran on the beach, while honing his character into a real maniac, especially in the KCOP-TV studios. He had a string of devious acts that still get the ire up, including breaking Raul Mata's guitar over his head, and losing a hair match to Victor Rivera, but then demolishing his foe with a chair after the buzz cut. Tolos would wield two-by-fours, chairs, and baseball bats, as well as hidden weapons, and even cleared ringside with a boa constrictor. But it's his epic feud with Freddie

Blassie that cemented his position as one of the greatest heels of all time. It was May 8, 1971, and Blassie was on TV getting an award for being Wrestler of the Year from the fans. Tolos had just won the Americas' title from Blassie, and was enraged. "I got hot. There was the doctor's bag there, and I opened the bag and found this powder — he was getting interviewed with his trophy. I threw the powder, I threw a lot of powder," Tolos told *RATNW*. "I got his trophy, and hit him over the head with it. We had a riot, had a riot in the studio." Blassie had been hit with Monsel's powder, and screamed, "My God, my eyes!" The fan favorite was taken to South Hoover Hospital, where Dr. Bernhart Schwartz, the state athletic commission physician, reported, "It is problematic how long he will be out. The injury takes several months to heal. I recommend that he retire, but I doubt that he will."

Of course it was all an elaborate work by L.A. promoter Mike LeBell and his bookers Jules Strongbow and Charlie Moto. But what a work. Blassie knew enough to stay out of the spotlight as they built to an epic showdown in the mammoth Los Angeles Coliseum on August 27. Walton feared the planning was too far out. "It was so far, far away. I thought, 'My God, so many things could go wrong and here I am doing the poster for this thing.'" The office totally stacked the card at the Coliseum to protect itself.

The promotion smartly kept them apart. Blassie would show up unexpectedly at shows, screaming for Tolos' head, his eyes still bandaged. "They never touched each other. They'd come close. You'd see cops coming, and grabbing Blassie, and straining to hold him back," said Walton. Tolos' car was badly damaged outside an event in Bakersfield. "We didn't expect the amount of heat we'd get. He had to get extra protection; we had to hire extra protection."

When Blassie and Tolos finally met, it resulted in a crowd of 25,847, paying $5 to $7 for a state record gate of $142,158.50. "The paper said it was 25,000 but it looked like 35,000 to 40,000," said Tolos. "It was a hell of a big, big, big card."

Walton was able to reunite Blassie and Tolos on his *WrestleTalk* radio show on February 7, 2003, just months before Blassie's death. Tolos was at his boastful best. "We had the greatest feud in professional wrestling," Tolos said. "You tell that to any fan, what was the greatest feud, and they'll say Blassie and Tolos. It was all kinds of matches, it wasn't just one fall, or two out of three. It was great super, vicious matches like the cage match, like Texas Death matches, Indian Death matches, stretcher matches where there had to be a winner. The hand had to go up. Those were vicious, vicious matches. There's no question about it, Blassie was one of the greatest wrestlers that I've ever wrestled and I've ever known. I am the greatest, so he was *one* of the greatest."

Blassie, no shrinking violet on the microphone, quipped back. "Top to bottom, you were, without a doubt, my toughest opponent. I'm saying this just because you're there, but every time I was matched up with you, I knew I was in for a hell of a night. And I'm telling you, too bad we didn't get paid!"

After finishing wrestling in the early 1980s, Tolos worked at Guy Martin Honda Oldsmobile in Woodland Hills, California. Today, Tolos lives in California, with his only son, Chris. His ex-wife of twenty years, Ingrid, isn't too far away. He is particularly moved by the show of concern following his stroke, and claimed he hears from friends "night and day," as he "met so many people through the years."

He does miss the spotlight. "Oh yeah. I wish I was still there." He also misses departed friends, and especially, his brother Chris, who died in November 2005 of cancer. The brothers were inducted into the tag team division of the Pro Wrestling Hall of Fame in 2007. "I liked being despised. That was it for me. It's very big. Even as I think about the guys I wrestled, it was really, really good stuff, good guys."

Mike Vachon, Mad Dog Vachon, John Tolos and Louie Tillet at the 2004 Cauliflower Alley Club reunion in Las Vegas.

The Egotists

Ripper Collins and Beauregarde.

BEAUREGARDE

Does it get any more despicable than threatening the Easter Bunny on live TV? It was the night before Easter in 1970, and Beauregarde was on Portland, Oregon's KPTV, telling viewers that he was going to let his evil minion, The Claw, loose in town. "All you kids out in TV land are not going to have any candy or Easter eggs tomorrow. I told The Claw to hide in the bushes tonight, and wait for the Easter Bunny to come by, and when he does I told The Claw to jump out and put the claw hold on him, and squeeze, and squeeze, and squeeze."

The Claw was Tom Andrews under a mask, and he hadn't been clued in on what Beauregarde was going to say. "I was just standing there. He was doing the interview. He came up with that, and I said, 'Uh, oh.'" Uh, oh is right. The phone lines lit up, and the station representatives threatened to ban Portland wrestling forever if an apology wasn't made. "I laughed my butt off," said Larry Pitchford, a.k.a. Beauregarde. "I had to come back on: 'No, no, easy, I'll keep him, I'll cage him. I won't let him kill the Easter Bunny.'"

That's just one tale of the nasty vitriol spewed by Beauregarde during his eleven-year career, spent mostly in Hawaii and the Pacific Northwest. Truthfully, he's almost forgotten by today's fans, but that shouldn't be the case. Beauregarde was a pioneer, both with his outfits and, more importantly, his music. At a time when very few grapplers came to the ring with any music, Beauregarde came out to a song, "Testify," that he wrote and recorded himself in 1970. He even made a music video, with him mouthing the words to the song as he wandered through Portland, throwing change to winos.

Greg Sage of Zeno Records has done more than anyone to keep Beauregarde's memory alive. As a seventeen-year-old, he played on Beauregarde's LP, and as an adult, he was able to reissue it as a CD. The first time he saw Beauregarde on TV as a teenager, Sage was transfixed. "He was doing an interview, and he had his face right in the camera, and so outlandish a costume on . . . it was just hilarious. I was just glued to it," he said. "He was so hilarious, and his insults so clever."

"I always did like music, all the time we were driving from town to town. I wrote a couple of poems. Then I thought, 'Hell, I could turn these into a song,'" explained Pitchford. The single of "Testify" became so popular in Portland that he was invited to record a full album. "I started the whole thing," he said of the Rock 'N' Wrestling connection. "I was the first rock and roller, and the first guy to record an album, record it, and sing it."

It's not like Pitchford planned it all. Born April 29, 1939, in Lima, Ohio, he wasn't a big wrestling fan. After high school, he and some buddies left for warmer climes, and eventually ended up in Hawaii and in the ROTC program at the University of Hawaii to avoid full draft notices. "I kept messing up with the reserves, so they drafted me into the regular navy. I failed my physical, so they let me out," Pitchford said.

Spotted at Dean Higuchi's gym by Neff Maivia, Pitchford was offered a chance to give pro wrestling a try, as Maivia wanted to open up a new promotion in the Philippines. Pitchford became "Eric the Golden Boy," and worked alongside Harry Fujiwara, Nick Bockwinkel, and Ricky Hunter. It was a crazy place to start a new career. "You couldn't get enough fans. Some of the places we went to, you flew to one of the islands where the airport was just a goddamn grassy runway. There weren't even paved roads in the town we went to wrestle in. Oh, man, it was really breaking new territory," he said. "So that folded. That was just a quick dry run, because we ran out of money and had to come back."

In Hawaii, Pitchford was paired up with Roy "Ripper" Collins, who had been working with the nickname "The Southern Rebel." "He used to pass

Beauregarde, the singer.

out this Confederate money, little fake Confederate money, and it was signed by General Beauregarde," said Pitchford. "Ripper looked at it and he said, 'Beauregarde, that's a good name.' I said, 'Aw, that's a faggot name.' He said, 'Now wait a minute, listen to me. One name stays better with you than two names — Liberace, Donovan, Fabian.'"

Collins was right. As a part-time valet and part-time partner to the likes of Collins and "Handsome" Johnny Barend in Hawaii, Beauregarde got lots of screen time. The Hawaiian promotion was a popular stopping point for talent on its way to or from the Orient, and Beauregarde worked with many of the greats during the measly ten shows or so a month. The rest of the time was spent on the beach. One of Beauregarde's gimmicks would be to bring high-school girls onto the TV show to show off the latest dance crazes. "I was young, nice body, good-looking. I could get girls any time," he bragged.

In Portland, the Beauregarde character really took off. "The thing that got me over so good in Portland was I got on TV, and I told everybody that I was related to all the greatest people in the world." He was Cleopatra, the Pope, Marc Antony, Julius Caesar, Al Capone, a Hell's Angel, a caveman, Nathan Hale. "Every week, I would rent a costume and tell everybody I was related to that person." Beauregarde would wear the same outfit for all the spot shows that week, then hand the bill to Don Owen.

"Beauregarde was a nifty little heat-generating machine during his stay here," said Dutch Savage, a former tag partner in Oregon. "Beau was a lot of fun even though we didn't associate too much outside of wrestling. We stayed at the same place and he was sort of a legend there. He had his room all painted up with the psychedelic stuff," Roger Kirby told *Ring Around the Northwest*. "He was single, and he had a waiting list to get in to see him as far as the girls were concerned. He was a fun guy to be around."

But when the five-foot-nine, 200-pound Beauregarde left Portland, whether it was Australia, Arizona, North Carolina, Japan, or California, it wasn't the same, and he wasn't a main-eventer. As time went on, he was dwarfed by the newer generation of wrestlers. "Everybody kept getting bigger, and bigger, and bigger. I wasn't that big. I had to wrestle Ernie Ladd a lot. Shit, Ernie was six-foot-nine, 320. So when the guy's 100 pounds heavier and a foot taller, it's just not believable," he said.

A short-lived marriage brought Pitchford to Florida, where he helped run a few towns for Eddie Graham's promotion. Pitchford worked construction, wrestled three nights a week, and saved up enough money for a nice condo on the ocean. He ran a drywall and sheet rock business for years, saved his money, and today can be found relaxing, fishing every day.

EDGE

Adam Copeland knows better than most how fickle today's fans are, especially toward a traditional baby-face. There he was, sailing along as Edge, one of the almost-top-guys in the WWE, his long blond hair and good looks setting hearts aflutter, when it all came to a crashing end: his private life became very public in the summer of 2005, and the fans turned on him. Those hard-fought battles with Triple H, Kurt Angle, and the tag team with the iconic Hulk Hogan were forgotten.

Caught having an affair with fellow WWE star Lita (Amy Dumas), who had been dating Matt Hardy for years, Copeland reverted to a heel role, almost by default.

Mike Mastrandrea

WWE champion Edge speaks his mind to John Cena.

Instead of denying the relationship, the pair played it to the hilt, sleazing it up and sizzling up the screen. "The Rated-R Superstar" finally vaulted to the top of the card, dethroning John Cena for the WWE world title in January 2006. The celebratory "live sex show" on the subsequent Monday Night Raw drew one of the show's highest ratings in years.

Having had significant runs on both sides of the somewhat rickety fence of babyface/heel, Copeland is uniquely qualified to address the business today. "To be able to do both is nowadays, not necessarily rare, but especially being a babyface today, a hard line to walk," Edge said. "The fans are so knowledgeable now that they can turn on you pretty quick. They sense things and they know. I always thought I was a better babyface, and now I think I'm better as a heel. It's funny, but it's more fun to be a heel."

That enjoyment factor shone through for the six-foot-four, 235-pound Edge when he first hit his stride in the WWE, initially teaming with his long-time friend Christian (Jay Reso, now known as Christian Cage). The two had grown up together in Orangeville, Ontario, and harbored the same dream of competing in the WWE. It took a while, but they eventually found their stride in a comedic tag team that won gold seven times in just a two-year span, dueling with the Hardy Boyz and Dudley Boys. Their sassy attitudes, daring moves and seven-second poses won the duo fans regardless of the ideological leanings of their foes.

The inevitable split with Christian came over Edge's King of the Ring win in 2001. The jealousy led Christian to turning on his old friend. Their feud was short-lived, however, as Edge was groomed to move up the card, and then suffered an injury. Tag title runs with Hogan, Rey Mysterio, and Chris Benoit would follow, along with runs with the Intercontinental belt.

Though he turned heel in 2004, the bad-guy Edge of 2005–07 is totally different than the fun-loving, frat boy who goofed around with Mick Foley and Kurt Angle in skits. This one is all about ego, and his aim is to push the right buttons to enrage the fans. "Edge has been an extremely good heel character for WWE, especially in a time when wrestlers don't want to embrace being a true heel," said Brian Fritz, host of the *Between the Ropes* radio show. "He relishes the boos and the negative reactions from the crowds, and doesn't play into them. He doesn't try to do something to get cheap heat. He doesn't try to do something cute or funny, where people would have a reason to cheer for him. Instead, Edge walks out with his smarmy grin bigger than a Cheshire cat. He exudes confidence in everything he does: his walk to the ring, the way he talks, and how he carries himself. He makes people want to hate him but for all the right reasons."

It was a well-deserved payoff for the thirty-three-year-old Copeland, a lifelong fan. "I've never really stopped watching tapes. I've always been a student of this. I grew up on it, and never stopped watching it. What I do now is what I do naturally. I don't even think about it. It just kind of happens." Getting him to rhyme off his favorite baddies can take a while. "I loved so many guys — Flair, Randy Savage was awesome, Ted DiBiase, Bob Orton Jr. — there's so many guys. Mr. Perfect, loved him. Rick Rude, so underrated. Rick Rude and Barry Windham were so underrated. Arn Anderson, Tully Blanchard, just so many, so many great heels that I grew up with."

He's gotten the chance to get advice from a few of those heroes, including Anderson and DiBiase, who have worked backstage for WWE. "In the last few years, I've really seen him come of age, so to speak. He's very good at it," said DiBiase. Still front and center in the action, however, is Flair. He had high praise for Edge in the summer of 2006: "The truth is, the first time I was in Toronto, our WWE champion — who I want to say is a great champion, a great guy, a great performer — was seven years old. I'm talking about Edge."

Edge admitted it is a thrill getting advice from The Nature Boy. "Ric takes me aside and tells me things that I never thought I'd hear. He considers Hunter [Triple H] and I to be the leaders now, that we are helping guys along . . . He said he was over in Australia doing press, and a journalist asked him whether he thought the old guys like Hunter and Edge are helping the young guys like Batista, and he went, 'Wait, Batista's older than Edge!' But that's the way I'm looked at now, which is a compliment. So Ric will take me aside just to tell me very positive, encouraging things. To hear that from a guy like that, you can't beat that."

"SUPERSTAR" BILLY GRAHAM

Was "Superstar" Billy Graham ever a true heel, with the white-hot hatred of the fans? Despite learning from masters of the art, like Abdullah the Butcher, Dr. Jerry Graham, and Ray Stevens, he doesn't think so. Instead, he believes he was the forerunner of today's characters, who want to be loved (and sell T-shirts) while still pissing off some people. Few played the tweener role better than the Superstar.

He's the first to admit that he evolved since he hit the big time in California in 1970. "I'm doing the hippie gimmick, but even though it's still black and white, some of the kids liked the gimmick," he said of days in the San Francisco promotion. "Then I went back to L.A., then the song 'Jesus Christ Superstar' came out and the rock opera *Jesus Christ Superstar*. I took that title, and began to really get into the tie-dye stuff. That right there began my blending into a real babyface character because of the interviews. I was still in my infancy in interviews in Los Angeles, my last run before I went to Minneapolis. I had the tie-dye, I had the physique, I had the sunglasses. I was beginning to develop my character, and it wasn't hardcore, I was too entertaining, see, kind of like Gorgeous George was. Of course, he was hated as a heel, but the people loved him because he was so entertaining. That began the crossover for me."

The six-foot-four, 275-pounder became one of those rare cats who stood

"Superstar" Graham prepares to wallop Andre the Giant with a table after an arm-wrestling challenge Thanksgiving night in 1975 in Norfolk, Virginia.

the test of time, said Johnny Rodz. "He was a character that was from the old time, and from the new time. He was old style, and then flamboyant at the same time. You put it all together, and that was his time. That's why he's a character that people recognize still today, more than twenty years later. He's a character that you just don't forget."

Superstar's biographer agrees that he was a good guy trapped in a bad-guy role. "I think Superstar really does have a babyface's personality," said Keith Elliot Greenberg. "He's an intelligent guy, he's a funny guy, and he kind of speaks in a way that he reaches out to people. He never would refuse to sign autographs. He likes people, and he connects with people. He's very curious about people."

Equally curious was Coleman's route to the top of wrestling as WWWF world champion from April 30, 1977, when he beat Bruno Sammartino, to February 28, 1978, when he lost to Bob Backlund. Born Eldridge Wayne Coleman in Phoenix, June 7, 1943, he was into weight training by the fifth grade, and was a standout in field events like the shot put. By his late teens, he was traveling in religious revival shows, preaching the Word, and performing feats of strength. He fell in with a different crowd though, was introduced to steroids, and built his body up even further while working as a bouncer. A fellow bouncer, Bob Lueck, suggested the twenty-six-year-old Coleman give the Canadian Football League a try. He tried out for the Calgary

Stampeders, got traded to the Montreal Alouettes, and just got into a couple of games. Coleman then seemed about to make the NFL's Oakland Raiders practice squad, but tore his Achilles tendon.

While Coleman was working as a debt collector for a Las Vegas casino, his friend Lueck called again, and said he'd started wrestling. Coleman drove to Calgary in 1970, and was introduced to Stu Hart. "He had no fat, and looked like he was holding regulation footballs in his arms," Hart once said. "He was the most impressive specimen I've seen in my life." With very little training, Coleman was thrown into a tag team with Angelo Mosca. "He was probably tailor-made for the business, and the business isn't on the up-and-up at all times," said Mosca. "He fits the bill real good. He was a lucky guy because he got some breaks along the way because he had this massive body. But he wasn't an athlete."

Coleman did his best to absorb it all, and thanks Abdullah for teaching him a lot about being a bad guy. In Phoenix, Jerry Graham rechristened him as brother "Billy," and Coleman had a new instructor in the fine art of heeling. "He told me his philosophy was, to quote, 'raise hell immediately after you leave that locker room door. On the way to the ring, start raising hell with the fans, and do not stop until you're back in the locker room.'" Jerry took him to Los Angeles, but got stuck in his usual boatload of trouble, so Coleman shipped out on his own for San Francisco. There, Pat Patterson took him as a tag team partner, while Coleman kept an eye on his hero, Ray Stevens. "At the Cow Palace, man, in the old school, you're labeled by what aisle you come out of, you're guilty by association," Coleman said.

Superstar got his first significant singles run in the AWA in 1975, but felt uncomfortable with promoter Verne Gagne's desire for workers to have legitimate credentials. He did have a series of bloody matches with Wahoo McDaniel. "When I got to Minnesota and I did the big thing with Wahoo, and I became the chicken heel, take the big beating, and leave the ring for a time out. That thing got so much heat that the fans started bringing rubber chickens to the matches, setting up that strap match angle we did," he said. "That Minnesota deal really began my influence of being a crossover heel, and yet being an entertaining heel and really a babyface at heart." The stage was actually set for a Superstar babyface run in Minneapolis, but he left the territory.

His first stint in Florida followed, and then he descended on New York, where he hit the heights for good. Despite being an excellent orator, Graham was given The Grand Wizard (Ernie Roth) as his manager. "He was very hard to hate, the Wizard, as a fan because he really never did any physical interference. He was a giant cartoon character," said Graham. "When

Dinner with announcer Gordon Solie.

we hooked up, it became pure entertainment at its finest with the Grand Wizard combing my hair, taking my shirt off, and all this and that, entertaining value."

In the ring, Superstar was still a heel, taking shortcuts and commiting evil deeds behind the referee's back. "The fans were so groomed, brainwashed, to hate cheaters that you had to get heat," Superstar said. "Then, I would say that, even with Bruno, the ultimate babyface in New York, I get e-mails from guys today saying, 'Man, I hated you, and I loved Bruno, until you came to New York and started cutting promos. Then all of a sudden, I realized, "Wow, this guy's cool."' So even with Bruno, I still had a lot of my babyface fans out there." Graham said WWWF owner Vincent J. McMahon used to tell him, "You're too entertaining. Why can't you be more of a heel?" His title defenses came against the likes of Ivan Putski, Dusty Rhodes, and Mil Mascaras.

The pinnacle of his title reign was a 1978 world title bout against National Wrestling Alliance world champion Harley Race at the Orange Bowl in Miami. The match went to a draw in the rain. "Graham could get over with his talk. Ability in the ring was limited," Race explained. "If he was going to be the heel, he had to be the dominant person, either that, or cut him off before he was coming into the ring, and then really stomp on him so when he did make the comeback, he would be the babyface. He was just a person gifted with gab, and it could go either way with him, depending on who he was working with."

Losing the WWWF title to Backlund — "He can't even cut a promo" — sent Graham into a tailspin, and within a year, he was digging ditches in Arizona. Once he collected himself, he would return as a karate master rather than a tie-dyed hipster. The abrupt switch masked an addiction to drugs, and his body breaking down from steroid abuse. The Superstar image of the '70s did return later in the '80s, though he was a shell of his former self. He had a decent stint in Florida in Kevin Sullivan's evil army, before turning true babyface for the first time. During the height of the WWF's national expansion, Graham returned, but is most remembered for allowing his hip surgery to be broadcast on the company's syndicated TV show.

An autobiography and DVD have allowed Superstar to share his stories to new generation of fans, including his plea for them to sign their organ donation cards — as a kidney from a twenty-six-year-old woman killed in an auto accident saved his life.

He is somewhat wistful about his earlier days. At the top of his game, no one talked better than Superstar, and certainly no one looked better. His legacy leads directly to the likes of Hulk Hogan, Jesse Ventura, and Scott Steiner. But it isn't the same. Though he was a babyface at heart, he is a little wistful about his heel work. "It's a lost art. The old school, man, they had a price to pay," Graham said. "You've been doing this thing, and you've been getting beaten up, shot, carved, cars destroyed — there was a price to pay. If I was wrestling today, just for safety's sake, I'd love not having the line blurred."

ROGER KIRBY

To escape from being pinned, Roger Kirby developed a regular routine where he'd get his foot on the ropes just as the count was hitting three. It would look like he'd been beaten, but the referee would acknowledge the foot on the ropes, and the match would continue. Sometimes, he'd pull off the same move three or four times in a single bout, infuriating the fans. It worked so well he earned the derisive nickname in Kansas City of "Bottom Rope" Kirby.

He just saw it as part of his job of making a living. "What made me a great heel was the ability to want to make money. The ability to make money was the willingness to look bad to be successful. I watched so many guys who wanted to be [big], and they'd eat guys up, beat 'em, and squash 'em, and want to know why they weren't drawing a thing," Kirby explained. "It was the ability to make everybody look good, whether they were doing a job for you, or whether you were in the main event."

Roger Kirby and Lord Alfred Hayes.

Willis Kirby learned those lessons under the tutelage of Dick the Bruiser and The Sheik in Indianapolis, not too far from his home of Dunkirk, Indiana. "Me having a halfway good body, and being a good athlete, they both fell in love with me, and just requested my presence everywhere to do jobs for them," Kirby recalled. A Golden Gloves boxer who was "about halfway tough," Kirby attended a wrestling show at his high school after he'd graduated in 1957. The heel team of Roy Shire and Ray Stevens was getting the best of Bobby Managoff and his partner. Managoff was being choked. "All my friends are there. All I could hear was 'Kirby, Kirby, Kirby.' There's the adrenaline rush. I'm up on the apron, and almost pulled Bobby Managoff's head off with the tag rope, because I ended up with the tag rope. Roy Shire kicked me upside the head, and when I hit the floor, it almost tore my ear off." At home that night, his mother revealed that his cousin's husband was actually a minor pro wrestler named "Cowboy" Dennis Hall. Kirby was at Hall's doorstep that Sunday, and was soon wrestling as "Wild" Bill Baker. Four years later, he was working full-time.

Stretching to make five-foot-ten, and having to jiggle the scale to crack 230 pounds, it was a constant battle to be noticed. "For as small as he was, he didn't back down from anybody," recalled Kansas City announcer Bill Kersten. "If he went to a bar and somebody challenged him, he'd accept it." After explaining that nobody's that big when they are lying on the mat, Kirby summed up his demeanor: "I was very aggressive because I was small, and I stayed in shape so I could be aggressive."

With his blond hair, handlebar mustache or beard, and a more-than-passing resemblance to Buddy Rogers, "Nature Boy" or "Rip" Kirby worked mostly as a heel, and took on every world champion from Pat O'Connor on up. He made his mark in territories like Georgia, Florida, Oregon, Minnesota, and Kansas City, where he stayed for the last ten years of his career, and still lives nearby today.

Add an extended run in Mexico, time on top in Puerto Rico, and six trips to Japan, and you have a real world traveler. Just don't talk about South Africa. Bill Howard booked Kirby there, despite the dangers of being in Johannesburg in the early 1980s. "Kirby was there three or four months. All I got was a postcard from him. And on the postcard it said, 'What a thing to do to a friend,'" laughed Howard, who had nothing but praise for Kirby, aside from his penmanship. "Roger was the best there ever was. Roger could work. Roger could do everything that they're doing today, and probably even better. He had impeccable timing, his punches, his kicks, everything looked good, perfect. He had the body, the looks, the arrogance. He should have made more money than he did."

Kirby considers the pinnacle of his career his year-long run as NWA junior heavyweight champion. It was 1971, and Kirby had a couple of broken ribs. His wife was from Louisiana, and he went there to recuperate. Attending the matches to see some friends, Bill Watts convinced him that he was the man to take over as champ while Danny Hodge went to Japan. Kirby beat Hodge on May 20 in New Orleans, and held the belt until September 10, when he lost to Ramon Torres.

Hodge called him a "first-class" hand who knew how to get everyone riled. "He even got to me, just the walking, strutting, the showmanship was great," said Hodge. "He had the right personality, the right actions, the right steps. He was the right man."

As the junior champ, Kirby worked an extended program with Tom Jones, whom he actually started out with in Indiana. "We sold out everything we touched," claimed Kirby. "A lot of the places there would be maybe 100 white people and 2,000 black. Every night that I wrestled Tom, there wasn't a person in that building that knew he couldn't beat me. But I always worked out a finish to where I got my hand up, I kept the belt. We went back two, three, sometimes four times. We'd end up where it was in a cage or lumber-jack match. The last match wasn't a championship match, and Tom would always get his hand up to put Tom right back where he should be."

By 1985, Kirby just couldn't do it any more. "Probably a couple of years longer than I should have," he said. "I tell people I had a twenty-one-year paid vacation." He briefly refereed for the WWF in Kansas City, and worked a few shots in 1986, but gave it up. "I wanted to be remembered as a top wrestler." For the next twenty-one years, he worked at the *Kansas City Star*, initially driving a truck, and later working as a carpenter. Healthwise, both knees have been replaced (he used a knee brace in the ring for years, and it made a convenient weapon as well), and both hips, as well as his shoulders. Now retired, he putters around his house with his third wife, tinkers in the garage, and keeps up with his three kids and his extended family.

"NATURE BOY" BUDDY LANDEL

Pete Lederberg Collection

"Nature Boy" Buddy Landel.

One night in Evansville, Indiana, "Nature Boy" Buddy Landel stepped into the ring to take on "The Invisible Man." "This is back when I was doing my chemistry experiment," Landel said, referring to his use of recreational drugs. "I'd lock up with myself, I'd shoot myself off, I'd give myself a hip toss, I would sell invisible punches, take hip tosses over the top rope. I guess you had to have been there, but it was funny."

Though it's the only time it happened in the ring, the matchup against himself was a constant one for Landel. Today, at forty-five years old and admittedly out of anything close to wrestling shape, he can honestly examine his missteps and mistakes. His legacy? "If Buddy's here, if Buddy's in his right mind, Buddy can draw money as good, or better, than anybody," Landel said. "But the thing is I was just undependable, and I was unreliable. If I was there and I showed up, you can count that we were going to sell out."

Landel figures he abused drugs for ten to fifteen years. "There's something about the adulation of a crowd, either cheering your name or booing you, and then you have the admiration, and the adulation of people swarming you, and all that. Then you go back to the hotel room, and there's just nothing," he said. "I don't blame anyone or anything, it was just me having an addictive personality. I couldn't just do a little of nothing, I had to go over the top on everything that I did. I'm kind of a shy person in my family life, and I think that's the opposite of my personality [in wrestling]. I could live out there in public, and I could live on the stage, a different person than I actually was. I was thinking to myself, back then I needed these substances to get my courage up to do these things. The rationale of a twenty-two-year-old guy in there with the world champion selling out every night, unless you put yourself in my shoes, you really can't, I can't expect anybody to understand that. I can only try to explain a little bit. I understand now that I didn't need that."

A fan growing up in Knoxville, Tennessee, Nature Boy Buddy Landel (his full legal name after changing it from William Ansor) had a sister who was dating Barry Orton. Knowing Landel was interested, they'd wrestle a little when Orton was visiting. Soon Landel was introduced to Boris Malenko, who would become his trainer. "I was seventeen years, and I was just coming out of high school amateur wrestling. I was in fantastic shape anyway. There were about thirty or forty guys that tried out, and I was the only one that made it," said Landel, who lived in an apartment with Bob Roop, and in the same complex with Bob Orton Jr. and Archie Gouldie.

He debuted in the middle of the promotional war between the Poffos and the Fullers. He was an insignificant cog in the wheel, a low-level, dark-haired babyface in the background. "All these guys were carrying guns and stuff. They were actually shooting with each other on television. I thought, 'What have I gotten myself into? Roop's telling me this thing's a work, except this part's real, about them fighting each other. . . .' I didn't know what the hell to think." In order to make ends meet, he slept in the store-front window in Randy Savage's gym in Lexington, Kentucky.

To get away from the chaos, he went to Bill Watts' Mid-South promotion. "I knew Buddy before he got in the business in Knoxville. I knew his folks. In fact, when he first went out to Watts, he called himself Buddy Roop," said Bob Roop. "I liked Buddy. If you think about it, imitation is flattery." His sister came up with the name "Landel," and he started using that in Memphis. It was also in Memphis that he got the call that would change his life, and allow him to shine.

Tom Renesto Sr. phoned from Puerto Rico, where he was booking, and asked if Landel would consider bleaching his hair and coming in as a heel. Landel was quickly thrust into the spotlight, even if he didn't realize it. "We did six hours of TV in one day, six shows in one day. I really didn't know what they were doing because I had just been a babyface for two or three years. I was down there with Crazy Luke Graham and Dick Steinborn. I was the hot opening on every show, and I was the close on every show, and running in two or three times. I remember asking Crazy Luke Graham, 'Do you think they're giving me a push?' 'Hell, kid, Ray Charles can see that.' I didn't know." For eight months, he learned from Renesto, who was formerly half of the famed Assassins team. "When I came back to the States, I don't know if I can say that I was a seasoned veteran, but I drew money right after that."

In Memphis, Jerry Lawler added the "Nature Boy" name to Landel. "What a talent this guy had. Great mouth. He just was naturally a great, great mouth," said Memphis announcer Lance Russell. "Lawler is amazing at that, and Landel was the same thing. Boy, you get those two guys working a mic, and you've got a couple of guys that know what they're doing."

Landel was then part of the massive exodus from Memphis back to Mid-South, where Watts was gearing up for a national run. "That was the school of hard knocks there," Landel said of the territory, with its long trips and hard-nosed boss. "If you ever worked for Bill Watts, you were two things: you were a good worker, or a great worker; and you were tough. Bill Watts didn't hire anybody who wasn't actually a tough guy." Terry Taylor was a frequent opponent there. "Landel was the type of guy that got real heat, and I mean in the ring and out," Taylor said. "Buddy was the kind of guy that really, in real life, people didn't like. He just couldn't help it. He had this air about him, and he was cocky. If you knew him, you knew it was all a smoke-screen, and all that stuff, but if you didn't know him, you wanted to fight him. Everybody did. And he wasn't tough at all, and everybody knew it. He was the kind of guy that everybody thought they could whip, and they wanted to, which is the perfect kind of heel."

By the time he got the call to go to the Mid-Atlantic area in 1985, Landel was one cocky twenty-three-year-old. "I knew I was good, I knew I was with great talent, I knew this was an opportunity of a lifetime, I knew I was in the driver's seat," Landel bragged. "I was like an artist out there, and my canvas was the wrestling ring. I could make you laugh, I could make you cry, I could make you hate me. I had learned how to pick one person out of the whole coliseum, and jump on that one person and get on them. That one person, by my insults and innuendos, would get the whole place going. I didn't have to work the whole building."

J. J. Dillon was assigned as Landel's manager, and the promotion started to fashion a "Nature Boy" versus "Nature Boy" feud with Ric Flair. The plan was aborted after a lengthy buildup and a three-month run, though Landel considers the matches the pinnacle of his career. "It never really took off as we had hoped it would," Dillon acknowledgd. "Part of it, I think, was Buddy having some personal problems, and the feeling being that there wasn't a lot of confidence to invest a lot of television time into something involving Buddy for fear this thing wouldn't follow through to fruition."

By 1986, Landel's personal demons had driven him out of the spotlight. He'd resurface on occasion: World Championship Wrestling in 1990; United States Wrestling Association in 1993; and most memorably, his last major run, in Jim Cornette's Smokey Mountain Wrestling, which also led to a brief stint in the WWF in 1995. Landel started the same day as "The Ringmaster" Steve Austin, but slipped and fell during a snowstorm after his third match with the company. He was out six months. "It was just one of those things where success eluded me again as far as wrestling was concerned." Landel credits his wife of twenty-five years, his two daughters, and his faith for cleaning up his act. "It's something that I still have to work on, because I'm wild as a buck, even today."

RANDY ORTON

Some people are just not cut out to be good guys. On August 15, 2004, Randy Orton beat Chris Benoit at the SummerSlam pay-per-view to become the youngest world champion in WWE history. But the next day, the twenty-four-year-old Orton was turned babyface, tossed from the Evolution heel group. He would lose the title a month later to Triple H.

Being so new to the business anyway, Orton just wasn't ready to try something so different, with so little warning. "That was a really hard way to get going, and to stay over. As a heel I was just starting to get some fire, and people were starting to respond to me. To turn me babyface, from being a dickhead to being 'Yeah, yeah, come on' — they didn't buy it, it wasn't really something the fans went with," he told Silvervision.co.uk. "It was kind of my fault — it was my fault and it was the writers' faults. It didn't bother me — I still had that title, I was a world champion, and the youngest ever."

Hindsight is 20/20, but there's little question it was a bad decision to make Orton good. "You can't book a smart, cocky, motherfucker like Randy Orton as a babyface. Oh God, he was the next Rick Rude," Kevin Nash told the Pro Wrestling Torch. "He should have been the guy walking to the building with two hot broads . . . Don't push him in a mustard suit on TV and think I'm gonna like him. If I'm an auto worker from Detroit, I'm gonna want to punch him in the face."

Dan Murphy, senior writer at Pro Wrestling Illustrated, agreed. "Randy Orton exudes a natural heel smugness. He's also incredibly physically gifted. Together, it makes it hard for fans to cheer him. He never comes off as the Ricky Morton-style face-in-peril, or the Hulk Hogan-style babyface with a cause. Instead, he comes off as the obnoxious upperclassman whose Daddy bought him an IROC while you were taking the bus to school. Like the great heels of the 1950s, '60s, and '70s, he is completely believable as the obnoxious jerk who just happens to be a tremendous wrestler."

Orton chalks it all up as a learning experience. "I'm sure I'll work babyface again in my career, but being a heel, I don't want to say comes natural

Randy Orton strikes a modest pose.

. . . but I guess it does come natural for me, I hate to say. Times ten, my personality out there is a heel, I enjoy it, I love it, and I'm growing as a heel every week," he told IGN.com.

Pro wrestling came naturally for the third-generation Orton, who was born Randal Keith Orton on April 1, 1980 in Knoxville, Tennessee, and raised outside St. Louis. With a grandfather, Bob Orton Sr., his father, "Cowboy" Bob Orton, and an uncle, Barry O, in the business, no one was surprised when Randy made the leap. But it didn't happen immediately. Though he was in dressing rooms from an early age, started amateur at age nine in grade school, and continued grappling at Hazelwood Central High, Mom and Dad did their best to keep Randy away from pro wrestling as he grew.

In fact, Randy entered the Marine Corps for a year after high school. But by age nineteen, he'd decided that he wanted to wrestle. He made baby steps with a couple local promotions, Dad pulled some strings, and with just a handful of matches under his belt, he was sent to the WWE training facility of Ohio Valley Wrestling. "What I've done is shown him how to wrestle, to do the things like I did, even though that's probably passé now. But still, it's a good sound base," Orton Jr. said in 1999. His grandfather, shortly before his death in 2006, beamed that Randy had a "style damn near like mine."

Within a year and a half, Randy was on WWE TV. Told to keep his mouth shut and ears open, he tried to soak it all in. He really couldn't help but get better working with so many veterans. Dubbed "The Legend Killer," Orton got the chance to face off with a veritable who's who from the past — spitting in Harley Race's face; dropping Jake "The Snake" Roberts with his RKO finishing move; beating down Sergeant Slaughter — and the present. He fought hardcore matches with Mick Foley, and almost stole the show against The Undertaker at WrestleMania XX. On top of that, he was positioned in the heel faction Evolution, with Triple H, Ric Flair, and Batista.

"Well, with Ric Flair, as far as being a heel, or a bad guy, it's . . . tougher to learn any more from anybody else . . . besides Triple H. So I was with two of the best heels, in my mind, and in a lot of other people's minds, in the business," he told NZPWI.com. "I learned from Ric, just that heel mentality and how to always be thinking, not have a mindset of what I'm gonna do and just do that, but to like being out there, and just be myself, and just have confidence in what I'm doing, and things like that are more important than how to execute a suplex perfectly, or how to make a power-slam look more spectacular. It's that psychology that I think a lot of guys that are my age breaking into the business don't really get, because they don't, they're not fortunate enough to learn from the right people."

"RAVISHING" RICK RUDE

If all you fat, out-of-shape sweat hogs keep reading, you'll get to hear about the one-time sexiest man alive, and his all-too-short life. This is, of course, the story of "Ravishing" Rick Rude, a man who made headlines the day he was born Richard Erwin Rood in St. Peter, Minnesota, on December 7, 1958. His father, Dick Rood, was co-captain of the football team at Gustavus Adolphus College, and a war veteran. "We had three girls. When Rick was born, the Minneapolis paper came out with 'Dusty Rood has son.' When he got off the plane in Minneapolis, he didn't even know Rick had been born," said his mother, Sally Chiaferi. "They were asking him, 'How do you feel

Mike Lano

Rick Rude oils up backstage at WCW.

about having a son?' He went, 'What?'"

Growing up with an athletic father, Rick was a workout fiend. But so were his sisters. "Rick used to say, when people asked, 'Why did you go into wrestling?' he'd say, 'Did you ever meet my sisters?'" recalled his mom. "We used to fight. All of us are tomboys. He was the only boy," said his youngest sister, Nancy, who was a competitive bodybuilder and would serve as Rude's valet in the early days of his career.

Robbinsdale High School is now legendary for its development of pro wrestlers. The legacy of Verne Gagne and Larry Hennig — at the school decades before — begat Rude, Barry Darsow, Curt Hennig, Tom Zenk, John Nord, Nikita Koloff, and Brady Boone in the 1970s. The school's gymnastics coach was also heavily into body-building, and shared his passion with a core group of students, said Koloff (then Scott Simpson), who was a year behind Rude. "We ended up with quite the reputation across the state of Minnesota of the 'muscleheads' from Robbinsdale High School."

Trouble usually found Rude, or else he found it. Koloff's fondest memory of Rude from high school was a postgame brawl at the state hockey playoffs against Edina High School, where Rick ended up on top of the opponent's starting goalie, who was still in full uniform. Koloff is as surprised as anyone at all the wrestlers from the school. "None of us ever really talked about getting into professional wrestling back in those days. It just wasn't a point of conversation." Illustrating Koloff's point — Rude graduated with a physical education degree from Anoka Ramsey Junior College.

As a bouncer at the notorious Gramma B's bar in the northeastern section of Minneapolis, the six-foot-four Rude developed a real reputation, especially for his ability to knockout a troublemaker with a slap to the face. "He was a big, good-looking guy," said Eddie Sharkey, who would train Rude for pro wrestling. "Of all the guys around, we had some big, tough guys. The toughest guys ever were Hawk and Rick Rude. Rick Rude was an arm wrestler and Hawk, no way could he put [Rick's] arm down or be as strong as him. We bounced together, Rick and I, so I saw him in action. Boy, he was tough."

Rude's first match was in 1983 at a card in Vancouver, British Columbia, but it was in Mid-South, in Jimmy Hart's "First Family" gang, where he started to develop as a wrestler. The chiseled physique was already there, thanks in part to enhancement drugs like steroids. "I figured Rick had what it took," said King Kong Bundy, who held the tag belts with Rude. "He wasn't an exceptional worker, but certainly adequate. With his great looks and body, and he had a good rap, I figured he would do very well." Hart said Rood was a good listener. "Rick had a great body, but his talking skills weren't very good back then, so we worked on that a lot," explained Hart. "He learned more and more, and got very visual. He learned it was more than just wrestling, it was having a lot of showmanship."

In Texas in 1985, Rood's sister Nancy was known as "Raven," and worked as his second. "It was a crazy, crazy life. We partied like rock stars," she said. "I was in Rick's corner, and they were running up, and spitting at me, throwing things. It was really scary. And when we went to leave there, my brother was trying to protect me getting me out of there. They hated us, they really, really hated us." Eventually, Nancy had to leave the business, but her brother was only beginning.

Up next were championship stints in Florida and Texas with Percy Pringle III as his manager. "The chemistry between us both in and out of the ring was instantaneous," Pringle wrote on his Web site. In Jim Crockett's expanding Charlotte, North Carolina, promotion, Rude was NWA World tag champ with Manny Fernandez. "Me and him were the hottest tag team there, no question," said Fernandez. "Rude was one of those quiet persons that you really, really had to irritate, or really get under his skin, for him to say anything to you, or retaliate at all."

The biggest stage of all called next, and Rude entered the WWF under the guidance of Bobby "The Brain" Heenan in May 1987 without having lost the NWA tag titles. Portrayed as the ultimate ladies man, Rude belittled the male fans with a striptease and bump-and-grind in the ring as part of his entrance. Celebrating his victories by kissing women in the audience got him into trouble as he laid one on Jake "The Snake" Roberts' then-wife, Cheryl. It touched off a fierce feud. "He could be very dangerous. He had a very, very volatile temper," said Roberts. "I don't know if it was the 'roids, the personality, or a little of both. I don't care. I just knew that I didn't want to piss him off, because he'd explode in heartbeat. Sometimes you didn't see it coming, so that was dangerous."

Rude's mother said that her son had a passion for what he was doing that extended outside the ring. "Most of his gimmicks were his own ideas. He would go to any extent," she said. "He was doing the thing with Jake The Snake, and Jake's wife Cheryl, and he had her picture on the front of his pants. We were in Las Vegas, and we found this snake skin. He bought this snake skin so he could use it in the ring with Jake, and say, 'Here's your snake.' I don't know if he ever did that, but that was his plan."

After an Intercontinental title reign and a run as challenger to the Ultimate Warrior's WWF world title, Rude abruptly left the company in 1990, out of action with a torn tricep. He worked in Japan before returning to World Championship Wrestling. His career peak was in 1992, when he headlined against Sting, held the U.S. title and the WCW International world title. "He had an underlying thing inside of him that when he looked out at the people, and flipped them off, or something, he meant it. I think people can see that," explained Sting. "Then he'd blow his snot all over his opponent. He was just vile. I think that's the way people looked at him."

A back injury in Japan during a match against Sting in the fall of 1993 ended Rude's active career. "He was thirty-five years old, and in the second year of the biggest contract he ever signed," Rude's wife Michelle told the *Wrestling Observer Newsletter*. "And then it basically ended. That just killed him. He was a great entertainer, and it really hurt him that he couldn't perform."

Over the next few years, Rude would resurface at the Vince McMahon and Titan Sports trial over steroid distribution, and as an announcer involved in storylines in ECW, the WWF, and WCW. On April 20, 1999, Rude died suddenly at a hospital in Alpharetta, Georgia, after suffering a cardiac arrest at home. According to his mother, he still harbored a dream of returning to action. "I think he thought he could go back. He was working out to that end. I was going, 'My goodness, you'll end up in a wheelchair' because of the injury in his back." Rude left behind a wife and four children. "To this day, my daughters and I have never really gotten over it. And Rick's dad. You never get over the loss of a child. It's not like it's supposed to be."

BOBBY SHANE

"Cowboy" Bob Kelly remembers it as one of the best pitches he ever got. In 1971, Bobby Shane and his wife Sherri arrived unannounced at the wrestling office in Mobile, Alabama, and proceeded to make a case to Kelly and promoter Lee Fields to be given a chance as a bad guy. "I didn't know him at all, and Lee didn't know him either. We didn't know anything about him," confessed Kelly. "He had the crown, the cape, the whole nine yards that he was going to wear . . . the cigar and all that. . . . He convinced me that he could get the job done. I told him we'd use him as a heel, because he wanted to try, and use his wife as a valet."

What transpired in the Gulf Coast territory was the transformation of the white-meat babyface "Boy Wonder" into the "King of Wrestling." Kelly had an angle in mind for Don Fargo, but elected to use Shane instead. "He put the sleeper on me, and just left me laying," said Kelly. Ken Lucas, sleeperhold expert, came out to wake up Kelly. "That really shook the people up, got him over. 'He just left him to die!'" While their feud flared, another was building between Shane and Lee Fields, whose active career was done. Shane won the first match, and Lee admitted to the fans he was too out of shape. Kelly publicly helped his friend get back in shape, and together, they bested Shane. "He was just a natural-born heel. There just ain't no doubt about it," said Kelly. "He was one of the masters. I'm just so glad that I got to work with him, kind of help him get started as a heel."

Born Robert Lee Schoenberger in St. Louis, Missouri, on August 25, 1945, his parents took him to wrestling at a young age. In his teens, he was helping to carry ring jackets and run errands. Tutored by St. Louis regulars like Rip Hawk and Bobby Bruns, Shane succeeded despite his small five-foot-nine, 200-pound stature. "I didn't like him when I first met him because he was Sam Muchnick's pet," recalled Bill Watts. What Shane lacked in size, he made up for with a desire to learn and a love of the business. "He ate, drank, and slept wrestling. He was always thinking about new angles and gimmicks," wrote Jack Brisco in his autobiography. Seattle-area promoter Dean Silverstone corresponded with Shane for years. "I discovered there was another wrestling zealot besides me. Bobby Shane not only knew the name of the timekeeper in Kansas City . . . he knew his wife's name."

After a couple of years of community college at the advice of Muchnick, Shane went to Portland, Oregon, and debuted as Bobby Schoen. When he arrived in Kansas City, promoter and Shane foe Bob Geigel saw someone who wanted more. "He was a dedicated person, about wrestling, about his profession. He worked out a lot, and he trained a lot," said Geigel. "He'd ask people questions because he wanted to improve." Stints in Georgia, Nebraska, Hawaii, California, and the Mid-Atlantic would follow for the youngster, until he convinced Kelly and Fields that his ideas would work.

In late 1971, Shane headed to Florida, where he really hit his stride as a bad guy, winning the Southern title, the TV title twice, and the tag team titles on three occasions. According to Alfred Ticineto, Shane's number one devotee,

Pete Lederberg Collection

Bobby Shane and Miss Sherri.

Shane proved to be a popular heel, and the Tampanella Cigar Factory even named a stogie after him ("Shane — a truly fine cigar" was the ad slogan).

Shane was shipped to Atlanta in 1973 as a part of the war between Paul Jones' NWA Georgia territory and Ann Gunkel's All-South Championship Wrestling, and he helped book the NWA circuit with Jerry Jarrett. That experience led Jarrett to suggest Shane for the booking job in Australia in early 1974.

Upon returning to Florida in late 1974, Shane picked up where he left off as one of the area's hottest heels, and he had a new role helping book the territory. However, it was destined to be a short, tragic run.

His last match came on February 19, 1975, in Miami Beach, when Shane and Buddy Colt defeated Tony Parisi and Dominic DeNucci. Coming back to Tampa, Bill Watts flew the babyface plane, and Buddy Colt had the heels. "When the match was finished, everybody went back to the airport, and they were following each other in the plane," said DeNucci. "Bill Watts was right in front, and I was right behind, and I could hear the radio, and everything. Then we got a call, please stay away from downtown Tampa airport, the wind is very, very bad."

Colt was piloting a Cessna 182 with Bobby Shane, Gary Hart, and Mike McCord (Austin Idol) as passengers. He headed toward Peter O. Knight Airport on Davis Islands, but the sky was thick with clouds. "I start thinking, 'I'm probably where I shouldn't be,'" Colt told a Tampa newspaper. "It seemed like a split second. We hit the water." The plane was just 300 feet from shore, and broke in half. Colt, Hart, and McCord swam through Hillsboro Bay to shore. Shane was later found, still buckled in his seat. In its report on the accident, the National Transportation Safety Board listed "Pilot In Command — Attempted Operation Beyond Experience/Ability Level" as its number one probable accident cause.

Shane was just twenty-nine years old. "Had he been about five inches taller, there's no telling how far Shane would have gone," Muchnick said at the time of the tragedy. "He went as far as he could." His death still makes his colleagues wonder, "What if?"

"There is no doubt in my mind that he would have been the best we had to offer in the wrestling business," said Kelly. "If he had stayed alive, he would have been Ric Flair before Ric Flair."

"EXOTIC" ADRIAN STREET

Courtesy Adrian Street

A young workout fanatic.

Liverpool Stadium was a rough place, the type of arena where the wrestlers had to fight their way to the ring. It was not a place where "Exotic" Adrian Street found his recently recorded LP, complete with a fold-out poster, in much demand. Conspiring with opponent Jon Cortez, Street decided to try something new. After parading to the ring in one of his fancy-dan outfits, Street saw that Cortez had a copy of his record. Though he usually tried to never acknowledge his opponent before a match, Adrian gave him a nod of approval for his obvious good taste.

"Next thing is, he starts to rip up the poster into pieces, and throws it all over the place," Street explained. "He gets a hold of the record, and breaks it over his knee, smashes it up, and throws it to the people. I'm screaming, and shouting, going nuts. Jon says to somebody, 'Get me another record.' The people were running, and lining up in bloody hundreds to grab the record, and bring it down to Jon. They were bringing them down, and he was breaking them up, showing me the poster, breaking them up. I made more money than night than I had wrestling in about six months on the records, just to break the damn things up. Now I couldn't care less what they did with them. I was just interested in the money, and getting rid of the bloody things."

It was key to one of Street's philosophies about the business. "You've got to give the people a chance to react to what you're doing, and give the people a chance to perform," he said. "The only difference between the wrestler and the people is that the wrestler is paid to perform, and the people pay to perform."

Courtesy Adrian Street

Street with his father in 1974.

Born in Brynmawr, South Wales, on December 5, 1940, he left school at the age of fifteen, heading off to London to try to become a wrestler and avoid working in a coal mine like his father. Instead, he struggled to get by, working in a factory, sweeping up Wembley Stadium, and sleeping on park benches when he couldn't pay for a room. A bodybuilder from the age of eleven, his dream of bulking up to 200 pounds to be a wrestler wasn't compatible with his meager diet, and he actually lost thirty pounds. Desperate, he found himself boxing in a touring carnival for a pound per bout.

At the local gym, he'd horsed around with the cauliflower-eared veterans of the British mat wars. Unable to break onto Dale Martin's main circuit,

Street took whatever bouts he could, debuting in 1957 as Kid Jonathon. Within a couple of years, he was invited to bigger venues, and started working under his real name as "Nature Boy" Adrian Street. But success didn't truly find Street until he found his image.

Emerging from the dressing room, Street would pause just outside the doorway, allowing the commoners in attendance to take in his long, blond hair, elaborate outfit, and garish facial makeup, complete with embedded sequins and rhinestones. "I'd go in the ring looking like a French poodle, and I'd carry on like a French poodle, but as soon as the bell went and I'd done my little bit of prancing about, and the time was right, I'd turn from a French poodle to a pit bull," Street said.

Playing up an unmanly character was a challenge, but Street always knew what he wanted to portray. Interviewers would hone in on his sexuality, but "The Exotic One" would answer ambiguously. "Whenever someone infers that I'm effeminate, it makes me want to scream." Over the years, various characters like Goldust (Dustin Rhodes) and Rico Costantino used Street's gimmick. In Rico's case, he actually went to study from the master.

In 1969, Street met Linda Gunthorpe Hawker, who would become the woman wrestler Blackfoot Sioux, and later his valet, Miss Linda. Linda added a different dimension, and more mystery. She would allow him to step on her back on the way into the ring, straighten the robe of her "perfectionist pansy," and occasionally interfere by pulling a leg or bringing out a foreign object.

Street and Hawkes set off for the North American market in 1981, beginning in Calgary, then heading to Mexico and Los Angeles before finding a real home in the southeastern U.S. Promoters and bookers didn't always know what to do with him. "Adrian would do anything for attention. He would have shown his private parts on television if he thought it would have done him some good," British promoter Max Crabtree said in *The Wrestler*. As the booker in Florida for a time, Bob Roop admitted he didn't understand the gimmick: "It didn't feel like the kind of solid, long-term heat that you needed to draw with as a bad guy, I didn't feel that type of gimmick could carry it. That might have been my limitations as a booker."

Street has no problem explaining the nuances of what he was trying to achieve. "My idea of a bad guy is possibly different than a good many others. To me there's no reason why a bad guy's got to get cheap heat all the time, where he's got to growl and scream at everybody, jump in the ring, poke somebody in the eye, kick them in the balls as the first move, and scream and shout until his eyeballs pop out. My own way of doing it was to go into the ring, and wrestle, and show the people what a good wrestler I was," he said.

Adrian Street checks the dental work of Davey Boy Smith.

Rip Rogers was the heel in a year-long feud with Street in the Florida, Alabama, and Mississippi areas. "You had to go with the flow with Adrian. Me and Adrian never talked over a match," Rogers said. "All that mattered was the finish, and what we were coming back with. The rest was ad lib out there. No pre-arranged bullshit like they there is today." Terry Taylor was the good-looking baby-face working with Street in the Mid-Atlantic territory. "Adrian was a guy who looked like he couldn't bust a grape, and in real life was probably one of the toughest wrestlers around," he said, explaining the problems working with Street's style. "It was very difficult, it was very awkward, different timing, different execution of moves. In the old days, when we prided ourselves on having good matches with anybody, Adrian was the kind of guy that, if I had a match with Kamala one night, he was limited by what his character would let him do. Adrian was limited, honestly, by what he could do. But he knew exactly who Adrian Street was."

By the late '80s, Street had settled in the Gulf Coast region, where he still resides today. He and Linda make a living primarily by fashioning custom-made ring attire through their Bizarebazzar.com Web site. Street also taught wrestling at his Skull Crushers Wrestling School, which blew away during a hurricane a couple of years back. He still takes occasional indie bookings as well, despite having battled off throat cancer in 2001. Retirement is not on the horizon, he joked: "I can't do nothing. I'm not intelligent enough to do nothing."

Monsters Kane and The Great Khali battle at WrestleMania 23.

The Monsters

James C. Melby Collection

Jerry Blackwell.

CRUSHER BLACKWELL

It's the dropkicks that everyone remembers. Not too many wrestlers who weigh in at more than 400 pounds could launch picture-perfect standing dropkicks into the chests of their opponents. With a bushy beard, short legs, and a roly-poly stomach on a five-foot-eight body, Jerry Blackwell defied logic as well as gravity. "I think one of the most phenomenal things that he do was throw dropkicks. For a man that size to throw dropkicks!" marveled Dewey Robertson. Kansas City promoter Bob Geigel simply said that Blackwell was "amazing" for a man his size.

Nicknamed the "Mountain from Stone Mountain," Blackwell broke into the business in his native Georgia at the relatively late age of twenty-five. His early days in the South were under his real name (as well as, briefly, the masked Canadian Bumblebee in Tennessee), until he was brought north to the WWWF and made into "Crusher" Blackwell. With Freddie Blassie as his assigned manager, Blackwell worked a program with Louis Cerdan, a.k.a. Gino Brito, who was asked to teach the newcomer.

"He worked out pretty well. If he made a couple of mistakes the night before, you could be sure that the next night, if he made a mistake, it wasn't the same one. He was a quick learner," said Brito. "If you could jump the house 500 people a show, it was great. We knew we could do it with him. We went into the program, and worked some sort of story around it. You build him up just from a preliminary, and we made him into a main-eventer in just a short while."

Blackwell's size, which fluctuated between 375 and 450 pounds, was almost enough to make him a heel on its own. One of Blackwell's gimmicks was to drive large nails into a two-by-four using only his head; the feat accomplished, he'd lift his face, the blood dripping from his forehead. Visually, it was chillingly perfect. For interviews, he developed a quiet, whispering voice that was ultra-serious, and drew the viewer in.

His in-ring work was like a whisper too, said his colleagues. "He was so easy to work with. He splashed me and didn't even hurt me," Mike Davis told journalist Scott Teal. Scott Casey told Teal a similar tale. "I'll never forget one night in Kansas City in the Memorial Auditorium. He said, 'Scoop slam me.' I said, 'What?' He was 410 pounds. . . . He went up like a feather, but boy, when that weight got up there, he didn't feel like a feather. I barely got him over without killin' him."

Arriving in the AWA in 1979, Blackwell found a home, and stayed until 1986. He had an epic feud with The Crusher (Reggie Lisowski) over their common moniker, had a bodyslam challenge with Dino Bravo, and battled other babyfaces like Verne and Greg Gagne, and Brad Rheingans. "Jerry was just totally a different style, but for the size of man he was, there was nobody better. He had a different way of doing things, but he was phenomenal," said Greg Gagne. Blackwell's most famous feud was with Bruiser Brody (Frank Goodish), and it lasted for years.

As Sheik Ayatollah Blackwell, he held the AWA tag team titles with fellow American turncoat Ken Patera from June 1983 to May 1984. They were managed by Sheik Adnan Al-Kaissy. In his autobiography, Al-Kaissy talked about Blackwell's shortcomings. "He ate like a pig, and really never tried to lose any weight as far as I could tell. And, despite the fact that he ate tons of junk food, he was very sensitive about being so overweight. Traveling with him was always an adventure. We stayed in the same room together, and it was insane living with him. He would sit up all night watching TV, eating chips, and drinking Coke, until he fell asleep when the sun came up. Meanwhile, I would be up by five in the morning and out the door for my morning workout. I had to babysit him wherever we went, and it was really tough."

When Al-Kaissy and Patera turned on Blackwell, he became a fresh-off-the-farm, aw-shucks good guy. "Jerry was the type of guy that his size and just his demeanor in the ring made him a big, huge, super natural heel," said Harley Race, who often saw Blackwell in St. Louis, where the big man was Missouri champion on two occasions. "But when he turned babyface, he became one hell of babyface, because he was that dominant, dominant heel."

Health problems caught up with Blackwell by the mid-'80s. "I had seen Jerry in his younger days. He really got over in Kansas City, and in Minneapolis too," said Ed Wiskoski, who would battle Blackwell as Colonel DeBeers. "The only thing was, when I finally got to work with him, the majority of his career was behind him. He had severe diabetes. He wasn't taking care of himself. He couldn't hardly move anymore. Here was a big fat guy that used to dropkick you on the chin, and just couldn't do it anymore."

In late 1987, Blackwell returned to Georgia, where he was involved in a couple of local promotions — he was "Mr. Big" — before calling it quits a year later. He worked as a security guard after a business failed, and as his health faded, he fought diabetes, gout, and gangrene. He also divorced following the death of his son. A car accident in December 1994 further crippled Blackwell, and he died from pneumonia in Dawsonville, Georgia, on January 22, 1995, at the age of forty-five.

"BLACK ANGUS" CAMPBELL

Wrestling manager Percival A. Friend wasn't exactly impressed when he walked into a hotel in Calgary, Alberta, in 1971 to hook up with a new charge named "Black Angus" Campbell. "Now, I had never met him before. And I look over at a table and there's this monster sitting there with the long beard and his hair pulled back in a ponytail. He looked like nothing you'd ever seen before. I said, 'Good Lord, what is this world coming to?'"

Of course, the fearsome character turned out to be Campbell. He might not have looked like much physically, with his craggy appearance, unkempt mane, and buggy-whip arms. And his Irish brogue was barely understandable. But his unique style caused headaches for North American opponents throughout the 1970s.

"He was a wrestler, brawler type, not as extreme as Bruiser Brody, but somewhat similar. He was a very talented individual — basically, a tough ol' guy," said former NWA champion Harley Race, who worked with Campbell in the Central States territory. "The look, the accent got him over. His strength came from his legs — he could pick damned near anything up." Including Kansas City, Missouri, TV announcer Bill Kersten. During one angle, Kersten found himself on the receiving end of a Campbell attack. "An amazingly strong man. He was nobody to mess with. He picked me up by the head without any bracing or anything, and then slammed me. I was sore for three months," said Kersten.

Campbell was a veteran of the European scene before he moved to Calgary in 1971, where promoter Stu Hart was on the lookout for foreign-bred talent, and already had imported Les Thornton and Geoff Portz. Born Francis Patrick Hoy in Enniskillen, Northern Ireland, Campbell worked as a steeplejack before cutting his teeth in wrestling on

Black Angus, North American champion in Calgary.

the English equivalent of the "bring 'em on" carnival circuit. "Wild Angus" formed a tag team with wrestling brother "Mad" Jock (Harry Strickland), and fared well in weeks-long wrestling tournaments throughout Europe.

"Everybody knew we were tag partners in Europe, Mad Jock and Wild Angus — I was the mad one, always losing my temper too quick," laughed Strickland. The two big heavyweights had decidedly different styles. "For a twenty-three-stone man, I could stand in front of an opponent, and literally leap off my feet, and dropkick them under the chin," said Mad Jock. "[Angus] would just pat me on the shoulder and say, 'Keep it up, Jock, keep it up. You're doing good.'"

Most important, when he crossed the Atlantic, Campbell perfected the methods that would set him apart — a lot of European uppercut forearms, where he'd swing up and under an opponent's chin, and a heavy dose of tosses and suplexes. "He knew about submission wrestling," Race said. "He liked to jack around with you a little with that stuff. Ninety percent of it was his English style of working, the Greco-Roman throws."

Campbell shot to the top almost upon his arrival, and was two-time North American champion for the Calgary promotion in 1971. A year later, he headed to Kansas City, where he won the territory's heavyweight crown. In addition to his grappling skills, he liked to aggravate fans by implying he was concealing some kind of illegal goo. "He would take his thumb and his finger and run it inside his tights like he was getting something. Then he would rub it in his hair, and sling his hair in the guy's eyes. Of course, the guy would fall out of the ring, and grab at his eyes. It worked beautifully," Friend said.

Once he'd felled his adversary, Campbell took on a truly horrific appearance. "He'd open his mouth wide, throw his hair back, and he had this smile ten yards wide, and all the saliva would come out," Kersten recalled with a shudder.

Campbell was a tough guy as needed — "He just had ungodly strength for the way he looked . . . He would fight a grizzly bear with a stick," said former tag partner Roger Kirby. But he had a soft side, as well, and passed the wee hours on long road trips singing everything from "Tie Me Kangaroo Down" to gospel music. "He would play guitar and sing even though he wasn't a great singer. He would play acoustic guitar and his favorite song was 'Country Roads' by John Denver," said Jennifer Geigel, one of his daughters.

After nearly three years together, when his manager accidentally slugged him with a briefcase, Campbell turned on Friend and worked as a fan favorite for a while. In Portland, Oregon, though, he reverted to his old ways as the hard-hitting, villainous Rasputin. He held the Pacific Northwest title in 1974, and feuded with Dutch Savage in coal miner's glove matches.

Campbell made another swing of the States in 1977, capturing the Central States TV title, before returning home for good. He won the European heavyweight championship in June 1978, and continued to tour Australia and Japan, where he tagged with the great Billy Robinson. He wrestled into the 1980s, and passed his time fishing and enjoying the outdoors before he died in Stranraer, Scotland, in April 2005.

"It's a shame he didn't come over from England sooner because he would have been in demand absolutely everywhere," Friend said. "He looked like your worst nightmare, but, boy, he was one of a kind as a wrestler and as a person."

"MOOSE" CHOLAK

Tales of "Moose" Cholak's tough-
ness, bulk, and ungodly strength
permeate wrestling lore like mos-
quitoes around a bull moose in the
woods — even near the end of his
days. Filmmaker John Dolin went to
Chicago to film Cholak for his
Wrestling with the Past series. Cholak's
body had been beaten down
enough that he had to rely on a
wheelchair to get around his tiny
Chicago home. Yet, he never complained when asked to wear his
moose head (nicknamed Alexander)
for the interview, which was outside
in typical Chicago weather. "He
wore it in, literally, a thirty-miles-
per-hour wind. It kept slipping. He
kept rushing his dialogue to get it
out. This thing is ninety pounds on

Moose Cholak, before . . .

his body in a wheelchair," said Dolin. "He did not complain, he was totally
cooperative, just a real gentle spirit."

Fellow Chicagoan Angelo Poffo worked with and against Moose. "He was
a real tough wrestler, big and heavy," Poffo said. "I had a Cadillac, and when
he sat in the front seat on the passenger side, after he got out, my car leaned
to the right. That's why nobody wanted to take him anywhere."

Dominic DeNucci teamed with Moose Cholak in Indianapolis. "He was
so clumsy, and he was strong like a bull. One time, I was in the corner, and
he threw the other guy to me, and I grabbed him. I was behind the turnbuckle, and the guy was in front of me. He came in from the other corner,
and he hit him, like a football tackle. Shit, he almost killed me and I was
behind him!"

Rene Goulet finds himself laughing almost too much when trying to tell the
tale of an interview at Chicago's Channel 44, where he and Don Fargo, a.k.a. the
Legionnaires, had challenged Moose to a boxing match. Cholak and Goulet practiced the punches backstage. On camera, it worked out differently, and Goulet hit
Moose three times before Fargo interfered, hitting him with a wooden board in
the head. "The Moose fell down, and he gigged himself, bleeding. He turned

. . . and after.

around to the camera, 'Don't worry, Mama, I'm okay. But those guys are going to pay!'"

To the fan sitting at home watching Cholak from the Marigold Arena on the DuMont Network, or at ringside, the sheer size of the 350-pound man topped with a monstrous bullmoose head was unforgettable. Future manager Percival A. Friend was one of those captivated. "I was in awe of the size of this man but totally mystified by the huge moose head, capped off with a cape of actual fur from the same animal, which adorned his own head and shoulders. The rack of antlers had to be at least three feet on each side, and weighed around 125 pounds," Friend wrote on his Web site.

Born of Croatian heritage on March 17, 1930, Edward "Moose" Cholak became a wrestling star at Chicago Vocational High School, went to the University of Wisconsin, and played football in 1949 and 1950. He entered the navy for the Korean War, serving as an engineer. In 1952, he achieved a first by becoming All-Navy heavyweight champion in both boxing and wrestling. While in the navy, he met famed native wrestler Don Eagle, who convinced the six-foot-four Cholak to give the mat game a try. From 1953 to 1987, Cholak worked an estimated 8,000 matches, primarily throughout the Midwest, never far from his Chicago home and the Calumet Beach Inn tavern he inherited from his father. From 1976 to 1996, he worked for the city of Chicago as an engineer as well.

Known at various times as Moose, Golden Moose and Yukon Moose, some clever promoter came up with the idea of billing him from the non-existent town of Moosehead, Maine. Cholak didn't have to do a lot in the ring to be impressive. His size and strength were no gimmick, and at one point he ballooned to 450 pounds.

"He could really eat," said frequent tag partner Paul Christy. "One time, he entered an eating contest in downtown Chicago. He won the contest, came back to his bar, and ordered a large-size pizza." Christy stressed that his friend was not a simple man, and could talk about everything from opera to religion. "He was brilliant, but he didn't want to bring it up a lot of the time, but we made a lot of long trips together."

Family was important in Cholak's life, and he was with his wife Arlene for forty-five years, until his death on October 31, 2002, in Hammond, Indiana. His pneumonia developed after suffering a stroke a week before. They had two children together, Kathleen and Steven. "He would take our son, Steven, everywhere," Arlene Cholak said when her husband died. "If he was wrestling nearby, he would pile all the neighborhood kids in the car. There were times when I didn't think they could fit another kid in the car."

ERIC THE RED

The name Eric the Red stirs memories of a beastly man with long, red flowing hair, decked out in Viking gear, throttling opponents. The name Erik the Animal recalls a wild man, dressed in furs, and carrying a stinky old bone that doubled as a weapon on unsuspecting noggins. But the name Erik Hansen brings nothing but smiles to the faces of his old colleagues. "God bless Eric the Red. This is the only wrestler that could drink with Andre," said George Steele.

"Eric the Red and I had a lot of funny, funny stories together when we traveled. We went in to Oklahoma together, and Bill Watts really took a liking to us, yet we gave him a lot of grief. We aggravated the shit out of him. He'll tell you that. They had to split us up. They put one on the north end, and one on the south end," said Bruce Swayze. Watts does, in fact, say that: "When he came to work for me, he had the greatest sense of humor, was totally incorrigible, morally even beneath Bill Clinton. But he was so funny about it. He loved to poke fun at me."

There was just something about the six-foot-one, 340-pound Hansen that endeared him to people. "Eric the Red should have been a babyface. His demeanor was such you just had to love the guy," said Ron Martinez, the son of Buffalo promoter Pedro Martinez. "Bruce [Swayze] was correct, anybody that met him truly was taken by the big lug."

His oldest son, Kim Hansen, who worked around southern Ontario as Leif the Viking with his dad, called Erik a social butterfly. "He could get the party going. If there were any women around, it didn't matter if there were pretty boys, big bodybuilders, or anything, they would just go right toward the old man. He just had that thing because he was fun-loving."

That fun-loving nature is partly how Erik and his brother ended up in Canada. In Denmark, their grandfather ran a pipefitting business, and, at his wits end by their exuberant lifestyle, decided to send them to Vancouver. In

Courtesy Wrestling Revue Archives

Erik the Red chokes the Canadian Wildman with his bone.

the new land, Hansen became intrigued by the local All-Star Wrestling pro-motion. A special challenge had been issued to anyone who could stay in the ring with esteemed shooter Karl Gotch for a certain amount of time. The cash prize was too much to ignore, and Hansen talked promoter Rod Fenton into giving him a chance.

"He was the guy that Karl Gotch couldn't stretch. Of course, that was kind of a misnomer, in that Erik was wanting to get into the business," explained Watts. "Some of the boys coached him. So what he did, he just stayed by the ropes and held on to them. And in the time limit — the time limit was so ridiculous that it didn't give Gotch the time to, quote, 'work on him.' It was a completely misdone thing, typical of Fenton. He just kept hanging on to the ropes. Karl couldn't get him to submit in the time. Of course, Fenton reneged on the money he promised."

But Erik Hansen was now in wrestling. He just didn't know anything. As a rib, he was shipped off to Japan as Viking Hanson where he was smartened up to the business after beating up one too many Japanese wrestler.

For the rest of his brief career, he didn't go out of his way to do much more than he had to. But when he wanted to, he could really perform, showcasing remarkable skills for a man his size. "All he wanted was a twelve-pack, a room, and an arena rat, and he was happy," said Martinez. Nevertheless, he was a truly gifted big man. "He could do things with his body that no one else could do, until Vader, almost thirty years later." Swayze concurred. "I thought he was one of the best big men in the business. He was a guy that could walk on his hands. He could take a soccer ball and bounce it for five minutes, either foot."

Hansen's biggest runs came working with Johnny Powers in Buffalo and the Carolinas. "I think the key place he got over were my areas, where I was running promotions," said Powers, who exchanged the NWF North American championship with Erik the Animal in 1973.

Hansen found a home in Grimsby, Ontario, not too far from Niagara Falls, where he worked as a pipefitter while still wrestling. Well-known around town, Erik had five kids with his wife, Ignor. "It was a good thing that he was a wrestler, but it was a bad thing," explained his son, Kim. "Five kids living at home here, we'd only see him once in a while."

On November 18, 1978, Hansen was wrestling in Florida, and was NWA Florida tag champion with Pak Song when he was struck by a car. "I got the phone call, and I went down there first," said his son Kim. "I talked to some of the guys. I guess he was walking on the side of the road, and somebody came to pick him up, and he crossed the road. There were skid marks off the road, there were skid marks on the road. I can still remember it, because I went there and looked at it. So nobody knows exactly what happened, but nobody got charged."

KANE

The history of Kane in the WWE is intertwined with that of his fictional brother The Undertaker. While both have been portrayed as good and evil, only one of them was chosen to be a psycho-serial killer in the 2006 movie, *See No Evil*. But Kane, a.k.a. Glen Jacobs, acknowledges that he can't get away from the connection between the two monsters, even if they are on different rosters. "I think our fans, not just because of the craziness of the character, but because of the storyline between the two, we attract very dedicated fans," Kane told IGN.com. "The people that are Kane fans, they're always there. No matter what I do, they're always very supportive. So I would say, yeah, I attract crazy fans, and I also attract fans who are crazy about us and about me. Because Kane does have a history in WWE, a lot of people have been attracted to the mystery and the mystique."

In a storyline as old as Cain and Abel, the two brothers have gone to war together, and against each other. Starting off immediately as Kane in 1995 in a feud with the already-established 'Taker was a big coup for Jacobs, who had short stints earlier in the WWE as a fake Diesel and as Jerry Lawler's dentist, Isaac Yankem. Kane burst onto the scene under a mask, managed by Paul Bearer, claiming to have been horribly burned and scarred in a childhood blaze. Progressing out of Bearer's control, Kane became a Hannibal Lecter-type of intelligent monster. Essentially, through the years, the Kane storyline has progressed, yet his repertoire of moves hasn't.

"A lot of people may not like to hear it, but part of the appeal of pro wrestling is seeing oversized supermen throwing each other around the ring," explained Dan Murphy, senior writer at *Pro Wrestling Illustrated*. "Kane is the strong, silent type. You don't need much exposition from him. He's a big monster who is going to beat the heck out of people. That can make him an effective heel or an effective babyface. And WWE Creative has done a good job tweaking Kane's character through the years, gradually building to him being able to speak, then losing his mask, and turning him back and forth from heel to face. It's kept him fresh when so many of his contemporaries grew stale."

The six-foot-eight, 310-pound Jacobs exudes menace, with his slow, deliberate style, his sadistic scowl, and the flames that often surround his entrance. It is fun being evil, he admits, even if some fans are turned on by it. "Sometimes, the more heinous things you do, the more people like it," Kane told the *Ottawa Sun*. "It's a reflection of society. We're living in the era of the anti-hero. If you asked all the wrestlers, the vast majority of them would say they'd prefer to be booed. We get to go out there and have fun by upsetting people . . . it's so much more fun than being one of the good guys. You can pretty much do what you want."

Right from the early days of his career, it was hard for fans to have much sympathy for someone so physically huge. The former scholarship basketball player at Northeast Missouri State (he won letters in 1988 and 1989) didn't get into pro wrestling until he was twenty-five years old, but wound up dwarfing most opponents. His father was in the U.S. Air Force, and Jacobs was born in Madrid, Spain, but grew up in St. Louis. He had a job working at a group home for mentally challenged adults, which he kept as his wrestling career began under the name Doomsday.

Even as a good guy, Kane scares the beejeezus out of MVP.

Vincent Lagana

He made trips to Japan, and was working in Puerto Rico in 1994 when "Nature Boy" Buddy Landel found him, and telephoned Jim Cornette, who was running the Smoky Mountain Wrestling promotion in Knoxville, Tennessee. "I had called Cornette when I was down there, and I said, 'Look, there's a guy down here that is just fantastic,'" recalled Landel. "He had a lot of talent. I felt like he would fit in well in the dressing room." Sandy Scott worked with Cornette in a backstage capacity in SMW, and felt that he shared some of his lessons with Jacobs, who was known as Unabomb. "He came in. He was green. He worked for us, and we brought him along," said Scott. "He's a big guy, a big strong guy. But he listened, that's the one thing about the guy, he listened, and he wanted to do it. He wanted to improve."

A man that size does not escape the notice of the big leagues, and he was soon on the WWE roster. Initially, the Kane-Undertaker storyline seemed like it might be short-lived. But both have survived attempts to kill the characters — on and off screen. The litany of Kane's bizarre story twists — burying Undertaker alive in a ringside grave; stealing bride-to-be, Lita, and impregnating her; a Beauty and the Beast deal with Tori; attaching jumper cables to Shane McMahon's private parts; Mutt and Jeff tag teams with X-Pac and The Hurricane; beating up Pete Rose — would have destroyed a less enduring character.

"Being this character is pretty fun because I can do anything I want without getting arrested," "The Big Red Machine" told the *Calgary Sun*. "Doing things to people, and not getting into any trouble, is fun." The other fun that Jacobs enjoys? Video games. "Kane is probably the most hardcore gamer I've ever met," said WWE colleague Steven Richards. "There isn't a game that I've ever seen Kane start that he hasn't finished. He's very hardcore, and very intense."

Howard Baum

Jos Leduc: wild eyed and bloody.

JOS LEDUC

It always seems to come back to the axe. Every lumberjack worth his syrup has to have one; they just don't usually purposely cut their skin open with it. But Jos LeDuc was not your average lumberjack. In his hands, an axe was a way to deliver a message to his opponents: he didn't feel pain, and would do anything to win.

The most famous axe moment was in Memphis' WMC-TV studio in the late '70s. LeDuc was engaged in a feud with the beloved Jerry Lawler, and sliced open his own arm as a blood oath, vowing to get rid of Lawler forever. "The incident took everyone by surprise. I assumed that he was taking the axe as a prop," said Memphis co-promoter Jerry Jarrett. "The first time Jos cut himself was in a taped interview. I was able to stop the shoot as soon as he began. I advised that not only did I object to self-mutilation, but the television station would not air the incident. Later

Jos did the same thing on live television." Lance Russell was the announcer, and still finds it hard to believe that it actually happened. "Nobody was more stunned than I was," he said. "To see that right on camera, with him bringing that axe down, and that skin just peeling back, and slowly starting to spout blood out. What a shock that was!"

It was all in a day's work for LeDuc, who built a reputation with the fans and his peers for his unpredictability. In fact, he was so wild, it's hard to believe that LeDuc — actually Michel Pigeon — was once a security officer, working for Hydro Quebec. That was 1965, and the twenty-one-year-old Pigeon felt a need for something more. He befriended an eight-year wrestling veteran named Paul LeDuc, who encouraged him to try pro wrestling. After Pigeon trained under Montreal promoter Jack Britton, he and Paul LeDuc decided to become a tag team. The LeDucs headed to California, Oregon, and Calgary, where little brother Paul (five-foot-nine, 200 pounds) would be rescued by Jos (six-foot-one, 250 pounds). Wearing toques, checkered shirts, and work boots, and with thick French accents, they were prototypical lumberjacks. Altogether, they worked as a team off and on, for sixteen years. The pinnacle of their run came in Montreal, where they'd battle Johnny and Jacques Rougeau, Killer Kowalski and Don Leo Jonathan, and Mad Dog and Butcher Vachon. Jos legally changed his name and the LeDucs were such an institution in Quebec that when it was revealed, follwing Jos' death in 1999, that they were not brothers, a mini-scandal erupted.

In the mid-'70s, Jos LeDuc struck out on his own, and tweaked the act to play up his legitimate strength. He began doing strongman acts, honoring French-Canadian legends like Louis Cyr and Victor Delamarre. "People always loved visual stuff in Memphis," said his manager, Jimmy Hart. In one skit, LeDuc pulled a car with Hart on the hood around the Mid-South Coliseum; in another, he braced himself against a wall, and kept a car from going forward just with his legs. "People had never seen that before, because we played him up as a strongman. That was a great experience. People were really scared of him."

Yet while the fans were terrified, his co-workers loved him. "Jos was a gentle giant. Jos was a gentleman," said Ron Bass, who used to call Jos "Josh LeDuck" to get a rise out of him. "If you knew him personally, there was nothing that he wouldn't do for you. But in the ring, he was serious business all the way through. One thing about Jos LeDuc was those eyes, he had those piercing eyes, those wild-looking eyes. The expression he had was just unreal. What a powerhouse, and he knew what he was doing in the ring."

But a wild streak in LeDuc was deeply ingrained, said his son Robert J. LeDuc. "If you were to ask any one of the wrestlers, they could say nothing but great things about him. He was a great wrestler, he was very soft-handed in the ring, never hurt anybody, very generous in the ring when he sold. All kinds of great accolades. From my perspective, he was intimidating, fearful, this giant of a man. And wild. Even as a teenager, I partied with him — lots of women, drugs, and alcohol, it was wild, crazy. He ruled the roost with an iron fist."

LeDuc's career would run until 1988, when the WWF strangely tried to make him into The Headbanger, who head-butted his opponents so many times that he would get disqualified. His greatest successes came in the southern states, battling the Fullers in the Gulf Coast promotion, or tossing Jerry Lawler through tables in Tennessee. Frequent victim Dusty Rhodes summed it up in his autobiography: "[LeDuc] drew so much fucking money in the South and Florida, it is unbelievable." But LeDuc also worked the American Wrestling Assoication, teaming with Larry Hennig as The Axe and Double Ax, pulling a bus for the camera, in Quebec, and the Maritimes. Strangely, LeDuc was probably a babyface as much as he was a heel, but his style never wavered.

The youngest child from LeDuc's two marriages, Michele LeDuc Holmes, remembers just bits and pieces of her dad's career, particularly hanging out with him in the summers. She has the forty scrapbooks that her father kept, his flowery penmanship belying his in-ring nature. Her dad used to joke that he had a dog bone in his neck, "and if you touched it, his dog features would come out. He'd started growling. He would do that with kids, with people I introduced him to. He was a big teddy bear, really," she said.

In February 1999, in Montreal, LeDuc got sick with a lung infection. He moved to Atlanta to live with his ex-wife and her husband, his daughter Michele, and his grandson. "The Canadian Freight Train" lived just another month, his body giving out to complications from diabetes and the infection.

"THE MONGOLIAN STOMPER"

According to Bret "Hitman" Hart, to be a true, true great, you need to have a great look, wrestling ability, and be a great interview. And to Hart, Archie "The Stomper" Gouldie had them all. "[Gouldie] fit all three categories better than anyone I ever saw in the business before or since. He was just a phenomenal man to look at, he was a great athlete, he was a great worker, and he was a great interview," said Hart. "He was the best interviewer ever. He'd talk about coming out to my dad's house, and he'd tear it down brick by brick, and spike piledrive my mom on the highway. I remember him on TV and I'd get goosebumps on my arms."

But the irony is that while Hart may remember Gouldie for his interviews, the Stampede Wrestling promotion was one of the few that let the six-foot-two, 265-pound behemoth on the microphone. (And that was only after Gouldie had proven himself elsewhere.) Throughout the United States and Australia, he was The Mongolian Stomper, and usually had a mouthpiece speaking for him.

Gouldie found it hard to hold his tongue. "You wanted to let it out, unless you had a real good manager that could do it, you'd wish you were doing it," he said. Still, it meant he got to be a bad guy, which he always found to be more enjoyable. "It's really my personality. I had fun doing it. I couldn't see being a good guy, smiling, and signing autographs."

It was Pat O'Connor who came up with the idea in 1964 to turn the raw twenty-eight-year-old youngster with a junior football background from tiny Carbon,

The Mongolian Stomper flexes in Texas with manager J.J. Dillon.

Pete Lederberg Collection

Alberta (population 600), into the mysterious man from Mongolia. "He said he wanted a gimmick-type character in Kansas City, he had just bought the promotion. I went along with it, and it stuck with me. It worked well so I stayed with it," said Gouldie. It became a regular feat to see his opponents stretchered out of the arena.

The idea worked, said Ronnie Garvin. "The Stomper would murder guys week after week, after week, after week. Demolish them. He'd just got out there, and stomp, and stomp, and kill everybody. Boom and boom! He got heat, he got results. He got heat, and he drew money."

J. J. Dillon was one of Gouldie's many managers. (Others included Gorgeous George Jr., Don Carson, and Bearcat Wright.) In fact, it was Archie who convinced Dillon to switch from wrestling to managing, the

Archie Gouldie stomps on Angelo
Mosca at home in Stampede.

two having gotten to know each other during a summer tour in the Maritimes. "Archie was very intense — he looked intense when he was there for promos, he looked intense in the ring, he *always* was really a workout freak, and he always looked great, really looked great. His work was solid. He would use that stomp to the head, and it just looked like he killed people," said Dillon. It was a different era, when fans would suspend disbelief about where a wrestler was from. "We used to have some gibberish that we would use, like I was talking to him in his own language. It wasn't anything elaborate, just a sentence or two. I actually looked up some research on Mongolia."

Dressed in a fur vest, and sporting a tussle of hair on his shining bald head, the Mongolian Stomper struck an imposing figure behind his manager. One of his on-camera stunts was to flex a heavy-duty spring, like one from a car shock absorber, as sweat started to pour off his tensed body. In the ring, Gouldie knew more than he ever showed. He had tried his luck in Stu Hart's Dungeon when just barely out of his teens, then returned years later — in far better shape and more determined. He had survived. "I tried to work solid, believable. Of course, I was always able to keep going because I was fit. I didn't use a lot of wrestling holds, stuff like that. More or less just kicking, and punching, and tearing away," he said, calling it a "full throttle" style.

Though he worked with The Stomper in Calgary, Kansas City and the Maritimes, Leo Burke remembers Archie more for the workouts than anything. He saw Gouldie work out with football players, and do more laps than them. "We were doing push-ups, because we had a push-up stand that was at least three feet high, you put your legs on the bench, elevated. We'd go right down, deep. We'd end up, we were doing ten sets of thirty, which is 300 push-ups. God, what a workout we had. I could see the difference — I even lost weight. I was never sore, it's the weights that make you sore. It was no weight, but talk about good conditioning. I was in tip-top shape," said Burke. "He'd do that, then when he was done, he wanted to go play squash, handball, anything. He was almost psychotic as far as being conditioned."

Equally psychotic were the fans, said Gouldie. "Shoot, I couldn't count the tires I've had cut off, the windshields broken. I bought a couple of convertibles, which was a mistake. I went out one night in St. Joe, Missouri, and the top was cut off the convertible." There was no auto insurance for a wrestler;

the replacement roof came out of his pocket. In some places, he'd find a taxi stand, leave his car there, and take a cab to and from the arena.

His family (two sons and a daughter) suffered the wrath of those who hated their father as well. "They got into a lot of problems, especially in Dallas. I remember my kids were nine and eleven, and the other kids were beating them up in school and things like that," Gouldie said. He learned a lesson about taking his kids to matches at the Kansas City Auditorium, which had a place for wrestlers to park in the basement. "One night, I took my two kids because it was a special night. . . We were on last, and the last to get out of there. I went downstairs and got in my car. The overhead door was open. We got in the car, and started the car up, and drove over by the door, and just as I driving out through the overhead door, there were three men standing across the door. They had baseball bats, and a steel pipe. I always kept a pistol under the seat of my car. I got that out, and started shooting at the concrete walls. Bullets were ricocheting. The three guys took off out that door, and down that street. They were gone!"

Gouldie asserts that he has no regrets about his career, yet many a booker can recall him walking out on the promotion without notice. It was just his way. He would question the promotion's plans for him. "He would come to these conclusions, based on some minor thing, that they've got no plans for us," said Dillon. "Every time things got really bad, he'd go back to Calgary, where he had started, and Stu would always take care of him. That was kind of his safety net."

A frequent opponent in Calgary, "Cowboy" Dan Kroffat, thinks that Gouldie could have been a bigger star. "It's like a guy who played in the CFL who could have played on any team in the NFL, but he stayed in Canadian football," Kroffat said. "I don't think Archie ever reached the limits. If WWE was as big then as it is now, he would have been in WWE, and truly a villain, a real, solid, convincing guy that truly exemplifies what a villain is."

It was in Calgary where The Stomper had his main babyface run. Kroffat said it was inevitable, claiming, "The fans loved to hate him, is the best way I'd describe him. My biggest battle was to stay babyface when I worked with him." Gouldie is matter-of-fact about his days as a good guy: "It seems like if you stay in a territory a length of time, it's just going to happen that way. It just happens, so you turn over that way. I didn't mind that. In fact, in a lot of places where I had a lot of problems, I kind of enjoyed it for a while."

After his last major run, with Jim Cornette's holdout territory, Smoky Mountain Wrestling, Gouldie settled in Knoxville, Tennessee, where he took a job with the sheriff's department, initially driving the paddy wagon and then working in the guard shack at a prison. He continued to wrestle a handful of times each year, usually on benefit shows. In August 2004, he retired for good from the sheriff's department. It has given him more time for everything but rest and relaxation. "I did a 100-mile road [bike] trip in ten days," he said. "It gets harder to do every day, I'll tell you that."

GORILLA MONSOON

Courtesy Wrestling Revue Archives

The future Gorilla Monsoon, Gino Marella.

If you want to know how well the name Gorilla Monsoon fit Bob "Gino" Marella, veteran wrestler Lester Morgan offers an incident when Tony Garea, Joe Turco, and others were propping up thirty-five-foot-tall telephone poles at a work project in New Jersey. Morgan was sitting on top of a pole, trying to line up the next one. "Gino grabbed this one pole, picked it up, slammed it in the ground, and then grabbed both poles and started shaking them down, banging them into the ground. His wife Maureen yells, 'Les is on top of the pole, you fool!' I mean, he grabbed that pole like it was nothing. After that, I stopped agitating him," Morgan laughed.

Marella was an intelligent, giving, college graduate with a rich, full voice cut out for singing. He was also the least likely bloodthirsty, raw-meat eating, illiterate Manchurian manbeast you'd ever see. Gorilla Monsoon was the first big character heel — and the biggest physically — when the WWWF spun away from the National Wrestling Alliance in 1963. He remained one of the federation's leading bad guys till he changed his stripes in 1969. "He was so over in the early '60s," magazine editor Bill Apter recalled after Monsoon died in 1999. "His fierce growl and full beard persuaded people to take his gorilla persona seriously."

Always a big guy, Monsoon starred in football, wrestling, and track and field at Jefferson High School in Rochester, New York. He went on to Ithaca College, where he lettered twice in football, and set school records in the discus and shot put. He finished second in the NCAA heavyweight wrestling championships in 1959, losing by a single point in overtime, and represented the United States during a wrestling tour of Europe in 1960. "'Tiny' Marella was an unbelievable specimen," said college teammate Dave Auble, later a college wrestling coach. "I think he could do more pull-ups than anybody in wrestling. He weighed close to 300 pounds, but the guy was just a unique specimen, unbelievable arm strength. I think the guy could do thirty pull-ups, which was crazy carrying that much weight." A public school teacher by training, Marella seemed like a natural for the pro mat, sort of a latter-day George Bollas, an oversized legitimate wrestler. But the transition didn't come off easily. "Have license, will travel, but so far all I've gotten pretty much is the brush-off," he told Syracuse sportswriter Arnie Burdick in 1960. "I can't understand this pro wrestling riddle." Eventually, Buffalo, New York promoter Pedro Martinez used the 350-pounder more often. "I was proud of my success as an amateur wrestler but knew that Pedro was more interested in my physique than my technique," Monsoon acknowledged in one interview. "I was huge."

He got some work as a patriotic American who sang before matches, but his name was on the undercard until he became Gorilla Monsoon, whose initials of G.M. derived from "Gino," a nickname he picked up from scarfing bucket after bucket of fried chicken from Gino Garibaldi's restaurant. Even then, Monsoon was a tough sell because just about everyone recalls Marella as the antithesis of a villain. Beauregarde (Larry Pitchford) said Monsoon briefly practiced his heel work in the Pacific Northwest before heading back East. "He was good, but he wasn't a personality enough. He wasn't really that bad, like George 'The Animal' Steele. He didn't like to be the bad wrestler; he'd liked to have been a good wrestler, but he was too big, and not good-looking enough to be a babyface." Monsoon grew out his hair, added a chinstrap beard, and returned to Vincent J. McMahon's New York territory as a monstrous fiend with "Wild" Red Berry as his mouthpiece. "He was a nice guy, and a lot of fun," said Baron Mikel Scicluna, a longtime friend, who wrestled him for years in the WWWF. "Out of the ring, he was a nice guy. In the ring, he was a bad guy. He was very strong. But he was easy to work with."

In the early years of the WWWF, Monsoon was the top challenger to Sammartino's crown. "The old Madison Square Garden with Monsoon and Bruno, that was an event that had electricity in the air," Davey O'Hannon remembered. "He got on Vince's TV with Red Berry doing the talking for him — Red Berry found him swimming in a river in Manchuria, pushing

Gorilla Monsoon goes after "Crazy" Luke Graham.

away icebergs so he could swim. You didn't hear anything from Monsoon except five minutes of grunting, and being in the ring. He was really a convincing kind of guy in there." In 1964, Monsoon teamed with "Cowboy" Bill Watts to form a dominating, if short-lived, tag team that held the U.S. titles for about four months. "We didn't stay together too long because the office couldn't control us too well," Watts said. "When we got angry, which we did one night with [Chief] White Owl and [Argentina] Apollo in a little spot show, and guzzled both of them — Monsoon didn't like Apollo and I didn't care much for White Owl — things just got out of hand. They were the babyfaces, and the people were just sitting on their hands as we beat the shit out of them. So they didn't really like that team too well because if we got upset, there wasn't anything anybody could do with us."

Despite Monsoon's few public utterances, writer Jim Marr found a talented linguist when he dropped by Monsoon's New Jersey house for dinner and a story in 1967. "As a wrestler, Monsoon assumes the posture of an unlettered lout who can't speak a lick of English. In his wooing [of wife

Maureen], however, he was quite eloquent, murmuring endearments in French and Italian, and mixing in a few more in other languages."

Referee Dick Woehrle considered Monsoon a close friend who pulled his fat out of the fire more than one time. Woehrle got a kick out of refereeing a match between Monsoon and local hero Carlos Colon in Puerto Rico when his buddy came to the ring with paper-cup megaphones stuck in his ears. "The crowd is screaming bloody murder, they're throwing everything in the book at him, and he's pointing to his earphones saying, 'I can't hear you!'" After a ref bump and switch, Monsoon came out on top, and barely beat a mob rush by hopping a cab, with his wife half-hanging out the door, Woehrle said. "He could put the bad guy act over, but he was more or less a top-notch good guy."

The Gorilla didn't always know his own strength — he knocked out Pete Sanchez twice, once with an accidental kick to the head. That was more or less his style in the ring, though Sanchez said Monsoon sometimes snuck his amateur background out of the closet. "Once in a while, he used to have some fun — hook you, take you down, and kid around with you that way," Sanchez said. "I really loved the guy. Gino was a sweetheart of a guy." Morgan remembered being on the receiving end of one of his famous chops during a 1976 match in West New York, New Jersey. "I've still got the bruise on my chest from it. He lifted me up, and put me over the rope, then he realized he hit me a little bit too hard," Morgan said. "So I get back in again, he's got me in the corner, and he says, 'How do you feel?' I said, 'For just getting hit by a friggin' Mack truck, I feel pretty good.'"

Monsoon was a tag team champ in the WWWF with Killer Kowalski in 1963, and in California with Luke Graham and El Mongol in 1966. Sick of fan assaults, he became a hero in 1969 after a bout with The Sheik. "I got tired, literally tired, of being spit at, knifed, bottle whipped, and black-jacked," he told a Philadelphia newspaper in a candid moment. "I had chairs thrown at me, rocks, and had my car dismembered many times. I literally came to a point where I couldn't take that any more, and became a clean wrestler to avoid the physical abuse."

Though he ventured overseas frequently, Monsoon was most closely associated with the Northeast, and was an important backstage figure in the WWWF. At one time, he owned a piece of the promotion, and the "gorilla" position that oversees action from behind the entrance drapes was named for him. He handled a lot of the company's bookings in the 1970s. He spent that decade as a good guy before sliding behind the microphone when the WWF went national, and for years was the straight-man foil to heel commentators Jesse Ventura and Bobby Heenan. "The only thing I regret about becoming a professional wrestler is that I missed the opportunity to teach youngsters," Monsoon said in 1978. "Of course, there aren't many $100,000-a-year teachers."

When son Joey, a referee, died in a 1994 car crash, Monsoon stepped away from an active role in the business. He made some appearances as a figurehead commissioner before dying of heart failure in October 1999 at sixty-two. But his name still carries a lot of weight. Andre the Giant had two enormous recliner-style chairs specially built for himself and Monsoon. Morgan regularly takes the chair to fundraisers for causes dear to Monsoon's heart, remembering how Monsoon reached out to him after Morgan's young son died in 1975. "He helped raise money for the children's burn center, for ambulances . . . People have no idea how much money this man raised for diabetes and cancer research, and woman abuse and child abuse [causes]. He was just a great human being."

"APACHE" BULL RAMOS

In the wrestling world, more often than not, the Native Americans have been the heroes — whether they were truly blood Indians or just pretending to be. Then along came "Apache" Bull Ramos, who was bad to the bone, and proud of it. He described his debut in Australia to demonstrate his ability to turn a crowd. "When I jumped in the ring, everybody just started yeahing me and throwing me flowers, and all this stuff. By the time I finished wrestling that night, everybody wanted to kill me. I had a couple of people have heart attacks that night," Ramos recalled in 2004. "I was a heel all the time because the people never liked me. I was never a babyface."

His frequent opponent in the Pacific Northwest, Dutch Savage, called him the best heel he ever saw. "As far as getting red, raw heat, I'd have to say 'Apache' Bull Ramos," Savage said. "Ramos had this thing about him. It was like all you had to do was show up, and he'd get the heat for you. It was such a refreshing thing in the ring where you didn't have to do anything, he did it for you."

Wearing a simple headband around his brow, a vest, and bending the scales at a top weight of 350 on his six-foot frame, Ramos was a sight to behold. Yet for all his weight, colleagues said he could move with the grace of a dancer. "He was what we call a dream in the business," said Chavo Guerrero Sr. "He would lead the match. For his size, brother, he could take some awesome backdrops. The whole ring would shake like an earthquake. He was good. He had good timing. He was very athletic, not only for his size, but putting aside his size, he was athletic, period." Chavo's brother Mando appreciated Ramos calming him down in matches. "I wanted to explode. 'Hold it, hold it, come on, hold it. Just relax. I'll give it to you, just wait a minute.' Many times I had in the back of my mind that I wouldn't get my comeback."

Growing up in Houston, Ramos had an uncle who was passionate about his pro wrestling. He'd arrange for the family to go to the matches, sitting way up in the cheap seats, where a huge block of ice and a fan would serve as primitive air conditioning. Ramos had taken up boxing, but one thing led to another, and Houston promoters Morris Sigel and Paul Boesch decided he should be trained for wrestling. He was hooked up with David Weinstein, Danny McShain, and Cyclone Ayala for schooling. In his first session, Weinstein stretched Ramos so bad that he couldn't get out of bed for three days. But Ramos went back, though anyone who saw

Bull Ramos.

Pete Lederberg Collection

him in those early days wouldn't remember him. "When I started, I was around 200 pounds," Ramos said. "Then as I kept going, I'd get bigger, and bigger. The bigger I got, the better I used to wrestle and move."

Promoters tried to make him a hero, or an Italian. Ramos was having none of it. On his first trip to Australia, he was asked to portray a lumberjack. "I said, 'No sir, if I can't make it as "Apache" Bull Ramos, I'll get on a plane and go back to Houston.'"

During his two-decade career, Ramos would headline in just about every territory he'd work, at least for a short while. According to Gary Hart, who managed and booked Ramos, the big guy had the right temperament. "You've got to have guys to get people ready," Hart said. "A guy like Bull Ramos had a great look, couldn't talk, but was the type of guy that if I would get him ready to put someone over to work with the champion, Bull would do it right. If I would bring in Mil Mascaras, or the Blue Demon, or Doctor Wagner, or El Halcon, I knew that if I put him with a guy like Bull Ramos, or a guy like Tim Brooks, they would look the way they were supposed to look."

One of Ramos' epic feuds was with Mascaras, "The Man of 1,000 Masks," in Los Angeles. Their battles built to a hair-versus-mask match at the Olympic Auditorium in 1969. "That match was huge," recalled Mascaras to journalist Mike Mooneyham. "Bull Ramos was a very good heel. He knew how to make the fans hate him." Jeff Walton, the L.A. territory announcer and publicist, says the bout is still vivid in his mind. "The reason I remember it getting over so well was that Ramos had almost unmasked Mil by tearing his mask up in the early match, and kept vowing to finally unmask him," Walton said. "Both men worked very well together as Ramos could work the *lucha libre* style, as well as the catch-as-catch-can style along with Mil. Ramos was also a very good seller, and Mil liked that."

Ramos had other memorable feuds with Jimmy Snuka, Bruno Sammartino over the WWWF title, and Jose Lothario. "He was a good opponent most of the time," said Lothario. "He pleased the crowd the way he was wrestling. I consider him very good. As far as I was concerned, he was one of the best."

In the dressing room, and away from the arena, Ramos was well-liked by his peers. After his career ended in the early 1980s, he ran a wrecking service in Houston. Ramos led a fun-filled life, and even though he went blind, had lost a leg to diabetes, and was on kidney dialysis during the years before his death on May 29, 2006 at age sixty-nine from a shoulder infection that poisoned his system, he still kept his sense of humor. "I will really miss his phone calls. 'Hey, mano, you white trash, how's my boy up there in Washington?' he used to say," said Savage. "There are many men that come and go in this business, but Bull was special."

VADER

One backstage brawl can ruin a life's work. In August 1995, Leon White was involved in a dust-up with Paul Orndorff in Atlanta while both were employed by World Championship Wrestling. The massive White's years of aggressiveness on the football field and in the ring as Big Van Vader were no match for the veteran Orndorff, who diffused the tense situation with relative ease. White's reputation behind the scenes took a hefty blow, just another in a series of missteps that plagued his incredibly successful career.

"He just made so many dumb mistakes. He goes and tries to beat Paul Orndorff up. He goes and beats up a young boy in All Japan, and the mafia, they hold him down, and slice him up. So many dumb things have happened to the guy," said fellow popular *gaijin* in Japan Scott Norton. "The longer he's away from the business, the more they'll respect him. Leon, he's a massive guy, just what we call a real hard night, hard match to work."

Or, as his former manager Harley Race puts it, "Leon White was Leon's biggest enemy. He never really liked anything anybody did. Personality-wise, he was a big asshole."

Yet Vader will be remembered as one of the very best big men ever in professional wrestling. Carrying anywhere from 330 to 415 pounds on his six-foot-four frame, he could astound audiences with his power or his agility, defying gravity with thunderous moonsaults. He was violent and dominating, believable in the UWFI shootfighting promotion, or as a monster heel in the WWF.

Those with crafty minds for the business saw gold in those massive loins. "Here's a big, huge guy that could move. He had great credentials. He was impressive. He had his gimmick down. He understood his gimmick. He was a good guy to have," said Bill Watts. In a 1993 interview with the *Pro Wrestling Torch*, Paul Heyman raved about Vader: "When a man that size does a moonsault with a blown-out back, when a man that size does the things he does and is willing to do for other people, that impresses me a lot more than when a 230-pound guy does it."

Growing up in Lynwood, California, by the seventh grade White was working to help make ends meet at home, walking three miles to a bowling alley in inner-city Los Angeles. He was a highly sought-after recruit in football from L.A.'s Bell High School, and chose the wide open spaces and blue skies of the University of Colorado. The center was a two-time All-American, captain of the team when he graduated with a degree in business administration. He was chosen in the third round of the 1978 NFL draft, eightieth overall, by the Los Angeles Rams, the team he grew up worshipping. He signed a five-year deal, but was only active for three of those seasons, rupturing his patella tendon during a sweep against the Dallas Cowboys.

His football career done, he returned to Boulder, Colorado, and got a real-estate license, built townhouses, and owned and operated a car wash. He wasn't fulfilled, however. "I got bored stiff," White told the *Wrestle Radio U.S.A.* program. "I was gaining a lot of weight, and becoming way out of shape, and becoming a real businessman. But I decided to sell everything. The home, the car wash, condominiums, everything."

White left for Minneapolis, where former Olympian Brad Rheingans trained prospective pro wrestlers outside of town. As "Baby Bull" Leon White, he barely made a ripple in the AWA in 1986, but did get an invitation to Europe to work for the Catch Wrestling Association. Promoter Otto Wanz saw something in White, and through the regular work, the American made it to the top as CWA world champ. Up next, Antonio Inoki came courting, and actually bought out White's contract with Wanz.

Howard Baum

Vader lords over a beaten Davey Boy Smith.

Though Sid Vicious and Ultimate Warrior had apparently been considered, the role of Big Van Vader was given to White. Derived from Japanese folklore, where Vader was a top warrior who once fought for his village seventy-two hours straight, White was given a huge, black device for his head that shot smoke. In an unheard-of move, Vader, managed by a late-night TV host, beat Inoki in the main event at Tokyo's Sumo Hall in less than three minutes. A new star was born.

"He revolutionized what people thought of a monster heavyweight wrestler," said Japanese wrestling expert Zach Arnold. "He elevated the standards of what it meant to be an agile giant who could make fans believe that he could destroy everyone." Vader would again rise to be world champion in Japan, as well as in Mexico. "Years ago," Arnold continued, "Vader had an angle with Kenta Kobashi in All Japan in which Vader stiffed Kobashi over the eye, and Kobashi was bleeding hardway, only for Vader to continue pounding on the eye more. This kind of realism is what Vader could add to his style in Japan that he likely couldn't in later years in the WWF."

Fans in North America will remember Vader from his world title run in WCW, where he feuded with Sting, Ric Flair, and Ron Simmons. Sting said Vader was real stiff when he returned from Japan. "I'm the guy that tamed him," said Sting. "He just came out, and beat the crap out of me. It was like that for a long time, but by the time he got tamed, and we started to get things down and work out a match, we had some phenomenal, I think, really good matches. I always like working against the monster. He was a monster, and to be big as he was and to do a moonsault was pretty amazing."

"He was an incredibly strong man, without a doubt. Carrying that kind of mass, I always wavered between them, does he know his own strength or does he know it and just not care?" said Nikita Koloff, whose career Vader ended in the ring and in storylines. Vader's WWF stint, which began in 1996, never brought him the success enjoyed anywhere else.

In the end, Vader's public legacy is his dominance in Japan (where he still competes at age fifty), but to those in the know, his self-absorption lost him respect. "When I would wrestle Vader, it was a fight. It was just a brawl. It was just pecking rights," said Norton. "He was so worried about what was going on. And Leon, he was one of the best big men to ever wrestle, I don't care what anybody says. His attitude was horrible."

THE ZEBRA KID

There have been many zebra kids in wrestling over the years. But there was only one Zebra Kid. For twenty years, George Bollas traveled the world with his famous zebra-striped mask and ring outfit, an eye-catching piece of showmanship that belied the fact that he was one of the first agile big men in the business.

The son of Greek immigrants, Bollas was born in 1923, and grew up in Warren, Ohio, where his father ran a restaurant. He was heavy as a child — about 200 pounds by age twelve — so the gridiron became a natural calling. Tipping the scales at 318 pounds as a freshman, Bollas planned to play football at Ohio State in 1945, but instead was directed to wrestling. "One of the reasons he got into wrestling was the football coaches felt he needed to get a little more agility and quickness for football, and they felt wrestling would provide that type of training," recalled his son, George Bollas Jr.

Nicknamed "Dreadnaught," Bollas was an immediate sensation, credited with boosting attendance at Buckeye wrestling matches from seventy-five or 100 fans to about 2,000. "George has surprising speed and shiftiness for someone as big and heavy as he is," said Lawrence Hicks, one of his coaches. Bollas won the Big Ten Conference heavyweight championship as a

An unmasked Zebra Kid.

freshman, and repeated as a sophomore in 1946, when he also captured the NCAA championship.

Bollas' success caught the eye of promoter Al Haft, whose Columbus, Ohio territory was one of the most important in the country. Bollas appeared for Haft as the masked Mystery Man, and left school to wrestle full-time in 1947. "The main reason I think he got into the wrestling was his father ended up getting sick," his son said. "He decided to leave the university, and make some money for the family."

Initially working as George Bollas, he didn't get very far; the most notable event of his early career was a 1948 set-to with a referee in New York that earned him a suspension from the state athletic commission. Later that year, after a three-month stint in the Carolinas as the Intercollegiate Dark Secret, Bollas found the gimmick that would bring him world renown. Promoter Jack Pfefer, who was equal parts quirkiness and inventiveness, created the Zebra Kid, a play on the stretch marks characteristic of Bollas' weight fluctuations. "I think he was pretty proud of that," his son said. "He ended up grabbing the zebra part of it because someone made a comment where he went through one of his weight-loss periods, where he ended up having some stretch marks on his skin, and they mentioned that looked like zebra marks."

The 300-pound Zebra Kid made his debut in San Diego, September 14, 1948, beating Mike Mihalakis, and launching a career that would take him around the globe against legends such as Rikidozan and Lou Thesz. In a 1959 interview, Bollas acknowledged that his attire altered fan perceptions. "People always think I'm big enough to take care of myself — so they want to see me beaten. I was not a successful wrestler until I put on that mask and started getting really tough with my opponents."

Wrestling historian Will Morrisey, a professor at Hillsdale College who studied Bollas' career, said the mask was beneficial in more than one way: "Without the mask, George Bollas looked more or less like an average guy — admittedly, a very large average guy. The mask freed him from being George Bollas, immigrants' son from Ohio. Paradoxically, the mask made the fans see him, the great athlete and showman."

Bollas was an intriguing combination of speed and size. "Try to beat him in a footrace, forty yards. You'd have a tough time beating him," said veteran Phil Melby. Yet, when Bollas and Melby worked out together, the bulk came into play. "He'd get on top of me and I couldn't get out from under. I could sit out, but I wasn't strong enough to get out — he was so big," Melby said.

Paul "Butcher" Vachon, who toured Australia as Bollas' partner for several months in 1962, added that Bollas "was fat, kind of roly-poly, but he was one hell of a wrestler. He could move incredibly; he could move like a light-weight." The Zebra Kid had a bit of the hustler in him too, Vachon recalled: "He used to play handball. He'd go to the gym even in Australia, and he'd be hitting the ball, he was like 325 pounds, and he didn't look like an athlete at all. So he'd be hanging around the handball court, and get in a game with some guys, and they'd bring up, 'Well let's play for a few dollars.' By the time the day was over, he was the one who had the money."

The Zebra Kid taunted crowds to no end, and they responded in kind. A brick-throwing throng of about fifty attacked him in Columbus on June 13, 1957, following a match in which he won a controversial referee's decision from Bearcat Wright. "I made a mad dash for the street and the mob followed . . . I managed to leap into a cruising cab, but not before a rock had split my lip open," he said. The cab suffered about $100 in dents and bruises; Bollas was treated for cuts to his face and head.

The hood came on and off frequently — he did another stint as the Dark Secret in Columbus in 1953, and worked on and off as George Bollas in territories like Hawaii and Texas. While the gimmick made him a lot of money, he saw some downside in covering his head with a piece of cloth night after night. "I guess I'll have to take the mask off some day, anyhow," he said, revealing his identity for *Police Gazette* magazine in 1959. "It's no fun to wrestle in. It's so hot. It almost strangles me, and prevents me from seeing my opponents clearly." Outside the ring, his courtesy had a major influence on a young fan named Jim Morrison, who chased a car through a Philadelphia parking lot and side street just to get a glimpse of the famous wrestler. "He befriended me, and I told him, 'Someday this is what I would like to do,'" said Morrison, a.k.a. wrestler and manager J. J. Dillon. "He would write to me — he was in England and Japan a lot — he would write to me on this big, blue, eleven-by-fourteen piece of paper, and then fold it all down to fit in an envelope. And I've always been grateful to him."

In 1963, Bollas took his family to England, where he could return home the same night from a match virtually anywhere in the country. He also tried to promote matches in Greece with family relatives, a venture that failed miserably — he estimated that it cost him $5,000 to $6,000. He won it back with a heavier workload, and continued wrestling until 1968. As Bollas aged though, his health failed — his knees were shot from years on the mats, which prevented him from exercising and controlling his weight. He died in January 1977, but was hardly forgotten. In September 1998, Ohio State inducted him into its athletic Hall of Fame, located in the school's 20,000-seat Jerome Schottenstein Center.

"You can go down there now, and there are areas in the Schottenstein Center where they have murals of wrestlers who won the national championship," his son said. "He's there in the thick of things, and in the Hall of Fame, where there's a plaque for the first couple of years that he wrestled. It's pretty flattering."

Steven Johnson

Don Fargo chokes Luis Martinez.

The Technicians

Chris Swisher Collection

Don Fargo.

DON FARGO

Okay, pull up the chair. Time to tell some Don Fargo stories. Oh, and better send the kids out of the room for these. Let's start with former WWWF world champion Ivan Koloff: "I met him in California with 'Superstar' Billy Graham. We were on the beach, and he had these body piercings by his eyes, and this big black mark running down his arm. It looked like he'd been burned. I said, 'What happened?' He said, 'Oh, that's where I put my cigarette out.'"

Johnny Powers — "J.P." to friends — recalled: "At 2 a.m. in the morning, I get a call from the cops. This is in Greensboro. 'You know a Donnie Fargo?' 'Uh, yes sir — are you a policeman?' 'Yes, but this sorry guy here is on a motorcycle, and he is in trouble with his girlfriend, and he needed something to give to her, and he drunk all his money up, his paycheck from you.' There was a bunch of good-looking flowers in the front of a lady's house. So Donnie, at 2 a.m., drives up, makes tracks with his motorcycle, picks up the flowers, and goes off to make up with his girlfriend. But somebody got his license plate. Donnie says to the officers, 'Well, J.P. will tell you. J.P. will understand.' Also, he said J.P. will bail him out. Now, who else would do that except Donnie?"

Gun-totin' partner Nick Kozak was with Fargo at the U.S. Fast Draw Championships in Houston, and recounted: "When we pulled, we pulled a thumber; we pulled the gun from our waist, and, coming out of the holster, we thumbed the hammer back. There were guys who fanned it when they pulled. When the gun came out, they'd just with the left hand shoot the hammer back, and they'd fan. The guy who beat me was a kid out of Dallas, five-eight, five-ten, maybe, skinny, typical geek-looking guy. He jerked that gun out, and fanned it, it was like 25/100ths of a second. When Don seen this, he said, 'Did you see how fast that guy was? I'm going to try fanning it.' Don had his nice white shirt on, he put his gun in his waist belt, and practiced it a couple times, and it was faster than he was doing it. So he said, 'Oh, I think I've got this thing knocked!' He put a couple black powder shells in his deal, and we said, 'Go!' and he pulled, and fanned and fired. Well, the first time he did it, he pulled the gun out and without realizing it, the barrel was facing across his stomach. And when he pulled the trigger, the black powder fire burned the front of his shirt off, and just peppered his belly with gunpowder. He stood there and went, 'Fuck!' I'll tell you, we hit the floor."

Wasn't the only time that happened. Here's Jackie Fargo, his tag team partner in one of the great duos of all time, explaining: "This was in Tennessee, Nashville. He shot himself through the thigh. He was just out in the woods practicing quick draw. He had his finger on the trigger, and he pulled it, and he didn't clear the holster, and it caught him right through the thigh. It was real bullets. He went to the hospital, and he was laid up for a couple of months. Then I had to call my brother Roughhouse in for a couple months to take his place. Listen, I love him to death, and he was like a brother to me, but he was a goofball. He was a real goober."

You sure the kids are out of the room? Okay, you've been warned. Before he was Supermouth Dave Drason, Dave Burzynski was at a wrestlers' social in the Sheraton-Cadillac Hotel in Detroit. Here's his story: "Donnie Fargo walks into this party, and it was a nice casual party. People are laughing, and drinking, and talking, and stuff. He walks in, and immediately takes over the room. What he did was grab somebody's shoe. He goes over by a wood table, drops his pants, takes out a nail, and he takes his penis, and he puts it on this table, and starts pounding this nail into it. And he stood there, and pulled back, and this nail is through his penis on this table. It's like, 'Oh, God!' Everybody is shocked as hell. Lord Layton comes over, and says, 'C'mon, mate,' and gets him the hell out of there. It was eye-opening. Come to find out later on, he would do this all the time because he had his foreskin pierced. So he would freak people out, but it didn't hurt him at all."

Here's one that is more innocent, but no less mindblowing, from Gulf Coast star Terry Lathan: "He was a fabulous artist. One of the best artists I've ever seen. He did one of the Ten Commandments, Moses holding the Ten Commandments up in the air, this huge storm overhead. It is probably the most dramatic painting I've ever seen in my life. Picasso couldn't have done any better. The painting, when you looked at it, it floored you. How could this guy, of all guys, paint this scene of Moses holding the Ten Commandments? It was unreal."

Fargo did all those things, and a lot more we can't print, en route to becoming the greatest disguise artist wrestling has ever known. Born Don Kalt in Germany in 1928, he was raised in New York City and Pittsburgh, where he got into bodybuilding big-time. He got his real start for Al Haft's Columbus, Ohio promotion as Don Stevens, brother to Ray. He and Jackie tore up the tag team scene in the Northeast and the South during the 1950s; Jackie duly noted they were the first, great bleached blond tandem with wrestling egos in overdrive. When Don decided to break away, he morphed into Jack Dalton of the Dirty Daltons in the South and Southwest. He had championship teams with Kenny Mack doing a biker gang takeoff, Rene Goulet during a foreign legion gimmick . . . in all, about eighteen noms de guerre.

Lost in this merriment is the fact that Kalt/Dalton/whatever his name was an incredible worker who took each one of his characters to the max. "Every gimmick I did, I'm the only guy that lived it," said Fargo, who is working on a book about his multiple personalities. "I wore my legionnaire's outfit on the streets. I wore my cowboy and gun shit on the streets. I did all that. Nobody else did it. They would come to the matches, be who they were, and when they left, they went back to a normal life. Not me, I stayed in costume twenty-four hours a day."

Cowboy Bob Kelly, his best singles opponent in the Gulf Coast territory, said Fargo continuously reinvented himself so perfectly and completely that fans bought every bit of it. "The people didn't even know the difference. When he was Don Fargo, people never, ever told me that's Jack Dalton. If they did know, they never told me about it. But his appearance was completely different, and his wrestling was completely different. When he was Donnie Fargo, he wrestled a little more. As Jack Dalton, he'd come in the ring kicking and fighting," Kelly said. In just about every one of his covers, Fargo wrestled as a heel. "I was always a prick," he laughed. "All the time. Especially if I got into a crowd."

Lathan loved wrestling with Fargo, saying his moves were always smooth and well-timed, and his charisma was second to none. "I would put him in wrestling, not just on his ability, but his uniqueness, what Elvis was to rock 'n' roll," Lathan said. "He's just that unique. You could always count on him to draw a house. He was absolutely the most unique wrestler ever to live. And I'm glad to say he was a friend of mine."

Now retired and living in a trailer in the woods near Cantonment,

Florida, Fargo remains a hoot and a holler. He's been one of the big hits at Cauliflower Alley Club reunions in recent years, and he hasn't changed a bit. Idly chatting on the phone one day about his plans for a book, he said he hoped it would include a lot of pictures, when something suddenly diverted his attention. "That's what I want — pictures, pictures, pictures," he raved. "And I've got people sending me them from all over, wrestling fans . . . Goddamn! There's a rat. Son of a bitch! I got two big gol'-dang dogs just laying here watching this little, tiny baby rat. And they ain't doing a damn thing about it."

Let's finish with a tale Fargo tells about himself, and the time Greg Valentine was working as his brother "Johnny" in Pedro Martinez's Buffalo, New York territory: "One time, Pedro's kid [Ron Martinez] was doing the interviews. So we went to this one town to do it — I can't remember the name — and Ronnie was standing out front, getting ready to announce us, the Fargos, coming out to talk. We was supposed to walk out from behind the curtain. We come out naked. I mean, he went, 'Oh, no, man, cut! Aww, cut!' That's when they were still taping things. And he said, 'Get your damn tights and singlets.' We go back, and put on our tights, and everything. We had to start over again. We took a felt pen, and I put F-U-C-K on my chest, and Y-O-U on his chest and he announces us again . . . 'Fuck you!'"

The Legacy of Iron Mike

The Funks and the DiBiases have a deep, rich history, and the patriarchs of the wrestling families, Dory Funk Sr. and "Iron" Mike DiBiase, were great friends. But to the public, they were mortal enemies, battling off and on for years (including one hour-and-44-minute Texas Death Match). DiBiase battled both of Funk's sons, Terry and Dory Jr. "I can remember some of my earliest memories, anytime we went to Texas, going to Dory's ranch and spending the night," recalled Ted DiBiase, Mike's stepson. "Of course, any time company would unexpectedly show up, we had to go hide because my dad and Dory always had a big feud."

Both Dory Jr. and Terry lamented the fact that more people don't know about "Iron" Mike. "Mike DiBiase was a great help to me when I first started," said Terry Funk. "I had some of my first matches against him. He gave me some great advice, and was a great wrestler, both amateur and professionally. It was people like him who would open up your eyes, and make you

"Bulldog" Danny Plechas and "Iron" Mike DiBiase with a championship trophy in Texas.

realize there were some great people in this business, people who had values. But there is no tape on him and no one remembers him."

Dory Funk Jr. figures he worked with Mike DiBiase thirty or forty times, and said DiBiase was ahead of the curve, aerial-wise. "In those days, it wasn't everybody jumping off the top rope, and his finishing maneuver was off the top rope, landing on somebody's back. Not to say that there weren't some high flyers back in those days, because there were," said Funk Jr. "But Mike was a basic wrestler who also had some spectacular moves."

The son of Italian immigrants, Mike DiBiase was born December 24, 1923 in Omaha, Nebraska. His father, John, died when Mike was still young, so an uncle served as his male role model. At Omaha Tech High School, DiBiase starred in football, track, and wrestling before joining the navy, where he was stationed in Norman, Oklahoma, and won the Oklahoma AAU heavyweight wrestling title two years in a row, among other laurels. But his crowning achievement was the AAU national heavyweight title in 1946, which he claimed in New York City. At five-foot-nine and 230 pounds, DiBiase entered the University of Nebraska, and lettered four times in wrestling, and three times in football. His nickname came from battling back from a potentially career-ending knee injury. Turning down pro football for wrestling, he began his grappling career in the early 1950s. In 1959, he married woman wrestler Helen Hild, who had a five-year-old son named Ted, who would later follow in his stepdad's footsteps.

"I had ten years with him, from five to fifteen," said Ted DiBiase, who was prevented from seeing Mike wrestle. "We didn't go very often, because he was a heel. Back then, it was very protected. We went occasionally, but I watched on TV all the time. I fell in love with the business."

His peers tried to describe what made "Iron" Mike a great heel. He was "an aggressive guy" who "wasn't bashful in the ring," said frequent running-mate and sparring partner Bob Geigel. Harley Race said DiBiase was a big, husky-looking guy. "He could take over with wrestling, or he could take over with physical violence, and the people knew that. All he had to do was come up to his seat and snarl at the people, walk around the ring a little bit, and they hated his guts," said Race.

As Ted describes his stepfather, it's easy to see that he is detailing his own mannerisms as a heel as well. "He was a kind of guy that had a ring presence that told you, 'Don't mess with him.' He just had a presence about him. He wasn't wild, but it was just like a look, he had a look, and he had a presence that said, 'You'd better respect it' – that type of heel," said Ted. "Tough, but when the going gets tough, doing what heels do. To me, the greatest heel is what we call the proverbial chickenshit heel. You show the people that you are tough, you're rugged, that you can wrestle, that you're really a good wrestler, you're out there, and you compete, but when the going gets tough, and the babyface keeps outsmarting you, and whatever, you're forced to cheat to succeed. When you cheat and cheat, you get the big heat. Then when he explodes, and makes the comeback, you're on your knees, begging him not to kill you. People hate that."

In Omaha, DiBiase was a hero against the "Mad Russian" Stan Pulaski (Eric Pomeroy). "He could do anything, he really could. He could do dropkicks, head scissors, and everything," said Pulaski. "He had something that a lot of guys don't have, he just had a lot of natural ability. He was a good amateur wrestler, and really a nice guy on top of that. Everybody liked him, everyone around Omaha liked him because he was raised here in Omaha. He couldn't do no wrong, no matter what he did."

When he was thirty-nine, Mike DiBiase was almost out of wrestling. He had tried to run a nightclub in Omaha, sold insurance, and was considering operating a restaurant with his mother-in-law in Arizona. One last run in Texas beckoned though.

On July 2, 1969, DiBiase had just moved into a new apartment, eaten dinner, and driven 100 miles to Lubbock for a match with the 400-pound-plus Man Mountain Mike. Race, who was there that night, said that DiBiase looked exhausted and pale, but wanted to wrestle. "As I watched the match, I saw DiBiase grab his chest and fall. The referee froze, not knowing whether he should start the count," Race wrote in his autobiography. "I ran into the ring, and started administering mouth-to-mouth and CPR on DiBiase." Race's efforts kept DiBiase alive until the ambulance arrived twenty minutes later. The first hospital wouldn't admit DiBiase, and he expired upon finally arriving at the second. One artery was completely blocked, and there was scar tissue around the heart, proving there'd been other heart attacks – any warning signs had been ignored. "Iron" Mike DiBiase was buried July 5 in Willcox, Arizona.

Terry Funk brought DiBiase's wrestling bag to Ted, and the Funks were instrumental in his career. He never did get a chance to talk to his stepdad about becoming a pro wrestler. "I think he kind of knew it, but he was so against it that I never brought it up. So we never had a lot of discussion about pro wrestling," said Ted, who said he was smartened up to the business by his older brother, who refereed one summer, just as Ted would referee to start his career.

Would "Iron" Mike have been proud of Ted's wrestling career, which included headlining runs in Mid-South, and a star-making run as the arrogant, over-the-top Million Dollar Man in the WWF? "I think that if he would have lived to see me attempt to get into the business, he'd have probably killed me," Ted stated.

Ted DiBiase can only laugh — as only he can laugh, with that deep, maniacal, yet self-aware cackle that he used as the Million Dollar Man — at the irony he now faces as two of his sons train to be wrestlers under Race. A third will probably pursue it as well after finishing college. "My dad didn't want me [to do it] for all the same reasons that I didn't want my boys to. It's not the business itself, it's not the wrestling, it's the lifestyle. It's the ninety percent divorce rate. Of course, a lot of things have changed now," he added. "The difference now is the business is much more corporate. I said, 'That's the upside, guys.' The other upside is because of me, and my name, and everything, and because Vince [McMahon], he likes to see second- and third-generation guys make it. Now, he's not going to hand it to you. It's kind of like, you might get looked at because of who your dad was; the downside is there's probably going to be more expected of you because of the name. In terms of getting an opportunity, you'll get an opportunity, but you've got to produce. It's one of those businesses. They don't give you too many opportunities."

"MR. PERFECT" CURT HENNIG

Was ever a character more suited for a person than "Mr. Perfect" was for Curt Hennig? The vignettes that introduced him to the WWF audience in 1988 had him sinking hole-in-ones, hitting baskets from half court, smashing home runs, or effortlessly tossing a touchdown pass. Hennig's dad, Larry "The Axe," still marvels at it. "The character of Mr. Perfect is certainly something that pissed off a lot of people because there is no one really perfect, but he kept telling them he was perfect. He was. He could do a lot of things. In fact, everything he did, he did good. Consequently, that made him a good heel," said Larry. "It was the best [gimmick] that Vince ever had there. But he could do it. He could play golf, he could swim, he could hit the baseball, he could dive, whatever it was, he could do it, horseshoes, you name it, he could do it all."

In the ring, the second-generation star could do it all as well. "Curt Hennig gets A's in every subject that I would grade a guy — his working ability, the fact that he always made me look good before he beat me," said Lanny "The Genius" Poffo. "He never hurt me, he was always very safe in the ring, no matter what I did to him; you knew he wasn't going to hurt me

Curt Hennig.

because he was too coordinated, and he was very gracious, and he thought it was very nice that I would do a job for him, put him over. I always liked working with him, then when I got the opportunity to be his manager, if I'd been a jabroni for twenty-one years of my life in the wrestling business, I was a star for four months, and that's when I was the nemesis of Hulk Hogan and the partner of Mr. Perfect."

Hennig stood out in the day of musclebound monsters like Hogan and Ultimate Warrior, taking spectacular bumps. The six-foot-two, 235-pound Mr. Perfect eventually found his stride taking on other skilled grapplers like Tito Santana and Bret "Hitman" Hart. "With Curt Hennig, I was able to do slick moves that I wouldn't think of doing with most other guys," Hart wrote on his Web site. "He was my all-time favorite. He really was. When I think back to our incredible matches they sort of remind me of those 'Spy vs. Spy' cartoons in Mad magazine. We were similar in age, size, and background, and we had a similar look, except that Curt wore a mane of long blond curly hair. Both of us were second-generation wrestlers whose fathers were respected men in a tough business, and we shared an understanding of what it was like to have mighty big shoes to fill."

Born March 28, 1959 in Minneapolis, Minnesota, and growing up as the second son of Larry and Irene Hennig, Curt enjoyed a lot of golf, hunting, and fishing, as well as sports. He wrestled in high school, then junior college before he even talked about going into wrestling. "He had to get himself into a situation physically and mentally in order to do that, and then go out and pay the price," said his father, who helped train Curt, and hooked him up for Verne Gagne's wrestling camp, where the only other notable graduate was Brad Rheingans.

Hennig was a babyface from his debut on January 30, 1980. He was a good-looking young stud with talent to match. Besides Gagne's American Wrestling Association, Hennig had early stints in the WWWF as an opening match grappler, and in Portland, Oregon, where he latched onto "Playboy" Buddy Rose. "He always told me that he learned more from me than anyone else, not counting his dad. I'm talking about real attention to detail, and everything from Day One when he came out here to Portland," said Rose. In Portland, the Hennigs reigned as tag champs for a short while, which "The Axe" considers a career highlight.

In the AWA, after a championship tag run with Scott Hall, Hennig's frustrations with being unable to unseat the world champ Nick Bockwinkel were played out brilliantly, and a heel turn for the title win, with Larry Zbyszko's help, was a terrific swerve. Backstage, Hennig played negotiations with the WWF against his desire to be AWA champ. After dropping the belt to Jerry Lawler, Hennig left for New York.

As Mr. Perfect, he was Intercontinental champion twice, and battled Hogan for the WWF title. Compared to some of the silly characters of the day, Mr. Perfect was straightforward. "I am a wrestler," he once said. "I don't care about gimmicks. I don't care about ring entrance music. I just go out there, and do what I do best. I wrestle." Injuries derailed his career though, especially his back. Yet he returned again and again, in the WWF and WCW, despite doctor's orders and a lucrative insurance Lloyd's of London injury policy. Mr. Perfect's last big run came in WCW, where he was a member of the West Texas Rednecks, a character close to his true personality, friends said. Singing the parody song "I Hate Rap" to further a feud with a rapper group led by Master P (Percy Miller) led to an unexpected rise in popularity.

Hennig was a giving person, whether it was with fans, family, or wrestlers who needed a teacher. "I love to travel, I love to meet people," Hennig once told journalist Mike Mooneyham. "I love to be on the move. I love to be athletic. I love the fact that I get to release all of my tension, and I love the fact that I get to beat people up."

But as much as he is remembered for his generous nature, to friends, family, co-workers and strangers, Hennig was also a notorious ribber, perhaps one of the best ever at the backstage hijinks that helped ease the burden of constant travel. "He was a heckuva ribber. He liked to pull ribs," said Rose. "As long as it didn't hurt you financially or physically, a rib is fine." Larry Hennig said that Curt "was always that way. . . . Yeah, he liked to do it."

Locking suitcases to posts, putting Ex-Lax in drinks, hiding dead fish in suit jackets, and shaving eyebrows of sleeping giants were among the simplest of Hennig's ribs. "Curt could make you laugh at yourself, and before the joke was done, you would be laughing at him," Arn Anderson told WWE.com at the time of Hennig's death. But Curt was a good actor too, and could feign that he had nothing to do with a rib, said Ed Wiskoski. "He'd always imitate Charlie Chan: 'Oh, big investigation. We find out who do this. Me Charlie Chan. We find out. We call Mr. Fuji.'"

The last investigation of Hennig's career was a sad one. He was found dead in a hotel room in Brandon, Florida, on February 10, 2003. The Tampa coroner's office and the Tampa medical examiner's office declared acute cocaine intoxication the official cause of his death. Eulogies poured in for a beloved fraternity member — Randy Savage even wrote a rap song, "My Perfect Friend," for Curt — and the funeral was a packed affair. But questions still remained. "It's not quite clear to me yet, and it perhaps never will be. From my standpoint, it just looked like it was one of those one-night deals, got in with the wrong people," Hennig's father said. "There's still a mystery going on here. He left here with a couple grand, and he had a Rolex watch. That stuff was gone, that stuff was missing. That's still a blank." Recently, Curt's father elected to stop his private investigation of the tragedy to spare his family any more scrutiny.

Curt Hennig left behind a wife and four children, the oldest of whom, Joe, is beginning a wrestling career. But among the sorrow, there is celebration for the Hennigs. The Axe was inducted into the George Tragos/Lou Thesz Professional Wrestling Hall of Fame in 2006, and Curt in 2007, thanks in part to an impassioned speech to the voters by Hart. "Our book is going to have a beginning, a middle, and a double ending," Larry said. "There will be two Hennigs in the Hall of Fame."

THE MASKED SUPERSTAR

Count Blackjack Mulligan as one opponent grateful that Bill Eadie, as the Masked Superstar, locked him in his notorious cobra clutch. Mulligan

Courtesy Wrestling Revue Archives

The Masked Superstar.

remembered bleeding rivers of blood from an open head wound only twenty minutes into a scheduled hour-plus cage match as part of a big feud with Superstar in South Carolina. Referee Tommy Young wanted to stop the bout, but Mulligan would have none of it. "Bill ropes around and puts me in the old cobra clutch hold, and pushes his head against my head, and holds me in real tight, and squeezes, pushing on my head with his mask until it sort of cauterized it, just shut it down. He held me there, held me there, held me there. Finally it stops bleeding. To make a long story short, we continued the match. That's the kind of partner he was, the kind of a person he was — anything for the match."

When you talk about the real pros in wrestling, Eadie's name always comes up, even though it was years before most fans knew what he looked like. He started as Bolo Mongol in 1973, sporting a Genghis Khan-style hairdo with a tuft of hair in front and a ponytail in back. As Demolition Ax, he covered his face with menacing paint — it actually was moisturizing lipliner. In his best singles role, as Superstar, he sat quietly in restaurants with his family, watching in amusement as fans heckled other wrestlers. "I loved the anonymity, I loved the privacy," he said. "Guys like Ric Flair couldn't do that. I'd watch Flair get swarmed when he went out in public, and I'd just be sitting there minding my own business, chuckling to myself."

It's a good thing, of course — had Eadie ventured sans mask into public after, say, poking The Mighty Igor in the eye with a lit cigar, it would have been a lot tougher to hide his combination of technical skills and treachery.

"Bill was the sneaky type of heel, but he also was what I called the educated-type heel," said veteran Georgia referee Bobby Simmons. "He didn't just go out and yank hair and trunks and masks, but the things he did were very deliberate. One of the things he used to do would be to shake hands with his opponent, but cross his fingers behind his back. Now, that seems silly to a lot of people, but it got the message across about who he was."

The man under the mask was an outstanding athlete in high school and college. Eadie played football and track as a 165-pound high-school senior in Brownsville, Pennsylvania. At West Virginia University, he did a little bit of everything — tossing the javelin, running the 120-yard high hurdles in 16.3 seconds, and running 800-yard and one-mile relays. He was captain of the track team his senior year before embarking on a teaching career.

That was interrupted when Geeto Mongol (Newt Tattrie) chanced upon him at a show in Pittsburgh in 1972, and invited him for six weeks of weekend training in a converted barn. "He gave me the parameters and the basic education," Eadie reflected. "I knew I could always go back to teaching. I didn't know, if I turned down the opportunity, if I'd ever get another opportunity." Eadie became Bolo Mongol when Bepo — Nikolai Volkoff — departed, and the reconstituted Mongols kicked and smashed their way to titles for almost three years. After Geeto stepped aside, Eadie transformed overnight in the Carolinas into the Masked Superstar, a heel who stomped less and wrestled more. "Geeto told everybody we were specialists — eyes, ears, nose, and throat," Eadie joked. "When I got with Boris Malenko in Charlotte, we'd go down to the Park Center every Monday and work on wrestling for three hours."

Eadie's willingness to improve his craft impressed Rene Goulet, who knew him well from the Mid-Atlantic and New York. "He is one of the guys who really worked at it, he used to go in the gym to learn new moves, and stuff like that, which you didn't see too many guys do in our time," Goulet said. "As far as working, he was very good, excellent. He could have a match with anybody."

The mask hid facial expressions, meaning Eadie worked on other parts of his game to convey emotion. With manager Malenko's help, he became unusually articulate and well-reasoned for a bad guy. "The first thing he told me was to pay attention to the other heels in the territory," Eadie said. "If they're yelling and screaming, you talk. If they're talking, you yell and scream because you've got to be a little different." Employing his cobra clutch on all comers, Superstar said he would unmask, and pay $5,000 to anyone who could defeat him by pinfall or submission. "I was pretty sneaky as an individual. Probably the most heat I even had was when I burned Igor's eye. There was so much heat, I used it three times in different places. I got fourteen years out of it."

Superstar held a variety of titles in the Mid-Atlantic region. In Georgia, he held the National heavyweight title three times in 1981 and 1982, and added another stipulation to his matches — $1,000 to anyone could break the cobra clutch. Though he made a brief return to the Mid-Atlantic in a hero's role, he was set in Georgia, where his feud with Mr. Wrestling II became one of the best in the territory. "I had a good situation because Ole Anderson was the booker at the time and I could go to Japan twelve to fourteen weeks a year. So I had the best of all worlds, I could go to Japan, I could wrestle in Georgia, and I could take some time off."

Eadie made memorable forays north as Superstar, and was under consideration as a possible WWF titleholder after Bob Backlund. "He was a great worker," Mulligan said. "As far as Bill Eadie is concerned, he's one of the top talents there ever was in this business. He never really got his ado that he should have, he never got to do the big deal in New York that he should have." In the late 1980s, Eadie settled in as Ax of Demolition, a team that held the WWF tag team title for an unheard-of sixteen months. Today, he still wrestles on the independent circuit, and continues his educational work with at-risk youths and Inner Harbour, a nonprofit facility that treats troubled kids for a return to mainstream society.

"BIG" BILL MILLER

Every summer, Columbus, Ohio promoter Al Haft would host an amateur night, when fans could come down to challenge the professional wrestlers in his crew. However, Haft would only send up his best. "The ones that always got picked were Joe Scarpello, Bill Miller, and me," said Bob Geigel. With three pros with great amateur backgrounds, Haft knew the secrets of the squared circle would stay hidden. He was, however, concerned about lawsuits. "Al wouldn't come on and say, 'Don't hurt them.' But he'd say, 'Well, just pin them now, just pin them,'" explained Geigel. All three had the same standard response: "Al, I thought the guy was going to be too tough. I thought I'd have to extend him a little bit."

Miller didn't keep his fights confined to the arena either, said Don Leo Jonathan. "One night we were bothered by a bunch of guys, some kids. I stopped the car to get out, and Bill says, 'Don't spoil my fun. You just stay here.' There were four of them. I just sat there. I quite enjoyed it. He gave a lesson in respect in a hurry."

It all speaks to the legitimacy that Miller wanted to portray. When asked about the sport, Miller would respond that it was ninety percent wrestling and ten percent show. That only makes sense when one considers the serious athletic credentials that Miller brought to the table: nine letters (wrestling, football, and track, with discus and shot put his specialties) at Ohio State University, one of only a handful to ever get so many. He was on the 1949 team that shared the Big Ten title and went to the Rose Bowl the following year; he was a two-time Big Ten wrestling champion, and placed fourth in the NCAA tournament. In 1997, he was voted into the Ohio State Sports Hall of Fame, though he never learned of his induction; and in 2005, he entered the George Tragos/Lou Thesz Professional Wrestling Hall of Fame.

Raised on the Twin Pines Farm in Fremont, Ohio, Miller would grow into a monstrous six-foot-six, 290-pound behemoth. He was hard to miss at Ohio State, and Haft (who had his own ties to OSU), wanted him. "[Haft] took an interest in Bill when he was still in school. Bill had used his eligibility up, because he had a six-year course. So Al Haft turned him onto pro wrestling while he was still going to school," explained Bill's brother Danny, five years his junior, who later would be his tag team partner. Big Bill started pro wrestling after his undergrad work, but at the same time he pursued a degree in veterinary medicine. "He would remember times when he would end a main event at midnight, then have to drive back to Columbus, get back in at six in the morning, and then have classes at seven," recalled Dr. Chuck Miller, Bill's oldest of six children from two marriages. After graduation, Miller helped out with his new vet skills, but quickly realized there was more money in wrestling. To keep up his professional knowledge, he volunteered with vets in the towns where he was stationed for extended periods of time, like Minneapolis.

From the start, April 12, 1951, Miller got a huge push from Haft, and he

Courtesy Wrestling Revue Archives

An early posed Bill Miller with the WLW-TV belt.

was a main-eventer for the next twenty years. He didn't have to do a lot besides stand next to another human being to be cast as a heel. At times moody and gruff, his education and intelligence enabled him to retort to the best of the worst fans. "With his science and speed — he is unbelievably fast for such a big man — coupled with burning aggressiveness, he was all but unbeatable," recounted *Wrestling Revue* in 1962.

On May 1, 1952, Miller won the Ohio version of the old American Wrestling Association world title by defeating Don Eagle in Pittsburgh. Don Arnold upended him for the belt on September 2, 1952. "He was big and he was rough," said Arnold. "We got along great because we were both in the amateurs." Big Bill was recognized as world champion in Omaha as Dr. X in 1959, and a year later, in Verne Gagne's new promotion as Mr. M in Minneapolis. "Bill didn't change his style when he was masked as he was an unknown quality when he became masked," said historian James C. Melby, who compiled the *Bill Miller Record Book*. Miller was also as the Crimson Knight in St. Louis in 1970, and was unmasked by Dory Funk Jr.

Jonathan was a frequent opponent and tag team partner. "The Mormon Giant" recalled a riot in a small Ohio town. "Bill and I were on the floor heading for the dressing room. The police jumped in front of us, and one pulled his gun. Bill grabbed me by the shoulders, and turned me around, and kept walking to the dressing room. He says, 'You don't think he'll shoot us in the back, do you?'" Miller's son, Chuck, said his father's best tales were of almost being lynched in eastern Canada, and being hit with a torn-off piece of bleacher in Texas, resulting in a three-day hospital stay.

Given his size, Miller was a proponent of strength moves. But he was fast as well, and wasn't afraid of coming off the ropes with a precise knee drop. "He could work with a small guy as well as he could a big guy," said Geigel. "He'd work with anybody. He would and could." His various tag team pairings only doubled (or tripled) the mayhem, working with legit brother Danny, and their fictional sibling Ed (Eddie Albers).

As his career progressed, Miller started to wrestle less, but he still influenced younger generations. Dewey Robertson used to drive from Hamilton, Ontario, to Pittsburgh, to put over the likes of Miller. "He was wonderful. I'm sure he could take any of those guys today with one hand and club the shit out of them," Robertson said, still in awe of Miller's size. "You'd just have him give a flying mare, and he'd be halfway across the ring."

Larry Whistler was a fourteen-year-old kid at Pittsburgh's Civic Arena, long before he became Larry Zbyszko, protegé of Bruno Sammartino. In Miller, he found a sweet target. "I had a whole handful of Sweet Tarts, and I threw them at Bill Miller's head. You had all these Sweet Tarts bounce off his face and his head as he walked to the ring to battle Bruno. Then he came at me, but I ran away like a coward. I told him that story when I met him years ago."

No longer up to the full-time mat wars, Miller began working at the Ohio State Agricultural Lab, doing autopsies on animals. He wrestled occasionally until about 1975, mostly in St. Louis in the last days for promoter Sam Muchnick. "I purposely got out of it because I knew there was no chance of a wrestlers' union ever working, nor of anyone getting any medical or retirement insurance," he told radio host Mike Lano in 1992. Miller also worked for the federal government with poultry, meat, and large animal inspection.

It was while on that job that he was tripped by a high-pressure hose in Zanesville, Ohio, and fractured his back. While in surgery, he lost a lot of blood. His faith as a Jehovah's Witness precluded any transfusion, but he pulled through. He died March 24, 1997, of a heart attack after working out at a gym, as he was walking out of the facility. He was sixty-nine.

The Rogers-Miller-Gotch Backstage Mystery

The 1962 backstage incident in Columbus, Ohio, between the National Wrestling Alliance world heavyweight champion "Nature Boy" Buddy Rogers, "Big" Bill Miller, and Karl Gotch was perhaps the most talked about behind-the-scenes skirmish until Bret Hart knocked out Vince McMahon in 1997 in Montreal.

Layers of intrigue still remain to this day, largely because of the passing of Rogers and Miller, and the reclusiveness of Gotch, who shuns attention in Florida. "I don't know what the story is. It's unfortunate that most of those people are gone," said Fred Hornby, the world's leading authority on Buddy Rogers. "It's a cloud of mystery."

Here's an attempt to piece together what happened.

The card that night, August 31, 1962, was to feature Rogers against Johnny Barend in the main event. The final results from the Fairgrounds Coliseum looked like this:

Shohei Baba beat Johnny Barend
Antonino Rocca beat Fred Atkins
Frankie Talaber and Leon Graham beat Hank Vest and Angelo Savoldi
Magnificent Maurice beat Frank Hickey
Elaine Ellis beat Mary Alice Hills
Chief White Owl drew with Paul Stetson

According to historian Don Luce, who researched the history of wrestling in Columbus, $2,500 of the $8,000 gate was refunded.

Note that neither Miller nor Gotch were on the card. They both worked on the next show in Columbus, September 11, 1962, at Jet Stadium. In fact, Gotch went over Don Leo Jonathan for the Ohio version of the short-lived American Wrestling Alliance title on that show. Rogers didn't return to Columbus until 1969.

But on August 31, something happened in the dressing room, and Rogers was replaced in the main event. According to the *Columbus Dispatch*, Rogers went to the University Hospital, and filed charges (though no record of the case's conclusion seems to exist). The Nature Boy didn't work again for a week. How badly was he beaten? Did Gotch and Miller "beat the shit out of him" as Fred Blassie wrote in his autobiography? Or was it a lot less?

In a 1992 interview with radio host Mike Lano, Miller gave his side of things: "Well, Rogers had been ducking us, badmouthing us behind our backs, and one day here in Al Haft's dressing room we began issuing challenges to him, calling him a false champion, first in the dressing room, later to the boys and fans. We got him, Gotch and myself, in the dressing room, and I stood in front of the opening (the door wasn't closed). Gotch slapped him, then I slapped him, and he ran right past me, pushing me out of the way to get out of there. Then, as you know, he called up Thesz to complain. We never slammed, or crushed, or broke his hand in the doorway, and we only had the one confrontation like this – not two. So it only amounted to Gotch and myself slapping him."

In an interview with *Whatever Happened To . . . ?* Lou Thesz recounted what Rogers said in that conversation, and essentially confirmed Miller's account. "Buddy called me that night, and was talking in German about how they did this, and how they did that. I said, 'Well, what you should have done was just stand up and knock that Gotch right on his ass.' He said, 'What did you say?' I said, 'You don't have to take that shit from those guys. Fight back.' I was just having fun with him, because he was the gutless wonder."

Miller's 1992 story also is pretty consistent with his version of things from a 1964 edition of *Big Time Wrestling* written by Larry Matysik. "One night we caught him in the dressing room in Columbus. He was in his ring clothes, with pink trunks and a big cigar. I went up and asked him if he had ever made those remarks, and Rogers denied it. So I said that meant that he would accept my challenge, right there and then, and fight me in that room. Rogers just got up, and strutted away. I went after him, and grabbed him by the arm, and spun him around, and said, 'I was talking to you. Can't you hear? Are you going to fight me now or not?' And I slapped him across the face. Rogers quickly turned, and began to run away. Gotch went after him, and grabbed his arm, and swung him around, and said, 'What is the matter? Is my friend too big for you?' Then he slapped Rogers. Again, Rogers turned, and ran away and started to cry."

Matysik doesn't think that Miller worked him too much that night, that the big man was generally a straight-shooter. "My impression of Miller is he told the truth. He was not a BSer," Matysik said. "Miller opened up to me." From his perspective working in the St. Louis wrestling office, Matysik would still find himself talking about the incident a decade later. "It was a big part of the politics of the time, the stuff that happened with Rogers. I think he probably, in retrospect, played it for more than it was to avoid dates. But who really knows?"

Talking to the main-eventer that night, "Handsome" Johnny Barend, only confuses the issue further. What did Barend see? "They didn't beat him up. Three guys attacked the guy, three to one. He got away from them all," he said. The third man, Barend said, was Art Neilson, who wasn't booked on the card either. "They just went into the dressing room, and attacked the guy, just like that, period. I was wrestling that night in the main event, and they had to put Giant Baba in with me, instead of Buddy Rogers." According to Barend, Rogers got out unscathed. "Well, they couldn't have been too tough, because the three of them couldn't knock the guy down."

What is a lot easier to comprehend is why someone would have it in for Rogers. The champ's arrogance put off many of his contemporaries who saw him as a charlatan of the first order. And, following great wrestlers like Pat O'Connor and Lou Thesz as NWA champ, Rogers was a showman, not someone with legit credentials. Gotch was feared as one of the greatest shooters in wrestling history, and the six-foot-six Miller was an amateur champ in college.

Miller's brother Danny said Rogers was always looking out for himself. "Buddy told the promoters that he didn't want to be booked with Miller or Gotch because he couldn't defend himself against them if they wanted shoot at him," Miller said. Besides the professional jealousy, Danny Miller claimed that Rogers also badmouthed his brother's wife. Regardless, the animosity was certainly there between Buddy and Big Bill.

Bill Miller's son, Chuck, summed it up for all curious parties. "[Bill] said it got blown out of proportion, and became an urban legend. He said they came to blows. He said, certainly, Buddy Rogers would have suffered, from what my dad and what Karl Gotch said at that time, he would have been hurt if he didn't stop doing what he was doing. He didn't go into detail in all the communication that went on between them. They disagreed with the way things were going."

Paul Orndorff.

"MR. WONDERFUL" PAUL ORNDORFF

A lot of people watch wrestling on TV and figure, "I can do that." The difference is that Paul Orndorff was right. Orndorff, not a fan at the time, was lying on the floor watching Championship Wrestling from Florida in the mid-1970s after his football career hit a dead end. He called his father-in-law, who knew someone who knew Florida promoter Eddie Graham. During Orndorff's his first day of training, he went through round after round of Hindu squats before climbing in the ring for five minutes each with Bob Backlund, Bob Roop, and Jack Brisco. Then he got the privilege of a Hiro Matsuda front facelock. "I was so tired I was seeing stars," he remembered. But he came back each day for six months, and the brutal training left enough of an impression that he'd use the same techniques as a WCW trainer twenty years later.

"Mr. Wonderful" will forever be linked with the early days of Hulkamania, as he was one of Hulk Hogan's foes at the first WrestleMania, and a top challenger to the Hulkster's world title in the mid-1980s. "In my opinion, Paul's the greatest wrestling heel that there ever was. He could get real heat, not cheap heat, but the kind of heat where people wanted to kill him," said Brian Blair, a long-time friend and opponent. As Orndorff put it: "I liked being a heel. It came natural to me, and that's when I started making my money . . . Rough and aggressive, aggressive, aggressive," he said. "Same thing when I played football. One thing I loved to do was block."

"The Brandon Bull" overcame a childhood in a tough part of Hillsborough County, Florida, to become a football star in high school and at the University of Tampa, where he totaled 2,254 career yards and twenty-one touchdowns rushing and receiving. He scored twice in the team's 1972 Tangerine Bowl win, but the New Orleans Saints waived him in July 1973 after drafting him in the twelfth round. Orndorff estimated it took him three or four years before he felt truly comfortable in the ring, but it look a lot less time for him to square things with noted hooker Matsuda. After a few months of learning the ropes, he invited his father-in-law to a training session. "I got Hiro back and I mauled his ass. That's the way I was . . . I wanted it so bad and I wasn't going to be denied."

After breaking in around Florida, for about five years, Orndorff was mostly in Bill Watts' Mid-South territory with three runs as North American champion. "His work was excellent, he always stayed in very good shape, he was kind of a macho-looking guy, and he legitimately is a tough guy," said Roop, who was with him in Mid-South. "He knocked out Van Vader, and two or three other people . . . He actually was better as a good guy. He was good either way; he was very good in both ways, but better in my mind as a babyface." Super-intense and never shy about speaking his mind, Orndorff had a dispute with Watts about whether he'd lose to Junkyard Dog, and split in 1982. Despite the differences, Watts thinks highly of him. "Paul Orndorff was upset with me all the time, but he never did not do his absolute best in the ring," Watts said. "Paul realized later, he's one of the ones that called me back later, and said, 'I didn't realize what you were teaching me. I thank you so much.' I still respect Paul completely and tremendously. He was a great athlete."

Orndorff also had a front office run-in in Georgia in 1982, where he got a push as a popular National title champ. "I really liked him. He was a pretty fair talent and he was a good athlete. Everything about him was good," said booker Ole Anderson. But Orndorff skipped a card in Augusta because of an injury, and Anderson, a world-class talent at making a point, retaliated by tossing him out of the Omni in Atlanta. "Well, of course, he was pissed at me. He had a decent job. He was making some pretty good money, and he knew we were going to do everything we could to make him make even more money. And I just fired him." Incredibly, Anderson encountered Orndorff and Rick Rude, then with WCW, years later when they were motoring a boat on a lake near Anderson's house. "Paul said to me — again, I don't know if I got it, but I'm close — he said, 'You know what? I sure as hell wish you were back booking, in charge of this,'" Anderson said. "And to me, that was one of the nicest compliments that I ever received because, here was a guy who was so totally pissed at me."

Orndorff flipped between hero and heel a couple of times in the WWF. Entering the company as a bad guy in late 1983 after working in the Central States promotion, he teamed with Roddy Piper, wrestling with him at WrestleMania I against Hogan and Mr. T. Orndorff said he changed his style when he got to New York and saw a company full of slow-moving plodders. "I wanted to be different than any other heel that was there," he said. "I took a little bit from everyone I saw, and I could just go, go, go . . . I never got tired. I was aggressive. They'd never seen a heel like that." Blair, part of the excellent Killer Bees tag team, thought Orndorff was absolutely convincing as a heel. "Paul couldn't really talk like Ric Flair, didn't have that gimmick, but he didn't need one. He was just that good. People believed what he did." Case in point — during a match with Blair, a fan in Boston hurled a small bottle of alcohol in the ring at Orndorff, splitting his mouth open. "He got up, and he just beat the living daylights out of me," Blair remembered with a laugh. "I said, 'Paul, please, man, I didn't throw the bottle!'"

The Hogan-Orndorff feud became the top draw in wrestling in 1986 — it drew more than 60,000 to an outdoor show in Toronto, and headlined sell-out houses in Nassau, New York, and Chicago on the same night, August 30, as a waiting plane shuttled Hogan, Orndorff, and Bobby Heenan, his manager, from arena to arena. "There are very few guys like Orndorff . . . that are really athletes, that really can do what I like to do in that ring, which is have a great match," Heenan said. "Him and I worked together, we'd talk to each other, and then he goes and does something, and comes back to me. Very few guys that worked were as good as Paul Orndorff."

Hogan and Orndorff continued to battle until Orndorff switched allegiances once again, canning Heenan in favor of Sir Oliver Humperdink. But a severe arm injury essentially sent him into retirement at the end of 1987. He took a bad shot, and his powerful right biceps started to shrink noticeably, a tough blow for someone who prided himself on conditioning. "My whole right side, I couldn't pick up a glass of iced tea," he said. "I started a bowling alley, had two of them, then sold them." He returned to the national scene in 1990 with WCW, and worked there for most of the next five years before becoming a trainer at the Power Plant school. A member of the 2005 WWE Hall of Fame class, he's retired in Georgia, makes a lot of appearances at independent shows, and is openly disdainful of today's product. "To this very day, if I wasn't hurt, and banged up, and I could do the things I could do back in the '80s and the '90s, I'd be the hottest heel in the country," he said with characteristic bluntness. "You've got to do the psychology and make it believable."

BOB ORTON SR.

State Fairgrounds, Richmond, Virginia, February 11, 1966: Bob Orton, with more than fifteen years of experience under his belt, and as tough as a two-dollar steak, was finishing up a match with Boris Malenko (Larry Simon) against George and Sandy Scott when all hell broke loose.

Bob Orton Sr.

"They went out on the floor, and got some chairs, something like that, and all the people copied them and did the same thing," Orton said in his deep, gravel-filled voice. "We got down on the floor, and there they come. Somebody hit me from behind with a chair, and then they walked up to Malenko, and cut him around his stomach. I was out and [manager] Homer O'Dell come out, and pulled me back to the dressing room. Boy, my knees was tore all to hell, dragging me on that concrete. It's a wonder we didn't get killed. It was the worst I was ever in."

That was the kind of heat Bob Orton Sr. drew from 1950 to the late 1970s under his own name, as well as aliases like Rocky Fitzpatrick and the masked Zodiac. Born in 1929, as a teenager at Wyandotte High School in Kansas City, Kansas — a teammate and long-time friend was footballer-turned-actor Ed Asner — Orton got hooked on the Xanadu that was the Central States territory. "I learned from watching the greatest of all, Orville Brown, Sonny Myers, Dave Levin, the top guys when I was thirteen, fourteen, fifteen years old. I didn't know it at the time, but it was the best territory in the country. Matches out of this world." He turned pro at twenty and piled up an impressive travelogue during his first few years in wrestling, hitting the top of the card in places like Florida, Georgia, upstate New York, Ohio, Manitoba, and California.

Orton's first mega-break came when he tagged with Buddy Rogers in

1961 and 1962 in the Northeast, working to huge crowds in Madison Square Garden against good-guy tandems of Johnny Valentine and Antonino Rocca, and Valentine and Argentina Apollo. "I'd get in that ring and just look up like this, those Puerto Ricans would be ready to kill," Orton said with a barely perceptible upward turn of the chin. "You cannot explain it. I had it, and I don't know what the hell it was, or why, or how I did it, or nothing else. I had that charisma that they hated."

Orton knew every trick in the book, thanks to three great influences — Malenko, Rube Wright, and Lou Hines, with whom he worked at the San Francisco Athletic Club in the mid-1950s. He let his opponents know it, as well. Orton remembered a November 27, 1965, match against Lou Thesz in Roanoke, Virginia, where he decided to have his way with the aging world champ. "I told Larry Simon, 'Tonight, he's going to work my goddamn match.' Thesz wanted to do that headlock routine where he could rest, and didn't have a chance to get hurt. Larry's eyes go crazy. 'Oh, no, you're going to get us in trouble!'

"I took his leg, got up under his chin, reached up, and got a double-leg pick up. He hit his bad elbow on that hard mat, which was what I was trying to do." As Orton recalled with relish, he locked Thesz in a sugar hold, and tied him up for good. "He couldn't move nothing but his eyelids. I said, 'Send me a message with your eyelids like Morse code.' The rest of the match was good. I made him do everything. I got to the dressing room, and there's Malenko. 'Oh, goddamn, good match, good match.'" Thesz won the third fall by disqualification; Orton required a squad car for his getaway from the Starland Arena.

For all of his ability to brawl, Orton was considered a good worker. "He didn't 'chop meat,' but rather wrestled in a heel style and pace that he would set," said Sir Oliver Humperdink. "He didn't pull hair fifteen times in a match, or rake your eyes six times, but rather did it once when the time was right. He would wrestle almost a complete match, and never break a rule. People knew he could wrestle. But then he would take that one shortcut, and really piss them off." Dick Steinborn has fond memories of his match with Orton on the undercard of the famous 1961 show at Chicago's Comiskey Park, where Buddy Rogers beat Pat O'Connor in the main event in front of more than 38,000 fans. "Bob was a shooter and even gave [Danny] Hodge a run for his money. We respected each other in the ring, and I never felt him. He was that smooth."

Bill Dromo first met Orton in the Northeast in 1961, when he took a swift kick to the groin, courtesy of the tough-as-nails Orton. "He kicked me in the balls. I mean, he kicked me like you wouldn't believe. I just walked out," Dromo said. Later, when the two formed a tag team in Florida, Orton offered his own novel brand of an apology: "He said, 'Hey kid, I'm sorry about that there, kicking you in the groin. Didn't mean to do it, but you pissed me off,'" Dromo said laughingly.

Orton was the Southern heavyweight champion in Florida six times, Central States champion twice, Missouri heavyweight champion, and held all kinds of tag team titles. He returned to the East Coast 1968 against WWWF champion Bruno Sammartino as Rocky Fitzpatrick. He would have qualified for a world championship run, but the blunt-spoken Orton brooked little fast talk from promoters, and that probably hurt his career. "I could understand him," Dromo added. "A lot of people couldn't understand him — he had that 'I don't give a shit' attitude. If he liked you, he liked you. If he didn't, he told you so."

In 1972, Orton worked under a mask in Florida as Zodiac, a takeoff on the never-identified thrill-slayer who terrified northern California in the 1960s. Scary, darkened vignettes on TV were designed to elicit a sense of fear in audiences, and Zodiac had two Southern titles reigns, but Florida promoter Eddie Graham took the edge off the character. "Graham toned it down. It was supposed to be a real killer. We could have made a ton of money with it," said Orton, who also used the gimmick in Los Angeles. Orton's legacy lived on through his wrestling sons, Barry and Bob Jr., and grandson, Randy, a scorching hot star in the WWE.

In recent years, Orton, confined mostly to a wheelchair, kept in contact with buddies from his home in Las Vegas, keeping the phone lines buzzing with the latest news and gossip, his unique commentary on the difficulties of male-female relationships, and his musings on the state of the government. He died of a heart attack in July 2006, just a few days short of his seventy-seventh birthday, creating a warm outpouring from friends who missed his regular chats. "It wasn't even a question that he would be ninety years old," son Barry said. "It blows my mind. He was just so huge. Even though he wasn't mobile, he was bigger than life."

PAT PATTERSON

The roar of the paint and the smell of the crowd. Give that some thought, said Pat Patterson, and you'll come to understand what the wrestling business used to be about. "Everybody thinks it's backward, but I really accept and believe that. The roar of the paint to me was like you walk into the building, and you look at the building, and it's like wow. What a nice building, it's sold out. That's the roar of the paint. The smell of the crowd is having those

Pat Patterson.

fucking people yelling" — he inhaled deeply — "that smells good. You know what I mean? It's the crowd. You have to pay attention to the crowd when you're in the ring."

Given his history working backstage with the WWE off and on over the past couple of decades, Patterson is uniquely qualified to explain how the psychology of the business has changed too. The combatants today usually lay out their matches ahead of time. Then when they get to the ring, they are concentrating on remembering the sequences rather than paying attention to the crowd. "They forget that there's 10,000 people looking at them. It don't matter if they're yelling or not, they just want to do their stuff."

As for Pat, he had the stuff, and then some. He is considered by many to be one of the top workers ever in the ring, with one of the absolute best minds for creative finishes behind the scenes. His bump-taking was off the charts, but more important, he knew *when* to take those spectacular bumps.

Chavo Guerrero Sr. explains. He first worked with Patterson on the undercard of a big battle royal show at the Olympic Auditorium in Los Angeles. Patterson entered the ring, and held his nose, indicating that Guerrero smelled a little funky. "It embarrassed the shit out of me, because at that time, I'm small, I'm Mexican, I had a complex anyway. And you do it in front of a crowd of people! I'm getting hot," said Guerrero. "Then he says, 'Just go with it.' I'm saying, 'You son of a bitch.' He does it again. I go to lock up, and he goes, 'Ugghhh' and he holds his nose. But as he does this, I'm watching, and he's turning, and doing it to the people too, not directly but indirectly. At the right time, he tells me to give him a dropkick. By that time, I'm ready to kill him — not that I could have. I give him a dropkick and he takes a bump to the second floor, and those people, you could have mistaken them for being in the Superdome. It just popped, and I went 'Wowwww.' After that, the match was easy."

Born Pierre Clermont in Montreal on January 19, 1941, Patterson considered the clergy but was talked out of it. Instead, his adventurous nature took him to a church gym where amateur wrestling was taught. It was fifty cents to get in. He had a pro match at age seventeen against one of the other students, and was soon booked around Montreal on promoter Sylvio Samson's smaller shows. (His other wrestling connection? Roger Barnes, who later become Ronnie Garvin, used to date Patterson's sister.)

Like any kid, Patterson had his hero. "When I used to watch [Killer] Kowalski in Montreal, he was my idol," Patterson said. "Kowalski the big name, a big star. He had purple boots, a purple jacket, and I had the same thing. I came to Boston, and I was on the same card that he was — obviously, I'm in a preliminary match. I'm in the same dressing room as Kowalski, and I'm freaking out." He patterned himself after Kowalski really until the "Pretty Boy" Patterson gimmick developed around 1962. Wearing pink wrestling tights, pink lipstick, and rouge on his angular, high cheekbones, and puffing away on a cigarette, held in a long, diamond-studded holder, he had found a way to create instant heat. Over time, he learned to get the heat without the props, like his French poodle.

"He was a flawless heel, vicious, and aggressive, and did everything with precise timing," wrote "Superstar" Billy Graham in his autobiography. "To this day, there's never been anybody who can throw better mounted punches from the ropes. When his head was run into the ring post, it recoiled, with hair flying backward, like it was about to pop off."

Patterson used a few shortcuts to getting a crowd to react: he could scream and rant with the best of them on the microphone, his heavy French accent only adding to the charm; he would hide a mask in his trunks, and at the right moment, put it on behind the referee's back, and head-butt his opponent into oblivion with whatever was hidden inside; and he could bleed with the best of them, his blond locks soaked with sweat and blood.

"He was also of that era of the pure heel, and there was no fudging, you didn't cross that line. You remained a heel, period," said his former partner Graham. "It was just his timing, and his believability, his punches. His promos were the basic Ray Stevens, baddest bully on the block, just hardnosed. He was just so convincing . . . His accuracy, his timing, he just had the magic in him, he really did."

His first big run came in the Pacific Northwest in the early 1960s, but it is in the San Francisco promotion where he became a legend. Patterson is proud that he was able to stay on top for so long, and the city was home for many years to him and his life partner Louis Dondero. "In those days, you'd work in the same towns every week, and you see these people in the front row. 'Oh, Pat, we love you!' I'm like, 'God, what am I going to do this week? How many times can these people watch you?' Whether you're a heel or a babyface, it's hard to — I was hoping that one day I could leave San Francisco, but I was there about fourteen years. I thought that was a pretty good accomplishment to last that long in a territory." In 'Frisco, Patterson would form championship teams with Graham, Rocky Johnson, Peter Maivia, Moondog Mayne, Pedro Morales, Tony Garea, and Pepper Gomez, but it is his pairing with Stevens as the Blond Bombers that stands among the best teams of all time. Stevens and Patterson entered the Professional Wrestling Hall of Fame as a team in 2006.

While in San Francisco, he learned the philosophies of booking a territory from promoter Roy Shire. Patterson would book 'Frisco, and Florida for a short while, before ending up in the inner circle of the WWF after his in-ring retirement in 1984. He's an unsung hero, say those who worked with him in the WWF. "Much of the credit for the success of the WWF should go to Pat Patterson," said J. J. Dillon in his autobiography, adding that Patterson had the rare ability to communicate with Vince McMahon. "Pat was one of the most colorful, energetic, enthusiastic, funny, caring, and understanding individuals I've ever known," wrote Vince Russo in *Forgiven*. "I learned so much from him, and I think back then he was drawing from my energy. Pat and I always used to bounce ideas and angles off each other. To this day, I don't think he realizes what a thrill that was for me."

Though he retired from the WWE in the fall of 2004, Patterson would continue to be called upon by the company, especially for help with finishes. Content to travel, visit friends and family, and hit the golf course in his golden years, Patterson had a huge health scare in August 2006, when he was hospitalized for ten days following emergency heart surgery to remove a cyst from his main artery, but he recovered nicely and still has been helping out the WWE.

ANGELO POFFO

Lanny and Randy Poffo used to get hassled all the time by kids who hated their father, Angelo. Randy would be ready to fight, and Lanny would walk away. Eventually, Angelo and Judy Poffo sat down their two sons down for a talk. "I remember the big fireside chat," said Lanny Poffo, comparing it to the "birds and the bees" talk, "and I was shocked at both of them. I remember thinking, wrestling, okay, I can believe that; I've seen some matches that didn't look real to me. But what about Johnny Valentine? My dad said, 'Him too, but he's just better than everybody.'"

"It was not easy [keeping kay-fabe]. It was very difficult when the boys would get beaten up in school and stuff because their father was such a mean guy," chuckled Judy Poffo. The boys were "smartened up" as teens. "They were happy, actually, that he wasn't going to be beaten up every night. Everybody has their own way of looking at it, and that was theirs — and also thinking that they would be doing it one day too. They thought it was a gas."

In the end, all three Poffos did pretty well for failed baseball players, with Randy Savage having the most success on the field, playing in the minors before rising to world champion in the ring.

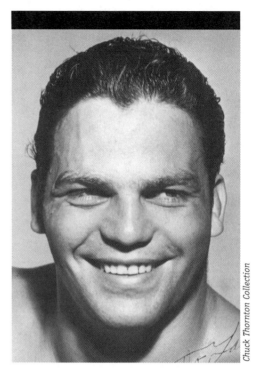

Angelo Poffo.

Angelo Poffo thought that baseball was going to be his ticket to success. He played his way onto the DePaul University baseball team as a catcher. "My catching was good, and everything, but my hitting was bad. So I had to give it up," recalled Angelo. At DePaul, Poffo studied physical education and played competitive chess. Before being hit by a baseball and getting plate-shy, Poffo played ball with George Mikan, who would later become the first big NBA star. DePaul is also where he met his wife of more than fifty years, Judy Sverdlin.

On July 4, 1945, while serving in the navy, Poffo set a world record of 6,033 sit-ups in four hours, ten minutes. "Somebody did about 5,000, and his abdominal aorta broke and he died. So I did 6,000, and I was so happy that I was still alive, I did thirty-three more sit-ups, one for each year of Jesus Christ's life," recalled Poffo.

Born April 10, 1925, in Downers Grove, Illinois, Poffo started wrestling at Karl Pojello's gym in Chicago's south side, directed there by classmate and amateur wrestler Carl Engstrom. "It wasn't a fantastic gym or anything, but Ruffy Silverstein was there," Poffo said. Silverstein, from the University of Illinois, would be Angelo's first opponent, in 1949 in Beloit, Wisconsin. Poffo put in time locally, wrestling in small-time "smokers," and doing occa-

The well-schooled Poffo learned all the shortcuts.

sional shows for Chicago promoter Fred Kohler at the Marigold Arena.

Like most beginners, it took a while to find his groove. He patterned his work after Professor Roy Shire, and first turned heel in Columbus, Ohio, in 1950, working many times with Frankie Talaber.

A good bump-man, Poffo was proud of his hit-and-run style in the ring, saying fans "don't like a coward." He wouldn't even get cheers from fellow Italians in the crowd. Once he was paired up with valet/manager Bronco Lubich, the fans' ire doubled. "I go out there to wrestle, and the guy was dumping me all over the place like Wilbur Snyder, who was a great worker and a nice guy. Then at the end of the match, Bronco would pull his leg, and I'd beat him, and I created a riot. It's that simple," said Poffo.

Kathy Lupsity, Lubich's older daughter, is thankful for Poffo's wise ways with the finances too. "When they'd go on to the next city, they'd like to get there really early, to relax, read the paper, eat . . . sometimes they'd catch a movie. But the biggest thing that he and Angelo used to do is to go down to the Merrill Lynch office, any close Merrill Lynch office, to talk to the guys about investment." Proving the best gimmicks have their basis in reality, at various times Poffo was nicknamed "The Miser" and "The Carpetbagger."

Poffo used an Italian neckbreaker as a finisher: "It was a front facelock, then I turned them around, jumped up in the air, and dropped them. Both of us would go down, but I'd cover." He won the Chicago version of the U.S. title in 1958, losing it to Wilbur Snyder in Detroit, where the belt stayed around the waist of The Sheik for years. In Indianapolis in 1966, Poffo was paired with Chris Markoff as The Devil's Duo, managed by Bobby Heenan. In 1973, he formed a regular team with Ken Dillinger known as The Graduates.

Falling back on his education at DePaul, Poffo eased out of pro wrestling, working as a physical education teacher in Chicago. (Yes, he did teach wrestling, but not eye-poking.) On one occasion, he had wrestled the night before in St. Louis, and driven back to Chicago to teach. He told his students that he was tired, and needed to sleep in his car, and let them run their own class. As the selections for teams were going on, Poffo started heading to his car. "Somebody says, 'I'll take Dago.' I turned around and told him I'm not playing. I used to play to try to control the game. He said, 'We don't mean you, Mr. Poffo. We mean Rufus, because he's blacker than the rest of us.' That made him a dago."

The family stayed together throughout Poffo's career, said Judy Poffo. "Traveling all over, and all that kind of stuff, every couple of months moving. Like our boys say, they enjoyed every bit of it. They went to foreign countries, they met many people. I probably, if I had not traveled with Ang, would never have been out of the state of Illinois."

When his sons were old enough to wrestle, Poffo bought into the Atlantic Grand Prix Wrestling promotion in the Canadian Maritimes with Emile Dupre in the mid-'70s, and then ran International Championship Wrestling out of Lexington, Kentucky, from 1978 to 1984. Promoting was not the most prudent move, said Poffo. "That wasn't very good. It's better to be a wrestler. Promoters die broke. If you don't draw, you lose money."

His last match was in 1991 against Luis Martinez, and Poffo did get to team with his sons on numerous occasions, as well as watching Lanny battle the evil Randy Savage in the family's promotions. "It was good for them, but they earned it the hard way. Lanny was a good acrobat, and Randy was a real good, hard worker." Now retired in Florida, Poffo, like any father, is pleased with the success of his sons. "That was great. I was very happy about it. And they kept their money like I did, so we're all fine."

PROFESSOR ROY SHIRE

Roy Shire is best known for running the northern California territory for twenty years, and helping wrestlers like Pat Patterson, Ray Stevens, and Billy

Roy Shire in his "Silver Adonis" robe.

Graham hit the big time. But before Shire used his brains as a promoter, he used his brains as a top villain in the 1950s as Professor Roy Shire, a super-educated, arch heel with a Ph.D. in dirty tricks.

Shire was born Roy Shropshire in Georgetown, Kentucky, in 1921, and raised in Hammond, Indiana, where he displayed a flair for showmanship as a regular performer in the Washington school children's theater — at fourteen, the eventual wrestling bad guy was Dick Deadeye in H.M.S. Pinafore. He wrestled in high school, the Amateur Athletic Union, and the U.S. Navy during World War II, before getting his start in Al Haft's Columbus, Ohio promotion in 1950.

Initially, Shire worked as a favorite nicknamed the Silver Adonis. But, after several months, Haft sensed that he could spin off his protegé into something bigger and better. Noticing that Shire always seemed to be reading the same textbook, he handed him a mortarboard and gown, and told him to learn how to strut. "I didn't think I was ready," Shire explained to Richard Hoffer of the Los Angeles Times. "And I was begging guys to take my place. They were laughing at me. So there I am, my first main event, and on TV, and I'm strutting into the ring. I'm trying to make people hate me, and they're laughing like hell. I was so embarrassed I could hardly wrestle."

But it worked like a charm. Tossing out ten-dollar words and mocking uneducated "peasants" in the crowd, Shire became a star across North America. "He was very impressive — he had that blond hair, he had a helluva body, and he was one helluva of a worker," said Don Fargo, who first wrestled him in Columbus. Shire was junior heavyweight champ in the Columbus territory, North American champion in the Amarillo promotion, and Texas tag team champion with The Great Scott in 1954. In 1957, Shire got into a huge feud with Dory Funk Sr. in Odessa, Texas, egged on when

Shire's manager, Bobby Wallace, cut open Funk's head with a cane on TV. Later that night, an arena match between the two led to a near-riot and police intervention. "I get the business everywhere I go," Shire acknowledged in an interview that year.

"Roy Shire was a big draw," said Terry Milam, who worked for him during his promotional years. "He'd go out, and say a big word, and tell you what it meant. But when you talked to Roy, you were talking to a guy that was wearing blue jeans, a white shirt, and if it was a little chilly outside, a blue jean jacket, and cowboy boots. And he spoke the same way he dressed, only a little more salty."

"Professor" Roy Shire.

Chuck Thornton Collection

Shire's character did have some unique qualities. One night in Ashland, Kentucky, he was tossed out of the ring, and landed in the lap of a high-school junior who had driven her mother, a rare Shire fan, to the matches. "Honestly, this is the truth. He reached up and pinched me on the cheek, and said, 'Thanks for rooting for me,'" said the future Dorothy Shropshire. "He went to the promoter; we were properly introduced. I became engaged when I was a junior. He insisted that I graduate from high school, and I graduated from high school, and five days afterward, we got married."

Once Shire was in character though, even his wife didn't know who he was, comparing the way he scrunched his face to NFL coach Jon Gruden, a master of spleenful facial contortions. "It was like Dr. Jekyll and Mr. Hyde when he got in the ring. It was even hard for me to recognize him," Dorothy said. "He had a way of scowling up his face — that, to me, is being intense."

Shire didn't back down from anybody. On September 9, 1956, he fought boxing great Archie Moore in Ogden, Utah, losing by a technical knockout. The two got into it again four years later, when Moore refereed a tag match with the Shire brothers — Roy and Ray, a.k.a. Ray Stevens. The duo also held the world tag title in the Indianapolis region in 1959 and 1960. "What made Roy so good was that he had a great sense of leadership in the ring, of telling a babyface to do this, or do that," said Pepper Martin, who wrestled him in the late 1950s, and later worked for him in California. "He was a great ring general, very, very smooth, and that's where Stevens learned to be a great worker, from Roy Shire."

By 1960, Shire was tired and hurting. As he related to Hoffer, he tore up his knee and loaded himself with painkillers so he could continue wrestling. "If it started to wear off during a match, I'd let the other guy beat on it so a limp would look realistic," he said. That October, he filed papers to start his Pacific Coast Athletic Corp., challenging the dormant San Francisco promotion of Joe Malcewicz, with the help of Johnny Doyle, among others. Using red-hot angles and good TV, the territory became one of the best and most profitable in the country. Those who knew him said Shire could be as stubborn and obstinate as a pack of mules, but also possessed a crystal-clear vision of what he wanted from his product. "He liked us, but he was a hard son of a bitch to work for, I'll tell you. He'd spit on the floor and make a puddle. Spitting all the time," Fargo recalled of his San Francisco run. Shire promoted for two decades, before changes in the business and general burnout sent him to a comfortable retirement at his Toe Hold Ranch in Sebastopol, California. He died of a heart attack in September 1992 at seventy.

Just what is Jeff Jarrett plotting?

The Connivers

TULLY BLANCHARD

Tully Blanchard had all the attributes of the traditional hero — son of the local promoter, a good-looking football quarterback, a small build perfect for winning sympathy against bad-boy behemoths. And none of it did him much good at the box office till he went for what came naturally. "Whenever he was trying to be a babyface, it was very contrived, and you could see through it," said Dr. Tom Prichard, who was with him in the Texas wrestling scene. "It was Tully's nature to be a heel. He was arrogant and he was cocky, just treated people horribly, and he was that guy. It wasn't an act. It was real, and that makes it so much better."

In fact, even though Blanchard was small by '80s standards, few wrestlers could fashion a more convincing match against more implausible opponents. Mid-Atlantic veteran George South appreciated the way Blanchard worked with the less nimble and much heftier Dusty Rhodes. "If you go back and watch every one of their matches, Tully puts Dusty over like a million dollars at the beginning. He lost to Dusty every night, but Tully was such a strong heel, he could come back the next week, and have a rematch," South said. "Tully had you believing that even if he went against Andre the Giant, you may not think he could beat him, but Tully sure believed he could beat Andre the Giant."

In fact, Joe Blanchard, Tully's dad, who ran the office in San Antonio, Texas, said one of the best contests he saw did pit Tully, at 210, against Andre for the Texas heavyweight title. "He ran, and dinged around, and the Giant missed him. It was good. Tully was a villain, and the people wanted the Giant to whip him, just paddle him."

An original member of wrestling's Four Horsemen, Blanchard had a clear idea of what he wanted to accomplish, estimating he'd control little more

Tully Blanchard comes off the ropes into Nikita Koloff as Ric Flair holds him.

than fifteen percent of a competitive match, and spend the rest of the time flying around for his opponent. "My goal was to make them scream," he said. "That was my goal every night for thirteen years. They don't scream when heels are beating up babyfaces. They sit down. They want their hero to win. They want their hero to be winning."

Born in 1953, Blanchard was in the wrestling game early, peddling peanuts and soda pop for his father's operation. First, he followed his dad's

Tully Blanchard, today.

other path — Joe starred on the football team at Kansas State, and for the Edmonton Eskimos of the Canadian Football League. Tully started at Southern Methodist University, and ended up as a wishbone quarterback at West Texas State from 1974 to 1976. But at five-foot-eleven, and no more than 200 pounds, a career as a pro signal caller was out of the question.

Though Joe hoped his son would find another line of work, Tully ended up refereeing for him in Southwest Championship Wrestling, and getting his face kicked in by old-timers who wanted to teach the promoter's kid a lesson. A couple of out-of-state sojourns to the Carolinas and Florida added some seasoning. In 1979, Blanchard did the unthinkable, turned heel, and eventually formed a snotty, hotshot tag team with Gino Hernandez. "He was a natural villain," Joe said. "They hated him even while they loved me." Blanchard turned on Hernandez in 1983, as well, igniting another hot feud. "When he turned heel, he became three or four times more valuable to the promotion that he was in than when he was a babyface," Nick Bockwinkel acknowledged.

By 1984, San Antonio was reeling after Vince McMahon's WWF snatched its timeslot on the USA Network, and Blanchard headed to the Mid-Atlantic, where intensity was more important than his size. "I was very fond of Tully," said TV announcer Bob Caudle, who was impressed at Blanchard's ability to attract heat. "They could really hate Tully. It wasn't his size. He was a good talker, and he was good at getting on the crowd. I think the fact he was such a good worker was the thing that really made it for him." Though a certified heel, Blanchard said he tried not to act like one out of the ring, so fans would understand that he broke rules as a last resort: "When I came into a building, I always signed autographs. I always smiled. I said, 'How are you doing?' I wasn't a bad guy. When I walked into the ring, I was the same way until I got outwrestled. I didn't cheat until I had to. I didn't heel till he outwrestled me. In essence, I said, 'I'm a chicken and nobody likes a chicken.'" Prichard said Blanchard didn't alter his style too much when he became a bad guy. "I think what made him a heel was he got a little more aggressive. He would keep you in the corner and work you over, but I don't think he really changed his style that much; it was more of that arrogance and cockiness coming to the fore."

Usually accompanied by valet Baby Doll — Nickla Roberts, an old friend from Texas — Blanchard's best singles run came in 1985, when he held the World TV title, the U.S. title, and squared off with Magnum TA in a famous "I Quit" match at Starrcade. Nikita Koloff credited Blanchard as one of the wrestlers who helped him learn the ropes. "I absolutely enjoyed working with Tully — just what we would call in the business a night off with him, because he was a consummate worker," Koloff enthused. "He had great, great psychology, really knew the business well, knew how to make the babyface shine, knew how to get a babyface over and keep his own heat."

Blanchard spent most of his time in tag team matches after 1987, sliding over to replace Ole Anderson as Arn Anderson's partner in the Horsemen. The duo went to New York in 1988 and 1989 as the Brainbusters, but Blanchard's return to the NWA was blocked by a failed drug test that essentially ended his career. At a low point in his life in 1989, he turned to God, and became a well-known lecturer and minister. He briefly returned to the WWE as a producer and agent in October 2006, but stayed only a few days before returning to his work as director of prison ministry operations for Champions for Life, an international outreach organization based in Dallas.

RIPPER COLLINS

It's doubtful that anyone ever got as much mileage out of butchering a language as Roy "Ripper" Collins. As enjoyable a performer as he might have been in other territories, he's a bona fide legend in Hawaii for his mutilation of the native tongue. "In Hawaii, he had those people gnashing their teeth. He would mess up the Hawaiian language on purpose. 'The King is going to Moo-i,'" recalled Don Leo Jonathan, with a hearty laugh. The irony is that the first time Ripper did it, while standing beside Lord James Blears for an interview, Collins just messed up the cities with his heavy, Southern accent. Blears encouraged him to keep it up. Fans dubbed him "The Yellow Rat," and would toss painted rubber rodents at him.

Football great Russ Francis, the son of Hawaiian promoter Ed Francis, loved to watch Collins. "He was one of the natural characters in life. He would have been an Academy Award-winning actor. He had such a great

Bob Leonard

Ripper Collins at his nattiest best.

sense of timing and talent," Francis said of the self-proclaimed King of Hawaii. "It was racial profiling at its best, with Ripper saying he was going to destroy the slow-witted Samoans or Hawaiians."

Given the extended interview time on the hour-and-a-half TV show in Hawaii, Collins really had a place to shine. Despite his small stature — five-foot-ten — and doughy middle, Collins exuded a cockiness and could talk people into the arenas. The schedule in Hawaii was a breeze as well, and the sun-loving Collins spent most of his week on the beach — heels went to one beach, babyfaces to another. "He loved Hawaii. It was his home. That was where he wanted to die," said Phil Watson, who made up the other half of the "Ripper and the Whipper" tag team in Hawaii and Nashville, Tennessee.

Hawaii was a long way from Muksogee, Oklahoma, where Roy Lee Albern Collins was born on October 8, 1933. Growing up, his mother ran a tiny restaurant in small-town Texas. He was already wrestling a little when he met woman wrestler Barbara Baker at a diner in West Virginia. "He was flipping around like he was gay. I thought, 'Wow.' I flipped out over him. I really fell for him," Baker said. "I think I just aggravated him to death, because I was really crazy about him. We started getting along and everything. I had to go to Texas, and he went along. I was booked there, he wasn't. We got married down there. We got married first at his mother's friend's home, and then we got married in the ring."

The newlyweds often would travel together from town to town, and would participate in many mixed tag matches. The couple was in California when they adopted their first of two baby girls; it was also where Barbara got a call to go to work in Hawaii, and her husband and new daughter came with her. "Then they wanted him to wrestle, and my God, we just didn't leave for seven years," she said. "Honey, he was like God over there."

Aside from Hawaii, Collins frequented the Pacific Northwest, where he feuded with the likes of Jimmy Snuka, Dutch Savage, and held the tag belts with Bull Ramos. "Ripper Collins may have been the best heel I had ever seen," said *Ring Around the Northwest* newsletter editor Mike Rodgers. "He made an immediate impression with myself and my friends when they talked about him filing his teeth. I think he borrowed a lot of his repertoire from

Ripper Collins at his bloodiest worst, going berserk after a match with Tommy Phelps in Amarillo, Texas.

Fred Blassie but it worked very well in the Northwest." Savage said that Collins was a man's man, who knew how to draw. "Ripper Collins was one of the better heels in the business, a great talker, and when he wanted to he could get a riot going in any town he was in."

As time went along, Collins turned up the "gay gimmick," coming to the ring in a long, pink, fur-trimmed cape with matching boots and trunks — yet to those who knew him backstage, it wasn't an act. Despite being married with kids, Collins was notorious to his peers, as well as the police; he spent time in jail in both Calgary and Louisiana for allegedly soliciting underage boys. Collins would torture anyone uncomfortable with his sexuality, pulling ribs, or rubbing himself suggestively in the ring.

To those whom it didn't bother, he was just another one of the boys. "Luscious" Larry Sharpe was paired with "Ravishing" Ripper Collins in Calgary. When they made their first trip together, Collins denied being gay. But Sharpe quickly added things up. "His mind was so much into the homosexuality though. I would go, and pick up a broad, and bring her back to the room. He'd open the door, and see me in there with her, and he'd go down, and sit in the lobby, and tap his foot until I'd come down at eight o'clock the next morning, all pissed off, like a hissy fit. He wouldn't come in the room with a woman in there." They also went to Japan together. "It was like taking my wife with me. He'd wash my tights, and hang them up, and do all the stuff that a female would do for you," Sharpe laughed.

Beauregarde (Larry Pitchford) considered Collins one of his best friends, and a mentor in the business. "He was a great person. He kept his gay stuff to himself, like Pat Patterson. That was their private thing," he said. "Inside the locker room, he never acted gay. He never put on any pretenses or anything. He was like a mild guy. He wasn't hot-tempered. He got along with everybody. A good joke teller — everybody would sit around and listen to Ripper tell jokes. He could tell jokes like a comedian."

The comedic role suited him well as a manager who wrestled, and as a TV announcer. In Los Angeles in 1971, his job was to contradict the famed Dick Lane in the KCOP studio show, while also ushering Gordon Nelson to the ring. "He could get heat all right," Nelson said. "He'd tell the people they looked fat, and people used to hate somebody like that." When Lia Maivia's Polynesian Pacific Pro Wrestling show aired on the Financial News Network in the mid-1980s, Collins was the lead commentator.

The relationship between Baker and Collins is a lot harder to describe than one of their mixed tag matches. "He even beat The Sheik, I don't mean in a match, I mean in orneriness," Baker said. "He could out-talk a preacher, except me!" To this day, Baker denies that Collins was a homosexual, and she insists that she still loves him. Yet around 1978, Collins just sort of drifted away from the relationship. As his physique deteriorated and he aged, Ripper wasn't in demand as much, and the money dwindled. "Eventually, I didn't hear anything from him. Would you believe that Social Security would not let me know where he was at, and I was his wife?" she asked.

Collins had returned to Hawaii, and worked at a security firm. Aside from helping out with Maivia's promotion, he tried his hand at promoting as well. What he couldn't do was resist the lure of the sun. On November 11, 1991, in Oahu, Hawaii, Collins died from melanoma, which started in his armpits. Baker didn't learn of her husband's passing until six months after the fact. That meant that none of his belongings made their way to his children. "His life was spent at the beach. He loved the sun. The darker he'd get, he'd tan beautifully. But I can see him in my mind's eye, as soon as I close my eyes, I can see him with his hands up the back of his head, his armpits showing up — because you know armpits don't tan — you know how white you get? He was very tanned. He'd be there trying to get a tan under his arms," Baker said. Collins had a traditional burial in his beloved Hawaii, with his ashes scattered out to sea.

CHRIS COLT

The story began with a young, eager, fuzzy-cheeked wrestling fan, anxious to ingratiate himself to his boyhood heroes by running menial tasks for them. It ended . . . well, it's not totally clear when, how, or even if it ended. But between those imperfect bookends rested the life, one beyond the reaches of even the most psychedelically deranged mind, of Chris Colt.

"Bizarre. That's the word you have to use," reflected former tag team partner Ed "Moondog" Moretti. "Chris was Chris because he was so bizarre, and because of the lifestyle he led. He was just sex, drugs, and rock and roll 24/7, and that was him. But when he hit that ring, oh man, it was magic."

In his fifty tumultuous and uncompromising years on earth, Chuck Harris, a.k.a. Chris Colt, as well as Paul and Chuck Dupree, flouted every wrestling and societal convention in the book. He incited riot after riot, pushed his physical well-being beyond any conscionable limit, and famously feuded with promoters, all the while leaving behind his calling card — a genius for wrestling.

"I would say that Chris Colt was probably the greatest wrestler that never made it. I'm not saying that as an insult, but a lot of people don't know who he was," said Lanny Poffo, his World tag team championship partner in the Detroit promotion in 1976. "He never ceased to amaze me with his imagination in the ring. He was an innovator. He was ahead of his time."

Dean Silverstone, who put Colt at the top of the card in the Superstar Championship Wrestling promotion in the Pacific Northwest, remembered him as "perhaps the most difficult individual I ever worked with in the wrestling business. He'd give me a lot of gray hairs and headaches. But it also took an awful long time to count the box-office receipts . . . He was spectacular in the ring. He was phenomenal."

A native of Idaho, Colt moved to Oregon when he was about five, and became a wrestling-consumed teenager, hanging out at local arenas to caddy for Don Fargo and others, and trolling for like-minded pen pals in the pages of wrestling magazines. "I knew when I was eight years old that I wanted to be a wrestler, and I used to save my nickels and dimes just to buy every wrestling magazine I could. I even read them during classes," Harris said in a rare, slightly worked interview. He swapped letters with future wrestling historian Tom Burke, then suddenly appeared as Magnificent Maurice Chevier from Paris in Burke's home area of Massachusetts around his eighteenth birthday.

There, Harris met Russ Grobes, who wrestled as "Golden Boy" Ron Dupree, and was about ten years older than Harris. The two became com-

Chris Colt takes to the air.

panions in wrestling, and their personal lives, on and off for a decade. In 1966 and 1967, they worked as the Dupree Brothers in Arizona and the Gulf Coast promotions. They quickly overhauled their image, and turned into the Hell's Angels, a couple of biker toughs who would resort to any tactic to win. "I think our team equals any in the country today, and with our 'Hells Angels' gimmick, it's different. Like you said, we are originals," Ron wrote promoter Jack Pfefer in August 1967. The two twice held the Detroit version of the world title in 1968 and 1969. They also headlined Arizona in the 1960s and 1970s as the Comancheros.

"Chris Colt was the embodiment of villainy, an arch-bastard among bastards," said Dale Pierce, author of a book on Arizona wrestling, who helped Colt with promotional photos. "He and Ron Dupree were not only master bad guys, but creative ones who were constantly finding new ways to cheat. They could take the most innocent or unimportant of objects and use it as a weapon. A comb, a pack of cigarettes, a string of hippie beads, a belt buckle, a pen, a popsicle stick, a pop bottle, a rock, a wrench, even mud from outside the arena one time, which they threw in Firpo Zbyszko's eyes."

Outside the ring, the pair was just as unorthodox. Greg Lake, who worked with the duo in the Northwest, was roused out of a bed one night after a show in Spokane, Washington. "It must have been about midnight or so. I heard a knock on the door at the motel. Ronnie and Chris come walking in, and right behind them there's a big white tiger like Siegfried & Roy. I was half-asleep and I must have jumped back three feet. They just walked around the room and left."

But Ron Dupree's health failed him at a young age. He suffered a heart attack that forced him into a role as manager of his brother, now named Chris Colt in a nod to the title of his favorite gay men's magazine. Dupree briefly recovered to wrestle Colt after a bloody and intense split in Arizona, and teamed with him as the Hells Angels to win the Gulf Coast tag title in 1974. On October 17, 1975, Dupree suffered a fatal heart attack doing ring announcing in Tacoma, Washington. He was forty years old.

As a single, Colt continued to shine, in large part because of his willingness to defy the norms. He was the one of the first wrestlers to adopt a rock-and-roll gimmick, painting his face, and using Alice Cooper's "Welcome to My Nightmare" entrance music as part of "The Chris Colt Experience" in the mid-1970s. "He said to me, 'The promoters and bookers at the time were stuck in a time machine of 1940, and could not see the changes taking place in society, and wrestling is a reflection of that,'" Burke recalled.

Colt's willingness to sacrifice his body — he loved to bleed — helped him tear down houses with Johnny Valiant for Dave "The Bearman" McKigney's Ontario promotion in 1982. "He was a zany kind of a guy, a risk taker, and looked like somebody out of a biker bar or a rock band. He looked like somebody that would be on a high wire or somebody that would be a lion tamer," Valiant said. "He just told me, more or less, 'Johnny, you can't give me enough bumps. I can take these bumps all night.' I would give him a lot of backdrops, and bumps, and slams, and throw him over the top rope. He just told me to keep doing it to him, that he could take it all."

Colt was gay, but wrestlers and promoters who knew him said he did not make a big deal about his lifestyle, and might have taught them a thing or two. "He was one of the first openly gay wrestlers," Poffo said. "This is where I learned a lesson. You would think a gay person can't fight. But Chris Markoff was hurting people in the ring, he was a really stiff guy . . . They had a fight, and Chris Colt beat him, and I couldn't believe it. Markoff tried to suplex him over the top rope, and it was like putting the cat out. He went 'reow' with quickness and ability. I never would have believed that a big guy like Markoff could lose to Chris Colt. You never know about these things."

But if innovation and talent were in Colt's dictionary, moderation was not. Bill Anderson, who met Colt in Phoenix, and later wrestled as his kid brother Billy, recalled Colt downed a case of beer and a bottle of Southern Comfort daily, like a thirsty dog lapping at a water dish. "He idolized Janis Joplin, Joplin and Joe Cocker, those were his people. Janis died at twenty-seven. I was around him at twenty-seven and he lived every day like this could be his last, just like Joplin. And he would have been the happiest guy on earth to choke on his vomit just like she did because that's the way he lived his life."

Anderson still shakes his head at the memory of a 1975 cage match in Phoenix, where Colt hallucinated in the ring. "Chris had taken some kind of junk. He got in the cage and thought he saw some giant spiders. It was just like he was envisioning giant spiders climbing in the cage at him. He was flipping out. He started a riot. I was swinging chairs to get out," Anderson said.

"Chris was always high. He used to say, 'I can't work if I'm not high.' This is not slander, this is true stuff," Lake added. "No kidding, one time he was sober and he said, 'Greg, I just can't work right when I'm sober.' He was just a crazy, wacko guy, but as crazy as he was, he was a nice guy."

Small by championship standards, and loaded with personal baggage, Colt bounced from territory to territory in the late 1970s and early 1980s. He finished in Alabama in 1986–87 as Chris Von Colt, a hate-spewing German. He soon disappeared from the mainstream wrestling scene, and his life took a nasty, downward spiral. He took roles in gay adult movies and landed in Seattle. Out of the blue, he called and visited old friends with supreme politeness, then, just as quickly, disappeared into the mist. He is believed to have died of AIDS in a mission in 1996. Unconfirmed reports suggest that he became a born-again Christian before he died. Like a wrestling version of Elvis Presley or Andy Kaufman, Colt's demise has become the stuff of endless rumor and lore. "Nobody knows for sure, and I think that's part of the mystique of Chris Colt. He was a mystery while he was here, and he is a mystery when he is not here," Silverstone said. "Knowing Chris, he would probably like it that way."

And everybody he touched misses him dearly. "I can honestly say he was one of he greatest workers I've ever seen. He didn't have the exposure, but as far as work, I'd rank him right up there with Ray Stevens and Pat Patterson. He was that good," said Moretti. "Politics, paranoia, and just Chris being Chris kept him from the big, big money, but they could not keep him from greatness."

"HOT STUFF" EDDIE GILBERT

Long before fantasy football was the rage, Eddie Gilbert was doing fantasy booking. As a kid in Tennessee, the son of veteran pro Tommy Gilbert was creating angles on his own. "It was like a fantasy wrestling league for himself," marveled lifelong friend Ken Wayne. "He booked stuff, and he wrote it all down in notebooks. Then, sometimes years later, he'd go find one of those books, and find an old angle that he thought of when he was fifteen years old, and rework it to where it would fit."

"Hot Stuff" Eddie Gilbert's career in wrestling didn't last nearly long enough — he died at just thirty-three in 1995. But everyone who watched him in action as a wrestler

Good before bad: Eddie Gilbert and Curt Hennig in their early days.

and a booker still marvels at his ingenuity. "He was not very big, but he was a thinker. Incredibly creative," said referee James Beard, who knew him from their days in Texas. "He was very basic in a lot of how he worked. He really believed in logic, and making fans believe what you were doing."

Given his bloodlines, Thomas Edward Gilbert Jr. probably was destined to follow his father into the business. "From the time he was in the second grade, his only thing was being a wrestler. His dad and I both tried to talk him into being anything else," his mother Peggy said. Eddie started off by writing articles and taking ringside photographs — and by his own admission, watching every move Memphis icon Jerry Lawler made. Contrary to popular opinion, he did not miss his graduation at Lexington High School to wrestle, and, though journalism held a little allure for him, it was nothing like taking bumps.

He debuted in 1979 in Malden, Missouri, and was a fan favorite at first, earning his spurs with a lot of blood. Gilbert teamed with Ricky Morton against Mr. Onita and Masa Fuchi in an infamous 1981 concession stand brawl in Tupelo, Mississippi. "Eddie and Ricky Morton really established themselves as tough country boys with that angle," said friend and Memphis manager Scott Bowden. "They went into that bout pretty boys — they left men who were fighting for America against the evil Japanese who had invaded their backyard."

Gilbert moved to the WWWF in 1982, mostly on the bottom half of the card, and his life changed the following year when he was involved in near-fatal car accident near Allentown, Pennsylvania, after a TV taping. Upon returning to Tennessee, he really found his niche as a cocky, upstart heel with a turn on tag team partner Tommy Rich that helped him earn a main event against Lawler. Since he yearned to be top gun in Memphis like Lawler, "that was a dream come true," he said in a 1992 interview with Paul Adamovich. Moving to Bill Watts' Louisiana-based promotion, Gilbert partnered with wife Missy Hyatt, a combination of beauty and sneakiness that shot him to the top ranks of wrestling. The "Hot Stuff" name, taken from a Donna Summer song, was always on his mind. "I wanted to be a heel," he said. "And I thought, 'Okay, everybody's got a nickname. Why can't I be "Hot Stuff" and why can't that be my song?'"

Gilbert constantly battled his small frame — at five-ten and about 210 pounds, he was coming of age in an era when 'roided-up freaks were making the covers of wrestling magazines, and he was familiar to pills himself. But he worked more of a big man's style. "I think Eddie always had something to prove because of his size," Bowden said. "However, his grasp of psychology rivaled that of Jerry Lawler's and Terry Funk's. I know Eddie's neck problems, stemming from his car accident, limited him a bit, but often you'd never know it, as he worked a very physical brawling style — especially in the early '90s."

One of Gilbert's great drawbacks was an impatience found in creative minds — he was forever hopping back and forth between World Championship Wrestling, Extreme Championship Wrestling, the Continental Wrestling Federation, and other promotions, though he always landed back in Memphis. "He was so creative that he became easily frustrated with management," Beard explained. Booking the dormant Alabama territory in 1988, Gilbert turned Dothan gates from $1,200 to $13,000, infusing midcard talent with clever, soap-opera-style storylines. "That's the biggest problem with WCW, is they'll start something, and then cut it out three weeks later," Gilbert said in an eerie forecast of the company's eventual woes. "The soap-opera syndrome, you don't cut it off; you blend it right into something else." His creativity became believable for fans in a legendary Memphis incident — Eddie, and brother, Doug, bickering with Lawler, took dead aim at him with a moving car. Lawler hit the windshield, and fell to the ground as the Gilberts sped away. Aghast viewers called the police to report the crime; Lawler appeared to TV to calm fans, and turn down the heat to "simmer" level.

If Gilbert had a second love besides wrestling, it was politics. He came from an active Republican family — his mom is an alderman and vice mayor of Lexington. Unknown to most, Gilbert worked from time-to-time as a sergeant-at-arms at the Tennessee state capitol on behalf of Representative Steve McDaniel, a family friend. Gilbert got his feet wet running for county clerk in 1994, though family knew his youthfulness doomed him. "If you're not up in years, you don't win," his mother reflected. "We knew that he couldn't win that, but he loved it, he loved the entire concept of it and he had a good time doing it."

Gilbert as Hot Stuff.

In 1995, Gilbert was booking Puerto Rico, and asked Wayne to come down for a tour in early February. During Wayne's second night there, fans rioted in Bayamon Stadium. Back at their apartments, the old Tennessee hands reflected on the evening, and agreed that they could turn that fan intensity into some cold, hard cash. But, the next day, Wayne knew something was terribly wrong when his raps on Gilbert's door went unanswered. Once he entered the room, he found Eddie dead on his bed. "I closed the door, and I stood here, and I cussed him for dying on me," Wayne said softly. "It did shock me because one of the things I talked to him about that Saturday night in Bayamon — if I see you walking around recreational drugging in a stupor for a day or two, I said, 'I'm outta here.' When he died, I searched the room and didn't find anything."

In fact, while Gilbert didn't do himself any favors with his hard living, his heart had been severely damaged in his auto accident years before, and he had long-standing problems with his blood pressure. Friends and fans always ask, "What if?" and in this case, it's probably justified. "I think if Eddie had lived, the business would have been a little different today. His influence would have helped a little bit. Maybe ECW would have done better; he might have gone back there because he was tight with [promoter] Paul Heyman," Wayne said. And while the family still deals with his loss, cards and letters remind the parents that their son made quite an impact during his life. "We still get things at Christmas time from people in Spain, and Germany, and all kinds of places," his mom said. "That helps us."

Chuck Thornton Collection

Dr. Jerry Graham in the beginning.

DR. JERRY GRAHAM

More than fifty years ago, a personable young Eagle Scout named Jerry Graham helped Phil Melby, his classmate and best friend, get a job alongside him as a night janitor at the Arizona State Capitol building in Phoenix. Melby's dad thought it was a prelude to greatness. "Jerry was a nice guy. He was a super guy. My dad used to say, 'He's going to run for governor.' He had a great personality," Melby said. "But the wrestling business ruined him."

Dr. Jerry Graham was pro wrestling's ultimate Dr. Jekyll and Mr. Hyde. He gave of his time and money more than anyone might suspect, founded one of wrestling's historic families, and mastered the art of audience manipulation like few in his time. But an addiction to booze and destructive behavior eventually left him living day to day in flophouses. "He was just constantly sauced, that was his problem," said Billy Anderson, whom Graham managed in California. "But when he got out in front of the crowd, he loved it. He would prefer to die in the ring than anywhere else. It didn't matter if there were five people or 500; he wanted to entertain at all costs."

Graham was born December 16, 1931, in Oklahoma, and grew up in Arizona amid future wrestling and political heavyweights. Long after outrageous behavior became his stock-in-trade, he regaled friends by explaining how he often ducked a night in the hoosegow. "All it took was just one phone call to my old Eagle Scout master, and he got me out of the slammer, no questions asked by the cops!" When friends inquired as to his Scout leader, Graham turned with a proud, stoic look, and blurted, "Senator Barry Goldwater!"

His first known attempt to kayfabe the world came at fifteen. He added three years to his age so he could drop out of Phoenix Union Central High School and join the U.S. Army paratroopers in June 1947, after six months in the National Guard. He earned a parachute badge, and departed the service exactly one year later at the 82nd Airborne Division at Fort Bragg, North Carolina. His mother Mary, a force in GOP politics, stepped in, and the truth ended his career before he shipped out. "They pulled him out before he went overseas because he was underage," said son Jim, part of the 82nd Airborne years later. Graham and Melby learned the wrestling game at the feet of the great Jim Londos, and Graham quickly found an outlet for his unique skill set. He parachuted into small Arizona towns as the masked Blue Terror, headed to a bar or lounge to stir up trouble, and led a hostile crowd, like a wrestling Pied Piper, to the arena.

From the fall 1952 through early 1957, Graham spent a lot of his time in Atlanta in a feud with beefy Chief Big Heart that ranks among wrestling's bloodiest. "Dr. Jerry Graham and Chief Big Heart were the biggest drawing cards I believe they ever had over there in Georgia," said wrestler Tom Drake, who promoted them in several cities for Paul Jones' Georgia office. "I never did see Dr. Jerry Graham come out of the ring where he didn't get bloodied up bad." In 1957, Graham got the call to go to New York City, and that's where the seeds of his renown and destruction were sown. He teamed with Professor Roy Shire, and later added Eddie Gossett as brother Eddie Graham, headlining card after card against Latino idols Antonino Rocca and Miguel Perez.

Graham brought Melby to wrestle in the Northeast that year, and his pal was astonished by what he saw. "By then, he believed his own shtick. He took me to a barber shop, one of those fancy joints. It was like thirty dollars. I said, 'Jerry, what are you doing?' He became a big shot, and believed his own write-ups. And you'd get him full of booze, and he'd fight a bear with a switch." In essence, Graham became his character. The top of his red convertible was always down, no matter the temperature, and a young Vince McMahon rode with him down the streets of Washington, D.C., flipping the bird at bystanders. "Jerry drove around in this '59 Caddy convertible with big fins, and when he was out in public, he'd light his cigars with $100 bills. I'm thinking, 'This is the life,'" McMahon told writer Joel Drucker in 1999.

In 1961, Dick Steinborn learned about Graham's preoccupation with turning heads when the Doctor drove Steinborn's new car to a popular Atlanta nightspot. As they approached the open parking lot near the lounge entrance, Graham stepped on the gas. "I thought we were going to crash. He

Dr. Jerry Graham later in life.

was headed for the valet parking attendants standing outside the entrance. I knew they were a goner," Steinborn said. Graham slammed on the brakes, and Steinborn swears he can still smell the burning rubber. The Doctor cranked the radio full blast, pulled his massive girth out of the car, and strode into the club. As Steinborn recalled, Eddie turned to him with a small smile and said, "Jerry just made his entrance."

Though he claimed that he gained weight to achieve the balance of a sumo wrestler, his drinking kept him over 300 pounds for a large part of his career. Still, ring psychology remained his calling card. He had a huge run in Calgary in 1962 and 1963 against Big Heart and Ronnie Etchison. In 1964, he brought Grady Johnson into New York as "brother" Luke, and stayed in the federation on and off through 1966; he introduced "brother" Billy Graham to the world a few years later. He held tag titles on eight occasions, and also had runs as Southern champion and Gulf Coast champion. Graham built up his heat with contempt — real, in a way — of fans. He bounced around the ring, propelling his ample body to all kinds of heights when the babyface made his comeback. And he believed in a big payoff — and that meant blood.

"He always thought the human condition — he used those words — and people in general were violent, and wanted to see bloodshed, whether it was for the sake of good or bad," said California wrestler Kurt Brown, who befriended Graham in later years. "So with whatever heat he built, he always felt that when it was time for the heel to get his ass kicked, he had to bleed. He believed in lots of blood and guts, but in a different way than Abdullah the Butcher or The Sheik. He thought fans were hungry to see the villain get his just desserts in a very violent way."

Anderson witnessed how Graham put that philosophy into practice in Los Angeles. Working as a manager, Graham went on TV and boasted about what his charges, Tim Patterson and Anderson, would do to Victor Rivera and Dominic DeNucci. "Rivera attacked him and hit him over the head with a board, and Jerry just bladed himself from temple to temple. It was so gory, but Jerry loved that. He loved the thrill of bleeding," Anderson said.

Graham attracted headlines of the wrong kind in August 1969, when he barged into Good Samaritan Hospital in Phoenix after the death of his mother. He took his mother's body, threw it over his shoulder, struck a nurse who tried to stop him, and tried to exit the premises. He fired a shot at a doctor, and kicked the door off a police car. Relatives committed him the next week to Arizona State Hospital. After observation, he was released and returned to Ohio, where he landed in jail about two weeks later, for leaving the scene of an accident. His three children in Arizona ended up in foster care. "It saved us," Jim Graham, now a teacher, admitted candidly.

Still, Dr. Jekyll still lurked somewhere inside his eccentric exterior. "Jerry was a great storyteller, a guy that had been there and done just about everything in the world. He could talk to you on any subject, no matter if it was politics or human anatomy," said Percival A. Friend, who had his first pro match with Graham. "Some guy asked him, he was just coming into the business, a real smartass, 'Oh, you're a doctor, are you, what kind of doctor are you?' Jerry turned to him and said, 'I'm a tree surgeon. You wanna get an arm removed?' The kid turned pure white." In December 1970, an Ohio newspaper blew Graham's villainous cover by noting he volunteered hours of his time to the annual Christmas drive of *The Advocate* of Newark, Ohio, near his home in Buckeye Lake, carrying bundles of toys, food, and goods to the needy. "My dad would do crazy stuff like walk into a bar in New York, and throw $3,000 in the air he just made at Madison Square Garden, and people would dive and go for that," son Jim said. "But my dad did a lot of positive things that people just never heard about. For him to pull fifty dollars out of his pocket and hand it to somebody was nothing. He loved helping high-school wrestling programs, and I ended up being the guinea pig for a lot of moves."

After Graham snapped in 1969, he pretty much bounced from territory to territory. Long removed from the spotlight, he worked some independent shows in California in the 1980s and early 1990s for promoter Ed Ahrens. A lot of the time, he couldn't pull on his boots without help. "There was still a very dynamic presence," Brown recounted. "The night I met him, he wrestled this kid, and it was a thirty-second match, but he had the people wanting to kill him." Driving Graham home after that match though, Brown and his friends encountered Mr. Hyde when the good doctor asked to stop for a couple of beers. "He came back with a couple of beers, but also with three bottles of hard liquor, and a couple of bottles of wine. He started downing them all, and letting out his war cry as we went down the highway, and he started throwing the empty bottles out onto the highway without looking to see if there were cars there. I was just praying we would get home without ending up in jail."

Graham's health failed in the mid-1990s, and he wound up in a nursing home, where he died unceremoniously, separated from his family, in January 1997. He is buried in a veterans' cemetery in Riverside, California. "I don't think about all of that stuff," Melby concluded. "He was my beloved friend, until he went and became another person who I did not relish being around. I remember Jerry from working out with Jim Londos, and having a beer afterward. God bless his memory."

RIP HAWK

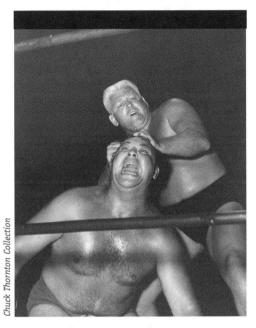

Rip Hawk rips into Louie Tillet.

Rip Hawk is best known for his legendary tag team with Swede Hanson, but the tough-as-nails wrestler also forged a memorable singles career. During more than thirty years in the ring, Hawk developed a well thought-out concept of what a villain should and shouldn't do, and colleagues still hold him up as a perfect role model for the sneaky heel.

Unlike a lot of his contemporaries, Hawk didn't yell or scream at the customers. Instead, he'd start out small and build the heat with one or two fans, as he worked over his opponent. "You just glare at them, and pretty soon they want to kill you. And because they're hollering at you, pretty soon every- body else is calling you an SOB and that. Pick out one or two, one on each side of the ring, and just glare at them. Pretty soon, you get them all going."

It worked out well for Hawk, who was Texas heavyweight champion in 1963, a four-time Eastern States heavyweight champion, and also had more than a dozen runs as a tag champ around the world before he called it quits in the early 1980s. Gerald Brisco had a pitched battle with Hawk in the Mid-Atlantic, but actually was a closet admirer, calling him "my hero."

"I hold Rip up with the best of anyone," Brisco emphasized. "Sometimes I would want to take a bump, and Rip would pull me up, and say, 'Not yet, kid.' He had the speed of a junior heavyweight. He knew how to look at the people and get heat. . . He got the most out of what he had than just about anybody I've been in the ring with."

An Ohio native, Hawk — real name Harvey Evers — was the son of a minor league baseball player. Born in 1930, Hawk participated in club wrestling as a teenager, and turned pro around 1948 after training with Karl Pojello, a top grappler and promoter who also managed The French Angel. That meant Hawk learned the hard way. "If you screwed up, you know who you had to wrestle? The Black Secret, and that was Karl Pojello. He was tough. He was a tough wrestler."

Uncle Sam came calling during the Korean War, and Hawk entered the Marine Corps, which patriotic promoters added to his billing after he finished with the service. With a stocky, low-to-the-ground build, and a nasty streak, Hawk — the nickname came from a Chicago promoter who noted his sharp features — became a wrestler fans loved to hate. "They didn't take to me as a good guy. People just didn't care for me," he said. "I think it was the way I carried myself at that time. I guess I was just miserable to the people. I wasn't really miserable; it's just the persona I had."

Hawk got a break wrestling Fred Blassie in Georgia in 1956, and then made a big name for himself in St. Louis. There, former world champion "Wild" Bill Longson suggested Hawk employ the piledriver, a hold he used for years, but had been shelved by state athletic commissions across the country. "I said, 'Well, I can't use that; it's been banned.' He said, 'It's been so long ago, they'll forget about it.' So I used it for the first time in St. Louis, and it got a great reaction — they kept calling me 'Bill Longson, Bill Longson,' 'cause they didn't forget where it came from," Hawk reminisced.

Hawk headed to the Carolinas in 1961, where he hooked up with Hanson. In addition to their mayhem, Hawk was the territory's top singles heel for years against headliners like Brisco, his brother Jack, and Thunderbolt Patterson. Hawk never considered himself a dirty wrestler — he was more of a psychologist, using little tricks of the trade to manipulate crowds. "You have to psychoanalyze people. You can have a hammerlock on a guy on the mat and you don't have to do anything bad. Just sneak like you're going to do something and glare at those people, and they're going to call you everything in the world."

If anything, public recognition of Hawk's skills as a singles heel might have been overshadowed by his tag team role, according to Sandy Scott, who wrestled him dozens of times in the Mid-Atlantic. "They looked at Swede as the punisher, the big guy, and I think it took a little away from Rip because Rip did the wrestling," Scott said. "In the ring, he got into that sneakiness. Rip did it in such a way where the people would burn. They'd say, 'Damn it!

You didn't have to do that, and you did it.'"

The piledriver came into play during one program with Brisco, who was in line for $1,000 after pinning Hawk during a time-limit challenge match. Gary Hart, Hawk's manager, counted out $100 bills one by one, but dropped the tenth one on the floor. When Brisco reached over to pick it up, Hawk locked him in a piledriver as Hart scooped up the cash. Years later, Brisco could still laugh when reminded of the angle — "Yup, they got me."

Hawk introduced his "nephew" Ric Flair to the Mid-Atlantic in 1974, winning the Mid-Atlantic tag team titles, before winding down his career in Texas and California. "Finally, in Oklahoma, I decided to quit. Everything was in slow motion," he said. Hawk settled in Hereford in West Texas, where he taught wrestling at a local YMCA for years. "I still run the kids' program. I don't want to retire. I think it keeps you young."

Steve Johnson

The perennial champion Triple H.

TRIPLE H

One of the most astute students of "the game," and a heavy behind-the-scenes player in World Wrestling Entertainment, it's not a surprise that Triple H has given a lot of thought to his character, and its evolution through the years. He really does feel he's best as a bad guy.

"To be honest, I enjoy being a heel more than anything else. To me, it's a great time for it. The hardest thing in this business is to stay one way or the other. If you're a (babyface), if you're not creative enough, people start to dislike you. If you're a heel, it's easy for people to start liking you, especially if you're doing a lot of badass stuff," he told journalist Alex Marvez. "Toward the end of my run as a heel, people were starting to cheer a little bit. It was just an inevitable fact. This babyface turn and then turning back to heel was great because I think people bought into the fact I had turned (babyface). When I turned again, it was like, 'That bastard. I hate him.' It puts me back with heat and I like that."

Given the booking-on-the-fly methodology of the last decade though, a current fan will read the above insight and wonder, "Which heel turn is he referring to?" (It was in 2000.) Such is the business today. Like few others, Harley Race can understand what it's like to stand at the top of your chosen profession and look down. He credits Triple H for working so hard: "He's in that super-position, where he can work with your super-hot heel at the time, he can work with your superstar babyface at the time. He's in a perfect, perfect position."

While many have disparaged Triple H for staying on top so long, and using his real-life courtship and marriage to Vince McMahon's daughter Stephanie to keep his political influence sharp, his peers insist he is someone who shares. "[Triple H] has an amazing psychology for the business," Randy Orton told IGN.com. "He understands how to tell a story, and you just pick his brain the best you can while riding with him."

Growing up in Greenwich, Connecticut, Paul Michael Levesque really dreamed of two things: bodybuilding and pro wrestling. He used his paper-route money to join the gym, and built himself up from a 135-pound "beanpole" to a competitive bodybuilder. But he knew wrestling called. In a gym, he met champion powerlifter and former wrestler Ted Arcidi, who told Levesque about Killer Kowalski's wrestling school.

Kowalski sized-up his new six-foot-four, 260-pound student, who still worked as the manager of a Gold's Gym, and liked what he saw. "I can spot these guys by the way they perform in the ring. And he had so much athletic ability, Hunter, that I said 'This guy's going to make it.' And he sure did," Kowalski said. Levesque bluffed his way into a one-year deal with World Championship Wrestling under Eric Bischoff, and worked as Terra Rizing and then French aristocrat Jean-Paul Levesque. He credits Terry Taylor and Jody Hamilton for really helping him develop as a worker.

When his deal expired, Levesque jumped to the WWF in July 1995, and was another arrogant prat, this time an American one (reportedly designed to annoy Vince McMahon's Connecticut neighbors) named Hunter Hearst Helmsley. Given his recent role on the top of the company, it's easy to forget that he was in midcard feuds with Henry Godwinn and Mark Mero until really hitting his stride in the D-Generation X faction with Shawn Michaels, Billy Gunn, Road Dogg, X-Pac, and Chyna in 1997.

DX marked Triple H's first real babyface run, since the gang was a collection of the coolest, anti-authority guys (and one really big girl) in town. "What makes DX great is that it's fun," Michaels once said. "If you worry about what you are going to do in the ring, you forget about what you really need."

Since then, "The Game" has bounced all over the map, and been willing to play whatever role necessary, from world champion to fall guy, from heir apparent of the WWE's fortunes to a vampire in the movie *Blade III*. "He's the hardest working guy we have on either roster. He is a lifelong student of the game," WWE announcer Jim Ross told the *Between The Ropes* radio show. "I think the guy gets a lot of undue criticism. A lot of guys have beat him. He's beaten a lot of guys. He's at the house shows. He works hard. Anybody who pays their money to go to a live event sees that he's there. He busts his ass. He's worked through injuries."

"[O]ne of the things that I'm proudest of all I've accomplished in the business . . . [is] to be able to work with a wide variety of guys, whether it's Foley, or Austin, or The Rock, The Undertaker, Big Show, Jericho, all the way down to Taka, just numerous guys," Triple H told writer Mike Mooneyham. "And there's a part of me that wishes it was still the old days, because I would love nothing more than to make a trip to Japan, and work with the top guys there, and go to different places. I love that challenge, to go to the different places, and work with the top guys in those places, and have great matches with. That would be the best to me. That's the challenge of it."

JEFF JARRETT

It's fair to say that there were a lot of skeptics when Jeff Jarrett, the old-time "Golden Boy" of Tennessee wrestling, debuted as the lead bad guy in the NWA-Total Nonstop Action promotion in 2002. Whether an upstart company could challenge the WWE, and whether Jarrett was the wrestler to do it, were interesting, but open, questions.

But Jarrett willingly assumed a traditional heel role, as the company he founded with his dad upgraded its talent and provided the only nationally televised wrestling alternative to the WWE. "You've got to stay true to your character, you've got to have emotion, and you've got to be smart. That isn't cocky; that's confidence," he said. "At the end of the day, this business is about conflict. Regardless of what shape, form, or fashion, it is about conflict. You have to have good versus evil." Tennessee veteran Randal Brown watched how Jarrett put that philosophy into practice, as a successor to heels like Jackie Fargo and Tojo Yamamoto, not long after TNA celebrated its fourth anniversary in 2006. "He grew up watching those guys, and he really, really does a great job," said Brown, who built TNA's six-sided rings. "His interview skills as a heel are kind of average, I think. But in the ring his stuff is really very good. He knows exactly how to get over as a heel."

For as long as Jarrett has been a part of wrestling, it's hard to believe that he would only turn forty in 2007. The son of wrestler and promoter Jerry Jarrett, "Double J" broke in by refereeing as a teenager, and got his baptism of fire in 1986 when "Nature Boy" Buddy Landel and Bill Dundee battered him, prompting his father to come to his rescue. Given Jarrett's bloodlines, wrestling was a pre-ordained profession for him. "When you have any kind of athletic ability, coupled with your dad owning the territory and being surrounded by great talent, you have to be a sheer idiot not to be able to go on," said Landel, who helped with the young Jarrett's training. "But when somebody hands you the ball, you can fumble it or you can run with it, and God knows he's run with it."

Jeff Jarrett does the Fargo Strut.

His father thought the family name was probably a hindrance to Jeff — and to his brother, Jason, who was in the construction business. "Early in their lives, I was able to explain that people would expect so much more from them than they would an outsider," Jerry told Tennessee wrestling historian Tim Dills. "We discussed it so much before the fact, that when they each got into the businesses, they were well aware that they had to work longer and harder just to get on level ground. They were both aware that not only did they have to be good at whatever they did, but that they had to be humble in the process. I'm proud of both of them and their achievements in their respective businesses."

Jarrett stuck to Tennessee for his first couple of years, and won the Continental Wrestling Association tag title with Billy Travis before he turned twenty. When the Tennessee office entered an alliance with World Class Championship Wrestling and the American Wrestling Association, Jarrett started to expand his horizons to Texas and other stages. But it wasn't until late 1993 that he became known on the national stage as the self-confident, Fargo-struttin', guitar-pickin' Double J, who schemed to use the WWF as a springboard to country and western fame in Nashville. That's when he made his first run as a heel, and he said it came natural as his Tennessee accent. "I was a good guy for the first seven years of my career, and I busted on the scene with WWF in 1993 as Double J, and never looked back. That's who I am, for good or bad. That's who I am."

The highlight of his time in the WWF was three runs in 1995 with the Intercontinental championship, part of a feud with Razor Ramon. After contractual issues with the company, Jarrett started hopping back and forth — Memphis in 1996, then to WCW, then back to the WWF in 1997. That's when he dropped the musician gimmick, shaved his head after a match to X-Pac, and ended up pairing with, and against, women in matches — Debra McMichael, Miss Kitty, and Chyna. On his way out of the WWF, he dropped his Intercontinental title to Chyna at the No Mercy pay-per-view in October 1999. "It was a business deal. I wrestled and performed my last match without a contract," he said. "They paid me the money that was owed to me." Brown, who has known Jarrett since he was a kid, thought the loss to Chyna was a blow from which Jarrett's career has been slow to recover. "I think he's done some things that have hurt his credibility," he said, referring to that match. "He does a better job than most heels. But he just lacks the credibility factor that he needs to do it. He has to do something to right it somewhere along the way."

Opinion is divided on whether Jarrett is better as a favorite or as a heel. While he's been the top dog in TNA, some colleagues think his guitar-across-the-noggin practice ran its course a while back. Dennis Condrey of The Midnight Express had a match with Jarrett in Alabama in 2006 when he was the bad guy, and Jarrett was the hero. "He is still very good in the ring today," Condrey said. Still, "I think he is better as a babyface. As a heel, he gets the wrong kind of heat." "Fallen Angel" Christopher Daniels believes Jarrett has "a strong heel presence. It's a role he plays that gets the people motivated to see him beat up every week. His character keeps the people wondering who's going to beat him up next, and they want to watch, and see that happen week after week. It also makes for some potential matches down the road, and matches people want to see."

Jarrett won the National Wrestling Alliance heavyweight title in 2002, and became the "King of the Mountain" when he reclaimed the belt in 2004 against A. J. Styles. He'd hold it six times through 2006, including a defense against Dory Funk Jr., who was NWA champ when Jarrett was two, before taking a much-needed ring hiatus in late 2006. Still, Jarrett was a key figure in front of, and behind, the camera as TNA matured from a tiny Nashville-based operation to one seen in more than 100 countries. "When you do take a deep breath and step back, and look at just how far we've come, it boggles my mind sometimes," Jarrett said.

"I think that what keeps Jeff going is that it's in his blood. I think he loves what he does," added Sting, a long-time friend. "He's going to want to be a part of wrestling, I think, forever. I can see Jeff going into bigger stock, bigger ownership, more involvement corporately, maybe even involved with TV."

Man on the Moon

Courtesy Wrestling Revue Archives

Andy Kaufman pulls at Jerry Lawler's hair.

In the last twenty-five years, pro wrestling has become a nice fallback gig for B-list celebs, a place where they can rehab a stalled career, or earn a quick paycheck. For the most part, promoters, hoping to add paying customers from the mainstream, are glad to have them. How else to explain Mr. T standing in arms with Hulk Hogan? Or David Arquette as WCW world champ? Or Kevin Federline doing whatever he did in WWE?

But they're no Andy Kaufman. In 1982 and 1983, Kaufman, the performance artist cum wrestler, feuded with Jerry "The King" Lawler in the most exquisite example you'll ever find of a Hollywood star who understands what drawing "heat" is all about. "I think he was just enthralled by the control that the heels had — that by taking a pose or lifting a hand, they could control the mood of a crowd," said Lance Russell, the voice of wrestling in Memphis, Tennessee, who was in the middle of it all. "It fascinated him so much that when he first came down to Memphis, and got up there, and was able to do in the ring what he had seen all of these guys do, I think it was a real rush for him. He was just absolutely enthralled with it."

Interestingly, the reaction from other wrestlers to Kaufman's entry into their profession was positive because they knew he was in for the performance, not the payoff. "I did think it was a good idea; everyone was talking about it," said Dennis Condrey, a Tennessee headliner at the time. "Whenever they wrestled, everyone in the back was going to make sure they watched it, because it was entertaining."

Kaufman grew up a wrestling fan, and, if you didn't know it, you could probably figure it out with one gander at his unique, quirky act, where he was often the only one on the inside of an inside joke. "I'm not a comedian, never claimed to be a comedian, and I never claimed to be funny," he insisted to glitterati chronicler Kay Gardella. "And that's where the confusion came in. I'm an entertainer." Part of his shtick included wrestling women as the self-proclaimed intergender champion of the world, and that led indirectly to his march on Memphis. Kaufman hung with wrestling magazine editor Bill Apter, who doubted New York promoter Vincent J. McMahon would sanction a man-versus-woman match in Madison Square Garden. Ah, but Tennessee, Apter told his friend one night – heck, they'd book anything down there! Kaufman was on the phone with Lawler almost immediately. "Of course we jumped at the chance, being a local territory back then, 'cause that was a big deal for us," manager Jimmy Hart, Lawler's arch-nemesis, explained to *Pro Wrestling Daily*.

Back up a second. We're talking about a star of the TV hit *Taxi*, not some cauliflower-eared hand bouncing from territory to territory in search of a booking. Russell, who knew TV from the inside as a program director, is still incredulous a quarter-century later. "I frankly couldn't believe it when I heard he was going to do this. What kind of sense does it make for a guy who was, at the time, that popular in a comedy show on national television to come down, screw around in the ring, and not know whether anybody is going to take a shot at him?"

Lawler entered the scene when he rescued one of Kaufman's female victims, setting up a man-versus-man match, April 5, 1982, before 8,091 fans. After a few minutes of hide-and-seek, The King finished off Kaufman with a suplex and a pair of piledrivers that sent his adversary to St. Francis Hospital. In the kind of delicious irony Kaufman loved, he didn't have to fake his injuries – he legitimately strained his neck. As Lawler recounted to Kaufman biographer Bill Zehme: "Later on he said, 'First of all, the suplex knocked me out. Then both of the piledrivers jammed the heck out of my neck.' And I said: 'Well, you didn't hit, did you?' He said, 'Yes, my head hit both times.'" Condrey was among the backstage gang that ran into the ring to corral Lawler. He seconded Lawler's version, saying Kaufman's head was not where it needed to be for a proper piledriver. "Lawler had actually put it on deep and Kaufman was hurt, and came out with a neck injury," he recalled.

The details of the feud, which ran more or less through late 1983 in different incarnations, are well known, thanks to *I'm From Hollywood*, the 1989 documentary that traces the Kaufman-Lawler battle, and Milos Forman's 1999 biopic, *Man on the Moon*. Not to be forgotten is the infamous July 28, 1982 episode of *Late Night with David Letterman*, when Lawler slapped Kaufman in an unscripted moment that reinvigorated the bad blood, and checked in at No. 93 on *Entertainment Weekly's* list of "The 100 Greatest Moments in TV History."

What's significant beyond the matches was the way Kaufman got fans going in a chicken, cowardly, arrogant way that perfectly fit the Tennessee-heel philosophy. "This is a bar of soap. Now, does it look familiar to any of you?" he smirked during one promo, instructing local rubes on proper hygiene techniques. "The fans just couldn't believe he was here, but it was not a heartbeat between the time they were sitting in wonderment and the time he was developing genuine heat with every one of them," Russell laughed.

"Kaufman's heat was intense," added Memphis manager-turned-columnist Scott Bowden. "After Lawler delivers the first piledriver [in the first match], I believe you can hear Ms. Lily, the old black lady who sat ringside every week at the matches and often tossed her cane into the ring, screaming, 'One more time, one more!' Caught up in the moment, she clearly wanted Andy dead — or at least to suffer a broken neck." As veteran Mid-South star Danny Davis related to *The Courier-Journal* of Louisville, Kentucky: "He took it very seriously. . . . The fans were always irate — they wanted to kill him. He had them in the palm of his hands."

In the short run, wrestling didn't do much to help Kaufman's career, but that is beside the point. In 1984, not long after the program with Lawler petered out, Kaufman died at thirty-five from aggressive lung cancer. "Unlike today, Andy risked his reputation by appearing on wrestling, which was largely considered one of the lowest forms of entertainment by the mainstream press, and masses, even though there were plenty of 'closest' wrestling fans," Bowden observed. "Sure, the Lawler match got them both a lot of press, but really, Andy had nothing to gain by wrestling. If anything, wrestling probably hurt Andy's career, while Lawler gained plenty." In fact, Lawler said he got a cool $150,000 for playing himself in *Man on the Moon*.

And the little legacy Kaufman forged in Memphis has carried over, for better or worse, to Cyndi Lauper, Jenny McCarthy, Jonny Fairplay, and all the celebrities who had a later brush with the mat. "I also think that that was one of the things that helped create sports entertainment as it's evolved into today," Lawler told interviewer Shannon Rose in 2000. "It's one of the first times that anybody from Hollywood came into wrestling, and was involved in a storyline so to speak. We all know what has happened since that time."

JAKE "THE SNAKE" ROBERTS

'Tis the night of Christmas 1982, and all is right with Championship Wrestling from Florida. Kevin Sullivan is in for a drubbing against Dusty Rhodes in their Loser Leaves Florida match, and his henchman Jake "The Snake" Roberts has been banned from the building. Santa Claus is in the house too, handing out candy to the kids. But what's this? Santa's at ringside! He's just handed Sullivan a weapon!

"I loved it, I loved being that fucking sneaky, and that fucking sick to do that," said Santa, er, Jake the Snake. "Dressing up as Santa Claus, and handing out candy for hours, knowing that if somebody actually recognizes you, you're fucked. Santa's going to get reamed, and the reindeer can't even save his ass. Working your way through the crowd, handing out candy, and stuff,

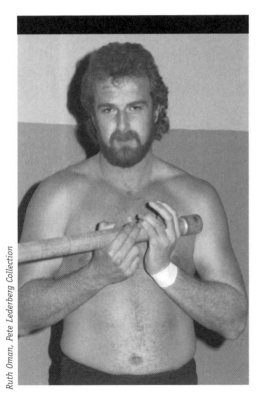

then at the right time, getting close to ringside, and handing the gimmick in to Kevin, and then fucking all hell breaks loose. I remember the police coming to the back afterwards saying, 'This has got to be it. The end of the world is here. Listen to the crowd outside — We want Santa, kill fucking Santa.' I remember reading the paper the next day, and four or five Santa Clauses were beaten up because they'd walked down the street Christmas night. That kind of tells you the end of time is near."

Perhaps Roberts didn't, in fact, bring on Armageddon that night in St. Petersburg, but he sure knew how to make hell for his opponents. With one of the most devious, twisted minds in wrestling history, Roberts messed with viewers, his sinister

A young Jake Roberts.

voice and wicked smile serving as a type of hypnosis. "He never raised his voice, because he didn't have to raise his voice," said Bubba Dudley. "He was pure, intense evil. You listened to him whether you wanted to or not. He had the ability to completely captivate an audience."

"I think Jake Roberts was a sadistic mystery. I think that's what scared people about Jake, because they never knew what Jake was going to do next," Roberts said of his ring personality. "I never thought about what I was doing, I just did it. That's where I've been very fortunate. Same with interviews. I never thought about interviews, I just fucking let it fly. I was smart enough to know — never say something on

Delivering a DDT to Sting, as Nikita Koloff looks on in vain.

television that you're not going to do. Never say you're going to kill somebody, because if you don't do it, you're a piece of shit. You don't come through, you fell short. I went on television and said I was going to make somebody miserable, I would make them wish they were dead. Hell, I can do that pretty easily."

The son of wrestler "Grizzly" Smith, Aurelian Smith Jr., born May 30, 1955, had a strained relationship with his father. Roberts attributes a lot of his personal issues with drugs and alcohol to his perverse upbringing, his father never smartening up the family to the fact that wrestling is a well-done work. "He worked it all the way, and then some. It's sickening. How can you do that to your own child?" Roberts asked. Grizzly Smith and Luke Brown were the Kentuckians, and had a lengthy feud with the masked Assassins (Jody Hamilton and Tom Renesto Sr.). "The Assassins, to me, were the fucking ultimate. They scared me to death," Roberts said. "I just knew those guys were chasing my dad down. 'Dad, you've got to quit wrestling! Those guys aren't going to give up!'"

Trying to gain favor from his father, Roberts decided to get into wrestling too. (His half-brother would wrestle as Sam Houston, and his half-sister was Rockin' Robin.) He only learned the secret to the business in 1975, twenty minutes before refereeing his first match in Alexandria, Louisiana. "I was pretty heartbroken." For the first couple of years, he used the name Jake Smith Jr., before adopting Jake Roberts. He was a babyface at the beginning as well. The Vancouver, British Columbia territory was desperate for talent, and Roberts was desperate to learn. He found an early mentor in Moose Morowski. "[He] basically led me through the process and made me a star, and got me over. In the process, we got to where the PNE [arena] was selling out, which they hadn't done in years." Bobby Bass was the heel Texas Outlaw working against Roberts in B.C. "Jake was a hell of a hand. He got over real well in Vancouver as babyface, believe it or not," said Bass. "He was tall, skinny, just had the trunks on, big bushy hair, like an afro."

A trip to Japan and a stint in Calgary, where he was North American champion and feuded with Big Daddy Ritter (Junkyard Dog), further seasoned Roberts. In Louisiana, Roberts really came into his own. A new, deadly move, the DDT, came about as the result of a botched move in the ring against The Grappler (Len Denton). The Grappler stepped on Roberts' foot while he was in a front face lock. Roberts fell and Denton was knocked out. "It was an accident, but accidents happen for a good reason, don't they?" asked Roberts. "It was pretty obvious that we'd found something. I don't think we really talked about it. I think I went away by myself. I think his talking about it was, 'What the fuck was that? You nearly fucking killed me.'" The Grappler is comfortable with his legacy, and praised Roberts. "He was a very good worker — great promo — but a good worker too. He was a natural in there," said Denton. "He never did train with weights, he never looked like he was that athletic. He was just a big guy."

After a run in the Mid-Atlantic territory, and a return to Bill Watts' Mid-South area, Roberts was called up to the WWF. There, he first started bringing a snake to the ring, wearing trunks that looked like snakeskin, and slithering into the ring. Yes, it was cartoonish, but the snake was feared in a way that Frankie the parrot or Matilda the bulldog weren't. Even during job matches, Roberts was booked brilliantly. Each match would end with the DDT, then his snake, Damien, slithered on his beaten foe. The Snake was given plenty of interview time as well. "I always tried to say a phrase, or two or three words that the people have heard before," Roberts explained. "To me, it's like a subliminal thought. If I say, 'I'm the one your mother has always warned you about,' everybody's heard that line. If I say that at the beginning of the interview, your brain starts going, 'Yeah, I've heard that before, so it's true.' Once I get you doing that, I can go anywhere I want, and I can drag you with me. I'm in. I've got you in, and you want to believe me. The other thing is you don't scream, you don't yell. That's pretty easy. If somebody screams at me, I turn the son of a bitch off. If you're screaming at me in my face, man, I didn't hear a word you said. You walk into a room with a thousand people and you scream, nobody listens. But you walk into that room, and you say [whispering] 'I've got to tell you a secret,' every fucking ear in the place is straining to hear what you have to say."

Roberts had that mysterious charisma that people bought, whether as a heel or a face. He believes that it is inevitable for a character like his to be cheered, which derailed a feud with Hulk Hogan in the WWF at the height of Roberts' run. "Here's the funny thing about people: They want to love you, if they fear you," he said. "If they fear you, or they respect you, they want to love you, because they don't want to be sitting there buying a ticket for somebody they're scared of, for somebody that's a possibility of beating them at whatever they want to do. So they want to be on the winning side, they want to have the winning team."

In the WWF, Roberts would have memorable battles as a heel against Ricky Steamboat and Hulk Hogan. A Honky Tonk Man guitar shot during a Snake Pit interview segment turned Roberts babyface, but also legitimately ruptured two discs in his back, to which he credits his descent into painkiller addiction. As a good guy, Roberts fought Andre the Giant, Rick Rude, Randy Savage, Earthquake (who "squashed" Damien) and Rick "The Model" Martel, who blinded him with his Arrogance perfume, forcing Roberts to wear hideous contact lenses until their blindfold match at WrestleMania VII. "The blindfold match was a fucking hoot. That's one of the matches that I get the most comments on," said Roberts. The crowd was in their hands, as the combatants would just have to stop, and point, and the crowd would direct them in their actions, despite the fact that the hoods were gimmicked, and both could see.

Another regular foe was Ted DiBiase, who concurred that Roberts was not a classic babyface. "He didn't all of a sudden become like the squeaky-clean good guy. He was the same character, but the people cheered him," said DiBiase. "He wrestled the same way, but the people cheered him instead of booing him. That's just knowing psychologically what to do, and how to get that out of people."

Jake the Snake left the WWF in 1992, and slid into World Championship Wrestling for a short feud with Sting. A return to the WWF in 1996 as a

Bible-spouting preacher is best remembered for provoking "Stone Cold" Steve Austin's comeback line, "Austin 3:16 says I just kicked your ass." Roberts' battles with drugs and alcohol have been well-documented, including in the documentary *Beyond The Mat*, but The Snake has worked regularly since leaving the spotlight, despite an artificial hip. In Mexico, he was a feature performer, and lost his hair to Konnan. In Great Britain, Roberts ran a school, and worked around the United Kingdom and Europe.

He still has an undeniable presence, whether it's cutting a promo on Randy Orton on Raw before taking an RKO, or showing up unexpectedly as a referee in TNA for a Monster's Ball match. Even on the independent scene, he cuts an impressive figure, and works as much as he wants. The Snake may be smiling, but perhaps it is best to still use caution. "Just because I'm smiling doesn't mean I'm happy. . . . When I'm smiling is when I'm most dangerous."

LARRY ZBYSZKO

Get Larry Zbyszko going on his masterful technique of stalling — delaying the actual physical contact in the ring with his beloved opponent by yapping at fans and constantly bailing out of the ring — and you are in for a rant.

"There is no such thing as stalling. There are people like [journalist Dave] Meltzer and some guys who became pioneers of the mark/stooges, and they came up with term," Zbyszko spat. Simply put, he was there as the eras collided, and the mid-'80s ushered in steroid monsters who were very limited in what they could do. "Things in the business changed to suit the inability of the new wrestlers. Basically, what was invented was a lot of entrances, music, pyro, and the favorite move of the modern-day wrestler with no ability, the clothesline. But because they didn't know psychology, and they couldn't work a match, and they couldn't build a match, all they did was have an entrance."

Enter "The Living Legend" Larry Zbyszko, with his epic betrayal of his mentor and trainer Bruno Sammartino in 1980 still fresh in fans' minds. Given Zbyszko's high position on cards, by the time he would hit the ring, fans had already seen a couple of matches. He took a different approach than the beastly mountains of the day. "I knew the psychology of getting to the crowd, which takes time. It takes a few minutes. The match tells a story," he explained. "If I chose to do what everybody else did — tie up, start taking bumps, and flopping around — my match would have been like everybody's else's. All I did was stay the same. I took my time. I set up the beginning of the match so people would hate me, and get the story and the idea. Then when something did happen, whether it was three, four minutes, or five minutes down the road, the place would go through the ceiling, the place would go nuts. That somehow became known as stalling."

Born of Polish descent in Chicago, and raised in Pittsburgh, Larry Whistler got into pro wrestling around 1973. Of course, like any kid in Pittsburgh, his hero was Sammartino. But Whistler took it one step further, and started stalking Bruno about 1971, driving past his house just for a glimpse of the champ. On a couple of occasions, he burst into his hero's backyard to seek out advice. Eventually, Sammartino realized that the easiest thing to do would be to train his tormenter. They

Courtesy Wrestling Revue Archives

Zbyszko has Greg Gagne up for a piledriver.

started working out in Bruno's basement gym, with the promise that Whistler would turn pro after school. He attended Penn State, and continued the amateur wrestling that he had begun in grade school.

The pro wrestling workshops happened in Newt Tattrie's barn outside Pittsburgh. "He was just out of high school," said Tattrie. "We trained him at the gym. I was running some shows, and I put him on a few of the shows." After a brief foray to Vancouver, British Columbia, for schooling in the Gene Kiniski/Sandor Kovacs-run promotion, Whistler was brought into the WWWF as Larry Zbyszko, Bruno's protegé.

Unlike a lot of others who found the established guard cold to newcomers, Zbyszko was welcomed with open arms. "Because Bruno was such the man, the superstar of the time, and so politically strong, and because I was his protegé for real, everybody else in the business then was wise, and smart, and very nice to me so they wouldn't get heat with Bruno," he said. "Everybody would be nice to me, help me out, and give me their advice, and go out of their way to enlighten me. I had guys like Jay Strongbow, [Arnold] Skaaland, [Gorilla] Monsoon, the list goes on and on, because I was politically correct before political correctness."

His first big angle was being a part of Spiros Arion's turn on Sammartino in 1974, when Arion decimated the student to get to the teacher. After a short stint in California in 1975, Zbyszko returned to the WWWF, where he would capture tag team gold with Tony Garea.

The turn on Sammartino is perhaps the most famous in wrestling. Zbyszko is a little reluctant to talk about it, as he is working on his autobiography, which he said will reveal all the luscious details. "It wasn't a long time coming, because if you remember, Bruno was retired. He was doing broadcasts. So that's the only hint that I'll give you," he said cryptically. But the facts are these: the protegé started showing signs on TV of being ready for the next stage; he challenged Sammartino to a scientific match; Sammartino reluctantly accepted; in the match, Sammartino hardly performed any offensive moves, and eventually Zbyszko clocked him with a chair (exceedingly rare at that time).

It worked because people could understand the mentor-protegé relationship, said Sammartino. "It was supposed to have been just a workout, and the idea was that he felt at that stage of our lives that I was over the hill and he was coming into his prime, and he felt that if we had a workout where we were trying to out-maneuver each other, that people would have new respect for him, and not just look at him as a protegé of Bruno Sammartino," the ex-champ told *Pro Wrestling Radio*. "When he got a little frustrated because people started getting him a little bit, why I got mad because a lot of people don't know is, he really clobbered me with that chair. I mean, he hit me so damn hard that I was really bleeding bad, and I did — I got very upset and angry with that, and I lost a lot of respect, and after that I just had a completely different feeling about Larry."

Even Leigh Montville of the *Boston Globe* found the time to weigh in. "He is a creep, this Larry Zbyszko. He is a creep of Shakespearean proportions, eyes darting behind that handsome face, wheels turning, creepiness oozing from his every action. He would do anything to succeed. He would sell his mother swampland in Florida. He would steal the March of Dimes canister from the neighborhood variety store counter. He would kiss and tell. He is not just a creep. He is a *real* creep."

Zbyszko laughs when the piece is read to him. "The guy was real close too, he was pretty on for what Larry Zbyszko was," he admitted. "If anybody does learn anything, and gets a lesson from Larry Zbyszko in the time that he was a wrestler, because in the old school that I came from, more people believed. People believed, they had heart attacks, and *died*. Larry Zbyszko survived after that for twenty years, and is still going with reaction, because people believe — not in wrestling — but what I stole from all the greats was no matter what they thought of professional wrestling, people believed that Larry Zbyszko was a real asshole in real life."

Yet the WWWF run came to an abrupt halt. Zbyszko never really got a major run against world champion Bob Backlund. Just one day, he was out. Stints in the Carolinas and Georgia would follow, and eventually, Zbyszko found a home — and a wife — in the American Wrestling Association. The Minneapolis promotion had resisted, for a time, the changing of the business. Zbyszko was fooling around with his nunchucks one day in the locker room when promoter Verne Gagne saw him, and started to promote him as a lethal martial artist. He'd be a key figure in Curt Hennig's AWA title victory over Nick Bockwinkel, handing him a roll of dimes to nail the champ. A Zbyszko-Bockwinkel feud followed.

"We had very good matches, but it's kind of hard, because it's a heel match. Even though I might have been the babyface by this time, and he had become the heel, and now they want to see me beat him up. [He's] not going to get as much sympathy pounding on me as a babyface is," explained Bockwinkel, who praised Zbyszko for having "that little magic of being an irritant."

After a run as AWA world champ, and a feud with Sergeant Slaughter, Zbyszko started venturing into World Championship Wrestling, but kept up occasional appearances in the dying AWA out of loyalty to new father-in-law Gagne — Zbyszko married Kathy Gagne in 1988.

In WCW, he would team with Arn Anderson as The Enforcers for a decent run, and retired the Western States title (which he says is still in storage). At the age of forty, he had arthroscopic knee surgery, and WCW elected to put him in the broadcast booth. A second career was forged, and soon crowds were chanting "Larry! Larry! Larry!" when he'd come out to the announcer's table. Recently, he has played an authority role with TNA, which runs close to his Florida home. Working one day a week did wonders for his golf game, as well, and he's played regularly ever since. "I'm very good at golf," said "The Living Legend" modestly. "I've been playing on the professional circuits. So even if people don't watch wrestling, or know who the hell I am on TV, after they play a few holes with me, they're in awe of my greatness."

Compared to many of his peers, Zbyszko led a quiet life, and largely left the drinking and partying to others. He got his high a more natural way — getting booed. "It's a feeling you can't explain. It's an addictive feeling that no drug could produce."

The Tough Guys

Bob Leonard

It's Bad News for Mr. Hito.

BAD NEWS ALLEN

"Bad News" Allen Coage had to think hard about it, but there was at least one person who cheered for him when he was at his nastiest best — his mama. "When I used to go to Madison Square Garden, a lot of my immediate family would come down. The people would be booing and screaming at me, and she's walking up and down the aisles, 'Oooh, that's my son! That's my son!' My sister is trying to grab her: 'Look, mom, you can't do this!'"

Born in New York City in 1943, and raised in Queens, Coage brought legitimate streetfighting skills to the squared circle, and his equally legit background in judo — he was bronze medalist at the Montreal Olympics in 1976, competing in the over 93 kg/205-pound range as a heavyweight. "I thought that was the pinnacle of my judo career, to train all those years just to get there was, I thought, quite a feat," said Coage. "Even though the American officials in judo tried to keep me off the team, I wound up going to the Olympic trials, and I beat everybody, and I made the team, so there was nothing they could do about it."

Convinced to give pro wrestling a try, in 1977 Coage attended the New Japan Pro Wrestling dojo. Eventually, Coage spent fifteen years with NJPW, usually under the name "Buffalo" Allen Coage. "For me, training for wrestling was a lot easier than judo itself. Judo was a real hard, rugged sport. When I trained in Japan for a year [for judo], it was really, really tough. So when I went back, this time I was getting paid to do it. Before I was doing judo because I loved it, and I didn't get paid for it."

New Japan was a good place to learn because under Antonio Inoki the company stressed a harder style. "My thing was to really make it look legitimate, make everything that you did make sense so people could actually believe what was going on. Apparently, I guess it worked, because a lot of people just hated me with a passion — which is good. I knew I was doing my job," he said. Much of his roughhousing was based on the fighting he grew up watching on the streets of Harlem. "My style was punches and kicks, so I always tried to use a certain amount of hand speed, like it's almost like you're picking somebody's pocket. They never see you coming. That was more or less my style, hand speed. I always concentrated on that."

His work looked stiff, but Coage insists it wasn't. "That was always my thing, the illusion, make it look stiffer than it was." Coage's favorite opponent, "Dynamite Kid" Tommy Billington, talked about their bouts in Stampede Wrestling in his autobiography. "[Once] he got you in the ring, it was as if he didn't know you. I've had a lot of hard matches in my career, most of them in Japan, because that's how they like their wrestling, but the matches I had with Bad News were something else," wrote Billington. "Violence was a main feature of all our matches, and I could guarantee we'd both end up hurt. If Bad News picked something up to hit you with, a plank of wood, a chair or a bottle, you had to move fast, because he would hit you. He didn't care."

In 1986, Coage got the chance to get on the big stage of the WWF. He spent two and a half years there as Bad News Brown, and was mostly miserable. "They handcuffed me. They pretty much didn't let me do what I should have done," he said. "They really held me down." He made a memorable early dent by winning the battle royal at WrestleMania IV, turning Bret Hart babyface in the process, and further established his lone-wolf status by walking out on his teammates in two straight Survivor Series events.

Jake "The Snake" Roberts worked a program with Bad News. "I had no problem at all working with him. We had a great time," said Roberts. "He got fucked there because Hogan couldn't work with him. I think Hogan was a little scared of him, and Bad News couldn't get up and down. His knees were bothering him. But I knew not to make him get up and down."

However, Allen made his fans from that run. He was a badass in a cartoon world. "He was the complete and total asshole," recalled TNA star Samoa Joe. "Even other heels hated him. He never had a friend. He couldn't be a face if he wanted to."

Yet in October 1985, Allen had a brush with the right side of the law in Calgary. When an angle he worked, throttling Archie Gouldie's "son," got out of control, announcer Ed Whalen quit. A short while later, promoter Stu Hart sold Stampede to the expanding WWF. When Stampede re-started, Whalen insisted on "Good News" Allen. "They brought me back as a face, but eventually they turned me back into a bad guy. That was more my style," Allen explained. The artist was back to his proper medium. "I always liked to work with the best babyface around, because I liked to draw a picture that's clean-cut, to look at it and say, 'Okay, this is it, this is what we're looking at.' You don't want to do some modern painting where you try to figure out what the heck is on the canvas."

A proponent of clean living — his wife, Helen, said he never smoked or drank — Coage died suddenly March 6, 2007, of heart failure, prompting a show of affection from both the wrestling and judo communities. "He appeared gruff, and in the wrestling world, his persona was that of a very gruff person," said Jim Bregman, the only American to win an Olympic judo medal until Coage. "On an interpersonal relationship, he was actually a very gentle and kind man."

MARIO GALENTO

There's a plaque hanging on the wall of Smokey Ford's home in Pensacola, Florida, that sums it up nicely. The award was presented posthumously to Mario Galento, and it simply states: "Gulf Coast Wrestling Reunion Presents Wrestling Personality of the Century — Mario Galento, 2001." High praise, indeed, but to just about anyone who knew Galento, it was appropriate. For a generation, he was an essential part of wrestling in the Deep South. With nifty clothes, finely slicked long hair, and an earring, Galento looked like a cross between a classy mobster and a pirate. But whether he was obeying the rules, or chucking them out the window, he had a unique hold on people. "I don't know how any promoter would not make money with Mario Galento," veteran Frankie Cain said. "He couldn't work, his punches were lousy, but he had that down-home philosophy that people believed when he said things like, 'I'll beat him out of the bushes, and stomp the snot out of him.'" As Smokey, who remarried after his death, put it: "I've heard people sit there — in fact, I was one of them — calling him, 'You long-haired son of a bitch you,' then, when he got out of the ring, run and pay two dollars to get a picture and an autograph. He had a great personality. No one had one just like it."

Galento's real name was Bonnie Boyette, and he was born June 17, 1915, in the western Tennessee town of Alamo, one of five children in a sharecroppers' family. His childhood was about as tough and wild as it got in the backwoods in the '20s and '30s. His daddy made moonshine, and Galento started sipping it, the beginning of a long battle with alcoholism. He dropped out of school in sixth grade, and rode the rails on and off for years, living as a hobo. "He always had a roamin' blood. He never liked to stay in one place," Smokey said. He got into wrestling more of necessity than anything else, working for the Welch family promotion in Tennessee for a few extra bucks. "His momma and poppa was having it pretty rough, and he wrestled for them once a week to buy milk for his baby brother because they had a baby brother that was sick. That's how he got into it," Smokey recounted.

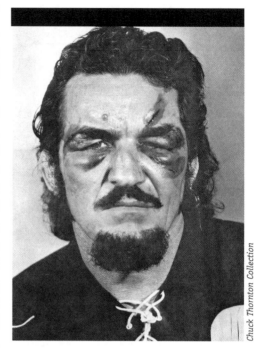

Mario Galento.

Boyette's nickname of "Butch" came from work as a butcher, and he served in the Seabees from 1942 to 1945. He returned to Welch's in the late 1940s, and, despite a lack of formal training, first hit the old Gulf Coast promotion in 1952 as Butch Boyette. He got the name "Galento" from his mentor, the great Al "Spider" Galento, in Tennessee, and it was off to the races. In 1954, already pushing forty, he worked as the Masked Flash in the Mobile, Alabama territory; after an unmasking, he was formally identified as Mario Galento from New York. Lean and raw-boned, he held a ton of titles in Tennessee, Georgia, and Mississippi in the 1950s and the 1960s, most notably winning the Gulf Coast championship six times from 1957 to 1968. "He was probably the first, full-time, always-here heel that they worked a lot of angles with. Nobody had ever stayed the way he did," said former wrestler Michael Norris, a Gulf Coast wrestling historian. "He just drew money like crazy."

Galento's appeal went far beyond titles and headlines. His look was unique for the era, his microphone work was first-rate, and those played a part in landing two movie roles, Frontier Woman in 1956 and Natchez Trace in 1960. "When you met him, you remembered him. That's the best way I can put it," said Tennessee veteran Buddy Wayne, whom Galento helped break into the business around 1953. Galento was more of a brawler than a wrestler, biting, stomping, and kicking his way to the top. Billy Wicks, one of his closest friends, said Galento loved to slug it out and draw real blood in the ring. "He wanted to show how tough he was, and he was a tough son of a bitch," Wicks said. "He'd look you right in the eye and he would say, 'You'd better believe it.' It was like, 'Oh, God, this guy's serious.' He was always high-strung anyway, so that was no act. If he told you he was going to do something, dammit, you'd better believe he was going to do it." That strange brew, a combination of sincerity and roughhousing, kept him going for years. "He was unorthodox. You just never knew what he was going to do," added "Cowboy" Bob Kelly. "Most of the time a guy could be coming toward you and, with ninety-nine percent of the boys, you know what he's going to do before he gets there, by his actions. He was just jerky. People believed Mario, no doubt about it; they believed he was a rough, tough customer." Need more proof? Galento, wound as tight as a fist under the best of circumstances, almost always carried a gun, and shot and wounded a Memphis tough named Sonny Byrd during one fracas.

Barbara Galento, a daughter from his first marriage, worked as a pro, as did Smokey, his second wife, who was twenty-seven years his junior. The fire in his eyes flared one night when he was put in a cage so he couldn't interfere in one of his wife's bouts. As she came to the ring, an obnoxious fan shouted, "Here goes Mario's whore." As Smokey recalled: "I mean, he was mad, and he wasn't playing mad. He was trying to tear the cage, and he couldn't get out." Smokey lost the bout, whereupon Galento was freed so he could tend to his defeated wife. At that point, a woman approached Galento, called him "monkey boy," and handed him a banana. "He went over to that man who had called me 'Mario's whore' and he walked up to his face, and said, 'My wife's a whore?' Well, the man's mouth fell wide open, and he shoved that whole banana down the man's throat. I thought, 'Oh gosh, we're going to jail.'" A police officer talked the spectator out of pressing charges. Galento also averted jail in Georgia in April 1965 after slugging Billy Hines with a roll of coins and bloodying him on live TV. Columbus Police Chief Clyde Adair, unwise to the ways of wrestling, saw the crime and headed out after him. As Smokey said, her husband beat the heat by hopping a promoter's plane out of town to his next gig, and authorities had to wait until he returned the next week to charge him with disorderly conduct and a $77 bond.

Galento's remarkable hold over people wasn't confined to wrestling — he legitimately dabbled in hypnotism and showed off his skills one night on a late-night bus ride across Tennessee. "He was weird-looking with that long black hair and beat-up face. He was sitting a couple of rows in front of me next to a young lady," Dick Steinborn said. "About thirty minutes later, I saw the girl rest her head on his left shoulder. I left my seat, and sat directly behind him. I was amazed — he had hypnotized her. He kept bringing her out of it, and then requesting the post-hypnotic suggestion which was 'white cross.'" Years later, Atlanta booker Leo Garibaldi capitalized on Galento's talent during a program with Paul "Butcher" Vachon.

Galento worked a fair amount as a fan favorite, as well, and stayed in the business through the early 1980s, even after a series of heart ailments. "He went in there full blast, and he always stayed in great shape," Wayne explained. "He'd do 200 deep knee bends even before he got in the ring. He could tire you out in two or three minutes, and then beat the hell out of you." When Norris was breaking into wrestling, he borrowed a mask from Galento at a house show in Dothan, Alabama. By then, Galento was in his mid-sixties, "but you'd have never known he was that age," Norris said. "He was in great shape, still with the jet black hair, and the earring, and everything. He looked like he just stepped out of a time tunnel from 1958 or 1959." Galento died in January 1989, taking with him one of his prized possessions. Smokey once made him a belt proclaiming he was the Senior Citizen World Champion. "It meant the world to him," said Smokey, pleased that her husband turned to the Lord in later years. "So I fastened it around his waist. It was buried with him."

STAN HANSEN

When Stan Hansen first toured Japan in the mid-1970s, he was intrigued with the crowd reaction elicited by his tour leaders — Abdullah the Butcher and Tiger Jeet Singh. Their wild styles got him thinking about ways he could keep fans there on the edge of their seats. "In the Japanese market, the fans weren't like the American fans that were yelling or booing. All their reaction came from action. Abdullah and Jeet Singh, those were the two guys that I saw in Japan, and said, 'You know what? I want to develop a style of my own.'"

Hansen succeeded beyond anyone's wildest imagination. By the time he retired in 2001, he could lay claim to revolutionizing wrestling in Japan, and

Stan Hansen has a hold on Bob Backlund.

had made a huge name for himself in the States, with a mixture of brutality and inexhaustible energy. "I thought he was blowed up the first two minutes, but then he never stopped, same pace, he'd be out there for an hour," marveled Ron Bass, who held the All Japan Pro-Wrestling International Tag Team title with Hansen. "I'd say, 'Dang, boy, how you do that?' He'd be almost dying in the dressing room, but you would never know that. Stan was just full of energy, full of excitement."

A Texas native, Hansen was a star footballer at high school in Las Cruces, New Mexico, before playing college ball at West Texas State. A fling with the Baltimore Colts didn't work out, so he tried his hand at wrestling, in the mold of former West Texas Stater Terry Funk. "I had not really considered wrestling," he said. "But the Funks had gone there and that's how I got to know the Funks." Borrowing a little from Funk and Dick Murdoch, he debuted in 1973, and won the Tri-State version of the U.S. tag team title the next year with Frank Goodish, the future Bruiser Brody, before booker Bill Watts split the team. "They were holding each other back," Watts recalled. "I said, 'You guys are going to be phenomenal singles, but you're different, and you guys are a bad influence on each other as a team. I'm breaking you up.'" They left the area, and Hansen became an immediate star as a single.

Rick Martel first met him around 1975, and was impressed with what he saw from the 300-pound wrestling cowboy. "The thing that characterized Stan the most, and it showed at an early age in his career, was his hard work. This guy would just go out and work hard, just give it all," Martel said. In 1976, Hansen took his bullrope and tobacco chaw to the WWWF against Bruno Sammartino. After a missed slam, Sammartino suffered a broken neck that wrestling scribes eagerly attributed to Hansen's clothesline lariat. The accident set up a big June rematch at Shea Stadium in New York, and, in the strange world of wrestling, enhanced Hansen's image, according to ex-tag partner Larry Sharpe. "It certainly made him an instant heel. I was in Japan when that happened, and, I mean, it made the headlines in the Tokyo news-paper the next day," Sharpe said. "He was deserving of that opportunity if someone was going to get it. He had a great work ethic. I'm glad he got whatever good came out of that unfortunate incident."

Hansen's biggest mark as one of the great monster heels of his generation came overseas, though. On one tour of Japan, former NWA champ Jack Brisco sensed promoters were getting ready to turn to Hansen as their top guy, and urged him to get his share of big paydays. "Jack kind of smartened me up as to maybe I should be a little more focused on business," Hansen acknowledged. To Brisco, it was an easy call. "He was so big compared to those Japanese, he was very convincing, and young, and full of fire. You'd go to the ring, and people would scatter to get out of his way; they were scared to death of him — he had that ol' bullwhip, tobacco coming out of his mouth, screaming and hollering."

Hansen dominated the sport in Japan in the 1980s and 1990s as the top foreign draw for the promotions of Shohei Baba and Antonio Inoki, with four stretches as All Japan Triple Crown titlist. "Brody and I, as we went over there, we just went out and kicked butt until they stopped us, and they weren't used to that, I don't think, and that basically changed the style of wrestling in Japan because they had to fight back. They did fight back, and it's really evolved greatly for Japanese wrestling."

Back home, Hansen starred in Georgia, and also returned to the WWWF against top gun Bob Backlund. U.S. promoters and wrestlers generally shied away from him after seeing his reign of physical terror in Japan. "Everybody knew I was going to Japan eventually, and they were hesitant to give me that opportunity, and I understand that. It's just the way it was," Hansen said. In 1985, Verne Gagne did bring him into the AWA for a series of memorable scraps with Martel, who was more amazed than ever at his rival's condi-tioning. "I remember coming back after the matches all blown up, like you had been in a gunfight. Stan, when he dropped those elbows, he was always really stiff and snug. You knew you'd been in the ring with that guy afterward," Martel said.

Hansen won the AWA title from Martel, but he and AWA honchos were not on the same page, or for that matter, the same chapter. He had commitments in Japan — in all, he made 130 trips there — so losing a title match in a Midwest arena was not to his advantage. "What Verne didn't realize was that the dynamic of the way that the business was set up had changed, because of the powerful impact of someone in a foreign country," AWA legend Nick Bockwinkel said. Hansen said his role in the Japanese wrestling hierarchy played a part when he no-showed a title bout with Bockwinkel in 1986. But the AWA's failure to promote him was much more important. "I didn't ask for it, never thought I'd get the belt, but if they gave it to me, then I felt like it ought to be promoted," he said. "I was there six months, and they're giving me squash guys on TV. Do something with me, make the belt worth something." Legend has it that Hansen returned the AWA belt from Japan with a tire track or two on it. He just laughed at this and said, "There's more good stories out there about how they got the belt back. I just let everybody tell the story and everybody can figure it out." More notorious than his AWA stint was his legendary bad eyesight. "He probably accidentally beat me up as much as the guys he beat up on purpose," Sharpe joked. "It was hard for him to see, and now you add in a chair, or a whip, or something like that flying around, you were always getting nicked with this, or nicked with that."

The only physical danger Hansen faces now is being hit by a foul ball. His son, Shaver, is a shortstop at Baylor University, and another son has college baseball aspirations as well. Much trimmer than in his fighting days, Hansen still makes regular trips to the country where he was named *Fuchinkan*, or unsunk battleship. "It was hard, it was really hard physically to do that, but that's the style I developed, and I think that's why I kind of got a niche. And whether it was before 200 people, or 10,000 people, I think the people in Japan always said, 'You know what? Stan Hansen goes out and he doesn't change his match.'"

JBL

John Layfield is an author, financial commentator, former world champion, color announcer in the WWE, and just about anything else you can imagine. In the beginning though, referee and wrestling insider James Beard can tell you, he wasn't much of anything. Layfield walked into a show in Dallas one night, unannounced, out of nowhere, and claimed he had a little wrestling training with Brad Rheingans. "We were short a wrestler, so we said, 'We're going to throw this kid in and see what he can do.' He went to a twenty-minute draw with Rod Price, and it was great," Beard said. "He is one of two or three guys in my career who had a grasp of things from the very beginning."

Layfield's transition from college football player, to wrestling under-study, to respected financier is one of the wildest rides any wrestler has gone on in recent years. Under-standably, he has a hard time believing it too. "One of the neatest things that ever happened to me was at WrestleMania [in 2005]," he said. "Hulk Hogan walked by and said, 'Hey, champ!' Something's wrong with that. I said, 'I'm holding this belt for you.'"

JBL gives Rey Mysterio a hello at a WWE press conference as Booker T approves.

A Texas native, Layfield was a terrific offensive lineman at Abilene Christian University. Clearly a rah-rah guy even in college, he won the coaches' spirit-leadership award two years in a row, was a second-team Division II All-America pick as a junior, and made the first team as a senior. He's a member of the school's All-Century team. He went to training camp with the Los Angeles Raiders in 1990, but, by his own admission, wasn't big enough for the pro game.

He did pretty well as John Hawk in the Dallas-based Global Wrestling Federation, wrestling as a worked cousin to Barry and Kendall Windham. He had a brief feud with Kevin Von Erich over the North American title. Based on his work ethic, Beard recommended him to Bruce Prichard in the WWF front office, and Layfield joined the federation in late 1995 as Justin Hawk Bradshaw, a brawling Texas tough guy in the mold of Stan Hansen. "He studied tapes, he did everything he could; he wanted to know everything. John's very interesting and very intelligent," Beard said. But Layfield had trouble finding his niche and went through a couple of characters, including a revamped "blackjack" tag team with Barry Windham, oldest son of Blackjack Mulligan.

Dr. Tom Prichard, who was with the WWF at the time, said a combination of politics and performance probably limited Layfield's push in the mid-to-late '90s. "At the time with Shawn Michaels and those guys who were running the show, he wasn't part of that clique," Prichard said. "Initially, I think there was a lot of potential but he didn't register to a lot of people who were booking at the time as being in the same category as Steve Austin or The Rock as anything like that."

Layfield's break came when he started to team with Ron "Faarooq" Simmons in 1998. The two worked as part of The Undertaker's Ministry of Darkness, before spinning off to form a slug-it-out, beer-swilling duo called the Acolytes Protection Agency. That pairing, which became a fan favorite, revived both men's careers, and Layfield said it worked because it was rooted in real life. "I had a great time with Ron Simmons. He's still my best friend. He was best man at my wedding. I was a beer-drinkin', fun-lovin' Texan. I still am."

Despite his self-image, Layfield also became a self-made stock-market expert, and wrote a book in 2003 on investments for the common man. "I have read so many financial books that are so boring, or ones you need a calculator or accounting degree to read, and I realized that there is a market for people to have a common-sense approach to financial management for 401(k)s and to find out everything out there that is available to them," the banker's son said.

Layfield's big break came after Brock Lesnar quit the federation following WrestleMania XX, and a host of injuries knocked out a lot of the competition for the top slot. He was ready with a new gimmick that became JBL, which he called a cross between Ted "Million Dollar Man" DiBiase and J. R. Ewing, the sleazy oil tycoon from *Dallas*. "It kind of happened," Prichard observed. "The field narrowed and the characters changed to where he had enough backers who said, 'Why don't we give this big son of a gun a run with it?' It was a circumstance that he took advantage of."

Initially, fans seemed to be a little bit ambivalent about Layfield, who won the WWE championship from Eddie Guerrero at the Great American Bash in 2004. "I was a mid-card guy in a tag team," Layfield explained. "All of a sudden, they stuck me in the main event of a pay-per-view, and most people didn't feel like I deserved to be there. So it took several months, of a lot of matches, and wrestling against some really good wrestlers."

Layfield also worked hard at becoming an old-school heel that fans disliked in and out of the ring. "I'm a classic bad guy," he said. Acting like he was running for president, complete with an attendant cabinet was "a 180-degree turn, completely different" from his old brawler look, he said. It got him in hot soup in 2004, when he gave a Nazi-style salute during a match in Germany that created a minor furor, and cost him a spot as a CNBC financial analyst.

Overcome by injuries, including a broken back and a herniated disc, Layfield hung up his boots in 2006, and moved behind the microphone on Smackdown! In fall 2006, he completed the transition to financial guru by joining Northeast Securities as a senior vice president, working on investment baking. "John is a savvy financial guy with an incredible sales talent," Robert A. Bonelli, the president of the company, told *American Banker* magazine. "You need more than just a marquee name in order to make it in the financial services industry. John has substance, and he is going to continue to develop it here."

THE MISSOURI MAULER

Brian Berkowitz, Pete Lederberg Collection

Wrestling fans who saw Larry Hamilton, a.k.a. the Missouri Mauler, pound opponents into oblivion might be surprised to know he was a guitar-strummin' good guy for a little while. "Larry is a superb, well-conditioned wrestler without using gimmicks," the *Chillicothe Constitution-Tribune* of Missouri said in 1957. "But he has now parlayed his natural singing voice [and] has composed several original ballads in which he musically lambastes some of the mat game's roughest personalities."

It was a brief promotional ruse, though Hamilton did like his music. A huge, whirling dervish of a man,

The Missouri Mauler Larry Hamilton, right, with his masked brother Jody, The Assassin.

Hamilton was one of the toughest competitors around during his thirty-plus years in wrestling. A championship Golden Gloves boxer in his hometown of St. Joseph, Missouri, Hamilton was struck with wanderlust at an early age. The older stepbrother of Jody "The Assassin" Hamilton, Larry lied about his age — born in 1932, he was just sixteen — to serve an eighteen-month stint in the U.S. Army when he was a teenager. Later, instead of working on his father's farm, Hamilton followed the urging of promoter Gust Karras, and took his athletic prowess in boxing, football, and basketball to the athletic training carnival circuit.

"He'd get out there with those big old country farmers, and they'd want to posse up on you because you're fighting and kicking the shit out of their hometown favorite," Jody said. "That's basically where Larry got his wrestling experience and background."

Hamilton had long hair and sideburns when Karras got him into the music angle a few years later, but he changed into a bleached blond with close-cropped hair when he and his brother became Southern rednecks in New York in 1957 and 1958. Billed from Georgia, they had a huge program against Antonino Rocca and Miguel Perez that drew the largest crowd to that point — 20,335 — to Madison Square Garden.

Amid it all though, Hamilton was a bit of a contradiction. In 1958, at the height of his unpopularity in New York, he bared his soul in a remarkably candid interview with Gay Talese, the famed New York Times writer. "It's lonely," Hamilton said of his life. "You're on the road going from town to town, and, after the show is over, you're back in a hotel room." In fact, there was only one salvation in his life — the same friend he plucked while lampooning the likes of Rip Hawk and the Dusek Brothers. "After a match, I play this guitar here. I'd go nuts without it. It's a miserable life."

Hamilton believed he was born to be a villain. "I sometimes think I'd like to be a hero, but my style — aggressive — is more a villain's style. I take every advantage." Inconveniences like a seven-pound auto water pump that whizzed by at his head in Newark, New Jersey, were offset by the fact he was making $60,000 annually by the age of twenty-seven; he said he cashed in $4,200 for the Rocca match alone.

His evolution to The Mauler was gradual — by spring 1961, he was referred to as Rocky Hamilton, the Missouri Mauler, in Nebraska, where he became noted for wild antics such as attacking Dick the Bruiser with a chair in one match, and being led away in handcuffs by police after going berserk against Ernie Dusek. By 1965, the "Hamilton" was more or less discarded, except for some return appearances in his home area. "He wrestled a real crazy style, a windmill style, fists coming from every which direction. He was just a rough guy who didn't get many holds, just all kicking, and punching, and kneeing, and all that — moving all the time," said Bob Orton Sr., who wrestled with and against him in several territories.

The Mauler worked around the world, but became best known for his work in the Mid-Atlantic, Florida, and Georgia, holding the Southern heavyweight championship six times from 1966 to 1970, and the Eastern States title twice in 1970 and 1971, among a laundry list of singles and tag championships. He regularly identified himself with Jesse James, an Old-West outlaw that he admired. "Larry was a whole different kind of heel, a scary guy. I think he convinced people he was crazy," said Les Thatcher. The Mauler even had Thatcher snookered during a TV match in Waterloo, Iowa, in 1963. "He said, 'Throw me out.' Okay, so I threw him out of the ring, and he came up with his head over the apron and this look on his face and he started running in place. I thought, 'Holy smokes, what did I do wrong?' I honestly had a little fear in my heart. I thought, 'He's going to clean my clock.' Never mind what the fans thought — I was sold."

On the personal side, The Mauler could be impatient, intolerant, and his eccentricities nearly got him and some partners poisoned, according to veteran Tinker Todd. With Hamilton and Boris Malenko (Larry Simon), Todd entered a restaurant in Richmond, Virginia, after a tough night of grappling. The trio was immediately recognized. "So Larry, instead of keeping his mouth shut, he starts shouting at the cook. We all got No. 5, the lasagna, and we go back to the hotel, and it started! All night long, I'm running to the toilet — they put something in the food." Simon and Todd got some relief at an all-night drugstore, but the Mauler unaccountably decided to cleanse his system with 7-Up. "The next day he was so sick, it was unbelievable. We were working the next night in Roanoke and we drove over there. He couldn't make it that night, he was so bad; he spent all night in the shower room. He took everything so serious. I got along well with him because I understood the man and I respected him, but he had no patience."

Hamilton left wrestling in 1982, quitting en route to a minor show in Mississippi. "He was ready to get off the road. He was tired. He had had it," Jody said. The Mauler turned around, went home, and never stepped back in the ring again. After his career was over, Hamilton, a devout Catholic, became a successful bail bondsman before he died in 1996. "He was a very complex person, actually," Jody said. "He was extremely good-hearted. He had tremendous compassion for older people. He had tremendous compassion for weak people, disadvantaged people, and that's not a characteristic that would come across in the Missouri Mauler's persona. But, then again, he was the Missouri Mauler."

SPUTNIK MONROE

Sputnik Monroe was a two-fisted drinker, and a two-fisted brawler. He had tattoos on both arms, and a white streak down the middle of his jet black hair that gave him the appearance of a skunk, which is exactly what a lot of fans thought he was. If you were lucky, he wasn't wearing his ring that

Sputnik Monroe offers up a scalp massage.

spelled "PUKE" in raised letters when he took a swing at you.

And he just happened to be one of the most unlikely champions of integration that the South has ever seen. It's there in writing at the Rock 'n' Soul Museum in Memphis, next to his wrestling tights, sequined jacket, and cape: "Sputnik Monroe played a major part in destroying the color lines in Memphis." Or, as his son Bubba put it: "He integrated the black people with the white people in Memphis, Tennessee. How much more powerful can you be?"

Monroe was the porcupine, and the southern social establishment got pricked. Billy Wicks, his best opponent in 1959 and 1960 in the Memphis territory, remembered Monroe's outrageous antics. "He was down on Beale Street, kissing little black babies, and doing things like that was not accepted. Sputnik, that was his way of life. He liked the challenge of doing certain things society and culture didn't want people to do. He was going to do it his way," Wicks said.

Roscoe Monroe Brumbaugh was born in Dodge City, Kansas, December 18, 1928, and got into the athletic training circuit after a stint in the U.S. Navy. He and a friend visited a carnival in Wichita, Kansas, and found they could make five dollars for every minute they stayed with the carnival brute. "They had a big-bellied guy named Bill Ely. He was a pretty tough old guy, but the 'Sweet Man' beat him," Monroe said, using his own pet nickname. After a few years, he transitioned into the pro game in places like Kansas City and St. Louis, working under guises such as Pretty Boy Roque and Elvis "Rock" Monroe. It wasn't until a 1957 incident in Mobile, Alabama, though, that he became "235 pounds of twisted steel and sex appeal with the body women love, and men fear." Fatigued after a cross-country trip from Washington state, Monroe picked up a young black hitchhiker in Greenwood, Mississippi, to help with the drive. At the TV station, an older woman blasted Monroe as "a nigger-loving son of a bitch." In response, he threw an arm around his newfound buddy, and kissed him on the cheek, prompting the woman to invoke the recently launched Soviet satellite: "What he really is, is a goddamned Sputnik."

That was just dandy with Monroe, who grew up with a black nanny in Kansas. When he got to Memphis, he stretched matters to the breaking point. On one occasion, a car show in Memphis was for whites only, so Monroe called the president of the show, and thanked him for making him rich — you see, the Sweet Man planned to open a blacks-only auto agency in Mississippi to sap money from the Memphis economy. About ninety minutes later, Monroe saw a TV announcement that everyone in Memphis — black or white — was welcome to attend the show. Another time, Monroe was arrested after lying down in the middle of the street. "I did it just for the hell of it," he laughed. After an arrest for vagrancy on Beale Street, he showed up in court with a black lawyer. He regularly trooped into the black section of town to hand out discount wrestling coupons, and, when crowds overwhelmed Ellis Auditorium, he threatened to walk out unless his 1,000-member contingent was seated properly. Blacks had been confined to the balcony, but the building manager opened up a new stage to accommodate the traffic. "I was put in jail numerous times, had a lot of street fights," Monroe said.

Danny Goddard began an unlikely lifelong friendship with Monroe by heading his fan club as a teenager in the 1960s, and said Monroe had the same amazing appeal to black fans in Atlanta. "I remember he always had a crowd of black people following him, and he always took the time to spend with them and treat them differently. I remember growing up in Atlanta in those days of segregated restrooms. Boy, he was right in the middle of that, spending time with them. But he's always pretty much done what he wants anyway."

Monroe wrestled as a good guy occasionally, but being a bad guy was definitely in his blood. "In his younger days, he was one of the most innovative heels in the business. I've been in this business for around thirty-five years and I don't know many heels I'd put in my top ten who were better," said Robert Fuller, who was a little kid when he first met Monroe (working for father Buddy Fuller's Memphis office). On the mat, southern star Tom Drake characterized Monroe as strictly a brawler. But Drake also thought Monroe's rough-hewn image was guaranteed money in the bank. "He was the best agitator that ever came down the pike. When he got in that arena, he was hell to pay, he was a brawler, and a hellraiser, and an agitator. He was hell on wheels. Wrestlers all liked to have him on the card because when he was there we made a lot of money," he said.

"He was always trying to hurt you in a subtle way, like 'I didn't mean that. I'm dropping my shinbone across your Achilles tendon, but, oh, I didn't mean that,'" Wicks added. "He was tough, very tough. He'd fight a buzz saw. He was a professional wrestler twenty-four hours a day. He was his character, and he was going to let you know it, and he didn't take any baloney."

Monroe didn't take any shortcuts either, preferring to take a pounding to draw blood, rather than nicking himself with a blade. "My dad busted him hardway forty times," Fuller said. "That was one of his biggest deals. He'd use the blade two or three times, and then he'd say, 'Hell, I don't want to continue using the blade because it don't show a black eye when I'm done.'" He had some great moments with championship belts, winning a Cadillac tournament in Georgia in 1964, and swapping the Tennessee title with Wicks in 1959. The grand finale with Wicks came on August 17, 1959, with Rocky Marciano as special referee in front of a state record crowd at Russwood Park. Newspaper accounts put attendance at about 14,000, though fire marshals fixed it at 18,000; the house yielded a nice $750 payday for the main-eventers. In the third fall, Marciano ruled the contest no decision, and slugged Monroe and his second. "There was just something about Sputnik — it was kind of like magic," said former referee Tommy Fooshee, best man at one of Monroe's weddings. "I liked the attitude he had on life. He was colorful, but no matter what happened, he took care of business."

On the road, Monroe earned a reputation as one of the most fascinating storytellers in the business. Former NWA champ Gene Kiniski always tried to bum a ride with Monroe just to hear him talk. "I remember many times I'd be going from Miami to Tampa, and I'd say, 'Sputnik, how'd you get here?' 'I drove.' 'Can I ride back with you?' Just to kill some time. It'd get so boring." Case in point — Monroe liked to relate the story of a match he had with Greg Peterson in front of prisoners at a penitentiary in Atlanta. "I was pissed off because I said, 'There ain't no way you can entertain these guys. You bust both eyes and you're not going to impress a bunch of murderers and robbers, you know?' We went out to the ring, and on the cement steps was a bunch of guys made up like girls. And then I snapped. So when Greg and I got in the ring and went around a little bit, I turned him over on his hands and knees, and jerked his tights down, and went to funkin' with myself, and they tore the bleachers down."

Traveling with Monroe could be an adventure, though. Johnny Valiant once hopped a ride with him from Atlanta to Statesboro, Georgia, and back, as Monroe warned, "I'm not stopping . . . this is an express!" After their matches, Monroe grabbed a case of beer, while Valiant picked up a six-pack or two. On the way home, Valiant felt the call of nature. "Uh, Sputnik," he said meekly, "I gotta go." Sputnik's answer? "Aww, kid, I told ya, this is an express! I don't stop for nobody! Go ahead, hurry up, hurry up." A few beers later, Valiant asked for another roadside stop. Monroe growled, "Aww, jeez, kid, damn, that's why I don't take nobody! Go ahead. You see, kid, that's why I'm the Lone Ranger. I don't bother nobody, but nobody bothers me." After arriving in Atlanta, Valiant paid for his share of the gas, and had one final query. Valiant remembered, "I said, 'Sputnik, can I ask a stupid question?' 'Yeah, kid, hurry up, I gotta go to the strip show, what is it?' I said, 'How come I took two leaks on the highway. You drank a case of beer and you never stopped one time.' He said, 'I got it right here, kid.' I said, 'Where?' 'Right here!' As Valiant recalled, he looked at a pool of liquid on the driver's side floor and exclaimed, "Damn! I thought it was a transmission leak."

Randy Colley got to know Monroe in Texas, and recounted how he feared Monroe was going to cost him his life in a simple matter of restaurant choice. One time, Colley moaned to Monroe that he couldn't find a good pork barbecue place, so, in his brusque manner, Monroe took him to a shabby dive in the black section of town. "We're the only two white people, and there are probably thirty, forty black guys in there, in their construction clothes — just nasty. He hollers, 'Bring us a plate of barbecue over here. I told this kid if he wants some good barbecue, he had to come over to Niggertown to get some,'" Colley recalled with a shudder.

"It sounded like a beehive had been shaken. Everything was buzzing. I'm thinking, 'We're dead, we'll never make it out of it. It all started with a plate of barbecue, but they're fixing to kill us.' He got to talking with them, and we sat there and drank all afternoon. They kept buying beer. We couldn't pay for the barbecue. And we left with a sack of barbecue ribs and stuff. Everybody loved him. He could go in anywhere and say anything."

Years of drinking, smoking, and hard living took their toll on Monroe, who had his last match when he was seventy; in frail health after losing half a lung and his gall bladder, he died in November 2006 at seventy-seven. At the family's request, Goddard, a pastor, presided over a graveside service in Alexandria, Louisiana. "It was a beautiful morning, the sun was shining, the temperature was just right," Goddard fondly recalled. Monroe's death prompted an outpouring of memories about his one-man revolution in wrestling and Southern society. "Sputnik was a good example of how the rock and roll spirit was something that wasn't confined to music," said Memphis cultural historian Robert Gordon. "Sputnik turned it into this kind of social justice, which was very powerful." But Sputnik knew that, of course. A few years ago, in better health, he and wife Jo Ann took a trip back to Beale Street, and Monroe got choked up just reminiscing about it. "People were hugging me and kissing me for what I did for them. Many of them were young and didn't know what kind of a wrestler I was or anything. And it's kind of hard to handle when people come up on the street and hug you and kiss you for something you did forty years ago."

Howard Lapes

Blackjack Mulligan beats Ricky Steamboat senseless.

BLACKJACK MULLIGAN

Blackjack Mulligan is a force of nature. Like a cyclone, it's easy to get blown away by the power of his words, and sucked up into his vortex. Ask a question, and he's a boulder rolling down the hill, unable to stop. At an early stage of his career, he found that getting heat from the fans was the same way — once it starts pouring in, it's pretty hard to turn off.

It's 1971, and he's facing WWWF champion Pedro Morales in a title match in the Boston Garden. In Blackjack's corner is The Grand Wizard (Ernie Roth). Mulligan isn't that far removed from his football days, but at six-foot-nine, 345 pounds, pro wrestling seemed a natural. The heat is rising in the building, as Mulligan dominates the much-smaller Morales. The Grand Wizard hands his charge a blackjack, and Morales is down.

"One, two, I pick him up by the hair. They couldn't stand that. Unbelievable heat. They couldn't believe it. Here's a Hispanic being tortured by a big white guy and a funny-looking guy in a head wrap. I pick him up for the second time, and don't cover him, one, two — that's when they start coming unglued," recalled Mulligan with a shudder. "I picked him up by the hair the second time, and that's when they slashed me across my leg, and they slashed me across my arm. [Gorilla] Monsoon was refereeing the match. God bless him, Gino can't see thirty feet. He can hardly see the guy. But he did grab the guy to get rid of him."

Mulligan knows now what he didn't know then — it is possible to go too far. "One would have been enough, but no, I had to do two pick-ups. I had control of the situation, the people are horrified that this guy is going to get beat," he said. "I'm picking their little guy up, and they are going nutso. At that point, the heat should have been controlled and stopped. But it didn't. We kept on with it, and went one more time. It was too much. So you can go too far with these situations. The situation got out of control."

While in recovery from the stab wound, Mulligan got a call from Red Bastien, one of his wrestling heroes, and a mentor from their days together in Minneapolis. "You've got to understand how to control this heat. We got you ready, put you in the biggest slot in the world, and you let it go too far. Everybody's in a quandary, scared to death of you, because they don't know what's going to happen, what you are going to do," Mulligan recalled Bastien saying.

That Mulligan got to that slot, and stayed on top for so long in various territories, is a testament to his talent, his interview skills, and to his love of the business. Growing up in Sweetwater, Texas, Bob Windham was exposed to the wrestling promoted by Dory Funk Sr. out of Amarillo. But football called first, and after playing at Odessa High, he attended Texas Western (now UTEP) for two years. It was there that he was first exposed to performance-enhancing drugs. "I've been a steroid guy since the day I was in college. . . . They used to give us steroids in the dressing room," he said. "It was a Dianabol pill, it was a doctor-regulated situation." Windham, who also served as a Marine in Guam, would have brief flings trying to get on the AFL squads in New York and Denver, until a compound fracture of his left leg ended his career. According to Windham, the owner of the Jets, Sonny Werblin — who was also president of Madison Square Garden — suggested he try pro wrestling. He'd already heard about the riches to be earned from Wahoo McDaniel, who wrestled in the off-season from football.

For six months, Windham learned in Mexico and Corpus Christi, Texas, along with some others from Joe Blanchard's San Antonio, Texas promotion. Windham was dispatched to Verne Gagne's AWA for further schooling. "The first time I showed them that in Minneapolis, they went 'Quit taking so many bumps. Don't go down. Stop at the knee.' What a lesson process it was there," Windham remembered. Butcher Vachon was one of those veterans who showed Mulligan a thing or two. "The problem with Blackjack Mulligan, he was so damn tall. It was hard to get him to take a bump because his whole top part of his body would come around and take the bump, but his feet were still starting to come over from the other side. His legs were too long," said Vachon with a chuckle.

Dale Hey would later find fame as Dale Roberts in the Hollywood Blonds and as Buddy Roberts in the Fabulous Freebirds. But in the late 1960s, he was assigned to take the ring from town to town for AWA shows along with Windham. "Bob was just breaking in, and basically I was too. We were both doing jobs. We'd drive around together on these looonng trips together, heck, all the way up to Winnipeg. We became pretty good friends on the traveling end of it," said Hey. "I remember they booked us against each other, and he wanted to be a heel, and so did I. We had two matches against each other, and I let him be the heel in the first match, and I was the heel in the second match. That was funny because we were both fighting to see who was going to be the heel." It was Windham, though, in whom the AWA saw potential, naming him the promotion's 1970 Rookie of the Year.

A man so big and so strong-willed could only be held down so long. He was invited to New York, where promoter Vincent J. McMahon insisted on a name change. The Mulligan surname came from Windham's great-uncle who had been a fighter in Sweetwater. But after the stabbing, it was clear that Windham still needed some more schooling. Mulligan was paired with Blackjack Lanza in Indianapolis, and a legendary team was born. "Well, Lanza and I with [Bobby] Heenan, a blond manager, another new-looking thing came together, this thing went nutso, this thing went crazy. We had so many problems, it was unbelievable. Here's where we couldn't stay together, it couldn't last, because territories couldn't handle it," Mulligan said. The Blackjacks would tour around, though it wasn't a team destined to last. "We worked Texas together a little bit, but this team, every time it got together, it created problems of heat. These people, we go to New York, and they give us Lou Albano, and that even got nutsier than before. I went, 'Oh, my God, I'm back in the same situation where I'm going to get killed!' Well, with myself as an individual, I could control."

As a single, he had a heated, bloody run against McDaniel in the Mid-Atlantic territory, before one last stint with the Blackjacks as WWWF tag champs in 1975. But when Jim Crockett Promotions lost Johnny Valentine and Ric Flair to injury after a plane crash, it created a void that Mulligan could amply fill. He was the top heel in the promotion, thanks to lots of TV interview time, with epic battles with Mr. Wrestling (Tim Woods), Paul Jones, Rufus R. Jones, Dino Bravo and Ricky Steamboat. But in 1978, Mulligan did the unthinkable, and turned babyface to battle Flair.

Once he'd gotten a taste of the right side of the fence, there was no return. "I'm not a bad guy, but I come off as a bad guy," Mulligan said. "But I'll tell you, once I switched babyface, I couldn't go back. It was impossible to go back. I tried to make a move like that. I didn't want to do it anymore.

Once I got a taste of this Dusty Rhodes babyface stuff, who wants to ever go back? It was ridiculous. It was so easy it was silly."

Mulligan is more than happy to expand on his "babyface rap," which he perfected, along with Rhodes and "Superstar" Billy Graham. "We changed the face of this business because we could do promos, and talk, and get heat in promos where the other guys didn't know how to work the camera. They hadn't had that camera time. Once we had created a character, or an aura of a character around us, we found out that we could talk them into the buildings," Mulligan said, freely admitting that he stole from Thunderbolt Patterson. The days of the two-out-of-three fall matches were going, and Mulligan, Rhodes and Graham realized they could do more with less. "The charisma of the business was changing, because we would stop, slam a guy, take a look at the people, find out they was cussing and screaming at us. Well, we found out that we could kill time by doing that. And I'm indicting myself as much as anybody else, because Dusty, myself, and Billy Graham had the biggest to do with the changeover of this business, diluting the business to what it is now."

The Superstar doesn't disagree. "I can't ever forget Blackjack Mulligan, almost seven-feet tall, wrestling Kevin Sullivan, five-feet tall, and Blackjack has to spend most of the match on his knees — and he's still as big as Kevin Sullivan on his knees! But the entertainment value, he was still able to get sympathy because he was an entertaining babyface," said Graham.

After his Mid-Atlantic run ended, Mulligan took his act to Florida, and then, at the end of his career, back to the WWF on two occasions, during one of which he worked under a mask as a part of the Machines. He and wife Julia would see their children involved in wrestling as well, with Barry and Kendall Windham becoming wrestlers, and his daughter marrying Mike Rotunda. After his last run in New York, he ran into legal trouble with his real-estate holdings, and spent two years in a minimum-security prison for a federal counterfeiting conviction; Kendall got twenty-seven months. Now, the Mulligans run a car dealership in Florida.

During his career, Mulligan had two stints as an owner too. From 1980–81, he owned Knoxville, Tennessee, with Ric Flair; the promotion included some southwest Virginia towns. "All these small territories, they were finished. The TBS program, and Vince bowling over everybody, those little territories were gone," he said. The other was the Amarillo, Texas territory, which he bought with Dick Murdoch from the Funks just before the WWF expanded nationally. "It was more for me a break," Mulligan said. "Barry was going to West Texas State, so I went out there so I could watch the football season. It was the most expensive football season that I ever watched in my life!"

The Blackjacks were inducted into the WWE Hall of Fame in April 2006. Mulligan, bad knees and all, still gave a powerful — if short — induction speech. He's wistful on the past. "The only regret I have is that I'm not twenty-one years old. I wish I could do this again, I really, really do. I watch these guys now, and I swear to God, it would be like taking candy from a baby."

Death in the ring

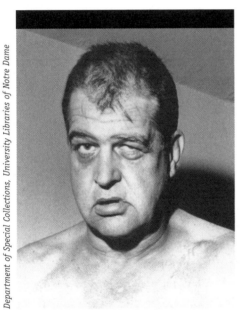

LaVerne Baxter.

Almost since the inception of pro wrestling, heels have taken out their anger on referees – berating them, shoving them, and even slugging them because of allegedly unfair judgments. It's a tried-and-true brawling tactic. But one night, it turned deadly.

Friday, March 1, 1940: the Seattle Civic Auditorium was the scene, and the key players were veteran bad-guy LaVerne Baxter, fair-haired favorite John Katan, and a fifty-year-old referee named John Stevens. Baxter, a big man at 220 pounds, was employing his standard fare of rule-breaking tools, when Stevens disqualified him and awarded the match to Katan. Naturally, Baxter started to whine and complain. The usual post-match shenanigans ensued; the wrestlers resumed their tussle, their seconds joined in, and Stevens got caught in the middle. Somehow, he got tossed into a ring post, and then Baxter added a couple of stomps for good measure. Stevens crawled through the ropes on his hands and knees, rolled onto the floor, and died in front of 1,400 spectators who weren't sure what they were seeing.

The death of Stevens, who left behind three daughters, shocked and outraged segments of the Seattle community. George Adams, secretary of the State Athletic Commission, immediately banned all wrestling in the city pending a review of the incident. In an editorial, the *Seattle Times*, no friend of the mat game, screamed, "We killed a man!" because the citizenry itself had tolerated pro wrestling. Coroner Otto H. Mittelstadt and prosecutor B. Gray Warner launched an investigation into Stevens' death with an eye toward fixing blame for the fatality.

Did Baxter, who'd spend three decades as a top heel, actually kill a man? Witnesses at Mittelstadt's inquest thought so. "Stevens took blows hard enough to kill anyone," testified Howard Foster, a lawyer and wrestling fan. Mrs. Jack Zander said she stood on her chair, yelling that Baxter was killing Stevens "because you could see that the referee was unconscious. I don't see how any man could stand those kicks without injury, or death . . . That was no show. Baxter was so angry, he lost control."

In fact, an autopsy determined otherwise. Stevens had a bad heart, and died of heart disease. "Nobody else is to blame but the State Athletic Commission," Chief Little Wolf Tenario declared at the inquest. "They never should have let him in the ring." Prosecutor Warner agreed, stressing the need for a stricter overseeing of physical exams. "It should be a condition precedent to any contest that the referees must be as physically fit as the contestants and subject to the same check, so tragedies of this type will not reoccur," he said.

The investigation did provide a rare behind-the-scenes look at the business, and Baxter's testimony in particular was fascinating. Dressed in a black cowboy shirt and grey business suit, the Iowa native explained that Stevens wanted to take what is now called a "ref bump." In fact, Stevens asked to be dragged around the ring at the end of a different match just a couple of weeks before the fatal incident. "I took him by the hair, and threw him around the ring, and he went right on out," Baxter explained. "Then, last Friday, Stevens asked me to throw him out into the second row of seats. I didn't think that was right. The referee is supposed to leave the ring right after a bout. I told him I wouldn't do it."

But after Stevens was pushed or shoved into a corner, Baxter decided to break out a common heel maneuver. "I kicked at him twice, because I thought it would be good color and might make good stuff for a return match if I protested at the decision," he said. "He couldn't get hurt on those kicks. I had nothing against that man. You could put anything between that kick and him, and it wouldn't have broken." His wife at the time, Helen Mildred Baxter, also pulled back the curtain on her husband's role, testifying that he played the part of a villain so he could "make more money."

Baxter was free to go, of course, and continued his nefarious ways into the early 1960s – *Ring* magazine once declared him "the roughest wrestler in the country." In the aftermath of his match in Seattle though, it was clear that excess heel work, of the kind still seen today in every arena in the country, had disastrous consequences. Commissioner Adams vowed to impose harsh penalties – just as in boxing – on wrestlers who made physical contact with referees. Officials banned wrestling in Seattle for more than five years – it wouldn't return until 1945. And one final piece of evidence introduced at the inquest placed a sad tag on the price of a little "rough stuff." Stevens was paid three dollars for officiating two bouts the night he died.

MAGNIFICENT MURACO

Ruth Oman, Pete Lederberg Collection

Don Muraco, the bearded Florida champ.

Don "The Rock" Muraco is uniquely qualified to explain how the business changed in the 1980s. He'd been a top star for the WWWF, its Intercontinental champion on two occasions, and a challenger to Bob Backlund's world title. Then the Hulk Hogan era began, and business expanded. The heel's role changed as well, moving away from the scorching white-hot heat that was the norm to a tamer "It'll be fun to boo the bad guy" mentality. The regular trips to the same towns were gone in favor of long, cross-country tours.

"I don't know if cartoony is the word. It took away a lot of the creative, a lot of the creative input that guys had, because it would be the same match every night, the traveling, and everything else. There was no variety," Muraco explained. "You didn't think anymore."

Wrestlers would be paired up like dance partners, competing against each other regularly: Muraco versus Jimmy Snuka; Muraco versus Tito Santana; Muraco versus Hulk Hogan. "The travel, the work days, and you're working with the same guy every night. After awhile, it doesn't seem like it, but you kind of lose your inspiration," he admitted. "But you find things for the big shows, when you can make the big money. But on some of the intermediate shows, you just follow."

Few would ever call Muraco a follower. He totally went to his own beat, which was pretty much dictated by the surf. "He really was born in Hawaii and his beach-bum character was not a gimmick," wrote Jack Brisco in his autobiography. "He loved the surf, and when it was up he would take off to wherever it was, regardless of what program he was involved in. He would call Eddie Graham and say, 'Don't book me for the next two weeks, I'm going surfing.' It used to drive Eddie crazy, but that was Don."

Muraco was a wrestling fan growing up in Hawaii, but not a huge one (even though his parents once rented an apartment to Freddie Blassie). He left the island to go to college at Glendale in California, a chiseled 265 pounds on a six-foot-two body, but dropped down at school. "Living on my own, college food, busted vein, and my nose bleeding like crazy, I was down to about 210, 215. Living with four other guys in a surf hut didn't bulk me up either." The next year, he went to Santa Monica City College and technically studied sociology, "but mostly football and surfing though."

Like most stars from Hawaii, it was Lord James Blears who convinced him to give wrestling a try — Muraco had gone to school with Blears' son Jimmy — and Blears dispatched him to the Vancouver office to work under his old partner Gene Kiniski in 1970. Muraco, who used Don Morrow as his name in the early going, credits men in Vancouver like Dean Ho, "Bulldog" Bob Brown, and Steve Bolus, and wrestlers from Portland, Oregon, like Beauregarde, Tom Andrews, Lonnie Mayne, and Mr. Fuji for teaching him how things worked. Muraco was a fast learner. "As soon as I started it, I was into it. I pretty much thought it would be a career."

A handsome babyface for the first few years, Muraco worked Los Angeles and returned to Hawaii before venturing to the AWA for the first time, where his real name was adjusted to Morocco. "Don came to Minneapolis and he was 220 pounds, and lean as could be. Gosh, he was young," recalled journeyman Bill Howard. "He was freezing to death because it was so cold in Minneapolis after coming from Hawaii. He wanted to go back home so bad. He was making $30,000, $40,000 way back then, in the '70s. He didn't care. He wanted to go back home where it was warm!" Muraco laughed at the description. "I went to college in California for a few years, but I wasn't ready for that Midwest life, that's for sure."

So it was off to Florida, the scene of some of his most memorable clashes with heels like Ivan Koloff and Dusty Rhodes, and where he first hit his stride as a "Magnificent" heel. Koloff loved working with Muraco, even in a series of bloody cage matches. "We appreciated each other, respected each other. It was just the idea that we'd go all out to try and make it a good match, compliment each other. When a person does that, you can't help but have a good match because both guys are trying so hard to make the other guy the star," the "Russian Bear" said. There was a lot of talent to offer advice for Muraco. "I'd spent so much time there as a babyface, big programs with Jack [Brisco], Harley Race, Koloff, Pak Song, a lot of tag teams with Bob Armstrong. I did good business in Florida," he said. "I had been over as a babyface, so they were just looking for something, and pretty much between Eddie, and Buddy Rogers, and Jerry Brisco was in the office at the time. It was a pretty good collaboration."

Having the experience as a hero helps you to be a heel, Muraco said. "You need a good understanding of either side to make a good anything." A balance always has to be struck. "I think it's a coordinated effort, the promotion, heel, babyface, talent, the whole game plan — getting a guy over, getting both guys over, getting some, getting this, getting the right angle."

Muraco was taught to listen to the fans. "You had to play it by ear back then, manipulate the crowd, because it wasn't the high-speed it is today. It was more of a gradual story, longer. Guys like Dory Funk Jr., and Johnny Valentine, that whole different school," Muraco said. "I'd been exposed to different styles in the different parts of the country: San Francisco, Minneapolis, Florida, those are three totally different atmospheres."

By the time a young Larry Sharpe got a chance to work with Muraco, the Hawaiian was a skilled tradesman. "His biggest ability was to take a guy of lesser talent, and be able to make a match out of him, whereas most people wouldn't be able to do it," said Sharpe. "Guys in general that he would get thrown in there with, he could carry pretty well and make a match out of. His psychology was good."

"Muraco was excellent at playing to the crowd. I always got a kick out of his personality because he was doing that laughing-in-your-face type of thing to the crowd," said Mickey Doyle. "He was good with the crowds, cynical."

After putting in time in far-off locales like Australia, New Zealand, and Japan, Muraco was indeed ready for the spotlight when the WWWF brought him to the Northeast. "Captain" Lou Albano was assigned as Muraco's manager. It was new to Muraco, but he accepted it. "[The WWWF managers] did their part. The people were educated in that direction. It helped, I don't think it detracted much," he said. Albano praised Muraco's professionalism. "He did his job well, got out there, and also verbally, he could get out there and express himself. He did a lot of takes himself, where he didn't have to count on just the manager," Albano said. "People accepted him as a villain and that was it."

Both Intercontinental title wins came at the expense of Pedro Morales, and Muraco's memorable string of bouts with Snuka led to a spectacular leap by Snuka off the top of a cage in Madison Square Garden. But it's Backlund for whom Muraco has the most praise. "I always thought that he represented the belt and that image as world champion, and the stuff he did, maybe not as dynamic, and exciting, and charismatic as a lot of guys. But at the time, and in the position he was, he was an excellent, great representative with the WWWF title," Muraco said. "I wrestled him for hours and hours, up and down, all over the world in fact. I did two hours with him in one day, an afternoon in Washington, and that night in Philadelphia. I spent a lot of time in the ring with him . . . tremendous stamina."

With the changeover from WWWF to WWF, a new booker in George Scott started bringing in his own talent. Muraco was shuffled downcard. "I just didn't fit into the guys he had. . . . He had his crew of guys. That's neither here nor there. I still made money after that." Muraco would work on top with Hogan, team with "Cowboy" Bob Orton, and have a weak face push under the tutelage of "Superstar" Billy Graham that died when Graham needed surgery. "I probably could have done more than what I did," Muraco said. "At that time, I wasn't too enthused. I was burned out. Being a baby-face was an awkward position there."

As the 1980s came to a close, Muraco hit the few remaining territories, and was North American champion in 1988 in Stampede Wrestling before returning to live in Hawaii. He also held the forerunner of the ECW World title on two occasions in 1992–93, being flown in for shots. In 1991, he started working as a longshoreman to support his two daughters and one son from two marriages. Recently, he graduated to a clerk's position — "pushing buttons, registering containers when they come in, check over containers when come off the street, and when they go back on the street."

Magnificent Muraco still gets recognized, though his jet-black hair has gone grey, and he doesn't move with the same grace he once did. "Hawaii's a small place. I was on the original wrestling here with Ed Francis and those guys, and the transition when it came with cable," he said. He has also worked a little with the local promotion as his son gave a shot at following in his father's footsteps.

Does he miss it all though? "I miss surfing more," Muraco laughed. "Physically, it would be a joke trying to get in the ring to perform. It's just not happening. That's why I got out in the first place — I wasn't moving the way I wanted to move. That was seventeen, eighteen years ago. You can imagine what the body is like now."

DICK MURDOCH

Howard Baum

Dick Murdoch bites Dusty Rhodes.

You walk into just about any honky-tonk in West Texas, and you'll find a Dick Murdoch, a big ol' opinion-ated redneck, and proud of it, a little long in the paunch, and heavy on the character. But *the* Dick Murdoch — now that was some-thing else. Murdoch joked, fought, loved, argued, and drank his way through forty-nine years, leaving behind mayhem, memories, and a trail of busted-up Oklahomans.

"He was one of a kind, no doubt about that," said veteran Dusty Wolfe. "When he was a heel, every-body would look at him, and say, 'That's the son of a bitch that lives next door. I wish he'd put up a pri-vacy fence. When he comes home at night, I wish he'd quit running over my trash cans.' When he was a babyface, he was the guy everybody looked at, and said, 'Well, when I walk in the bar, he slaps me on the back, and says hello. I know I don't have to worry about watching my back.'"

As captivating as he was in real life, Murdoch was even better in the ring, where contemporaries regard him as one of the best workers of his genera-tion. As the son of ex-grappler Frankie Murdoch, he grew up around the business, and learned a thousand little tricks of the trade to get audiences going. How good was he? Referee James Beard said Murdoch went through one match in Dallas with Virgil (Mike Jones) employing exactly one — count 'em, one — hold. "He got a hold of a headlock, and went twenty min-utes with nothing but the headlock. It was wonderful. He had me working my ass off for twenty minutes doing everything I could to tell the fans, 'He's about to kill him with this headlock.' Everybody in the place was sitting on the edge of their seats. Virgil went over, and won with Dick still holding him in that darned headlock."

Born August 16, 1946, Murdoch wrestled as an amateur at Caprock High School in Amarillo, Texas, toted wrestling bears around the streets for his dad, wrestled a little in Texas and Kansas City, and got his first real taste of action as

Don Carson's brother "Ron" in the Gulf Coast region in 1965. "From then on, everything we touched turned to gold," Carson recounted in *Whatever Happened To . . . ?* That's also where Murdoch learned to drop his famous big elbow — he flinched one night when a locust flew at him in the ring in Tennessee, and retaliated by crouching . . . waiting . . . waiting until the bug settled down, then smashed him with the elbow. "That was a classic," Carson said.

Murdoch's tag team with Dusty Rhodes as the Outlaws was one of the best of the late 1960s and early 1970s. After the Outlaws, Murdoch was all over the world as a singles star, probably more often as a bad guy than a good guy. He held the Central States championship, the Missouri championship, and various belts in Japan, Puerto Rico, and Australia. Despite carting around 270 pounds, a good portion of it in his big beer belly, Murdoch could do just anything promoters demanded. "He just had that ring presence. He was a bumper, he was a brawler, he was a wrestler — long before character development became a focus of sports entertainment, Murdoch was all of the above," said Jerry Brisco. "I think if anybody was ever overlooked, it was Dick Murdoch. I think because of his character, because of his personality, Dick Murdoch was never taken as serious as he should have been."

Of course, then he might not have been Dick Murdoch. Not too many other wrestlers could put on a show in the ring, and serenade their opponents at the same time. Killer Karl Kox, his mentor and close friend, said Murdoch broke out in verse even as he was sweating on the mat. "He'd sing to you as you wrestled him. He'd sing country and western stuff to you. Remember 'Lucille'? Murdoch used to sing that in the ring. 'You picked a fine time to dropkick and beall.' He'd sing that to you as you wrestled, see? 'You picked a fine time to dropkick and beall.'"

Dallas TV announcer Bill Mercer said Murdoch's routine came naturally. "He just had a mean-looking streak about him. They would do those crazy, bad things to people in the ring. He always had that aura of being above the rules, and being beyond the rules, and doing nasty stuff to the guys, and always being in trouble with the referees." Dick Slater knew Murdoch almost all of his adult life, and teamed with him late in their careers as The Hardliners. Like Brisco, he was amazed at the big man's ability to handle any situation in the ring. "He had a flamboyant style, but he could adapt to anything they threw at him. He could be serious, but he could be funny when he wanted to be funny. You didn't know what he was going to do from one minute to the next, in life and in the ring." But you knew it would be fun, Slater added. "When you went with Dickie, you were out every night going somewhere having a few beers here and there. He was a classic card."

Murdoch and Adrian Adonis were WWF tag team champions as the North-

South Connection in 1984; if anything, Murdoch didn't fit in as well in New York because he outshined the competition, according to Davey O'Hannon, who knew him from Texas and the Northeast. "For a big guy, he flew all over the place," O'Hannon said. "He was a really good heel. But here's another guy that wound up with people liking him. He was 'Captain Redneck,' and, man, they just loved him. They tried to hook him up with Adrian, but he just did not get over as well up here, and the reason why is he was probably too good a worker in the ring." Stan Lane, who worked for Murdoch when he briefly owned the Amarillo, Texas office, concluded: "He was loud, he was brazen, he was a redneck. Great, great worker. His stuff was always very, very believable."

One thing the son of Texas could not abide was Okies. Brisco, and his brother Jack, are from Oklahoma, and Jerry joked that he'd say the magic word in Murdoch's presence, then run like hell. "It was brutal back and forth. Murdoch respected us, and we respected him, but no, you didn't want to say 'Oklahoma' too loud around him." Traveling with him near the Oklahoma border, Wolfe said Murdoch always made sure that the call of nature was answered on Sooner ground. "I've been in the car with him, the truck with him, when he'd pull off the side of the road, just across the Red River, so he could piss on Oklahoma. Really," Wolfe said. "I said, 'Dick, I've got to pull over.' 'No, no, no, we've got to cross the Red River. Then I can pull over.'"

Take a little rowdiness, throw in some chow, and a drunken Okie, and, well, you've got a Murdoch field day. Kox recalled how he and Murdoch accompanied Bill Watts to a Texas-Oklahoma football game one year, when Watts' Sooners took it on the chin from the Longhorns. "Watts got drunk, got nasty, and everything. We're taking him back to the airport to meet his pilot. Watts had his own plane in those days. He stopped and wanted us to get some fried chicken. He got a bunch of fried chicken in a box, and dropped it on the ground. Dickie got out, picked up the fried chicken, and rubbed dirt all over it. I got Watts in the car, and Dickie put it back in the box, and gave it back to Watts. I imagine Watts ate it on the way home."

Murdoch wrestled some in the 1990s, headlining cards in Puerto Rico in 1992 as Universal and TV champ. His last appearance on the big stage was at the 1995 Royal Rumble, and, appropriately, he later did promotional work for Coors, as well. Never one to listen to doctor's orders, he suffered from high blood pressure and had a fatal heart attack in June 1996. "He didn't take any goddamn medication at all," said Kox, who still bemoans his loss. "Damn Dickie, he was good every place he went with me. I enjoyed having him around."

DUTCH SAVAGE

Whether he was in the ring, trying to get a storyline across, or whether it was in the dressing room, acting as a promoter for one of his Pacific Northwest towns, Dutch Savage took things seriously. "When he got in the ring, he was all business. No matter what was said outside the ring, when you got into that ring, he was business," said Sandy Barr.

"He was very conscious of the business. Some of the guys he'd get after, if a guy would do anything to hurt the business, Dutch was all over them," recalled Don Leo Jonathan.

Savage's gruff nature was easy to portray to the fans, and his in-ring skills shone. "I was a no-nonsense, articulate heel on the mic," Savage said. "I polished my work up to where it had to be believable. I could slap a punch right off the end of your nose, or come off the top rope with a stomp right to your face — ask anybody who worked with me, they wouldn't feel it. That was the key, making believers out of the

Courtesy Wrestling Revue Archives

Dutch Savage.

people, not the boys. I hardly ever, ever, ever potatoed one in my life."

While Savage didn't hurt opponents, he did piss off a great many of them. "Dutch was a fantastic business guy, very smart," said Moose Morowski, who feuded and teamed with Savage. "If I owned a territory, I would have gotten him to be my booker. A lot of guys couldn't stand him, but he had a great mind for the business." Count Ed Wiskoski among the people who didn't always see eye to eye with Savage backstage: "A fantastic worker, but a miserable son of a bitch to work for. You couldn't ask for somebody better in the ring, and somebody who had impeccable timing on the microphone, knowing how to sell a match to come back with. He had it. He was just such a miserable son of a bitch after that."

Such is the life of Frank Stewart, who was born in Scranton, Pennsylvania, June 9, 1935. He grew up in Maryland, and went to school at Marshall University in West Virginia before moving back home to work. A high-school chum of Stewart's in Elkton, Maryland, was Luke Brown, who was wrestling in Canada as Man Mountain Campbell (and would later be half of the Kentuckians). When a knee injury ended Stewart's football career, Brown convinced his friend to give it a try. Stewart made his debut in Georgia in 1962 as Lonnie Brown, and got beat up for months, slowly learning the trade, and putting weight and muscle onto his six-foot-four frame. The name Dutch Savage came along in Kansas City, and he worked as "Mr. X" in Tennessee as well.

Savage moved to the Pacific Northwest in 1966, and split his time for the rest of his career between Vancouver, the Oregon/Washington territory, Hawaii (as Dutch Shultz), San Francisco, and Japan. He'd work with ten different world champions, and almost every top name in the business during his thirty-five-year career.

He was also a top-notch tag team wrestler. Savage's favorite pairing was with Jimmy Snuka. "We were tag team champions off and on for seven years," he said. "We would make the heels look like seven million dollars. That way, when we made our comebacks, they were wild and furious. Jimmy could sell rugs to an Egyptian." Other successful teams were formed with Mario Galento, John Tolos, Bob Brown, and Don Jardine.

During the course of his career, Savage evolved into a very convincing babyface, with bloody battles against the likes of Bull Ramos and Killer Karl Krupp still in the minds of many fans. What those fans didn't realize, however, is the stroke that Savage was developing behind the scenes. In 1972, he started buying into the Oregon and Washington area, ending up with one-third of the territory. Savage also had a percentage of British Columbia's All-Star Wrestling. "We had the hottest territory in the nation there for almost eight years in the Portland and Washington territory," Savage bragged. "My end of the territory, Washington, was outdrawing Oregon 50–1."

There were many ups and downs along the way, however. "A lot of times, if you had the right group, and everything ran smooth and tight," Savage recalled. "Everybody was interested in making money, not just for themselves alone but for the territory. You don't run into that group very often. When you do, the territory hums. That's why, in the Northwest here, it ran so well for so many years. Your whole outlook when you're coming into it is that you want to make money no matter where you go. If you're a team player, you will. If you're an individual, all you'll do is create heat for the guys underneath, they won't like you at all, and they won't work with you.

They'll start bad-mouthing you in the cars, and to the boss, behind your back. Pretty soon, you're on your way out, and you wondered what happened. The problem I had with a lot of promoters is that they paid too much attention to the boys. The boys were only as loyal as their next payoff. That's the truth."

Savage was involved in the business end of wrestling until 1980. After his career ran down, he dabbled in real estate, but found a real calling doing drug and alcohol seminars at schools, which led him deeper into his faith. Today he has a different kind of fame on TV, with a show called *Dutch's Corner* on a public access station. "I teach King James scripture. I do not teach denominationalism, I do not teach religion. I teach straight scripture," he explained.

"DR. D" DAVID SHULTS

Bob Leonard

Dr. D sports a "David Shcultz" t-shirt.

What you see is what you get with "Dr. D" David Shults. He really is a strapping, country redneck hillbilly from Madison County, Tennessee, just outside Memphis. He really is a tough son of a bitch who scrapped his way through the wrestling profession before finding an even tougher calling as a bounty hunter. A proud man, he was unafraid to stand up for his profession on December 28, 1984, when he slapped 20/20 reporter John Stossel on the left ear in a dingy hallway in New York City's Madison Square Garden. And he's unafraid to speak his mind these days either.

It's December 2003, and Shults is in New Jersey at a fan convention. As the snow piled up outside during one of the Northeast's worst blizzards in decades, he let it all out, ripping the key antagonists in his story — Vince McMahon and Hulk Hogan. The inevitable question about Stossel and 20/20 came up almost immediately. "Vince McMahon was happy that I slapped John Stossel," Shults explained in his gruff, raspy, southern twang. "He shook my hand, congratulated me, everything. I did exactly what he wanted me to do. He knew I was going to do it. The guys in the dressing room knew I was going to do it."

Watching a tape of the incident, the smiling face of Mr. Fuji (Harry Fujiwara) is evident along the aisle. Fuji said that Stossel was asking for it. "I was there laughing, we all laughed. He made trouble on his own, and David just protected himself and the business," he said. "He was a hero, you'd better believe it. He's a good man who protected the business."

The tape that aired of Stossel's piece on the expansionist-minded WWF was pretty standard stuff for the day, concentrating on the color of the mat game and the growing business. But Stossel veered from the question-and-answer format with a bold statement to Shults' face: "I think this is fake." With one right hand, Shults did more for the WWF publicity machine than Cyndi Lauper ever did.

Chris Cruise, later a TV wrestling commentator, was working for the WWF in media and public relations at the time. "I started the day after the Stossel piece aired on 20/20. I started, and that morning we were inundated, absolutely inundated. Of course, our response was 'no comment,'" Cruise said in an interview with the *Pro Wrestling Torch*. "I was sickened by [the feature]. The fact is, you can say just about anything about these guys, and they're just not going to respond physically. That's just not their style. So when Dr. D did that, I was really sickened."

No doubt, McMahon picked the right man for the job. On the WWF's farcical *Tuesday Night Titans* show, the blond, curly-haired Shults had been portrayed as one tough backwater hick, with a (hired) inbred family, and a passion for shotguns. "Schultz continues to obliterate opponents with his Southern Piledriver, and twisting leaps, and subsequent elbow smashes from the second rope," explained a WWF program, using its chosen spelling of his name, and listing Roddy Piper as Shults' manager. In fact, Shults wasn't that far removed from 1974, when he was a good-sized country boy with homemade tattoos, courtesy of his three brothers. He was fresh out of the army, delivering for a welding company to the house of former wrestler Herb Welch, who took a look at the 220-pounder, and offered him a chance to grapple.

"He was sixty-seven years old when he trained me, and I would drive forty-five minutes to work out, and when I would come home after two hours, my wife would have to come get me out of the car, and pull me in the house," Shults said. "After three months, he told me that I would never make a dime in the business, that I was too rough on his wrestlers. Of course, I didn't know any different. I was fighting for my life."

Eventually, Shults was smartened up to the business, and debuted in Missouri in December 1974. Defending himself against hostile crowds became a regular occurrence. In 1978, he met a young Terry Bollea, who introduced him to steroids, taking the six-foot-three Shults from 220 to 300 pounds. While many blame steroids for side effects of aggression and anger, those who knew Shults don't; that's just the way he was.

"He didn't let it go in the dressing room. In other words, drop your gimmick in the dressing room. We're here, we know, you're working, don't act like you do. But that was just him. What you saw on TV was what you got," said

"Playboy" Buddy Rose, who was so hated in the Northwest in 1981 that he managed to turn Shults babyface when he tried to recruit him to his "army."

"He was very, very temperamental. If he liked you, he liked you. If he didn't like you, he let you know," said Leo Burke, who worked with Shults on top in Stampede Wrestling, and in the Maritimes, where Shults worked as David Von Shultz. Maritimes promoter Emile Dupre concurred: "He was not exactly the easiest to get along with. He could be a handful. But he was good, especially when you had TV. He was a good speaker, and he was good in the ring. His problem was outside the ring." In his book, "Dynamite Kid" Tom Billington called Shults a "short-tempered bastard."

It was all part of being a bad guy. "Being a heel was natural to me. I loved being a heel. I would not ever be a good guy," Shults said. "I'm a bad guy at heart, I don't like anybody. Everything's wrong. The government's wrong. Everything's wrong with me. I bitch and complain about everything . . . If you give me the world, I want a turnip patch on the outside."

"The Hitman" Bret Hart credited Shults with teaching him more about ring psychology than anyone else he knew. "Dave was one of the most charismatic and gifted blabbermouths of them all," Hart wrote in a *Calgary Sun* column. "He and Ed Whalen were often the highlight of the show with their hilarious back-and-forth banter."

Shults' friendship with Hogan got him more than jacked up. It helped get him into Verne Gagne's American Wrestling Association, where he headlined against Hogan before both jumped to the WWF, crippling the Minneapolis-based promotion. Though he once called Hogan his best friend in the business, things changed. Today, Shults spits venom over the Hulkster: "I really have no comments about Hulk Hogan, except when he started in this business he was sleeping in his van and didn't have a room or anything, he stayed in my house. Then later on, he acts like he don't know you, he don't know anybody — to me, he's a piece of garbage."

The myth that exists today about Shults getting fired over hitting Stossel is just that — a myth. To let the heat die down, Shults was sent to New Japan Pro Wrestling after the incident. (Stossel would eventually collect $425,000 in an out-of-court settlement with Titan Sports, and the slap helped to propel his career.) Instead, it was Shults' temper that got the best of him. In September 1984, he had an altercation with a fan, and was berated by actor and wannabe-wrestler Mr. T. It left a bad taste with Shults, who let it simmer until February 1985, when Mr. T and his entourage wanted to come backstage at a WWF show in Los Angeles. Shults wouldn't let them. "I told him I was going to make him shine my shoes in L.A., called him a 'boy,' tried to get him to come in the ring with me. He refused," explained Shults. "The next time I went to L.A., they hog-tied me, and put guns to my head, and drove me out of the L.A. Coliseum because Mr. T was scared I was going to beat him up or something. But they actually hog-tied me, my legs behind me, I mean, my back, handcuffed me, throwed me out of the building with guns drawn to my head. I don't know why; I said, 'Hey, I'll go. No problem with that.' They didn't like that. They wanted me on the ground and hog-tied me. But that was okay."

Shults' wrestling career floundered, his bad rep and temper leaving him few places to work. With a family and a home in Connecticut, he got a license to be a private investigator, which led to work as a bounty hunter. "I got into it because I needed to make money. They needed somebody to pick up a motorcycle gang member, the Diablo motorcycle gang. Everybody was scared of the guy. I went and picked him up, and made great money. After that, I picked up over 1,500. I picked up murderers, rapists, bank robbers. It's great money if you can live to stand it." Having risen to be the number two bounty hunter in the world — paying for information is key, he said — Shults lives quietly with his wife in Connecticut.

DICK SLATER

Long-time promoter Jim Barnett gave Dick Slater the name of "Mr. Unpredictable," and the big Floridian thought it fit him like a glove. "You never knew what I was going to do in the ring — that was the deal," Slater said. "If you wrestled the same style every single night, people would get bored watching you. Me, I'd change. I'd be completely different one night and completely different the next."

Slater was at his unpredictable best in the 1970 and 1980s, earning status as one of the top heels in the business. "Dick Slater was a great heel. . . . Tough, tough, tough guy," Mid-Atlantic star Don Kernodle recalled. "Not a wrestling tough guy, but a fighter. He wasn't a great shooter in wrestling, but he would knock a great shooter out before he knew what hit him."

In fact, Slater was considered world-championship material at one time because he could work a variety of styles, and defend himself in just about any situation. But, according to Slater, Charlotte, North Carolina-based promoter Jim Crockett insisted that Ric Flair hold the National Wrestling Alliance championship strap, and that was that. "I couldn't fight politics so I just went along with the flow," he said. Slater played off the decision though — in 1984, he had his own world championship belt made, and strutted around the Carolinas as kingpin, touching off a program with Flair.

Slater wasn't much of a pro wrestling fan growing up in Florida, but he was into amateur wrestling and football big-time. He started on the mats in the Amateur Athletic Union — training with professionals like Hiro Matsuda and Bob Roop to improve his skills — and landed at the nearby University of Tampa, where he wrestled, and played football. "I'd go to football practice in the afternoon, and wrestling practice at night. That was a tough life." Slater got to know wrestlers like Mike Graham and Dick Murdoch though, and had his first pro match in 1972. His choice of careers was pretty much forced on him when Tampa announced it was dropping football because of cost and academic considerations after the 1974 season.

Dick Slater delivers a smash to Dusty Rhodes.

He estimated that it took him about three years to be fully comfortable in the ring, but when he did, he racked up a pretty impressive resumé, with more than two dozen singles and tag belts to his credit, some of them multiple times. His first tag title came with Dusty Rhodes in 1973; twenty-two years later he won the World Championship Wrestling tag title with Bunkhouse Buck (Jimmy Golden). His preferred stamping ground was Georgia, where he was state champ four times in battles against Mr. Wrestling II and Paul Jones. His tag team with Bob Orton Jr. was one of the best in the South in the 1980s, as well. "I wrestled as a babyface the same as a heel. It was the same style; I never changed anything. I could adapt," he said. It also was easy to see flashes of Terry Funk's style in Slater, maybe too much so for promoter Bill Watts. "I think Dick Slater was an awesome heel, then he got infatuated with Terry Funk, and started copying Terry Funk," Watts said. "He would walk like Terry Funk, he would act like Funk in the ring. That's not how he started out." Still, the bond was pretty much unbreakable — Slater and Funk lived together for a while, teamed up in Japan, and even helped coordinate stunts together for *Rocky V*.

Slater also booked for Watts, Joe Blanchard, and Paul Boesch in Texas and surrounding states, but that wore him out quickly. "I got so brain dead I had to go down to the [Florida] Keys and go fishing," he laughed. A controversial angle involving a white man and a black woman perked up things when Slater met Linda Newton in an Atlanta nightclub. He got her to be his valet, named Dark Journey, in Watts' Texas-Louisiana promotion. "I got stalked. We got stalked. They were following me out of the arena and into the car. But we drew good money with that." Slater also worked for the WWF for about a year in 1986 and 1987 as a forgettable rebel character, but after wrestling a brutal stretch of more than 100 non-stop days, he tired of that, and returned to Florida. "Dickie was a paradox, really. He was just a big raw-boned, tough guy," said former NWA referee Tommy Young. "He was over well, a good heel, a good work ethic, a good interview, but he's had a lot of personal problems."

Part of what also held Slater back was a series of serious back ailments that cause him pain to this day. "Had it not been for the back problems he experienced, no telling what heights he may have hit," said Sir Oliver Humperdink, who knew and managed him in Florida. Slater has been through almost a half-dozen operations for ruptured vertebrae, and now suffers from flat-back syndrome, loss of curvature in the lower back. He's been on pain medication for years, and blames the pills for a well-publicized altercation with his girlfriend in 2003; Slater pleaded guilty to a lesser charge. He was arrested in January 2007 for allegedly violating an order related to the earlier case; Slater told authorities that drugs might have played a role in that. In the meantime, he is shopping a book on his career, called *A Thousand Lives*. Despite the pain and turmoil, "I wouldn't change it for a million years. I had some great, great years wrestling."

STAN STASIAK

Early in his career, Stan "The Crusher" Stasiak used a bearhug as a finishing hold, which was perfectly acceptable for a big lug from an industrial town in Quebec. But when he switched to the heart punch as a finishing move — and perfected its delivery, often with his taped fist — Stan "The Man" shot up the cards.

His opponents can still picture the move in their heads today, and speak highly of Stasiak's painless delivery of the potentially deadly move. "He'd get you in a position where he'd put your left arm over your head, sort of holding it. Then he'd turn you around from the referee, and give you a heart punch. He'd just use it once," recalled Moose Morowski. Paul Diamond's recollection is similar: "You take your left arm, put it behind your back, way back, and give him a target to hit on your chest. Boom! He'd hit your heart. He just got you, but you'd sell it like crazy."

Ed Wiskoski explained that the heart punch was as much about the psychology as anything. "You just had to draw back, and get your arm back behind your head, and people would go fucking nuts. You'd get away and skate out of the ring," Morowski praised Stasiak's timing. "When he'd pretend to be using it, the people would want to jump in the ring. When he used it, it was the finish. He didn't use it for a high spot, he'd only use it for a finish. It got over real well."

Never has another grappler been so associated with the heart

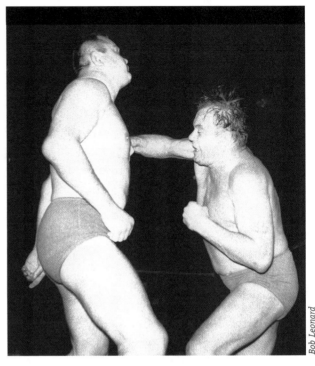

Bob Leonard

Stan Stastiak drives a heart punch into Gene Kiniski.

punch. "There's actually been a few people try to imitate it, but no one can quite do it right," said his son Shawn, who had a short run in the WWF and WCW in the late 1990s. "There's only one way to do it, and it remains a secret in the Stasiak family."

In the 1950s, George Stipich was a youngster in Arvida, Quebec, with great potential for a career in hockey. But he had a fascination for pro wrestling, and regularly attended shows. Another French Canadian, Rene Goulet (Robert Bedard) recalled meeting Stipich in a dressing room in Jonquiere on an Eddie Quinn-promoted tour of the smaller towns, and being quizzed on becoming a pro wrestler. Goulet later learned that Stipich dropped his hockey dreams, and his job at the aluminum mill, to give wrestling a go. "After he went to Montreal a few times, he was discouraged," explained Goulet. "[Billy] Red Lyons told him, 'You should get on the bus, and go back to Arvida, and get a good job and work there.' To make a long story short, a few years later, Stasiak came to work in Toronto. . . . He said to Red Lyons, 'You know, I never took that bus back home.'"

Of Croatian descent, the twenty-one-year-old Stasiak started wrestling in 1958, and took his name from a well-known wrestler of the 1920s and 1930s. At six-foot-five, 270 pounds, the "Arvida Assassin" ground it out for a few years, doing what it took to get known. Paul LeDuc met him in

Calgary, and Stasiak lived with Paul and "brother" Jos LeDuc for a while. Stasiak's size was natural, stressed LeDuc. "He was not an addict of body-building or training with weights. He was big. He hated the guys that trained in the gym, he said he was not flexible [when muscled]."

Even so, early in his career, Stasiak's ability with the crowd was evident, said LeDuc, recalling a hot feud between Stasiak and Calgary promoter Stu Hart: "Stu showed him his fists, and Stan jumped out of the ring and cracked up the house. That's the way he was. He didn't want to match too much with Stu. He was playing with the crowd. He was fantastic with the crowd."

Stasiak was in Texas when promoter Don Owen convinced him to give Portland, Oregon, a try, and the rest, as they say, is history. Though he would work in dozens of other territories, from Calgary to Australia, from Texas to Toronto, and hold the WWWF World title for nine days, it's the Pacific Northwest where Stasiak was best known (and he started being billed from Buzzard Creek, Oregon). While on both sides of the heel/face fence, Stasiak was a six-time Pacific Northwest champ (1965–71, 1979), and an eight-time Pacific Northwest tag team champ (1965–69, 1979–82).

"Stan was one of those sweet guys. He loved the Northwest, and the fans ended up loving him," said another Pacific Northwest regular, Pepper Martin. Stasiak broke the mold in Oregon, which had traditionally been a smaller man's territory. "He was a good talker. He gave a good interview," said Martin. "Whatever 'it' is, he had it. He was also a very good worker, he had a charisma about him in the ring, and the fans, obviously they disliked him, and he got over."

Wrestler Sandy Barr became one of Stan's best friends. He tried to explain the dynamic between Stasiak and Owen, whose houses were really down in 1965 and 1966. But Stasiak volunteered to come in anyway. "He kind of saved Don's business. He was forever grateful to Stan for that, because he came down, no guarantee, nothing. Just worked for whatever was here," said Barr. "He told Stan, 'Stan, if you need a place to go, you're out and about, just give me a ring, and come right in.' But that got to be an old story because Stan made a home here. When he didn't have a place to go, he wanted to come home. Then in Don's mind, he became a piece of shit."

In a big man promotion like the WWWF, Stasiak was a natural, and he trotted in and out of the Northeast for years. The pinnacle of his run, of course, was his toppling of WWWF champion Pedro Morales in Philadelphia, December 1, 1973. He would headline against champs Morales and Bruno Sammartino in the mecca of Madison Square Garden six times, dropping the title to Sammartino in 12:14 on December 10, 1973. (Incidentally, Stasiak didn't get a rematch with Sammartino in MSG until

1976; in 1973, on the subsequent card, he fought Morales.)

It was common knowledge that Stasiak's run as champ would be a short one for Vince McMahon Sr., said WWWF regular Dominic DeNucci. "He was good enough to [be champion], but everybody knew, including Vince, they couldn't keep the belt on him because they knew he was not dependable sometimes, but only because of alcohol, not because he was a bad guy or anything."

Battles with booze would haunt Stasiak throughout his life. He was a fun guy to be around, good-hearted, and jovial. But once he'd been drinking, he was unreliable, and sometimes dangerous. "We go into a place to eat, and Stan is hammered out of the tree. Next thing you know, he starts a rumble with somebody," said Morowski. "Holy Christ, now we've got to get out of there! That night, I had to carry him into the hotel, because once he started drinking, he was one party guy. But in the ring, he always worked hard."

Dutch Savage brought his old friend back to Portland in 1978, and helped him clean up his act, and cement his reputation in the Pacific Northwest as a babyface. "That summer, because he tagged up with me, that was the best summer we had in Oregon in fifteen years. Stan and I had the belts. Got him all straightened out, got him back on his feet monetarily, doing real well," said Savage.

By the early 1980s, Stasiak's career had petered out. Around 1991, he was having marital problems in Texas, and Barr brought in his old buddy to be a color commentator for a few years. Later, Stasiask moved to Oakville, Ontario, just outside Toronto, and worked as a security guard, before retiring to the Pacific Northwest in 1994. He died of congestive heart failure on June 19, 1997 at the age of sixty.

"Tough" Tony Borne delivered the eulogy at the funeral. "As a person, he was a very good-natured individual," said Borne. "He had his own way about him, but I think we all did in that respect. Stan was a real trooper."

RON WRIGHT

There's wrestling and then there's rasslin'. And out in the hills and hollows of eastern Tennessee and Kentucky, nobody practiced rasslin' quite like Ron Wright. Even though he did not spend much time on the national stage, folks who worked with him say Wright's brawling tactics and motor mouth earned him as much acclaim in his backyard as any world champ could hope for. "Ron Wright is, was, and will always be the king of the east Tennessee hillbillies," said Scott Spangler, a.k.a. Brian Matthews, former announcer for Smoky Mountain Wrestling. "People in east Tennessee loved to hate Ron Wright." You

Ron Wright bloodies Whitey Caldwell in his heyday.

won't get much argument from Wright. "I was pretty hated and I guess I still am," he said upon his induction into the Knoxville Wrestling Hall of Fame in Tennessee. "Looking back, it probably is deserved. I was pretty raunchy."

The raunchiness started innocently enough, when Wright was wrestling as a teenager at a Boys Club in his hometown of Kingsport, Tennessee, in the early 1950s. After a few years, he decided to step up his level of competition by squaring off with pros that passed through the area. "I kept challenging them, they kept rubbing my nose in the mat, stretching me out pretty bad, I kept on and on, I wouldn't quit," he explained to writer Gary Langevin in 1995. "Then a bunch of them kind of took a liking to me." Wright played some football in high school, but wrestling killed his amateur status. Though he turned in a couple of years with a semi-pro football team in Baltimore, he achieved more infamy as a bad guy. He held the Southeastern title three times, the Tennessee brass knuckles title twice, and did work some in the Carolinas and Florida, as well. For most of his career, he had a day job at a pressman in Kingsport, while his night job consisted of inciting riots.

"He was a meat chopper, but he played his part, and his promos were good," said Les Thatcher, who joined Whitey Caldwell in memorable wars against Ron and brother Don in the Knoxville territory. "He wasn't going to work a lot of holds, and if he did work a hold, he was going to cheat, or pull hair, or whatever. He was a badass; he was a barroom brawler."

He also was the perfect hellraiser for the territory. In backcountry Kentucky towns like Hazard and Harlan, fans shot at him for using brass knucks, a boot loaded with lead, and any other cheatin' thing he could dream up. "I guess I'd always go overboard with everything I done. I didn't have enough sense to take it so far and stop, I had to go all the way to the furnace with it. I guess that's why I drew as much money as I did; I just didn't care," Wright said. In Greenville, Tennessee, in the late 1960s, he ended up with almost 200 stitches to close a gash in his back. He bought a $30,000 twin-engine airplane to ease his travel burden in the 1970s; one night in Harlan, he found it burned to a crisp. Local authorities blamed irate fans, though Wright said he simply thought someone was trying to vandalize the craft and burned the evidence. "I only had about a $13,000 insurance policy on it, so I lost a lot of money on the deal," he told Langevin.

Ron meets up with his old partner Don Wright.

Wright reminded former NWA world champion Ronnie Garvin a little of Dory Funk Sr. "I can see Ron Wright out in Texas in the '50s and '60s, doing his thing out there. He was up there in the hillbilly country. He never took a wrestling hold in his life. But he had a lot of heat," Garvin said. "Nature Boy" Buddy Landel credited Wright with helping him during the early part of his career. "He was an excellent heel, just an excellent talker."

He stopped actively wrestling in the mid-1980s after an auto accident, and took a role in managing Tony "Dirty White Boy" Anthony in the Smoky Mountain promotion. His promos were still gems, full of fire and brimstone. "Listening to Ron rant and rave, I began to notice that Ron's speech patterns were reminding me the way an old-fashioned Pentecostal tent revival preacher would preach," Spangler said. "Even at his age then, ol' Ron Wright still had the people in the palm of his hand." When fans started getting restless during a feud between Anthony and Tracy Smothers over the burning of a Confederate flag, Wright, sitting ringside, didn't flinch a bit. "He just looked at me, and winked, and tapped the top of the blanket." After the show, Spangler asked Wright what he meant by the tap. "In that east Tennessee drawl of his, he said, 'Them ol' boys don't know who they were a-messin' with. I had my ol' nine-milly-meter under that blanket.'"

In his final match, Wright, with a hip and shoulder replacement, came out of retirement to pin Anthony as part of a dream matchup show in Johnson City, Tennessee. That day — August 12, 1995 — was Ron Wright Day in Kingsport. "Talking about a territorial heel, he was just fantastic," Landel said. "People outside of Tennessee, and around there, are not going to know him. But the wrestlers that sprouted out of there, such as myself, and Tim Horner, and guys from that region, we owe everything that we are to people like Ron because we stood on his shoulders for years."

The Foreigners

THE IRON SHEIK

Hold on, here — are we talking about the same person? Are we really talking about Khosrow Vaziri, the feared Iron Sheik, who became WWF world champ in 1983? "You couldn't get a word out of this guy," Johnny Valiant said of Vaziri's days in Verne Gagne's AWA. "He was a very quiet guy. He was 180-some pounds, and Verne had him set up the ring and had him refereeing." Jumping Jim Brunzell added: "He was very, very introverted when he first got in the business. He didn't drink, or smoke, and was very religious."

What's more, the beefy man who would swing heavy Persian clubs over his head for training was a quick-as-a-cat racquetball star, according to Rene Goulet, who knew him in the AWA and the WWF. "He was a helluva of racquetball player. He was playing racquetball up there in Minneapolis with one of the top guys in the country. One time, I challenged him. I used to play racquetball too. I told him I could beat him. He got pissed, and, man, he wiped my ass there. He was really good at that. He was a better racquetball player than wrestler."

It's hard to believe, given the way the Iron Sheik evolved over the years, but, as Kurt Angle might say, "It's true, it's damn true." The Sheik is not the same chap that entered the United States in 1969. The ultra-clean living got lost in the shuffle somewhere, the 180-pound frame is a distant memory, and when it comes to flapping the gums, well, "Captain" Lou Albano put it best: "The man is definitely a legend, a vocabulist. When he speaks, the words come out of his mouth. Where they come from, I don't know. But they come out. Don't

Howard Lapes

First he was known as Khozrow Vaziri.

know what he's talking about, but he talks, he talks, he talks."

Discerning fact from fiction with the Sheik is like trying to separate sausage into its component parts — it's a painstaking process, and it's unclear whether you'll come up with anything worthwhile. Still, it's worth a shot. The Sheik definitely was an Olympic-caliber amateur wrestler in Iran, starting in Greco-Roman at age fifteen, when he tipped the scales at 155 pounds. He did serve, apparently, as one of many guards for the former Shah. Contrary to urban legend, he didn't win any Olympic gold medals. He did not get to the Games; he lost a qualifying round match when Iran was fielding a team for the 1968 Olympics. Nor did he train pro wrestlers for Gagne. But he was AAU national champion in Greco-Roman wrestling in 1971 for the Minnesota Wrestling Club, and worked with some of Greco-Roman wrestlers there who were training for the Olympics. That's how he hooked up with Gagne, who sponsored the amateur wrestling club.

Greg Gagne started training in a pretty talented class with Vaziri, Ric Flair, Ken Patera, and Bob Bruggers, and has a clear memory of the facts. "He didn't know anything about professional wrestling," Gagne said. "One day, in fact, we went down to the TV studio and we were watching the matches. This is about two weeks into the class. He says, 'Nobody could beat me. Nobody could ever dropkick me.' And Verne turned and dropkicked him and knocked him out. He had a little different attitude after that." Valiant distinctly recalls the meek Vaziri hoping against hope that he might get a chance to change from hanger-on to wrestler. "They had all these guys like Ric Flair, and Ricky Steamboat, and all these other cats. Then he said to Verne, 'You think maybe someday I can do like sheik gimmick and make money?' He did it and he made a fortune. And he's legit."

After working as a midcarder in the AWA for several years under his real name, he headed to New York as Hussein Arab in 1979, just before the U.S. hostage crisis in Iran flared up. Never mind that the Sheik actually was aligned with the Shah, the object of revolutionary Iran's wrath — he had enough of a geopolitical connection to infuriate fans. "My heat was a natural because I was a real Iranian, and, you know, Ayatollah Khomeini keep the people over there 444 days," he said. "I was not involved with the politicians, but the people didn't like me carrying Ayatollah picture, Iranian picture. But I just say, that is my country, and I was proud."

He worked in the Carolinas and Louisiana before returning to the WWF, where he ended Bob Backlund's five-year reign as champ before dropping the title to Hulk Hogan a month later. He and Nikolai Volkoff, managed by Freddie Blassie, won the federation's tag titles at WrestleMania I in 1985. As a worker, "he never really caught on to the professional style. Later on, he got big, and

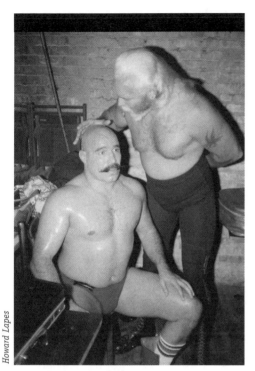

Howard Lapes

He shaved his head (being inspected by Jimmy Valiant) and became the Iron Sheik.

he couldn't move," Gagne said. Davey O'Hannon felt the Sheik was "kind of a vanilla guy in the ring," but showed signs of his Greco-Roman training. "He had a suplex for every occasion. He could suplex you from now to next week, and not do the same one twice." But that was secondary to the Sheik's antics out of the ring, where he dropped his proper bearings and lapped up Americanization. "What happened to Khosrow is when he got here, it was like a kid on Christmas morning, He said, 'Holy crap, look at all the stuff I've got at my fingertips. All I've got to do is, "Ptooey, U.S.A" and wave the flag,'" O'Hannon said. "New York did it to him."

Goulet remembered how the Sheik's mouth would drop when he encountered women not necessarily covered by a chador, as they were in his homeland. "He was about thirty-one years old and I don't think he had ever seen a woman before that. Every time he would see a woman, he would come and he would ask her, 'Are you a whore?'"

Brunzell had the distinction of wrestling the Sheik in the AWA, the Mid-Atlantic, and the WWF, and diplomatically said he thought Vaziri's character changed when he got into the goodies in the fast-paced Northeast. "He sort of sampled various products and it completely changed him. He was like a Dr. Jekyll and My. Hyde." What Brunzell was referring to, among other incidents, was a May 1987 episode when the Sheik and Jim Duggan — his arch-rival at the time — were busted for drug possession in New Jersey. The charges were dropped after the Sheik, who had been found with small amounts of marijuana and cocaine, completed probation and underwent drug testing.

Volkoff had firsthand experience with the Sheik's wayward ways when he woke up in a cloud of smoke in a Toronto hotel room one night. "The drugs. It was the Sheik and his party there. I told him, 'Sheik, what's wrong with you?'" But Volkoff got him back in spades — sharing a big bed one night, the big Russian simulated passing gas. The Sheik immediately got up and took a shower. "He is Muslim . . . he has to be clean, you know?" Volkoff said. A couple of hours later, Volkoff pulled the same trick, same result, same shower. "I love the guy, but Sheik likes to party, likes to drink," Volkoff laughed. "There is nobody like him."

The Sheik returned to the WWF in 1991 as Colonel Mustafa, acting as a second to American turncoat Sergeant Slaughter, and was inducted into the WWE Hall of Fame in 2005. He's now better known for his obscene and off-the-wall rants against Hogan, Gagne, Vince McMahon, Volkoff, and others, though he suffered a personal tragedy in May 2003, when his twenty-seven-year-old daughter, Marissa, was found strangled to death in a Georgia apartment; her boyfriend told police he did it. "He keeps screaming her name out. And he's still recovering from his surgery. So he hurts from head to toe," Vaziri's wife, Caryl, told the *Atlanta Journal-Constitution*. So probably his bark at age sixty-plus is worse than his bite, most people think. "He was okay; like I say, he got pissed off; sometimes, a guy would be afraid to talk back to him. Besides that, he was okay," Goulet said. "He was a gimmick all along. Matter of fact, that's not a gimmick, that's him."

IVAN KOLOFF

The first time Ivan Koloff wrestled Bruno Sammartino, he almost got himself killed. He filled in at a Pittsburgh TV taping as Red McNulty, an Irish villain with an eyepatch, and he gullibly bit on a veteran's advice to attack Sammartino when he was making the sign of the cross before the match. "I ended up doing it, and I remember Bruno looking up at me like, 'What's the crazy kid doing?' He threw me around, and I think he put the bearhug on me."

What a strange world this is. In January 1971, Koloff pinned Sammartino in the middle of the ring in Madison Square Garden, scoring the greatest wrestling upset of the era, and ending Sammartino's nearly eight-year reign as WWWF world champion. "Dead silence came down," said Lou Albano, who was in Koloff's corner that night. "They couldn't believe it."

In a business loaded with foreign heels, Koloff stood out from the pack during his heyday in the '70s and '80s, even winning academic admiration from social critic Paul A. Cantor of the University of Virginia: "I wish I had a ruble for every wrestling villain who was advertised as the 'Russian Bear.' But the greatest of all who bore that nickname was Ivan Koloff. Looking for all the world like Lenin pumped up on steroids, he eventually spawned a whole dynasty of villainous wrestling Koloffs." Koloff was more than hammer and sickle though. Ronnie Garvin considered his work to match his gruff Russian image. "Ivan was a good worker. He looked more Russian than

Ivan Koloff uses a backbreaker on Gino Hernandez.

a lot of Russians and he had a better accent. He probably didn't need it. But that was his gimmick, his style. He was very, very efficient."

Jacques Rougeau Sr. was instrumental in changing Koloff's nationality after seeing him wrestle in Japan. Impressed with his work, he suggested McNulty, born French-Canadian Oreal Parras, shave his head, and work for his brother Johnny Rougeau, who was running Quebec. Koloff fulfilled a few commitments, and then went to Ontario to tell his family about the big change. "I stopped in to see my brothers around the Hamilton area, had a few drinks too many, and I was telling them I had to shave my head. So next morning I woke up, I had toilet paper all over my head," he said. In Montreal, Koloff was billed as a nephew of Dan Koloff, a top wrestler in the territory thirty years before. "He was a very convincing guy," Jacques said. "He did great for us."

If there was any doubt about the demise of Red McNulty, Jimmy Valiant figured it out a few years later, when he encountered Koloff, half-asleep, in the Richmond, Virginia airport. Ever the ribber, Valiant tells the story of how he coaxed an airport employee to page Red McNulty. No reaction. He did it a second time — "paging Red McNulty." Koloff barely lifted his head, grumbled, "Red McNulty died," and went back to sleep.

Koloff grew up on an Ontario dairy farm in the Ottawa valley with nine brothers and sisters, and got hooked on wrestling when he first saw it on TV at a friend's house at age eight. But he also got into his share of scrapes before becoming a pro. He quit high school two weeks before graduating from eleventh grade after a suspension for playing ping-pong during class time. Later, he recalled, he and a brother served time for stealing cattle, a serious crime in an agricultural community. In 1960, he landed with famed Hamilton trainer Jack Wentworth, who gave him the McNulty name. Scarfing down food and protein shakes, he beefed up to 230 pounds within six months, and started working small shows. "I had super gains," he recalled. "I really wanted to wrestle. I wanted it bad." In Montreal, he set himself apart from the pack with a unique, fast-paced entrance and exit that he took to the WWWF. "They had me run from the dressing room, all the way to the ring, run around the outside of the ring about five times, and then while they announced me and my match, I'd jump in the ring as they announced my opponent, and attack him, beat him up, then jump out of the ring, and run around the ring three, four times, back to the dressing room. At 280 pounds! I was one blown-up guy. But it helped keep me in shape."

Koloff was touring Australia and Hawaii when he was called back to deliver the kneedrop heard 'round the world against Sammartino in 1971. He was a transitional champ, holding the belt for three weeks before dropping it to Pedro Morales. But it kicked off a rivalry with Sammartino that ran for years. "I wrestled Koloff — oh, my goodness, I don't know — fifty, seventy-five times," Sammartino said. "The reason why I enjoyed wrestling him so much was that after each match when I left and went back to the dressing room, I felt in my heart that the fans who came out and bought that ticket went home feeling they got their money's worth."

Though his reign was brief, Koloff continued to main event across the country. He was on top in the Mid-Atlantic for years, starting in 1974, and was a frequent visitor to the WWWF. "What a hell of a heel he was," said top Carolinas referee Tommy Young. "He wasn't real tall, but thick as a brick; great performer. He was very professional, knew how to get the heat, was willing to do whatever he needed to. I can't say enough about Ivan." Koloff held part of the world tag title in the Mid-Atlantic five times with teammates such as Don Kernodle and nephew Nikita, even though the days of kneejerk anti-Soviet sentiment were passing. "He was a very methodical type of person in the ring. He lived his gimmick to the fullest extent while he was in that ring," explained veteran Bill White. "The Russian gimmick suited him, and that's why he continued with it even after the Russian deal was over. He could make the people believe he could be that mean and that vicious, and that's what counted."

But Young was just one of many who noticed that Koloff was fighting demons outside the ring. "If he drank liquor, it was Lon Chaney turning into the Wolfman, just a totally different personality, mean, wanting to fight," Young said. Koloff traced his substance abuse to a youth where booze flowed freely, and a bad bump in a Minneapolis match that ruptured discs in his back. He took painkillers, sleeping pills, and muscle relaxers for about eighteen months so he could keep working, and turned to stronger stuff. "I ended up taking them and getting into situations where even the drugs weren't enough," Koloff said. "Looking back, I could say, 'Well, I deserve it. I worked hard. I get up every morning, and go to the gym, and work out. I work hard in the ring, so I need this for my body. It's okay then to not only take these drugs, but to find some relief in marijuana.' And if marijuana wasn't enough, then maybe cocaine."

He quit wrestling full-time in 1989 when Ted Turner acquired the Jim Crockett promotion and consolidated headquarters in Atlanta, though Koloff turned up in small promotions in the early 1990s with wrestling nephew Vladimir. His life turned for the better in 1994 when Nikita, a minister, persuaded him to attend church services and give his life to the Lord. Koloff ditched his vices — alcohol, drugs, and tobacco — and started a ministry in North Carolina with wife Renae. He appears at detention homes, prisons, youth groups, and churches, though he has laced up the boots for a few legends matches in recent years. "When I started straightening up, things started working in my life," he said. "Once I understood that, that it wasn't going to be on my power, it was going to be on His power, I now had a tag team partner who truly was a world champion."

THE GREAT MEPHISTO

Here's when you know that a wrestling gimmick is getting the job done. Frankie Cain was working on the West Coast in the early 1970s as The Great Mephisto, a mystical sort who invoked the supernatural, and touched his little finger and thumb together to make a point when talking. As it turned out, Mephisto's finger actions mimicked the sign of the ram, bringing him an unusual admirer — Anton LaVey, founder of the Church of Satan. "Anton LaVey thought I was a devil worshiper because of the sign of the ram and the name Mephisto means 'devil,'" Cain said. "He wanted to come on TV with me to be seen because it was going into millions of homes." They never got together, and though the Mephisto character was more about visions and auras than Beelzebub, the memory gives Cain pause. "It sounds mercenary, but if I had known what kind of money this guy made, I might have gotten in on it. This guy was a fan of mine."

If LaVey bought into Cain's work, he wasn't the only one. In the last half-century, few wrestlers have understood better than Cain how to manipulate a crowd with bad-guy tactics, whether he was Mephisto or an Inferno with his infamous "loaded" boot. "He got a ton of heat. He'd have people crying for me," Olympian-turned-wrestler Bob Roop said. "He had people scared to death that he was going to kill me with the boot. He convinced people that he was a seriously evil person and he was actually the nicest guy in the world. Is that not great acting skills?" That's exactly what Cain was striving for — the suspension of disbelief. "As Mephisto, I had such a bizarre interview. I was being a mystic and talking about spiritual guides and that you are blessed with certain powers that guide you through life unharmed," he said. "After a while, people started believing that I believed what I was saying." And his ring work was as strong as his reputation, according to southern stalwart Len Rossi. "He was unreal. Very good crowd psychology. He was a chief in the ring, a leader," said Rossi, who recalled Cain as almost a second father to his late son Joey. "He was straight as an arrow, no backstabbing. If he told you it was raining, you count could on it, and that's so rare in that business. He was wonderful." As Skandor Akbar, Cain's cousin and a star himself, put it: "Cuz was always a wrestler's wrestler."

Growing up on the streets of Columbus, Ohio in the '30s and '40s, Cain sold programs for Al Haft's wrestling promotion, hung around gyms, and soaked up everything he saw like a sponge. At five-foot-nine and 185 pounds, he was fit more to be the poundee, not the pounder. But he had the luxury of living in a Mecca for lighter-weight wrestlers, and picked up tricks by watching talents like Johnny Demchuk. As a teenager, he wandered from town to town with club wrestlers in unsanctioned "smoker" matches — no klieg lights, no ropes, just a flat twelve-by-twelve mat. "We had to get our heat by using holds, letting a guy get halfway out of a hold after fifteen or twenty minutes. That's where I really learned the art of heeling. The reason I wanted to heel is because you generate the heat, you generate the excitement, and I liked that, even though I was very young," he said. At the same time, he was boxing in and around southern Ohio, sometimes for real, and sometimes to make his opponent shine. "If I wasn't busted up from fighting, I'd take all the matches I could get for five dollars a night," he wistfully recalled. "We'd travel forty, fifty miles to these little towns."

The Great Mephisto

Most importantly, Cain cribbed from The Great Mephisto, a red-garbed lightweight hero who was the biggest attraction in the rich history of Haft's promotion. The story on Mephisto — his name appears to have been Julius Woronick — is that he was once a circus performer who lit a kerosene-drenched suit to set himself ablaze, before diving like a human torch into a pool of water. "His face was outstanding . . . one of the most interesting faces I've ever seen. Those piercing black eyes, that nose; he looked like the caricature of Mephisto," Cain said. "The way he moved in and out of holds, it was fabulous. I copied a lot off him."

In Columbus, Cain hung around Buddy Rogers, and helped to introduce Ray Stevens and Dr. Bill Miller to wrestling. He worked across the country in the 1950s and early 1960s before fashioning his own break with Rocky Smith by creating the Infernos. One of the big tag team draws of the time, they swept through the south and southwest from 1966 to 1969, as Cain broke out two gimmicks he perfected. His menacing built-up boot initially was an innocent heel lift he designed for a wrestler who had one leg shorter than the other. His fireball was a neat little trick he could hurl several feet in the air, compared with the momentary flash of most wrestling "fire." As their innovator, Cain relied on them sparingly to build maximum heat with the audience. "There was a proper time to use it. See, that boot was built to escape, to get you out of harm's way. It wasn't supposed to be used to stomp someone to death." Les Thatcher was a newbie starting out with Johnny Weaver and George Becker in the Carolinas against The Infernos, when he came to appreciate Cain's approach to the business. "I was just a young guy getting a break, and they could have been more concerned with getting Weaver and Becker over, but Frankie made sure that I was put over to look an equal so that it would help the angle draw," Thatcher said. "He is also one of three people I ever trusted to blade me over my career, other than myself. For all his fiery temper, he was a gentleman and a class act and businessman, and has been a friend ever since."

In 1969, Cain left The Infernos to become Mephisto, a bow to the hero of his youth, and teamed with Dante (Bobby Hart) before working as a single. "It was so unusual, such an unusual name," Cain said. "It was something different and a name the people could pronounce, but would sound mystifying." Mephisto's character contained elements familiar to fans of The Sheik — a prayer rug, an Arabian-style headdress, an attendant named Princess Shalina (his wife). But there the similarities ended. While The Sheik's matches were short and violent, Mephisto worked long, hard matches with the same calculated style he learned in Columbus. That enabled him to be the heel against much bigger workers like Johnny Valentine and Fritz Von Erich. "He always believed in the philosophy that you show people a heel can wrestle and that makes you hate them even more," Akbar said. "That's what made him stand out. With his lesser size, a lot of guys these days will say, 'My God, how could he get over like that?' He got over because he was tough, but he knew exactly when to do the thing and do it right." Wrestler-manager Izzy Slapawitz, who credits Cain for his break in wrestling, said he learned a similar message from his mentor. "If you watch a match with Frankie as Mephisto, Frankie would work holds. Yeah, he would kick and punch and do his shtick. But Frankie never got cheap heat. Frankie used high spots only when he had to use high spots. Frankie knew how to work a crowd."

Mephisto became Southern champion in Florida in 1970, U.S. champion in San Francisco in 1973, and Texas champion in 1974, among other honors. "Frankie Cain was a hell of a worker, very good in the ring, a very sharp guy, very smart," said Robert Fuller, even though Mephisto broke his ankle during a match in Fort Myers, Florida, when Fuller mistakenly moved at a critical juncture. "I worked with Frankie a bunch of times after that and he'd always tell me, 'Hey, kid, you know, when I tell you to do something, just do it.' I learned a lot of stuff from Frankie and one of them was the hard way." His California days were marked by sellouts against Pat Patterson, then a local favorite, and a KO of promoter Roy Shire following a dispute over wrestlers' payoffs. The knockout further eroded his standing with other promoters, whom he mostly viewed as a collection of "ruthless SOBs" anyway. "A lot of times he'd stand up for the boys, stand up for the guys and in essence hurt himself," Akbar said. "He did not prostitute his virtues to gain anything — no brown-nosing, nothing like that."

As a booker, Cain went to Australia in the mid-1970s and resuscitated a business that was on life support after promoter Jim Barnett pulled out. When Mid-South honchos Bill Watts and LeRoy McGuirk dumped the Calkin family territory in Mississippi in 1977, Cain re-established wrestling there, teaming future Freebirds Michael Hayes and Terry Gordy for the first time, and starting Percy Pringle (Paul Bearer) and James Harris (Kamala), among others. "Frankie is a real genius when it comes to booking. We were actually outdrawing the established promotion with the bigger names," Slapawitz said. "The guy just has a knack; he knows what the fans want, he probably knows every finish in the world. If Frankie speaks of himself well, he's still being modest."

After Mississippi, Cain wrestled, managed, and booked on and off for years in places like Oklahoma and Tennessee, and even teamed with The Sheik during a swing through Japan in 1980. He's also run a couple of clubs in Florida, where he is retired, but his heart still is in wrestling. Cain and wrestling writer Scott Teal are planning a book on his forty years in wrestling, and maybe some up-and-comer can learn how passionately he studied the business. "I loved it since I was a little kid," he said. "It was the only thing I knew how to do."

Chuck Thornton Collection

Mr. Moto.

MR. MOTO

Mr. Moto gave Mr. Moto a bad name. The original Mr. Moto was a crime-solving secret agent in books and movies of the 1930s. But, after World War II, "Mr. Moto" became universally despised as a fastidious wrestling bad guy played by Masaru "Charlie" Iwamoto.

Wrestling's version of Mr. Moto wasn't that evil, of course; his colleagues recall him fondly and remember the tasty sashimi he brought them to eat after the matches. Still, he was one of the earliest — and best — Japanese heels of the 1950s and 1960s, when memories of the bombing of Pearl Harbor were fresh in everyone's minds.

"When he first started, we all hated the Japanese because of the war. He was the first one to have the big, big sandals," said Mike LeBell, the long-time promoter in Los Angeles, who helped to get Moto going and later used him as his booker. "It was just great being able to root against the Japanese. It was mainly the Anglo population that we were asking, 'Come on down and let's kill this Jap.'"

Born in 1915 to Japanese immigrants in Hawaii, Moto carved out a successful career as a sumo wrestler, and also worked as a bouncer and a carpenter — construction was plentiful in postwar Hawaii. His son, Raymond, said star wrestler Kaimon Kudo told Moto during a trip to Hawaii that there was good money to be made in the States. "Kudo came back from the mainland and let dad know what was going on there. He had the sumo background, with the emphasis on balance and momentum, and it worked well for him."

He wrestled briefly in California as Charlie Chiranuhi before adopting the Moto guise around 1950. With a slightly saggy midsection that hinted at his sumo days, Moto was one of the first to bring sacred salt into the ring to ward off evil spirits and blind opponents. A supreme performer who infuriated fans with a mixture of Japanese rituals, comedic bits and downright wicked tactics, Moto dressed in flowing kimonos and clogs, wore tiny glasses, and looked for all the world like he had just emerged from Tojo's war council. "He would make them laugh a little, but then the people would want to kill him before he got out of the ring," said close friend Dick "The Destroyer" Beyer.

With faithful servant Suji Fuji, he appeared all across North America, causing mayhem in Canada, Texas, the Carolinas, and the Deep South. His titles included the Texas heavyweight crown and four runs with the Southern tag belts, mostly alongside Duke Keomuka, all while he was fanning the flames of anti-Japanese hatred. "I hated to ride with Moto and Fuji because you'd go into a restaurant, especially a truck stop, and you got some looks, take my word for it," said Tinker Todd, a regular roadmate in the early 1950s. Just walking through a drugstore one day in Florida, Moto took it on the noggin from a customer. "An old man passed us, gave us a look, and all of a sudden was belting poor Moto across the head with a stick, enough to bring blood," Todd said. "Moto just ignored him, he couldn't do anything in defense. He didn't want publicity. I asked the man what the hell he was doing. 'Damn Japs! Damn Japs!' He'd been someplace on the [Batann] Death March and said, 'I'll kill every damn Jap I can get my hands on.'"

Moto had trouble with ringside spectators, too; in March 1955, he was ripping a bandage off Fred Blassie's head during a match in Washington, D.C., when an incensed woman shattered her pocket mirror and slashed him in the leg with the broken glass. She was arrested; Moto was led away by police, bleeding. According to Houston promoter Paul Boesch, Fuji up and left after a series of near-riots. "Suji got ulcers and left for California. He just couldn't take the threats and screams of the fans anymore," Boesch told a reporter.

In California, Moto fell prey to Beyer's preschool son, Kurt, who, sitting ringside, couldn't stand the abuse that the sinister Oriental was inflicting on his dad. "Mr. Moto had my dad's mask turned around. There was blood everywhere. . . They were right in front of us, and [timekeeper] Jerry Murdoch looked at me and said, 'Kurt, your dad's in trouble. What are you going to do?' Without thinking, I grabbed the hammer from the bell and broke Mr. Moto's toe. Mr. Moto jumped all over the ring. [Dad] didn't know what was going on because the mask was turned around." Backstage, Beyer pleaded with his son not to take the in-ring action seriously. "You've got to understand that this is my business. Mr. Moto is your sister's godfather!"

Moto stayed mostly in California after about 1960, working long hours in the Los Angeles office, and wrestling from time to time, often as a good guy. After he retired, he moved to Huntington Beach, California, where he spent his retirement golfing and fishing until his death in 1991 at seventy-five. He's still remembered as the role model for the now-bygone Japanese heel. "He had the little goatee, he'd fix his hair, and he was perfect, just perfect," LeBell said. "But he was the nicest guy in the world."

TORU TANAKA

Complaints about a lack of ethics from the pro wrestling industry are legion. But according to the widow of wrestler-turned-actor Professor Toru Tanaka, the grappling game is lily white compared to the movie business. "When he got into the film industry, it was just unreal. It was so phony. People used and abused him because he was a nice person. He was a generous person, and people took advantage of that," complained Doris Peterson Kalani, who was married to Tanaka (Charlie Kalani) for forty-seven years, until his death of a heart attack on August 22, 2000, in Lake Forest, California.

For many of his film roles, Tanaka didn't have to do much more than be an incredibly imposing figure, dwarfing whatever protagonist he was matched with. It wasn't hard, given his 300-pound frame, making him more tank than man. That was essentially the role he played in pro wrestling too.

"He made Oddjob look like a fruitcake," said frequent opponent Larry Zbyszko, with an appropriate villainous film reference. "You couldn't hurt the guy. He was like a rock. He was one of the guys that really impressed me. Toru Tanaka was one of my most beloved bad guys."

Usually typecast as a Japanese thug, the Hawaiian-born Tanaka stood up against the likes of Arnold Schwarzenegger (*Running Man* and *Last Action Hero*), Chuck Norris (*Missing in Action 2: The Beginning*), Jeff Speakman (*Perfect Weapon*), and, perhaps most memorably, Pee Wee Herman (Paul Reubens) as a butler in *Pee-Wee's Big Adventure*. He also appeared on many TV shows, including

Toru Tanaka.

Airwolf, The A-Team, The Fall Guy and *Mickey Spillane's Mike Hammer*.

For both his film and wrestling career, the nice guy Kalani had to become a bad, bad man. Fans of his wrestling work in the 1970s no doubt still can picture Tanaka tossing salt into the eyes of his foes. "Tanaka was limited as heck as a worker, but he was a great guy," recalled Bill Watts.

Former San Francisco wrestling announcer Walt Harris remembered Tanaka coming by a TV station after Harris was through with the wrestling gig. "I didn't happen to be in and he left a note on my desk. 'Buddha bless you,'" said Harris. "He was a nice guy." Tanaka had a fun sense of humor too, and a regular joke became his expertise in the mysterious martial art of gundi; ask him to show a move or two, and he'd cock his fingers and fire a mock shot.

"He was just a gentle, good, soft-hearted island boy," Doris told the *Honolulu Star-Bulletin* after Tanaka's death. "And he had to work very hard all his life. It was hard not to be bitter when he got into wrestling and show business because he had to change his personality. He always told our kids, 'I'm your father at home and other people will not know the real me.'" Charlie and Doris had three children, daughters Cheryle Kalani and Karen Kalani-Beck, and son Carl.

Born in Honolulu on January 6, 1930, to Charles J. Kalani and Christina Leong Kalani (who was part Chinese), Tanaka began studying judo at age nine. In high school, he was a natural at many sports, and Doris credited his time on the football team with keeping him away from trouble. He would leave Hawaii for Utah's Weber Junior College (now Weber State University), and Tanaka met his wife at the University of Utah in 1952. Drafted into the U.S. Army in 1955, Tanaka would rise to the rank of sergeant, and excelled on the pistol team.

For four years, Doris and Charlie were at the base in Nuremburg, Germany. "A German friend of his started taking judo from Charlie. . . . Charlie was giving little demonstrations at the gym on the base. That friend told him about some wrestling matches that were around in the area," said Doris. "It was like being in a circus being married to him. We were married for fifty years. It was always sports and activities like that going on all the time."

After his discharge from the service in 1966, the couple moved to Monterey, California, where Charlie ran a judo academy. Dominic DeNucci worked with Tanaka early in both of their careers in San Francisco. Tanaka had been doing jobs for the Los Angeles promotion, when San Francisco promoter Roy Shire brought him north in 1967. "Roy saw something in him, and started using him a little bit," said DeNucci. "He was good because he was aggressive, slow but aggressive. He was a rugged guy. It was not easy to push him over." Kalani said it was Shire who convinced her husband to be an evil Japanese heel, which meant all the usual shortcuts — kimono-like ring robe, salt in the eyes, and a lot of bowing. "Charlie was almost full-blooded Hawaiian," said Doris. "In wrestling, Hawaiian seemed not as exciting as Japanese, so they talked him into becoming a Japanese wrestler." Atlanta promoter Jim Barnett later added the "Professor" tag. When asked in 1972 about being typecast as a villain, Tanaka replied, "However people take me, that is up to them. Most people are mixed up, anyway."

Tanaka's most famous tag team partner was Mr. Fuji (Harry Fujiwara), whom he knew from high school in Hawaii. In his book, *Listen, You Pencil Neck Geeks*, Freddie Blassie explored the relationship between the two "Japanese" heels. "From Tanaka's point of view, he was passing time with Fuji because it made sense to team up with another Japanese villain. The two certainly had no great admiration for one another. Tanaka was a by-the-book guy, who looked at wrestling a means to make a living. He wanted to work his match, shake hands with everyone afterward, and save some money. He was a professional," wrote Blassie. "If you wanted to talk about an angle beforehand, you always went to Tanaka. He was the ring general, who'd lead everyone else in the match."

By the early 1980s, Tanaka's body couldn't handle the beatings in the ring any longer, and he moved into the film world on a more permanent basis. His first flick was 1981's *An Eye for an Eye*.

He and Doris separated for a few years, and when she re-entered his life, he was a shell of the man she knew. "We were separated for a few years. He went down, his body. He died . . . of Alzheimer's and Parkinson's disease. For such an exciting life that he had . . . the end was so sad. He would just sit and stare. He was very weak and had to be helped walking. So it was a very sad ending for him."

NIKOLAI VOLKOFF

In the 1970s and 1980s, Nikolai Volkoff represented the wrong side of the Cold War as a hulking Soviet menace whose charge was to bury Americans in general, and American wrestlers, in particular.

He was a fraud, but not in the way most fans would think. Volkoff was in fact a blood Russian on his mother's side. But the great secret is that Josip Nikolai Peruzovic, an elite Yugoslavian weightlifter, was raised in a small village until he was fourteen, read and studied philosophy as a teenager, and decided man was not destined to live under a communist regime. So, in 1968, when his weightlifting team prepared to return home after an international competition in Austria, Peruzovic walked to the Canadian embassy and defected to the West. "I was just so happy to

Ivan Koloff and Nikolai Volkoff.

Ruth Oman, Pete Lederberg Collection

Nikolai Volkoff heads to the ring.

get out from there," he recalled. "Those communist bastards. I hated them."

For two decades, Volkoff — he adopted his mother's maiden name — was a main-eventer who caricatured the Soviet system to do his little bit in undermining it. His passage from pensive teenager to Soviet heel was precarious — he fled without telling his parents and provided them with a kayfabed version of why he left the country. "If you said you don't like communism, that's why you escaped, you were done. Someone's going to Siberia. If you said you wanted see the world, you were young, you were impetuous . . . I wrote my mother a letter saying I would come back if there was a war."

Volkoff had size, athletic ability, and great bloodlines — he was trained by his grandfather, a one-time bodyguard for Austrian monarch Franz Josef. Veteran Newt Tattrie discovered him shortly after his exodus to Canada and forged him into Bepo Mongol of the Mongols championship tag team. "He caught on pretty quick. He was a good athlete and he was in good shape. He was very easy to train," said Tattrie, who worked as Geeto Mongol. With his size and foreign heritage, Volkoff was destined to be a villain. He joined the WWWF in 1974 as a protegé of legendary manager Freddie Blassie, and promptly took Blassie's sage geopolitical advice. "He said, 'If you hate Communism, that's how you destroy it. Tell people how good it is over there, so they know you're lying,'" Volkoff recalled. "If you say, 'In Russia, people buy cars only until the style wears out, then they drive it right to the junkyard to be melted down for military purposes,' then people know you are lying. Then you get the heat and the people say, 'That is ridiculous!'"

Volkoff was a major challenger to WWWF champion Bruno Sammartino, going to a fifty-three-minute curfew draw at a sold-out Madison Square Garden in March 1974 as part of program that lasted through the summer. He also held tag team championships in Florida and the Mid-Atlantic, and was Georgia heavyweight champion in 1975, sparking a feud with Mr. Wrestling II. He entered the Mid-South territory in the late summer of 1983 to run off Boris Zhukov, charging his fellow traveler was doing a poor job of following the Kremlin's bidding. "The fans responded to him real well," said Zhukov, who later teamed with Volkoff in the 1980s-era WWF as the Bolsheviks. "Nikolai had just a great ferocious look, big impressive looking guy, a behemoth. He had no trouble at all getting heat because he was so vicious in the ring."

Volkoff also employed an ingenious gimmick developed by promoter Bill Watts by insisting fans stand and respectfully observe his singing of the Soviet national anthem. With Blassie earnestly standing by, hand on heart, and the hated Iron Sheik as his tag team partner, Volkoff's vocals attracted enough debris from fans that Gorilla Monsoon once commented, "There's no need for a food drive when this guy starts to sing."

"Oh, the heat that drew," Volkoff remembered. "It was unbelievable. People hated me and they hated Russia." At WrestleMania I in 1985, Volkoff teamed with the Iron Sheik to beat Barry Windham and Mike Rotundo for the tag team championship he held as a Mongol fifteen years before. After dropping the belts, Sheik and Volkoff began a year-long battle with superpatriot Corporal Kirchner. "You couldn't manhandle that man. He was too strong," said Kirchner. "You worked with Nik how Nik wanted to work."

Volkoff also was a terrific chef and kidder — "He'd bring stuff and we'd cook in the room," Zhukov said. "Nikolai would carry all the stuff in his bag. He put a lot of garlic on, and then we'd go breathe in the Sheepherders' faces. Drove them nuts." Volkoff turned into a pro-American hero in 1990, as the Berlin Wall fell and the Soviet Union crumbled. He became a code enforcement inspector in Baltimore and lives with his wife on a sprawling, fifty-acre farm near Baltimore. Volkoff even became an American politician — he ran unsuccessfully for the Maryland General Assembly in 2006, a year after he was inducted into the WWE Hall of Fame. "When Russia was in power, I did everything I could to make them look bad. Then one day, Russia was gone, and I said, 'My job is done.'"

FRITZ VON ERICH

Fritz Von Erich has been lionized, criticized, vilified, and canonized over the years, primarily in relation to his Dallas wrestling promotion, his fervent Christian beliefs and the rise — and subsequent fall — of his family. But Fritz Von Erich was a headliner as a German bad guy before he ever was a promoter, even if he is not, as Kirk Dooley wrote in *The Von Erichs: A Family*

"The German Bomber" Fritz Von Erich in the 1950s.

Album, "probably the best professional wrestler ever."

The six-foot-four, 260-pound Von Erich's in-ring style wasn't pretty. He was a thumper, with a vicious growl and a feared finishing hold, the Iron Claw, where he'd place his meaty right paw over his opponent's skull and squeeze. "Fritz was a big sucker. Christ, his thighs were as big as the average guy's waist, and he had those size-fifteen shoes. Every time he kicked you, it was like going for three points from the fifty-yard-line," recalled Billy "Red" Lyons. "He was a rugged individual."

The football comparison is apt, as Von Erich, under his birth name of Jack Adkisson, was a lineman for Southern Methodist University in 1949, blocking for Doak Walker, until losing his scholarship for marrying Doris Smith, who would bear him six boys. He also played a couple of preseason games for the American Football League's Dallas Texans, until his knees could go no longer. Born in Leon County, Texas, Adkisson's family moved to Dallas when he was a teen. Besides football, he was a clarinetist and excelled at the discus throw. To make ends meet at college, he worked as a loan collector and a fireman.

Doc Sarpolis and Ed "Strangler" Lewis suggested that Adkisson give professional wrestling a try in the early 1950s. When his career didn't take off the way he anticipated, Adkisson devised a new persona, taking his grandfather's name, Fritz, and his mother's maiden name, Erich. "Back in those days, I couldn't do a damn thing without getting hurt," Von Erich told *D Magazine* in 1981. "People think of Fritz Von Erich, the great wrestler. They'd be amazed to find out I lost my first twelve professional matches." A win against George Pencheff started him off positively, until the next night in Corpus Christi, Texas, where Adkisson broke his shoulder in a bout with the same opponent.

Getting away from Texas seemed to do the trick for the rechristened Von Erich, and he, Doris, and son Jackie hit the road, from Boston to Iowa,

Fritz Von Erich administers his Iron Claw.

Minnesota, and Calgary, where Stu Hart would polish him into a solid worker. "Fritz was one of the first major big-name guys that wrestled everywhere. He was like a Hans Schmidt, a Don Leo Jonathan, a Dick the Bruiser. He worked in a lot of different territories," said Gary Hart, a constant thorn in Von Erich's side to the public in the Dallas promotion, and Von Erich's ally behind the scenes. "He was just a big, heavy-footed, raw-boned guy that didn't mind fighting. He was like a Johnny Valentine and a Don Jardine. He beat the shit out of you, and if you didn't beat back, he'd eat you up." After winning tag titles in Minneapolis with Hans Hermann in 1958, Von Erich would shortly thereafter introduce his "brother" Waldo von Erich (Wally Sieber of Toronto).

Based out of the Sunny Acres mobile home park, just outside of Niagara Falls, New York, Von Erich also found great success in the lower Great Lakes area. "A master of every dangerous wrestling hold, as well as the fastest and definitely the most vicious super-heavy-weight in wrestling, Fritz is responsible for more serious ring injuries to his opponents than any other grappler in modern wrestling history," reads *Wrestling The King of Sports*, distributed in Buffalo-area arenas, going on to quote Lord Athol Layton: "Von Erich is a crippler, and should be barred from the ring for life. He will gladly go so far as to cause serious injury to his opponent just to be declared the winner."

It was also at Sunny Acres where tragedy first struck the family, as seven-year-old Jackie was electrocuted in 1959. Away in Cleveland when the accident happened, Adkisson started to think about finding a permanent home to raise a family, which also included two-year-old Kevin. His first taste of ownership in a promotion came in the early 1960s, when Adkisson teamed with Lyons, Ilio DiPaolo and Dick Beyer to purchase the rights to run Rochester, New York, from Pedro Martinez. "Pedro wasn't drawing with it, so he offered it to us because we kept saying, 'You should do this, you should do that.' We bought it, and then we sold it back to him because we wanted to leave," said Lyons. "We bought it, and they were drawing $1,200, $1,500 in there. After four weeks, we were selling the place out."

Jonathan was with Von Erich in Indiana, just before he left to go take over the Dallas promotion from Ed McLemore. Jonathan doesn't remember Von Erich talking about his plans. "I think he was keeping it under his hat. He was a little disenchanted with things. You know how life gets. He wanted to do other things, to settle down. He went into Dallas, and he done all right."

Von Erich would run the Dallas wrestling office, later named World Class Championship Wrestling, until 1988, when he handed it over to his sons. But realizing that he had control (he'd hold the majority of his titles in his own territory), Von Erich began playing a different character, and turned babyface in 1967 after being outed as Jack Adkisson by Gary Hart. Bill Mercer would become the announcer for Von Erich's TV show on Channel 4, which would eventually find a much bigger audience in the expanding TV land of the 1980s. "He just didn't do all the goosestepping and the ridiculous arm-waving. He just polished his image by not doing some things like that," said Mercer. "He just became a guy who beat up on the bad guy, and just took away some of the unnecessary gestures that he had. But he still had that formidable, mean look about him. He wasn't exactly a handsome guy, and he had that face, kind of like Killer [Karl Kox], where you knew he was tough. But he upheld the rights of people and all that kind of stuff. He'd come in the ring and protect somebody. So it was just a transformation, an evolution of looking like a good guy with a bad face."

In St. Louis, he is considered one of the three top heels from the '60s to the '80s, along with Dick the Bruiser and Gene Kiniski. His German shtick wasn't pushed under promoter Sam Muchnick, said Larry Matysik, his promotions man. "Sam liked wrestling heels — guys who could wrestle and they were heels. Fritz Von Erich was a wrestling heel. He could wrestle and he could go and he was a heel," said Matysik. "Fritz had a beautiful way with the arrogance and the snotty pointing-the-finger."

In an interview with the *Fort Worth Star-Telegram* when Von Erich died in

September 1997 of brain cancer, Johnny Valentine explained Fritz's appeal to Texans. "He was the people's bad guy . . . They adopted him. If you're mean enough and tough enough, they get to where they respect you for that. I really loved to pound on him. One week, we would wrestle Fort Worth on Monday, Dallas on Tuesday, San Antonio on Wednesday and sell out all three places. People would be turned away. I don't remember who won or lost. It didn't make much difference. Even the winner was hurt."

As the rest of his sons — Kevin, David and Kerry were closest in age, followed by Mike and Chris — grew old enough, they followed their father into wrestling. The rest of the story is numbingly familiar to wrestling fans. The World Class promotion was a massive success in the 1980s, thanks to ahead-of-the-time syndication deals; the Von Erichs were pushed relentlessly as clean-living Christian stars, with the ex-basketball player David having the most talent, Kevin being the high-flyer, Kerry the pretty boy with the incredible physique, and Mike and Chris never measuring up. The millionaire Fritz knew no depth to what he would do to make a buck, and came out of retirement again and again to play parts in storylines. Battles with substance abuse and accidents would eventually leave Kevin the sole surviving son, along with Doris, who divorced Fritz in 1992.

The saga kept the Von Erich name alive through the years. A 2006 documentary, *Heroes of World Class*, has brought the sad tale to a new generation of fans, and Kevin's sale of World Class footage to WWE will likely result in a heavily pushed commercial package of products down the road. "As far as writing a book, one day I probably will," Kevin said. "Right now I haven't because the people I've talked to, in New York and in Hollywood, all want to tell the same story: big mean Fritz beat us up and made us all be wrestlers, and that's just not the truth. But that's marketable, and that's what they want to tell, and it's never going to happen that way."

WALDO VON ERICH

It's a spine-tingling transformation. One moment, it's a jovial Wally Sieber on the phone, laughing about the good times in his career. Then his voice drops a bit, becomes slightly more clipped and a whole lot more sadistic. He's Waldo von Erich again. As he says, "I enjoy twisting their arms, making them hurt and suffer," it's pretty easy to believe him.

That's the duality of Waldo. His peers have nothing but good things to say about him, praising his good-natured sense of humor, but his fans hated him with a passion.

"Waldo von Erich was the top heel in the NWF. He made more money

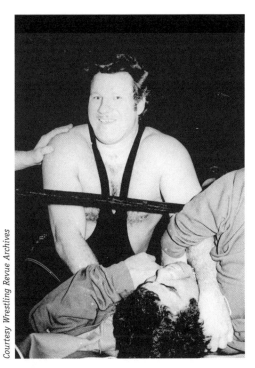

Waldo von Erich.

for us than anyone else," recalled Ron Martinez, son of Pedro Martinez, who ran the Buffalo territory where Wally Sieber first joined Fritz Von Erich's Aryan Army. "While not a great technical worker, his interviews were very strong for the time. People just hated him. He could P.O. the Pope." Waldo shared a similar memory: "Vince McMahon, the father, he says to me one time, 'You know, Waldo, I know what you're like, but I hate your guts when you're in that ring.'"

At six-foot, 265 pounds, sporting a World War II helmet and whipping crop, he portrayed the prototypical German, despite only being born in 1933 (in Toronto, Ontario) as the Nazis came to power. His finishing move was the blitzkreig, a kneedrop off the top rope, but von Erich was never known for action.

In the ring, frequent opponent Billy "Red" Lyons recalled von Erich "didn't do any more than he had to." Von Erich didn't disagree with the assessment. "I was very meticulous. You do too much and people don't have time to grasp it. I liked to do things and let it sink in so they know what the hell you're doing."

"Waldo wasn't a tough guy, as far as going around — I don't know if I ever remember him getting in a fight, or something like that," said Bill Watts. "But he could emote such hatred. He had that Nazi snarl, he had stuff down. He could just turn people upside down. He totally had control of his interview. He was a great interview."

Heavily into weightlifting, Sieber trained in Toronto at the Weston YMCA along with other future pros like Baron Mikel Scicluna, Dave "Bearman" McKigney and "Geeto Mongol" Newt Tattrie. It was his trainer, Red Garner, who influenced the 16-year-old the most, including in evil ways. A German heel almost from the get-go, Waldo von Sieber (or sometimes Baron von Sieber) used to have long, blond hair, and wore a monocle — and had his own wrestling brother, Kurt von Sieber.

He'd soon meet a true mentor in Jack Adkisson, who was four years older and much more experienced. "I wrestled a few places around Toronto, and Fritz liked me. I met him out in Minneapolis. That's where we started out as a tag team, the Von Erich brothers," he said. "When you're in with top guys right from the beginning, you learn pretty quick."

As a singles competitor, Waldo was on top just about everywhere he wrestled. He's perhaps best known for a series of battles with Bruno Sammartino around the WWWF. In 1964, they headlined Madison Square Garden three times, including an epic eighty-one-minute draw in August; in 1969; and again in 1975, when Waldo was victorious in one bout that was stopped because of excessive bleeding in front of 24,553 patrons, including attendance at the adjacent Felt Forum.

Waldo von Erich prepares for battle.

Steven Johnson

Waldo von Erich loved to do the TV spots. "When I'd get on there for interviews, they'd be so goddamn hot at me, you could hear a pin drop. Then the guys I'd be wrestling, they'd be in the room laughing like hell," he boasted. "Some actors are good, and some aren't. You have to feel it."

He also liked the feel of old cars. "I always loved old cars, I always had old cars. The first car I had, I was sixteen years old, a 1945 Passenger Cadillac limousine. There were only two in Canada." Today, retired from work as a certified reflexologist outside Toronto, he still has a customized Porsche 928S, and a sixty-year-old Rolls Royce. When not tinkering with his beloved vehicles, or coming up with inventions like his chair that reduces back pain, Waldo occasionally helps out with a wrestling school in nearby Cambridge where the current prized grads are WWE tag team, the Highlanders.

KARL VON HESS

Talk about living dangerously. It wasn't enough that Frank Faketty, aboard the USS Montpelier in World War II, raced to shove a hose down the barrel of an eight-inch gun to cool off a stuck shell that was ready to explode. It wasn't enough that he attracted sniper fire during hazardous military duty as part of the Underwater Demolition Corps, the forerunner of the Navy SEALs. It wasn't enough that he scraped out a hardened life taking on challengers on the dusty, athletic training circuit.

No, he had to adopt a full-scale Nazi guise in the uneasy years after World War II, and enter arenas in hotbeds of American patriotism with a galling Waffen SS appearance and a "Sieg, Heil!" salute. No wonder Von Hess, a master of minimalism, was shot at, stabbed, attacked, and burned en route to becoming a white-hot heel in the late 1950s.

"Karl Von Hess was absolutely wonderful," said Ted Lewin, wrestler-turned-author and illustrator. "He was very special because he didn't do a heck of a lot to make people angry at him. All he had to do was kind of keep turning and looking at the audience, and the audience would boo, and then he'd turn and look at them again."

"I did it because I was a performer," Von Hess told his hometown Nebraska newspaper, the *Omaha World-Herald*, after he retired. "It was the best way to make a lot of money. My business was to provoke you. If I had to spit in your face, I would."

Francis Faketty — he later officially changed his name to Karl Von Hess

Chuck Thornton Collection

Karl Von Hess.

— was born in Michigan in 1919 to Hungarian immigrants, and raised in a gritty, working-class section in south Omaha. His early life was a struggle — his accent made him prey for bullies at school and he coped with an abusive father who drank too much and took out his violence on Von Hess' mother. "There were times when it was upsetting to him, some of the things he had to do, like beat his father up to get him off his mom," his son, John Von Hess, said.

What Faketty had going for him was a remarkable physical gift. He took like a fish to water, training himself to swim in the swift currents of the Missouri River. "He was just an incredible human specimen for somebody who never went to the gym," his son reflected. "He used to swim across the Missouri River, steal watermelons, and bring them back with him. You can imagine what kind of feat that was." He later taught swimming and worked as a lifeguard — kids at Morton Park Pool in Omaha called him "Tarzan" — and started boxing and wrestling competitively.

After his valor in World War II, Faketty kicked around carnival and athletic training shows and worked with forgettable gimmicks like Mara Duba, the South American Assassin, who had a pet lion. He was in the Pacific Northwest in early 1955, at the same time Kurt Von Poppenheim was employing a less sinister German gimmick in the territory. When he went to the Carolinas that fall, he underwent a makeover to Von Hess, became an immediate sensation as an out-and-out Nazi, and was a key player in the talent movement between the Carolinas and Vincent J. McMahon's Washington office on the East Coast. He spoke forcefully, spewing hate, and even and even muttered a little German, like any faithful stormtrooper. Doctored publicity posters showed him with Martin Bormann and Adolf Hitler.

"Listen," he explained years later. "It was right after the war and I had tried everything. I played different characters, and then I came up with this gimmick of Von Hess and I played it right to the hilt." Despite the fact he could go toe to toe with almost anyone, Von Hess didn't use his grappling skills. He was hardcore — he kept wire in his trunks to choke people when he couldn't use the ring microphone to do it. He threw chairs.

"In the ring, you couldn't imagine Von Hess with any sense of humor at all, yet he had a very funny sense of humor," Lewin said. "Frank would live that, he would refuse to sign autographs and things like that, so he would keep that character out of the ring to a certain degree."

How intense was his heat? A fan named W. L. Lee slashed him with a knife in Florence, South Carolina, in January 1956, leaving a cut down the length of his back that authorities said required more than 50 stitches. "I remember it to this day," John Von Hess said. "My dad used to wear a very long trench coat with a hat, like a derby. And he came in and he turned around and the whole back of the coat was solid blood and you could see where the guy had raked him with the knife."

He and "Wildman" Jackie Fargo engaged in a series of violent brawls on TV in 1956 that drew howls of protest to the District of Columbia Boxing Commission. "I stuck a cigar right in his face," Fargo recalled with a laugh. "I was really upset at him and something was said and I just said, 'Screw you!' and pushed that cigar in his face. If I had it to do over after it was done, I wouldn't do it. But he walked away from it . . . He was a very good wrestler, very, very good. Nice fellow too. He could wrestle and he was pretty tough, too." So great was the outrage that McMahon calmed matters in *The Washington Post* by breaking the protection of the business.

"Von Hess is no Nazi. He uses that silly salute to point up the act that he is the villain," McMahon acknowledged in a candor rare for the age. Still, Von Hess set the Baltimore-Washington territory on fire in 1956 and 1957. A three-match series in Washington against frequent foe Antonino Rocca culminated in an outdoor show at Griffith Stadium; McMahon publicly credited Von Hess as Washington's top draw since the heyday of Jim Londos a quarter-century before. In New York, the state athletic commission directed him to put tape on his boots to hide a swastika. "Too much heat," explained Mad Dog Vachon, another long-time Omaha resident. "It was a dangerous job. He could get stabbed, or shot, or anything."

In the 1960s, Von Hess cooled off and later said he felt the WWWF was anxious to put him out to pasture; he had a brief stint with a version of the world title in Cleveland in 1963, but that was quickly dropped. He worked in several other territories, including Tennessee and Hawaii, left wrestling in the late 1960s, and operated trailer parks and other businesses with his wife Lenore, who died in 2005 after fifty-three years of marriage. In recent years, Alzheimer's disease has sapped his memories, pleasant and unpleasant. But he still remains the same vigorous force he was as a lifeguard and frogman, swimming regularly and exhibiting the appetite of "a mountain lion," John Von Hess said. "He always said, 'I'm a provoker. I know how to provoke people.' He would do it just to see the kind of reaction he would get. That's the way he was."

KURT VON POPPENHEIM

Beneath the glowering Prussian visage of Kurt Von Poppenheim beat the heart of an upholstery wiz. For Von Poppenheim, one of the most successful wrestlers ever in the Pacific Northwest, carefully built and stitched together furniture almost as often as he dismantled opponents during a twenty-seven-year ring career.

Unlike a lot of post-World War II German villains, Von Poppenheim had certifiable connections to Deutschland. His parents were German immigrants who never spoke English. The future Von Poppenheim was born Jacob Pappenheim in 1914, and raised on a farm in Sunnyside, Washington. After his father died in a horse accident, Pappenheim left school in eighth grade to help support his family during the Depression era, according to his daughter, Judy Sholin.

He later worked in area shipyards and started wrestling under his real name in the late 1930s, billed as a "brand, spanking new cleany" by the *Astorian Evening Budget* of Oregon. Pappenheim wrestled mostly on the West Coast in the 1930s and 1940s, and served as a gunner's mate in the U.S. Navy in the South Pacific during World War II.

After returning from combat, Pappenheim worked on undercards in the Northwest. In fall 1950, at the recommendation of Seattle booker Tex Porter, he segued into Kurt Von Poppenheim and the persona that would put him at the top of the card for years. Von Poppenheim approached the ring with the regal look of a Prussian nobleman — a swirling, upturned mustache, spade beard, a monocle and Iron

Courtesy Wrestling Revue Archives

Kurt Von Poppenheim.

Crosses on his garb. "He disappeared for a while and he came back to Seattle as Kurt Von Poppenheim," recalled John Buff, a long-time wrestler and referee in the Northwest. "I remember people hollering at him as he came to the ring, 'Hi Jack! How's it going? Where ya been, Jack?' He didn't bat an eye, and it wasn't two weeks before he made them forget about Jack Pappenheim. Oh, he was good."

While he was most closely identified with the Pacific Northwest, Von Poppenheim, ventured to Illinois, Texas, Tennessee, Missouri, and other territories during his career, packing his wife, five daughters, a son, a dog, a cat, and a bird in a little Nash car with a trailer. For several months in 1957, he worked out of the New York office as Eric Von Hess, brother to goosestepping Karl Von Hess. In a twist, Karl had adopted Von Poppenheim's pro-German character just a couple of years earlier. "He did that to a 'T,'" said Red Bastien, who teamed with Lou Bastien (Klein) against the Von Hess brothers. "I wish I had some tapes of those guys. If you had just one tape where you could see the match, you'd be amazed. When he got in that ring, he could stir up those people. He was good."

Back in Oregon, Von Poppenheim officially changed his name and became a major player in the promotion for 15 years, although undersized by today's standards — he was no more than 200 pounds. From 1952 to

1962, he held one-half of the Pacific Northwest tag team title with nine different partners, and was Pacific Northwest champion in 1959. "I always enjoyed watching him, which was the beauty of what he did, because he scarcely ever went anywhere," said J Michael Kenyon, the dean of wrestling historians and an expert on Northwest matdom. "You would see him week after week, in one role or another . . . upright and arrogant." He also had four good runs with the Pacific Northwest junior heavyweight title from 1954 to 1957, including a feud with Bastien.

Always a Prussian instead of a full-blown Nazi, Von Poppenheim's finisher was the German crossbow, a combination backbreaker and back-stretcher in which he drew back on his opponents' leg and chin. "He didn't look like anything special with his body, but he didn't have to do a look to get himself over," Buff said. "He had the look, and he had the psychology down pat. It took the character to get the attention, but then you could see what a good worker he was." Sholin recalled a woman in Portland, Oregon, regularly maintained a ringside seat so she could spit in Von Poppenheim's face. "People would spit at him and throw things at him, call him filthy names and he just kind of egged it on."

After he stopped actively wrestling in 1964, Von Poppenheim wanted to take a stab at promoting, but was blocked by the existing Don Owen promotion. He filed a $1-million lawsuit charging that the Portland office, a local TV station, and the state athletic commission were in cahoots, but never was able to claim a victory despite several court appeals.

Most surprisingly, Von Poppenheim was a master upholsterer, a craft he learned as a young boy from his father. He did work for the turn-of-the-century Pittock Mansion, a well-known Portland landmark. "He would go down in the basement, and spend hours and hours and hours. He made beautiful things. He redid all of his kids' furniture and he built furniture for the grandkids," his daughter said.

He also worked for the Portland Water Bureau and became something of a hometown celebrity. In later years, he developed dementia and passed away May 1, 2003, at eighty-nine. Said Buff: "Jack was one whose word was always good, was all business, and everyone around him knew where and what he stood for."

BARON VON RASCHKE

With a little more deference to an experienced wrestler, the German who terrorized rings from the late 1960s to the 1980s might have been "Baron Von Pumpkin." Jim Raschke was struggling to survive in the Midwest with a look as meek and mild-mannered as that of any stereotypical schoolteacher, which, in fact, he was. During a 1967 swing through the Montreal territory, veteran Mad Dog Vachon stepped in and growled, "You oughta be a German." Responded Raschke: "Well, I am a German." In the end, the Dog let Raschke keep his real last name, instead of calling him Pumpkin.

The change in Raschke's billings — and payoffs — was immediate, and friends are amazed at how he easily he managed his double identity. "Jim can just change in an instant. He can be the

Baron Von Raschke puts the claw on Cowboy Bob Ellis.

German, and he can be Jim Raschke," manager Bobby Heenan said. "He's the most remarkable human being I've ever seen, for a character, in this business, how he can just turn it off and on."

Fans didn't make the connection when Raschke goosestepped to the ring and locked opponents' temples in his feared claw, but he was a world-class amateur wrestler. He lettered for three years at the University of Nebraska, and won the Big Eight Conference heavyweight title as a senior in 1962. He took a bronze in the World Games in 1963. A year later, he captured the Amateur Athletic Union freestyle and Greco-Roman titles. He also landed a service championship in the U.S. Army, and was on track for the 1964 Olympics before an elbow injury sidelined him.

A junior high teacher by training, Raschke naively figured he had all the attributes of an American hero when he forwarded his resumé to Omaha, Nebraska, promoter Joe Dusek for consideration. "In retrospect, I'm not sure what he thought of that," Raschke chuckled. Dusek bit, though, and sent Raschke to Verne Gagne in Minneapolis, where he learned the trade while working on the ring crew, and as a referee, before hopping in the ring for the first time in the fall of 1966 with Johnny Kace.

His break with the rules came the next year, when he became Vachon's partner in crime. "It was really a piece of cake because although I had singles matches, I was with Mad Dog a lot, and he just said, 'Follow me kid; do what I do,'" Raschke said. Later that year, Vachon was injured in a car accident, but his heat just flowed on to his protegé. Vachon was just as complimentary of his teammate: "We were very successful together; not to diminish the prestige of my brother Paul 'The Butcher' when we were teamed together. As far as I am concerned, the Mad Dog and Baron Von Raschke, the oddest, more explosive tag team in wrestling history."

As a good guy, Raschke came across as timid and unimposing, but another side of him emerged when he turned into a bald, leering German. "It all became very natural, and I think it really helped me overcome a basic shyness. It became a tremendous outlet because I could say just about anything I wanted and get away with it." Frequent opponent Jim Brunzell called Raschke "sort of a natural. He was so good on the microphone, and there was so much heat on him, that by the time he got into the ring, he didn't have to do too much. But he was very, very limber for a big guy; he was extremely agile." Top those traits with his unique look, a sneer with wide ears toughened by years of wrestling, a frequent glance upward as though a higher power was directing his evil. "He was a gargoyle. He was all bald. He had that claw. He had the greatest rubber face in the world for that thing. He wore that big red cape. He is just such an interesting character," Heenan said.

Raschke's clawhold finisher also earned him a special niche among wrestling's most notorious heels. Former NWA champion Pat O'Connor persuaded him to adopt it, though Raschke put the move on ice during an extended stay in Texas in 1969 and 1970 because Fritz Von Erich and Don "The Spoiler" Jardine both used it there. When he hit Dick the Bruiser's Indianapolis territory in 1970, he broke it out for good.

"It was frightening!" laughed Kenny Jay, who was on the receiving end several times. "The fans responded to it because they knew it was all over when he put the claw on you. But I knew he was putting it on. I said, 'Don't hurt me, just put me to sleep.'" With confidence in his character, Raschke improvised his antics in the ring, according to the dictates of the audience. "Mostly, everything I did was mostly by ear. I had a good ear for what the crowd wanted. Nobody likes a sneak," he said. Even in retirement, asked whether he preferred to bend the rules right away, or wait until later in the match, Raschke replied with a classic heel attitude: "Who said I broke any rules?"

Raschke added his share of pro titles to his amateur awards: International champion in Montreal in 1967, world champion in Bruiser's promotion three times from 1970 to 1972, world tag team champion in the Carolinas in 1978 and 1979, and Georgia heavyweight champion in 1980. His only stumble came in St. Louis, where promoter Sam Muchnick refused to advertise the "baron" because he wasn't a real baron. "He demoted me," Raschke joked. Respected by friends and foes — "he was always a very courteous guy, inside and outside of the ring; just a helluva gentleman," Brunzell said — Raschke worked as a fan favorite for a while in the 1980s alongside Vachon, but preferred his allegiance to the dark side. "I was having too much fun, just beating up anybody."

Raschke slowed down in the late 1980s, managing the Powers of Pain in the WWF before retiring to the calm of smalltown Wabasha, Minnesota. In 2002, he was inducted in the George Tragos/Lou Thesz Hall of Fame in Iowa for his contributions to amateur and pro wrestling. Minneapolis-based writer Cory McLeod collaborated with Raschke and son Karl on *The Baron*, a play that debuted in 2007 that captured his career and unique walk through life. And, as Raschke concluded his TV interviews: "Dat is all da people need to know!"

TOJO YAMAMOTO

Here's a little thing that tells you a lot about southern wrestling legend Tojo Yamamoto: When a riot broke out one night in Huntsville, Alabama, he didn't hightail it to safety or hold his ground on the ring canvas. While referee Jerry Jarrett and other wrestlers tried to evict fans from the ring, Tojo took matters into his own hands. "Tojo was moving from fan to fan and breaking one of their fingers," said Jarrett, his long-time friend and later Tennessee promoter. "If it had not been so serious, it would have been comical that four or five fans left the ring screaming with a broken finger."

Tojo Yamamoto sends Man Mountain Link into the ropes.

For more than twenty-five-years, Harold Watanabe — Tojo to everyone — a native Hawaiian, was synonymous with wrestling in the Tennessee territory. He wasn't the first grappler to adopt the guise of a hated Japanese heel, but he was the most long-lasting, playing his part to the hilt decades after the United States and Japan became allies.

"World War II was long since over, but it was rekindled every time he came to the ring. He'd hit you with that chop. The first one, it'd raise blood blisters. The second one, it'd open them right up," said Tennessee hand Randal Brown. "When the ref turned his back, he'd hit you in the throat, and then walk around for three minutes pointing to how smart he was. Half the people wanted to kill him, and even the people who liked him wanted to kill him."

Tojo got into wrestling in the late 1950s as P. Y. Chung, the name he used in the Northeast and in the Carolinas. In 1961 and 1962, he worked in Florida as Tojo Yamamoto, assuming the names of a couple of Japanese war strategists, and homesteaded in Tennessee thereafter, with some exceptions, such as a stint as T. Y. Chung in west Texas in late 1967 and early 1968.

Exclusively a villain until late in the 1960s, Tojo held versions of the territorial and world tag team titles with a range of partners, and was junior heavyweight and Mid-American heavyweight champ as well. Len Rossi, who wrestled him countless times, said you had to earn Tojo's respect: "Tojo was a funny person. If he thought he could get away with it, he'd hurt you, but if he didn't, he would not. He had the sneakiness down pat. He was a master of that."

Tojo was the de facto trainer in Tennessee for up-and-coming wrestlers, such as Jarrett and Midnight Express star Bobby Eaton, and he didn't hesitate to use karate thrusts against his pupils — Jarrett said he still feels the effects of a brief singles feud after he and Tojo split as a tag team. "He damn near beat me to death with his chops each night. I ended the program as soon as possible."

The remarkable thing is that even into the 1980s, fans never seemed to tire of his evil Japanese gimmick. Rossi said the ethnic angle might have meant even more in Tennessee because Tojo was such a foreigner to the South. "If you were from the North, you were a foreigner here back then. Now, imagine someone from another country." Second-generation Tennessee wrestler Ken Wayne also attributed the longevity to the way Tojo perfected his persona. "He only had one style. But it worked so well for Tojo that I don't think it would have mattered if he was Japanese or not by the '80s. He just had this great face like, 'When I get there, I'm going to kill you.'"

In fact, while Tojo used a stomach claw as a finisher, he considered facial expressions to be more important than moves or holds. "He believed that the face was the mirror to the soul. He explained in great detail that unless you conveyed your emotions through your face, the fans would not believe anything you did," Jarrett said. Legendary Tennessee announcer Lance Russell, agreed, saying Tojo could turn an audience with a flicker of the face. "He didn't do any more than just cut his eyes, or drop eyebrows down — something like that. He just was an absolute master at being able to get across what he had in mind about being a sneaky Jap."

Inside, Tojo experienced his own sort of pain, though he didn't share too much of his personal life with fellow workers. "Tojo was perhaps the most 'old school' wrestler I ever knew. He believed in literally living your ring role both inside and outside the ring," Jarrett said. Some of his colleagues never knew he had been married and divorced. He wrestled until about 1986, and managed several wrestlers through the rest of the decade, even leading a sneak attack on Chris Adams' wife when the Tennessee and Dallas promotions combined. But he also suffered from severe diabetes and kidney problems that forced him away from the mat. On February 19, 1992, he shot himself in the temple with a pistol in his Nashville apartment. His driver's license said he was fifty-one, though most thought he was much older than that. All that was left was a hand-drawn will, and a note thanking an apartment manager for the kindnesses she had shown him while he was ill. "He was terribly depressed because he couldn't wrestle," said friend Nella Shaver, the only beneficiary in his will.

It was a sad ending, but friends remember Tojo for the realistic way he approached the business, something his trainees still preach. "His legacy was the intensity and seriousness that Tojo expressed about his profession. He would not have appreciated the style that is today's wrestling. He wanted the fans to really believe," Jarrett said. "Tojo, Jackie Fargo, and Jerry Lawler are the top three draws in the history of the Tennessee territory."

Notes On Sources

The primary source for this book is hundreds of interviews conducted with wrestlers, bookers, managers, promoters, referees, family members, and wrestling journalists and photographers during the last few years. Some of these interviews were brief; others lasted for hours. We're grateful to everyone for sharing their recollections.

The run on the publication of wrestling books has eased off a bit, but the world is richer for the market spurred by, but hardly begun by, Mick Foley. Our bookshelves are a testament to the volume of material out there, and many are cited in our text.

Each year, more and more of the past makes its way to electronic sources available online through archive sites. It's now possible to look up newspapers from 120 years ago without leaving the living room. However, a lot of legwork still had to be done, and, in particular, the Library of Congress was a wonderful resource, as was the Jack Pfefer Collection at Notre Dame, and the AAF Sports Library in Los Angeles.

The various fan festivals have provided marvelous opportunities to mingle with wrestlers of all eras. Thanks to those promoters who are doing their own part to keep wrestling history alive. It has been our pleasure to listen to and participate in a number of question-and-answer sessions at various conventions.

The WAWLI (Wrestling As We Liked It) Papers maintained by historian J Michael Kenyon have been invaluable. Here are a few other key Web sites and publications in our research:

Whatever Happened To . . . ?/Shooting With the Legends/ Crowbar Publishing — www.1wrestlinglegends.com

Ring Around the Northwest — $1/issue, Mike Rodgers, 2740 SE Lewellyn, Troutdale, Oregon, 97060

Wrestling Observer — www.wrestlingobserver.com
Wrestling Perspective — www.wrestlingperspective.com
Pro Wrestling Torch — www.pwtorch.com
Wrestling Revue — www.wrestlingrevue.com
GeorgiaWrestlingHistory.com
Mid-Atlantic Gateway — www.midatlanticwrestling.net
www.wrestlingclassics.com
Kayfabe Memories — www.kayfabememories.com
www.Oldschool-wrestling.com
www.lancerussell.com has video of Andy's Kaufman's wrestling days

Courtesy Wrestling Revue Archives

Writer/photographer Brian Bukantis is threatened by Bobby Heenan and Jimmy Valiant.

Photographers

Howard Baum, whose work has appeared in countless magazines since the early '80s, has both his original photography and his wrestling-based pop art available at his website. www.h-bombstudios.com

Bill Janosik was a freelance photographer for *The Wrestler*, *Pro Wrestling Illustrated*, and *Inside Wrestling* during the 1970s.

Andrea Kellaway is an up-and-coming Toronto-based photographer, who captures witty and powerful portraits. www.andreakellaway.com

Vincent Lagana is an Italian-based photographer who shoots professional wrestling and concerts. www.the-musicbox.com

Mike Lano has covered wrestling, boxing, MMA and TV/movie celebs around the world since 1966, and has many radio projects on the go. He is the official photographer for the Cauliflower Alley Club. wrealano@aol.com

Howard Lapes grew up in the Bronx, NY, and attended practically every live WWWF house show event held in the tri-state area (NY/NJ/CT) with his 35mm camera from the late 1970s to the early 1980s.

Pete Lederberg lives in Fort Lauderdale, Florida, owns negatives from other photographers dating back to about 1970 and has been shooting wrestling himself since 1987. http://home.bellsouth.net/p/PWP-flwrestlingpix

Bob Leonard shot images of Calgary's Stampede Wrestling from 1963 to 1989, and was recently honored by the Cauliflower Alley Club. bob.leonard@accesscomm.ca

Mike Mastrandrea is a Toronto-based photographer and has been shooting wrestling for over 15 years. His work has been seen in publications across the world. http://slam.canoe.ca/Slam/Wrestling/Gallery/mastrandrea.html

Collections

Canadian Sports Hall of Fame / Turofsky Collection — Lou and Nat Turofsky were two Toronto brothers who documented sport and culture in Canada in the first part of the 20th century. The non-hockey part of the collection rests in the Canadian Sports Hall of Fame. www.cshof.ca

Chris Swisher Collection — Includes the Lil Al collection of negatives and photos, negatives from part of the Early Yetter collection, the Detroit area from the '60s and '70s, negatives taken by Scott Teal from the '70s, the collection of photos and items from promoter Fred Ward of Columbus, Ga. www.csclassicwrphotos.com

Chuck Thornton Collection — Atlanta businessman and wrestling historian

Herschel "Chuck" Thornton has one of the world's foremost collections of vintage wrestling photographs.

Wrestling Revue Archives — Brian Bukantis is publisher of *Wrestling Revue* and curator of the Wrestling Revue Archives (www.wrestleprints.com). A photographer himself, he took the cover image of Bulldog Brower mauling Carlos Colon in London, Ontario, circa 1972, on a "Bearman" McKigney show. Other photographers in the Wrestling Revue Archives include Gary J. Kamensack and Brad McFarlin.

Department of Special Collections, University Libraries of Notre Dame — The photos in this book come from The Jack Pfefer Wrestling Collection, housed at Notre Dame. www.nd.edu

James C. Melby Collection — Jim Melby was one of the greatest wrestling historians ever. His passing on February 10, 2007, leaves a hole in our hearts, but his legacy lives on with the James C. Melby Award presented annually by the George Tragos/Lou Thesz Hall of Fame to a wrestling historian or writer.

The SPORT Collection, based in Toronto, is one of the largest and most significant collections of 20th century sports photography in the world. www.thesportgallery.com